Lecture Notes of the Institute for Computer Sciences, Social Informatics and Telecommunications Engineering   601

Editorial Board Members

Ozgur Akan, *Middle East Technical University, Ankara, Türkiye*
Paolo Bellavista, *University of Bologna, Bologna, Italy*
Jiannong Cao, *Hong Kong Polytechnic University, Hong Kong, Hong Kong*
Geoffrey Coulson, *Lancaster University, Lancaster, UK*
Falko Dressler, *University of Erlangen, Erlangen, Germany*
Domenico Ferrari, *Università Cattolica Piacenza, Piacenza, Italy*
Mario Gerla, *UCLA, Los Angeles, USA*
Hisashi Kobayashi, *Princeton University, Princeton, USA*
Sergio Palazzo, *University of Catania, Catania, Italy*
Sartaj Sahni, *University of Florida, Gainesville, USA*
Xuemin Shen, *University of Waterloo, Waterloo, Canada*
Mircea Stan, *University of Virginia, Charlottesville, USA*
Xiaohua Jia, *City University of Hong Kong, Kowloon, Hong Kong*
Albert Y. Zomaya, *University of Sydney, Sydney, Australia*

The LNICST series publishes ICST's conferences, symposia and workshops.

LNICST reports state-of-the-art results in areas related to the scope of the Institute. The type of material published includes

- Proceedings (published in time for the respective event)
- Other edited monographs (such as project reports or invited volumes)

LNICST topics span the following areas:

- General Computer Science
- E-Economy
- E-Medicine
- Knowledge Management
- Multimedia
- Operations, Management and Policy
- Social Informatics
- Systems

Xiaochun Cheng
Editor

Broadband Communications, Networks, and Systems

14th EAI International Conference, BROADNETS 2024
Hyderabad, India, February 16–17, 2024
Proceedings, Part I

Editor
Xiaochun Cheng ⓘ
Swansea University
Swansea, UK

ISSN 1867-8211   ISSN 1867-822X (electronic)
Lecture Notes of the Institute for Computer Sciences, Social Informatics
and Telecommunications Engineering
ISBN 978-3-031-81167-8   ISBN 978-3-031-81168-5 (eBook)
https://doi.org/10.1007/978-3-031-81168-5

© ICST Institute for Computer Sciences, Social Informatics and Telecommunications Engineering 2025

This work is subject to copyright. All rights are solely and exclusively licensed by the Publisher, whether the whole or part of the material is concerned, specifically the rights of translation, reprinting, reuse of illustrations, recitation, broadcasting, reproduction on microfilms or in any other physical way, and transmission or information storage and retrieval, electronic adaptation, computer software, or by similar or dissimilar methodology now known or hereafter developed.
The use of general descriptive names, registered names, trademarks, service marks, etc. in this publication does not imply, even in the absence of a specific statement, that such names are exempt from the relevant protective laws and regulations and therefore free for general use.
The publisher, the authors and the editors are safe to assume that the advice and information in this book are believed to be true and accurate at the date of publication. Neither the publisher nor the authors or the editors give a warranty, expressed or implied, with respect to the material contained herein or for any errors or omissions that may have been made. The publisher remains neutral with regard to jurisdictional claims in published maps and institutional affiliations.

This Springer imprint is published by the registered company Springer Nature Switzerland AG
The registered company address is: Gewerbestrasse 11, 6330 Cham, Switzerland

If disposing of this product, please recycle the paper.

Xiaochun Cheng
Editor

Broadband Communications, Networks, and Systems

14th EAI International Conference, BROADNETS 2024
Hyderabad, India, February 16–17, 2024
Proceedings, Part I

Editor
Xiaochun Cheng
Swansea University
Swansea, UK

ISSN 1867-8211   ISSN 1867-822X (electronic)
Lecture Notes of the Institute for Computer Sciences, Social Informatics
and Telecommunications Engineering
ISBN 978-3-031-81167-8   ISBN 978-3-031-81168-5 (eBook)
https://doi.org/10.1007/978-3-031-81168-5

© ICST Institute for Computer Sciences, Social Informatics and Telecommunications Engineering 2025

This work is subject to copyright. All rights are solely and exclusively licensed by the Publisher, whether the whole or part of the material is concerned, specifically the rights of translation, reprinting, reuse of illustrations, recitation, broadcasting, reproduction on microfilms or in any other physical way, and transmission or information storage and retrieval, electronic adaptation, computer software, or by similar or dissimilar methodology now known or hereafter developed.
The use of general descriptive names, registered names, trademarks, service marks, etc. in this publication does not imply, even in the absence of a specific statement, that such names are exempt from the relevant protective laws and regulations and therefore free for general use.
The publisher, the authors and the editors are safe to assume that the advice and information in this book are believed to be true and accurate at the date of publication. Neither the publisher nor the authors or the editors give a warranty, expressed or implied, with respect to the material contained herein or for any errors or omissions that may have been made. The publisher remains neutral with regard to jurisdictional claims in published maps and institutional affiliations.

This Springer imprint is published by the registered company Springer Nature Switzerland AG
The registered company address is: Gewerbestrasse 11, 6330 Cham, Switzerland

If disposing of this product, please recycle the paper.

Preface

We are delighted to introduce the proceedings of the 14th edition of the 2024 European Alliance for Innovation (EAI) International Conference on Broadband Communications, Networks, and Systems (BROADNETS 2024). This conference was originally scheduled to take place in 2023 however, it was postponed until 2024 to give the new conference committee time to organize and prepare. This conference brought together researchers, developers and practitioners around the world who are leveraging and developing smart grid technology for a smarter and more resilient grid. The theme of BROADNETS 2024 was "5G-enabled digital society".

The technical program of BROADNETS 2024 consisted of 49 full papers. The conference tracks were: Track 1 - Communications, Networks and Architectures; Track 2 - Smart City Smart Grid; Track 3 - Communication-Inspired Machine Learning (ML) for 5G/6G; Track 4 - Wireless Network Security and Privacy; and Track 5 - AI applications for 5G/6G. Aside from the high-quality technical paper presentations, the technical program also featured one keynote speech and two invited talks. The keynote speaker was Nithesh Naik from Manipal University, India. The two invited talks were presented by Princy Randhawa from Manipal University, India and Álvaro Rocha from the University of Lisbon.

Coordination with the steering chairs, Bhupesh Mishra, Sulakshana Chilukuri, Krishna Chaitanya Janapati and Praveen Kumar Devulapalli, was essential for the success of the conference. We sincerely appreciate their constant support and guidance. It was also a great pleasure to work with such an excellent organizing committee team for their hard work in organizing and supporting the conference. In particular, the Technical Program Committee, led by our TPC Co-chairs, Lakmini Malasinghe, Pushpita Chaterjee and Amit Mukherjee, completed the peer-review process of technical papers and made a high-quality technical program. We are also grateful to Conference Manager Martin Hochel for his support and to all the authors who submitted their papers to the BROADNETS 2024 conference and workshops.

We strongly believe that BROADNETS 2024 provided a good forum for all researchers, developers and practitioners to discuss all science and technology aspects that are relevant to smart grids. We also expect that future Broadnets conferences will be as successful and stimulating, as indicated by the contributions presented in this volume.

Xiaochun Cheng

Organization

Steering Committee

Imrich Chlamtac — University of Trento, Italy

Organizing Committee

General Chair

Ming Yang — Kennesaw State University – Marietta Campus, USA

General Co-chairs

G. A. E. Satish Kumar — Vardhaman College of Engineering, India
J. V. R. Ravindra — Vardhaman College of Engineering, India

Program Chairs

Bhupesh Mishra — University of Gloucestershire, UK
Sulakshana Chilukuri — Vardhaman College of Engineering, India
Vicente García Díaz — University of Oviedo, Spain
Xiaochun Cheng — Swansea University, UK

Technical Program Committee Co-chair

Lakmini Malasinghe — Sri Lanka Institute of Information Technology, Sri Lanka

Web Chair

Praveen Kumar — Vardhaman College of Engineering, India

Publicity and Social Media Chair

Amit Mukherjee — University of South Bohemia, Czech Republic

Workshops Chair

Pushpita Chaterjee — Howard University, USA

Publications Chair

Ruben Gonzalez — Universidad Internacional de La Rioja, Spain

Panels Chair

Osamah Ibrahim Khalaf — Al-Nahrain University, Iraq

Local Chair

J. Krishna Chaitanya — Vardhaman College of Engineering, India

Technical Program Committee

Xiaochun Cheng	Swansea University, UK
Abdulsattar Abdullah Hamad	University of Samarra, Iraq
Rubén Arístides González Crespo	Universidad Internacional de La Rioja, Spain
Jayanthi Ravindra	Vardhaman College of Engineering, India
A. Jaya Lakshmi	Vardhaman College of Engineering, India
Bindu Swetha Pasuluri	Vardhaman College of Engineering, India
Sangeeta Singh	Vardhaman College of Engineering, India
D. Nagajyothi	Vardhaman College of Engineering, India
S. Karunakaran	Vardhaman College of Engineering, India
A. Vijaya Lakshmi	Vardhaman College of Engineering, India
Krishna Dharavath	Vardhaman College of Engineering, India
Naresh Kumar M.	Vardhaman College of Engineering, India
G. Suryanarayana	Vardhaman College of Engineering, India
Jyothi V.	Vardhaman College of Engineering, India
Sreenivasulu Gogula	Vardhaman College of Engineering, India
Vijaya Lakshmi	Vardhaman College of Engineering, India

Contents – Part I

Communications, Networks and Architectures

Scalable Deep Learning for Categorization of Satellite Images 3
   C. Lokanath Reddy, T. Mukthananda Reddy, M. Mahendra Reddy, and M. Mohan

Mitigating Threats in PHY-Layer Authentication: A Proactive Defense
Against Membership Inference Attacks in Wireless Signal Classifiers 14
   D. Madhuri, V. Nikitha Reddy, M. Keerthi Reddy, V. N. L. N. Murthy, Saroja Kumar Rout, and Bijaya Kumar Sethi

Wearable Circularly Polarized MIMO Antenna: Design and Simulation
for High-Data Biomedical Sensing Devices 25
   Mallavarapu Sandhya and Lokam Anjaneyulu

Implementation of Antenna in Satellite Ground Station for Cubesat 33
   Kummari Harshavardhini, Vikas Kumar Ghanathey, SriSrujan Ryali, and Sulakshana Chilukuri

AESHA3: Efficient and Secure Sub-Key Generation for AES Using SHA-3 42
   Ankush Soni, Sanjay K. Sahay, and Parit Mehta

UWB Antenna with Integrated Quadruple Notch Bands 54
   Nallanagula Sanjana, Yellavula Jaswanth, Perumandla Sai Sushumna, and Sulakshana Chilukuri

Framework for Brute-Force Attack Detection Using Federated Learning 64
   J. Chethana Datta, S. Ananya, Mukund Deepak, Nishanth Mungara, and V. Sarasvathi

Differential Cascode Voltage Switch Logic (DCVSL) Level Shifter
with Logic Error Detection 74
   Azmath Noorain, G. Sanjeeva Reddy, Srimanthula Manish Goud, and Sangeeta Singh

Smart City Smart Grid

Robot for Transportation with an SMS Alert 85
   Pavani Arra, Ganesh Reddy, Santhosh Reddy, and V. Harini

Joint Design of User Association, Caching and Power Allocation for Delay Optimization in UAV-Enabled Networks 95
Gezahegn Abdissa Bayessa, Rong Chai, Yetmwork Gutema Lemu, and Qianbin Chen

Low Power VLSI Architecture for Rail To Rail Dynamic Voltage Comparator 114
S. Karunakaran, S. Srivardhan, M. Harshith, and K. SaiManish

Enhanced Semantic Communication in 6G Networks Using DCGAN 122
Sowmya Sri Nalluri, G. A. E. Satish Kumar, Dileep Kumar Arumulla, and Vinod Kumar Auti

An Efficient FR-1 MIMO Antenna for N78/77/48 Bands with Enhanced Isolation Using DGS 132
Manumula Srinubabu and Nuthakki Venkata Rajasekhar

A Study on Efficient Approaches for Distributing Workloads Effectively in Edge Computing Systems 143
Kavya Lingutla, Vennela Priya Penumuchu, Hima Varsha Nagisetty, Niharika Nunna, and S. R. Reeja

Real Time Phishing Detection Using Lexical Analysis and Visual Similarity ... 157
A. Gnanesh, Dasa A. Deepesh, Bhargav Hegde, Shreehari Vyasamudri, and V. Sarasvathi

Securing the Internet of Things: A Comprehensive Examination of Machine and Deep Learning Approaches Against Denial of Service Attacks 176
Deepak Singh and R. Uma Mageswari

Design of Single Cycle MIPS RISC Processor Using Re-timing Technique 189
Sindhe Sreeja, Gudipati Sneha, Guguloth Ganesh, and Sangeeta Singh

Prediction of Crop Based on Characteristics of Agricultural Environment Using Machine Learning Techniques 202
Madhavarapu Prathima Rao, R. Jegadeesan, P. Pranitha, D. Praveen Kuamar, and J. Krishna Chaitanya

IoT-Based Classification of COVID-19 Cases with Cardiovascular Disease Using Deep Convolutional Decision Trees 211
R. Amudha, M. S. Kavitha, S. Karthik, and Balakrishnan Biju

Communication-inspired Machine Learning (ML) for 5G/6G

Enhancing Maritime Safety with Deep Learning for Ship Identification 227
   K. Sripal, Kotra Akshay, Avula Shiva Sai,
   and Rebanamoni Sravan Kumar Reddy

Implementation and Analysis of PUF Architectures for Enhanced Security 231
   Sangeeta Singh, Azmath Noorain, G. Sanjeeva Reddy,
   and Srimanthula Manish Goud

Smart Drowsiness Detection System with Microcontroller Integration 241
   Satyarth Motupalli, J. V. R. Ravindra, G. A. E. Satish Kumar,
   R. Phani Vidhyadhar, Ramavathar Yadav Kanneboina,
   Varun Kumar Reddy, and Siddarth Tammineni

Innovative Motion Sensing System with Labview 249
   R. Phani Vidyadhar, J. V. R. Ravindra, G. A. E. Satish Kumar,
   Yanigandla Sandeep, Kanugula Ashwitha, Devansh Mantri,
   and Faldu Vishvakumari

Supervene Bag A Smart Luggage Carrier 260
   Krishna Chaitanya Janapati, J. V. R. Ravindra, Satyarth Motupalli,
   Veda Manogna Nanduri, Pavani Punem, Sameer Mohammad,
   Sujay Kapil Peddaraju, and Amit Lathigara

Enhancing Finite Impulse Response (FIR) Filtering with Distributive
Arithmetic (DA) and Residue Number System (RNS) Optimization 272
   Mentam Sunaina and G. L. Sumalata

A Wide Band Annular-Ring Loaded Circularly Polarized Microstrip
Antenna 282
   Samuel Nishant Muthyala, Pasumarthy Nageswara Rao,
   Kiran Mannem, and E. R. Aruna

Design and Implementing a PCI Express Serdes Block Using HDL 291
   Ravali Meesa and G. Surekha

Development and Realization of an FIR Filter Utilizing an Innovative
RNS Form with a Dual Modular Set 302
   Mentam Sunaina and G. L. Sumalata

Attack Detection in Smart Home IoT Networks: A Survey on Challenges,
Methods and Analysis 310
   M. Vinay Kuma Rreddy, Amit Lathigara, and Muthangi Kantha Reddy

AI Based Reliable and Secure Data Transfer in Wireless Networks 320
   P. Kalyanchakravarthi and Susmitha Das

Author Index 329

Contents – Part II

Wireless Network Security and Privacy

Design and Implementation of WiFi-Control Robotic Arm for Cleaning Blackboard 3
  Sanam Abhishek, Krishna Chaithanya Janapati, J. V. R. Ravindra, Satyarth Motupalli, Bondugula Karthik Reddy, Godugu Suresh, and Vatsal A. Dharek

Image Semantic Segmentation for Enhanced Communication 15
  A. Vijaya Lakshmi, Raparthi Rohan, Chirag Karthik, and A. Aravind Reddy

Performance Analysis of Dadda Multiplier Using Kogge Stone Adder 28
  B. Srikanth, Dodda Sai Pranathi, Padmaraju Sai Kumar Raju, and Vemula Sarika

Design and Implementation of Unsigned Serial Divider Using TG Logic 42
  G. Kavya, K. Shreshta Reddy, D. Vishnu Prasad, J. V. R. Ravindra, and Himanshu Rajeshbhai Dodiya

Speed Control of BLDC Motor Using Bi-directional Converter 51
  B. Raja Gopal Reddy, N. Karuppiah, Patil Mounica, Jaydeep Kumar, and Keval Jitendrabhai Dasadiya

Direct Torque Controller of SRM for EV Application Based on Neural Network 58
  Anuradha Devi Tellapati, Malligunta Kiran Kumar, Natarajan Karuppaiah, S. Ravi Teja, and Kambhampati Venkata Govardhan Rao

Performance and Analysis of Cuk Converter for Electric Vehicle Battery Charger Along with Resonant Converter 70
  Keval Dasadiya, Jayraj Chanv, and N. Karupaiah

Investigating the Effect of Compression on Face Recognition with OpenCV ... 79
  Mallellu Sai Prashanth, Ramesh Karnati, Muni Sekhar Velpuru, H. Venkateshwara Reddy, and Charmi R. Jani

Artificial Intelligence Research in Computer Network Technology 89
    Jhansi Bharathi Madavarapu, Arnold Mashud Abukari,
    Shailaja Salagrama, and Radha Krishna Yalamanchili

WSafe – A Women Safety Android Application 96
    Sai Prasad Reddy Kukudala, Gururaj L. Kulkarni, Kandur Keerthi,
    Pavan N. Kunchur, and Gangireddy Nitish Kumar Reddy

AI Applications for 5G/6G

Exploring CNN-Based Algorithms for Human Action Recognition in
Videos 107
    Shaik Salma Begum, Jami Anjana Adi Sathvik,
    Mohammed Ezaz Ahmed, Dantu Vyshnavi Satya, Tulasi Javvadi,
    Majji Naveen Sai Kuma, and Kommoju V. V. S. M. Manoj Kumar

Vision-Based Sign Language Recognition and Multilingual Translation
for Facilitating Deaf and Mute Communication 116
    S. V. Vasantha, A. Ashwini, M. Avinash, M. Yuvaraj, R. Manisha,
    and Shirina Samreen

Advanced AI Surveillance for Human Trafficking and Accident Prevention 124
    Shanthi Makka, A. Sowmya, Sanagala Vishwanath, Kattekola Snigdha,
    and Vankadaru Charan

Trust Forge: Harnessing Machine Learning to Build Trust on Social
Networks 135
    Kavitha Chitrala, Shanthi Makka, and S. Sowjanya

Database Under Siege: The Hidden Menace of SQL Injection Attacks 144
    Rajitha Ala, Attili Venkata Ramana, Vasantha Sandhya Venu,
    Kiranmai Bejjam, Sai Sriharsha Kanagala,
    Bheemeshwar Punyamurthy, and Ruchitha Sangeam

SearchScrapeAssistant Application Using RPA Tool 154
    S. Adityeshwar Goud, Sindhuja Ramala, PavanTeja Modugu,
    Ravi Kumar, Amit Lathigara, and M. Vinay Kumar Redy

LS-DYNA-Based Car Frontal Fascia Simulation During Collision 167
    Jalapudi Laxmi Prasanna, Kandukuri Vasantha Kumar,
    Burragalla Dhanraj, and Uday Kumar Madduri

Integrated Smart Footwear: Advanced Health Monitoring and Energy Harvesting 178
   Naresh Kumar, Boddu Mani Deep, Rejinthala Nikhitha, Talari Tarun Kumar, and Bhavikchandra Bosamia

Effective Low Leakage 6T and 8T SRAM Using CMOS 90 nm Technology 187
   V. Siddartha Reddy, G. Sumukh, K. Mahesh, P. Kalyani, and P. Bindu Swetha

Author Index 197

Communications, Networks and Architectures

Scalable Deep Learning for Categorization of Satellite Images

C. Lokanath Reddy[(✉)], T. Mukthananda Reddy, M. Mahendra Reddy, and M. Mohan

G. Pullaiah College of Engineering and Technology, Kurnool, Andhra Pradesh, India
chilakalalokanathreddy@gmail.com

Abstract. The analysis of satellite data has become increasingly challenging due to the vast abundance of satellite photos available in recent years. Understanding and extracting valuable insights from these images necessitates a comprehensive grasp of the underlying data they portray. The capability to identify and categorize objects within satellite photos holds significant importance across various domains, including land planning, ecology, military intelligence, and ocean monitoring. With their wealth of spatiotemporal information, satellite images serve as invaluable resources for global remote sensing applications aimed at addressing a wide spectrum of issues. This study aims to investigate the complexities associated with analyzing satellite data by developing a specialized workflow focused on mapping streets and highways to monitor urban development in cities. The study emphasizes addressing learning challenges through the configuration execution, and evaluation of deep neural network experiments. To achieve this objective, publicly accessible methods and information are utilized. The data acquisition pipeline incorporates preprocessing techniques to effectively handle inputs with varying sizes, resolutions, and spectral channels. Despite the significant potential of satellite imagery, its widespread dissemination is hindered by various challenges, including issues related to data distribution, volume, quality, and accessibility. These obstacles further complicate the study of satellite images. Additionally, satellite imagery finds application in monitoring oceanic and geographical data, highlighting its diverse utility. The proposed strategy is anchored in a scalable end-to-end approach for interpreting satellite imagery, aiming to overcome the challenges associated with analyzing large-scale satellite datasets efficiently. Through this study, we aim to contribute to ongoing efforts in harnessing the power of satellite imagery for addressing global challenges and fostering sustainable development.

Keywords: Hyperspectral remote sensing · deep neural networks · satellite images · Python · Google Collab are some of the index phrases

1 Introduction

In numerous visual tasks, such as identifying two-dimensional images, convolutional neural networks have proven to perform exceptionally well. As this paper uses deep convolutional neural networks to directly identify the spectral domain of hyperspectral pictures. In particular, the design of the production process has five layers by weight, namely the production layer, the production process includes the layers of production, production, production, and production. These five layers are applied to each spectral classification than certain conventional techniques (such support vector machines and deep learning models). In line with experimental findings derived from multiple hyperspectral picture datasets. The capacity to analyze object details using distributed photos has increased with the availability of hyperspectral images; yet, this has resulted in increased data processing costs. This study looks on the priority of key point analysis in Hyperspectral image categorization. Within this work, two exceedingly subtle maps—HYDICE as well AVIRIS—are used. The content of the drawing's major content was examined after a brief introduction to the main content analysis method. The findings indicate that only the first few groups contain significant information. An accurate classification rate of roughly 70% can be achieved by using the first few essential photos. This study demonstrates the results and efficiency of using the key point analysis technique as a preliminary step in hyperspectral image classification.

1.1 Existing System

In the classification of hyperspectral images, numerous techniques have produced good results. This paper investigates three elements of the three classification methods for hyperspectral images are available: supervised, semi-supervised, and unsupervised Classification.

1.1.1 Supervised Classification

Supervised classification involves training a model using labeled data, where each pixel in the hyperspectral image is associated with a known class or category. The process typically includes selecting representative samples from each class and extracting features from the spectral signatures of these samples. Common supervised classification algorithms include Support Vector Machines (SVM), Random Forest, Maximum Likelihood Classifier (MLC), and Neural Networks.

1.1.2 Semi-supervised Classification

Semi-supervised classification techniques leverage both labeled and unlabeled data. In this approach, a portion of the hyperspectral image is manually labeled, while the rest remains unlabeled. The classifier learns from the labeled data and generalizes its knowledge to classify the unlabeled pixels.

1.1.3 Unsupervised Classification

Unsupervised classification does not require any labeled data for training. Instead, it identifies clusters or groups of pixels with similar spectral signatures in the hyperspectral image. Common unsupervised classification algorithms include K-Means Clustering, Spectral Clustering, and Gaussian Mixture Models (GMM). These algorithms partition the image into distinct regions or classes based solely on the spectral characteristics of the pixels, without any prior knowledge of the classes present in the scene.

1.1.4 Disadvantages

The accuracy of distinct algorithms cannot be compared. It is irrelevant and the classification is 100% accurate. Whatever the kernel type, they are all the same. A quick and cost-prohibitive procedure is needed to create a house model.

1.2 Proposed System

It is demonstrated that the suggested model eliminates every drawback of the current setup. The system will use deep learning to examine the hyperspectral PCA image and the parsing model's structure, thereby increasing the accuracy of neural network findings. It improves every distribution result's efficiency. Hyperspectral images are expected to provide higher accuracy. The objective of this research is to categorize satellite photos. Four distinct groups are created from the supplied satellite pictures by the plan. Prior to classification, feature maps are retrieved from the input image and preprocessed. Convolutional neural networks use the basic structure of images spatial information, also known as topological information like adjacency and rotation about the structures in the image, is also considered. Now we'll go over the specifics of how the neural network's various methods interacts (Fig. 1).

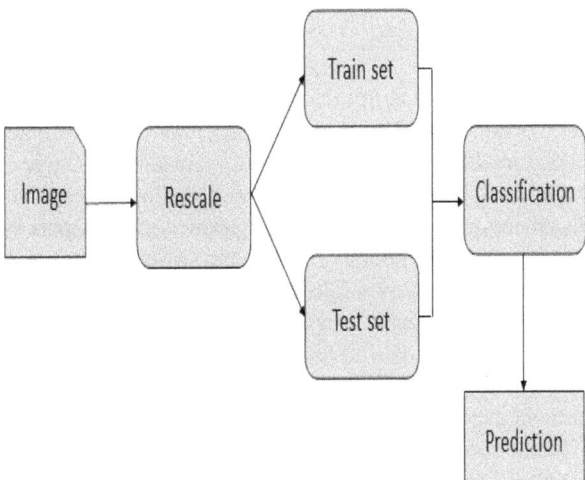

Fig. 1. Block diagram of system architecture

2 Motivation

Understanding complex global phenomena like urbanization, climate change headwinds, biodiversity research, and the social economy by stepping back and measuring overall processes at scale Images in the visible, mid-infrared, near-infrared, and ultraviolet spectrums of electromagnetic waves are captured using it. Image spectrometers can visualize a large number of pixels continuously and narrowly, so that every pixel throughout the range of wavelengths might get the entire spectrum emitted or reflected. As a result, High spectral resolution can be found in hyperspectral photos, multi-band capability, and a wealth of data. This system, also known as Global Monitoring, possesses uses in disaster relief, business control and accuracy agriculture. Earth observation information are collected using a variety of methods, which is able to broadly classified since final as well near-final (also known comparable to in situ sensing). Initially, there is that "the distance between the object and the sensor is greater than the sensor's linear size," and the second is that the distance is equal to the sensor's linear size. Image editing, noise reduction and dimensionality reduction, segmentation, and other techniques are used to process hyperspectral remote sensing images. Contains. Hyperspectral images, unlike ordinary pictures have a multitude of spectrum information that can reveal the chemical makeup and physical makeup of objects fascinating and cause image dispersion. The greatest advanced research in the hyperspectral field is hyperspectral photography analysis, in which Image categorization using computerized remote sensing is used to identify and analyze captured images of the Earth's surface and surrounding data, thereby identifying the characteristics of the image files and extracting the desired data properties.

3 Methodology

3.1 Image Quality

Interference impacts the data's quality due to noise and background obtained during hyperspectral image acquisition. The Hughes effect may be exacerbated by the small size hyperspectral picture data and the absence of domain names. People concentrated on spectral data and only used Spectral information was used in the early studies of hyperspectral image classification to carry out image classification. Support vector machines (SVM) and random forests (RF)), neural network, and so on. Manual analysis of satellite and aerial images was previously possible, owing to the scarcity of images; however, this is no longer the case. As a result, extracting relevant information from images has become a problem in today's big data environment. An important aspect of this problem is the annotated (or tagged)) process, which finds patterns and structures in satellite data images. This document explains how to interpret satellite images in order to categorize them into four different domains: water bodies, green areas, air, and desert. This translation has a wide range of applications. The proposed model has higher accuracy, which is supported by empirical results. A comparison with some deep learning models was also performed to ascertain whether component of the suggested model is optimal. This paper presents a network-based image classification algorithm that has been shown to outperform other methods. This new method not only improves classification accuracy but also lowers the model's training cost.

3.2 Neural Network

Although neural networks have been around for decades, they have only gained attention from the computer vision and machine learning communities in recent years. First, an overview of neural networks is presented. The author stated that "neural networks are computational systems composed of many simple, interconnected processes that process information, from dynamic responses to external inputs." Very roughly, one way to think of neural network algorithms as:

Based on the architecture of brain neurons Many people imagine networks as layers of neurons layered on top of one another or neurons) act as mechanisms of activation. The figure depicts a basic three-layer neural network. For a variety of vision-related tasks, the neural network can be thought of as learning models from raw data (pixel-related in our results).

The following definition of the objectives can be used for this purpose:

1. A concise examination regarding computer vision using neural network technology.
2. Create a deep neural network capable of generating semantically segmented picture maps by consuming data.
3. Compare various neural network models described in the literature. Developing and improving existing models to solve existing problems (Transformation)
4. Examine the network training on various datasets to determine its overall capabilities.
5. It analyzes existing satellite images in depth.
6. Deep learning models are used to interpret satellite images.
7. Compares the planned process with the state-of-the art technology (Fig. 2).

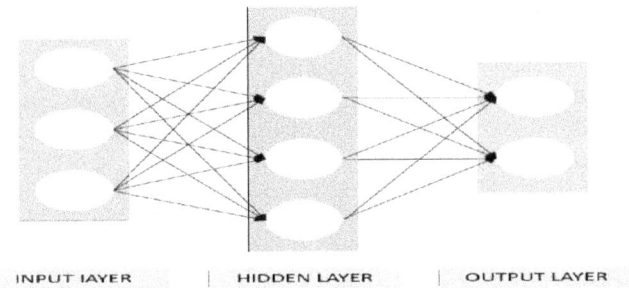

Fig. 2. Neural Network

3.3 Satellite Image Classification

In this study, dataset-RSI-CB256 was used. This is a public information collection that can be found at. This data is divided into four groups based on sensor and Google Maps snapshots. Each image is 256 × 256 pixels in size (Fig. 3).

It also distinguishes between common and distinct data t-distributed stochastic neighborhood embedding classes (T-SNE). High-dimensional data points can be mapped to two- or three-dimensional spaces using TSNE visualization. T-SNE preserves as much as possible the balance of high-dimensional data points in low-dimensional space.

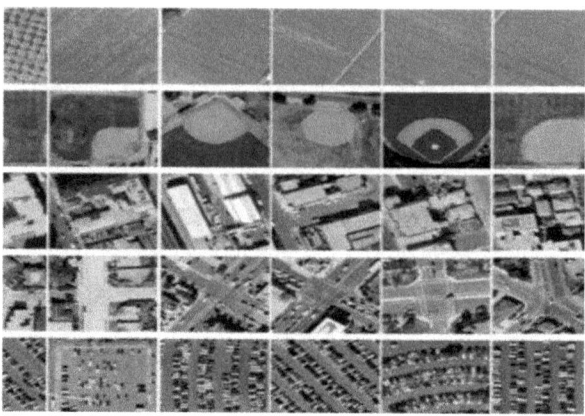

Fig. 3. Shows the category distribution of the data

3.3.1 Semantic Segmentation

Over the years, features have been defined in various ways, but the basic process has remained the same: analyze images to identify objects and determine their significance. Semantic segmentation, object location and detection, instance segmentation, and image classification are the most common learning problems arising from data visualization. The process of combining the image so that each group of pixels in the image in line with the item category among the entire assembly is then defined as semantic segmentation. The object class corresponds to the path and background in the current study. The pile can also be placed on homes, lawns, garages, and other fissile surfaces. The rest of this chapter discusses recent developments in semantic segmentation solutions and data applications for satellite/aerial imagery.

4 Implementation of Modules

4.1 Dataset

Using a same dataset for training and testing also critical to comprehend how the model functions on another. This section outlines the process for creating A second, far more compact dataset that will be used to evaluate the models used in this piece. Previous research's labels pertaining to using satellite or aerial photography to learn, for example, relied on Open Street Map, a project to produce and provide open-access geospatial data (street maps included) to anybody. Rasterizing vector graphic maps extracted from Open Street Map resulted in per-pixel labels. It was observed that prediction quality was impacted by the arbitrary nature of the conversion process utilized, and therefore also in this work. A similar technique is used to generate a road map from the road maps provided in the OSM database. Data selection and loading:

- Data selection is the process of selecting hyperspectral image data, which was used in this project.
- Hyperspectral images were used in this project.

- The file contains information regarding testing, training and visual effects. 2.1.3. Previous information (Fig. 4):

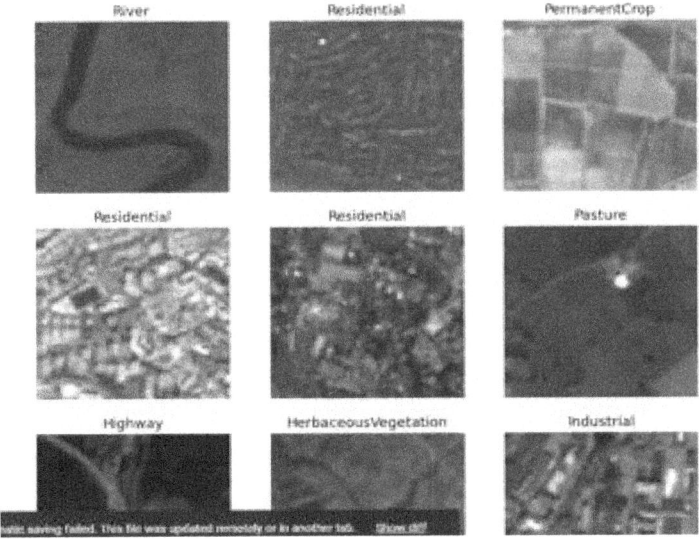

Fig. 4. Datasets

The preceding data has been enhanced by the addition of randomization and jitter compensation. We can improve it by utilizing the dataset's unique features. In the case of segmentation based on satellite images, for example, the orientation of the picture is unimportant. First of all, spins and spins can only be of assistance to broaden institution without having a negative impact. Further advancements can be made, for example, by accounting for the orbital parameters of a specific satellite photographer. Randomly rotate and jitter to increase the training size by 9000 times. To eliminate redundant data, the received data is first routed through a pipeline. This includes basic training set normalization and mean centering. Before feeding into the pipeline, the standard deviation is divided by the R-G-B image mean after it has been subtracted from each training set.

4.2 Split the Dataset into Training Data Testing Data

- The process of splitting the present data into two halves is known as data splitting, and it is usually done for cross-validation purposes.
- A piece of the data is utilized for the prediction model's construction, while another portion is used to evaluate the model's effectiveness.
- Generally speaking, the majority of the data is used for training and the remaining portion is used for testing when the data set is divided into training and test sets.

4.3 CNN

- Using appropriate filters, Convolutional Networks can effectively capture spatial and temporal dependencies in images. The design can be optimized for the image dataset by reducing the number of parameters and reusing weights.
- This is the process of forecasting based on hyperspectral images.
- Through enhancing the accuracy of each prediction result, this project will efficiently forecast data stored in the database (Fig. 5).

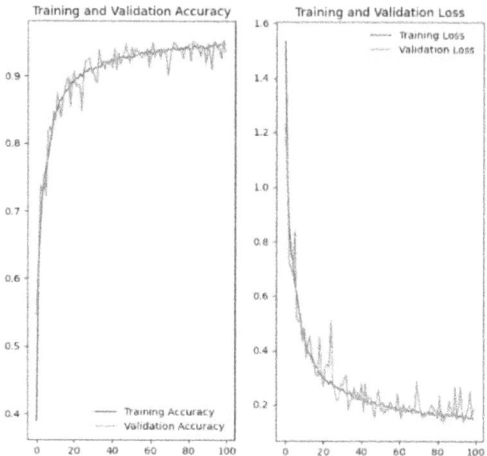

Fig. 5. Training and Validation Accuracy

4.4 Result Generation

Based on the entire distribution and result generation, the final result will be estimated. To assess the effectiveness of this method, use metrics such as;

- Accuracy
- Precision
- Recall
- F-Measure
- Confusion Matrix (Fig. 6)

4.5 Advantages

- High performance;
- Hyperspectral images improve accuracy;
- Time is reduced

```
Modified Deep CNN-BiLSTM with attention mechanism   Accuracy is : 95.8 %
classification_report:
              precision    recall  f1-score   support

           0       0.93      1.00      0.96       516
           1       1.00      0.92      0.95       484

    accuracy                           0.96      1000
   macro avg       0.96      0.96      0.96      1000
weighted avg       0.96      0.96      0.96      1000

[[515   1]
 [ 41 443]]
```

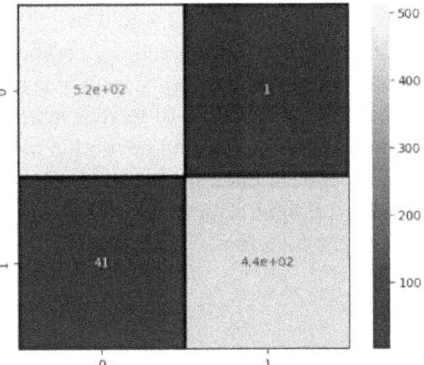

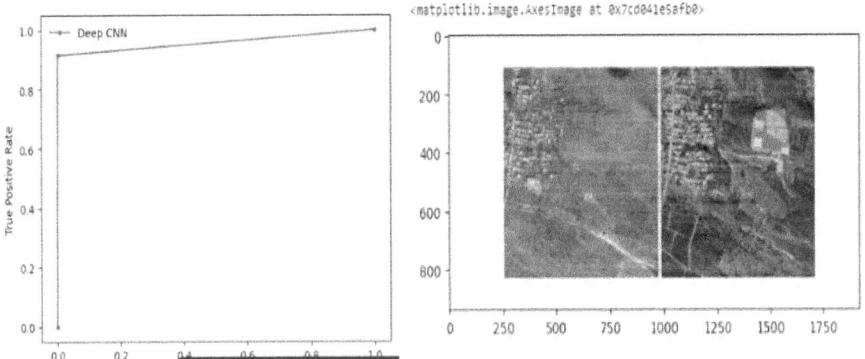

Fig. 6. Accuracy result of evaluate the effectiveness of hyperspectral images

5 Conclusion

The primary goal of this project is to use satellite image data to better understand the design, implementation, and evaluation of deep-water pipelines. The categorization and examination of hyperspectral pictures are crucial part utilizing hyperspectral image processing in our investigation. This article explains different approaches to the classification of hyperspectral images, such as supervised, unsupervised, and semi-supervised classification. Although the supervised and unsupervised classification methods discussed in this article have distinct advantages, each method's application has limitations. This research can be expanded by using different materials. It can also examine more than four satellite images at once. Other deep learning models can be defined as well. A fascinating study would be to investigate the effect of various bone structures on Efficient Nets. Image classification can also be done with multi-resolution remote sensing image models. Many data solutions are becoming increasingly expensive. Multiple problem solutions that make use of large amounts of data would be extremely beneficial. Introduction to the use of deep learning technology and the creation of deep pipelines for satellite imagery. This project started with gathering valid data and thinking about ways to improve deep learning models. A comparison of various neural network architectures listed in the literature. To understand the training network's overall capabilities, run it through various datasets. Using the standard testing method, the model was evaluated on samples from the unobserved Prague dataset as well as the Massachusetts dataset. These are compared to provide the final model evaluation.

References

1. Teng, M.Y., Mehrubeoglu, R., King, S.A., Cammarata, K., Simons, J.: Investigation of epifauna coverage on seagrass blades using spatial and spectral analysis of hyperspectral images. In: 2013 5th Workshop on Hyperspectral Image and Signal Processing: Evolution in Remote Sensing (WHISPERS), Gainesville, FL, USA, pp. 1–4 (2013)
2. Ke, C.: Military object detection using multiple information extracted from hyperspectral imagery. In: 2017 International Conference on Progress in Informatics and Computing (PIC), Nanjing, China, pp. 124–128 (2017)
3. Notesco, G., Ben Dor, E., Brook, A.: Mineral mapping of Makhtesh Ramon in Israel using hyperspectral remote sensing day and night LWIR images. In: 2014 6th Workshop on Hyperspectral Image and Signal Processing: Evolution in Remote Sensing (WHISPERS), Lausanne, Switzerland, pp. 1–4 (2014)
4. Pike, R., Lu, G., Wang, D., Chen, Z.G., Fei, B.: A minimum spanning forest-based method for noninvasive cancer detection with hyperspectral imaging. IEEE Trans. Biomed. Eng. **63**(3), 653–663 (2016)
5. Zhang, X., Zhang, A., Meng, X.: Automatic fusion of hyperspectral images and laser scans using feature points. J. Sens. **2015**, 9, Article ID 415361 (2015)
6. Kwon, H., Hu, X., Theiler, J., Zare, A., Gurram, P.: Algorithms for multispectral and hyperspectral image analysis. J. Electr. Comput. Eng. **2013**, 2, Article ID 908906 (2013)
7. Ma, Y., Li, R., Yang, G., Sun, L., Wang, J.: A research on the combination strategies of multiple features for hyperspectral remote sensing image classification. J. Sens. **2018**, 14, Article ID 7341973 (2018)

8. Binol, H.: Ensemble learning based multiple kernel principal component analysis for dimensionality reduction and classification of hyperspectral imagery. Math. Probl. Eng. **2018**, 14, Article ID 9632569 (2018)
9. Li, S., Song, W., Fang, L., Chen, Y., Ghamisi, P., Benediktsson, J.A.: Deep learning for hyperspectral image classification: an overview. IEEE Trans. Geosci. Remote Sens. **57**(9), 6690–6709 (2019)
10. Camps-Valls, G., Bruzzone, L.: Kernel-based methods for hyperspectral image classification. IEEE Trans. Geosci. Remote Sens. **43**(6), 1351–1362 (2005)
11. Camps-Valls, G., Bandos Marsheva, T.V., Zhou, D.: Semi supervised graph-based hyperspectral image classification. IEEE Trans. Geosci. Remote Sens. **45**(10), 3044–3054 (2007)
12. Hughes, G.: On the mean accuracy of statistical pattern recognizers. IEEE Trans. Inf. Theory **14**(1), 55–63 (1968)
13. Wang, X., Feng, Y.: New method based on support vector machine in classification for hyperspectral data. In: 2008 International Symposium on Computational Intelligence and Design, Wuhan, China, pp. 76–80 (2008)
14. Fu, A., Ma, X., Wang, H.: Classification of hyperspectral image based on hybrid neural networks. In: 2018 IEEE International Geoscience and Remote Sensing Symposium, IGARSS 2018, Valencia, Spain, pp. 2643–2646 (2018)
15. Li, J., Bioucas-Dias, J.M., Plaza, A.: Semi supervised hyperspectral image segmentation using multinomial logistic regression with active learning. IEEE Trans. Geosci. Remote Sens.Geosci. Remote Sens. **48**(11), 4085–4098 (2010)

Mitigating Threats in PHY-Layer Authentication: A Proactive Defense Against Membership Inference Attacks in Wireless Signal Classifiers

D. Madhuri[1], V. Nikitha Reddy[1], M. Keerthi Reddy[1], V. N. L. N. Murthy[1], Saroja Kumar Rout[1(✉)], and Bijaya Kumar Sethi[2]

[1] Department of Information Technology, Vardhaman College of Engineering (Autonomous), Hyderabad, India
keerthireddymugala@gmail.com, rout_sarojkumar@yahoo.co.in

[2] Department of Computer Science and Engineering (Data Science), Vardhaman College of Engineering (Autonomous), Hyderabad, India

Abstract. In a wireless signal classifier utilized for PHY-layer authentication, a membership inference attack is demonstrated as an adversarial machine learning method. Waveform, channel, and device attributes are among the private information that needs to be retrieved. There is a difficulty since varying channel conditions produce varying received signals and RF fingerprints. The attacker constructs a surrogate classifier by examining the spectrum in order to circumvent this issue. Subsequently, we employ this surrogate model to conduct a black-box Membership Inference Attack (MIA) on the designated classifier. Our findings reveal that the adversary can effectively discern signals and potentially extract radio and channel information utilized in training the target classifier. To address this potential threat, we have implemented a proactive defense strategy. In order to fool the opponent, this involves creating a shadow MIA model. In order to reduce the MIA's accuracy and prevent data from the wireless signal classifier from leaking, faults are intended to be introduced. This scenario holds significance as it sheds insight on potential vulnerabilities in wireless signal classifiers, particularly with regard to PHY-layer authentication. In order to enhance wireless communication system security, the proactive defense strategy highlights how important it is to anticipate and prevent adversarial machine learning attacks.

Keywords: Adversarial machine learning · Membership Inference attack · Privacy · Wireless signal classification · Defense

1 Introduction

The Wireless networks are dynamic, and machine learning (ML), which has shown to be a successful approach to solving complicated issues in wireless communications affected by factors including channel conditions, interference, and traffic effects, has successfully addressed this. In particular, recent advances in computation and algorithms have strengthened deep learning (DL), making it possible for it to efficiently capture high-dimensional representations of information on the spectrum [1]. The effectiveness of deep learning is demonstrated by a wide range of wireless communication applications, such as spectrum allocation, signal classification, waveform design, and spectrum sensing. However, there are unique security issues when ML/DL is integrated into wireless networks.

Due to adversarial machine learning (AML), attacks against ML/DL engines in wireless systems have expanded in variety. These attacks include those that facilitate clandestine communications, Trojan, spoofing, evasion (adversarial), and inference (exploratory). AML-based attacks function with small spectrum footprints, which makes detection more challenging, in contrast to more traditional wireless assaults such data transmission jamming [2]. Alongside security problems, privacy concerns are increasingly more common in machine learning (ML) solutions, particularly given the potential for adversaries to gain information from ML models. For instance, in a model inversion attack, adversaries have access to a machine learning model and particular private data, and they then use the model's inputs and outputs to deduce further private data. Another well-studied privacy assault is the membership inference attack (MIA), which has been applied to computer vision, healthcare, and commerce, among other data areas. MIA's goal is to ascertain if a certain data sample was part of the training set or not. MIA has been recognized as a significant privacy risk in the field of computer vision and related sectors, even if its potential application to the wireless sector is still unresolved (Fig. 1).

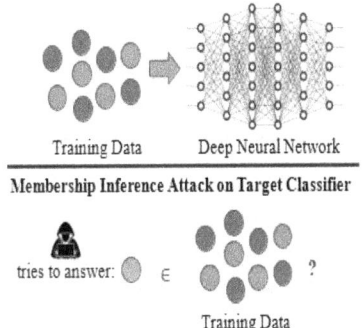

Fig. 1. Membership Inference Attack

Adversaries have particular chances to drop off over-the-air MIAs against wireless signal classifiers and eavesdrop on wireless signals due to the broadcast and shared aspect of the wireless channel. Since the target signal classifier's ML/DL model is trained using the waveform, channel, and basic radio device factors, they can therefore deduce information about these parts [5]. The present study describes the first-ever wireless application of Membership Inference Attack (MIA). Our aim is to introduce a goal for the aerial MIA machine learning (ML) technique, designed to function as a wireless signal classifier with enhancements from a deep neural network (DNN). This classifier serves the purpose of physical (PHY)-layer authentication for a wide range of diverse users, including Internet of Things (IoT) devices, such as those found in a gNodeB within

5G applications or network slicing scenarios. Service providers can utilize this classifier to authenticate users efficiently [6]. Using the Radio Frequency (RF) fingerprints found in received signals, this classifier helps determine if a user is authorized or unauthorized. These fingerprints show channel effects along with intrinsic characteristics of the user's RF transceiver. Then, requests for communication from approved users can be accommodated. This classifier could be used as an x App by the Open Radio Access Network's (ORAN) Near-Real-Time RAN Intelligent Controller (Near-RT RIC) [7]. Here, the adversary uses the MIA to ascertain whether the particular radio signal of interest is present in the desired classifier's training set after observing the target classifier's activity on the spectrum. The attack exposes whether particular waveform patterns, radio devices, or channel environments were utilized in training the wireless signal classifier. This breach of security could lead to further attacks exploiting the compromised personal data. For instance, adversaries could simulate the transmission of signals. This form of attack discloses whether a wireless signal classifier was trained under specific conditions, including waveform characteristics, device types, or radio environment settings [8].

The attacker could leverage the compromised personal information to carry out other attacks. Using a similar radio device type and waveform in a similar spectrum environment, for example, the attacker can fake signals that look to be coming from enabled users. Using signal classifiers designed for PHY-layer authentication, the adversary can steal communication resources thereby gaining network access or hindering other users' access. Wireless systems present distinct issues for MIA analysis and design than other data domains like computer vision. Even when an eavesdropper can see a provided signal over the air, the received signal differs from the signal received by the target signal classifier [10]. This leads to the data that the attacker collects and the data that the target signal classifier receives to fundamentally diverge from one another. The service provider uses its DL classifier to identify if the signal it receives in the context of RF fingerprinting is from an authorized user.

The DL classifier receives input in both phase and quadrature (I/Q) formats [11]. Based on the user's RF fingerprint, the categorization procedure takes into account the waveform, channel properties, and radio device. The adversary in a black-box MIA, or enemy unaware of the target classifier, is the focus of this work [12, 13]. Given the signal discrepancies that the adversary and the service provider receive, the adversary might not be able to use information about this classifier—that is, the underlying DNN model—to establish whether a signal is from an authorized user or not. The attacker builds a replacement classifier utilizing overheard signals as input to get past these barriers [14, 15]. The adversary can perform the MIA and ascertain whether the signal it received at the matching signal of the service provider was part of the signal's training data by utilizing this surrogate classifier.

2 Related Works

Recent research has increasingly focused on the intricate interplay between privacy invasion attacks directed at machine learning and deep learning models and the concept of differential privacy [1]. One such study by Rahman et al. delved into this relationship, with a particular emphasis on models built on neural networks. In order to investigate the trade-off between privacy and utility in the context of membership inference attacks, their study involved modifying the privacy budget [2]. Conversely, Wang et al. focused on developing a differentially private regression model in order to counteract model inversion attacks in regression models. To maintain utility and guarantee differential privacy, their method made use of functional mechanisms. Zhang et al. conducted research on obfuscation techniques, which involve the introduction of noise into input datasets for the purpose of training machine learning models.

Their results showed that, in comparison to non-private scenarios, data reconstructed by model inversion attacks showed increased blurriness when applied to obfuscated models [3, 4]. Park et al. continued this line of inquiry by examining the connection between model inversion attacks and differential privacy, specifically in the context of face recognition software based on neural network models [5]. With regard to model inversion attacks, they carefully examined the trade-offs between privacy and utility under various privacy guarantee levels [8, 9]. Furthermore, Jayaraman and Evans investigated the relationship between attacks that violate privacy and differential privacy definitions, focusing on membership inference and attribute inference attacks. Neural network and logistic regression models were used in their investigation. Their results showed that, in comparison to non-private scenarios, data reconstructed by model inversion attacks showed increased blurriness when applied to obfuscated models [3, 4].

Normalized Least Mean Square Algorithm

An adaptation process is always influenced by the stability, convergence time, and volatility of the LMS as well as the step size. An efficient method of overcoming the update step size is to normalize the input signal's variance, $\sigma_u(t)^2$. Therefore, the following equation shows the weight update formula:

$$w(t+1) = w(t) + \frac{\mu}{N\sigma_u(t)^2} x(t) e^*(t) \tag{1}$$

In consequence, the LMS algorithm's performance asymptotically does not depend on the number of taps N. This has a significant effect on convergence rate. More taps result in poorer convergence rates. Park et al. continued this line of inquiry by examining the connection between model inversion attacks and differential privacy, specifically in the context of face recognition software based on neural network models [5]. With regard to model inversion attacks, they carefully examined the trade-offs between privacy and utility under various privacy guarantee levels [8, 9]. Furthermore, Jayaraman and Evans investigated the relationship between attacks that violate privacy and differential privacy definitions, focusing on membership inference and attribute inference attacks. Neural network and logistic regression models were used in their investigation 2019) expanded on this idea by addressing vulnerabilities in deep learning models and suggesting countermeasures in the Proceedings of the 2019 IEEE Symposium on Security and Privacy [14]. Numerous defense strategies have been invested, such as: Differential privacy involves making it more difficult for attackers to deduce membership by adding noise to the model's output or by using strategies like federated learning. Adversarial Training: To improve robustness, train the model as an adversarial task against membership inference attacks [15]. Regularization Techniques: Reducing overfitting and complicating membership inference by using techniques like weight decay and dropout. Data augmentation involves adding artificial samples or perturbed data to training sets in order to make it harder for attackers to determine membership.

Ensemble Methods: To improve privacy and obstruct successful membership inference, combining multiple models or assembling [16, 17]. Private Aggregation of Teacher Ensembles (PATE): A method that protects privacy by training a student model with multiple teacher models, particularly in situations where sensitive data must be computed without dis-closing specific data points. The particular use case and threat model may influence the defense strategy selection [17, 18]. In order to protect sensing systems and deep learning models from membership inference attacks, researchers are constantly looking into new methods and improvements. Keeping up with the most recent findings in this area is essential for developing successful defense tactics.

3 Proposed Work

The study introduces the inaugural Membership Inference Attack (MIA) deployed over the air, aiming to infer training data and expose confidential details regarding waveform, device, and channel characteristics. Two MIA configurations are examined:

1. Various radio devices create nonmember signals, and
2. Both members and non-members' signals from the same radio device shall be distinguishable by the MIA.

The system extends the capabilities of Membership Inference Attack (MIA) by incorporating both original received signals and their corresponding noisy variations, taking into consideration the variations introduced by the channel. Extensive numerical analysis demonstrates the effectiveness of the MIA, indicating its ability to accurately deduce the membership of the training data used by the wireless signal classifier, as illustrated in Fig. 2.

Fig. 2. Depicting the Architecture

The research work represents a defense approach to keep the MIA away from wireless signal classifiers and show how this defense can significantly reduce the accuracy of the MIA. This work introduces the novel Membership Inference Attack (MIA). It is used to remotely attack a wireless classifier with the goal of gaining insights from the training set and disclosing personal data regarding the properties of the device, channel, and waveform. Two distinct situations for the MIA are examined: (i) testing the MIA's capacity to discriminate between members and non-member signals coming from the same radio device, and (ii) creating nonmember signals coming from other radio devices. Structures Create a diagram that takes into consideration the noisy changes of the channel fluctuations. Encompassing numerical findings demonstrate the notable success of the MIA as well as the accuracy with which it can identify which training data belongs to the wireless signal classifier. A defensive method is described to protect wireless signal classifiers against the MIA, showing how effective it is in significantly reducing the attack's accuracy.

In our test scenarios, a single service provider (e.g., a gN-odeB in 5G or beyond applications) and IoT user equipment (UEs) represent authorized consumers. Channel circumstances, device-specific phase shifts, and transmit power effects all impact each user's signals. Regarding user classification accuracy, the intended deep learning (DL) classifier consistently demonstrates great accuracy, nearly hitting 100% in many scenarios. Using the spectrum data and classification results, an adversary simultaneously constructs a surrogate classifier to categories the signals it receives. A Membership Inference Attack (MIA) is then used by the adversary to determine whether a signal received at the adversary is related to a member of the training data or not. We take into account two situations: The radio equipment that yields member signals can also generate non-member signals, or signals that are not part of the training dataset. Other radio equipment is the origin of non-member communications. As an example, the MIA accuracy in the first case is 77.01% at a low Signal-to-Noise Ratio (SNR) of 3 dB and 88.62% at a high SNR of 10 dB. One MIA produces training signals, and another radio device emits non-member signals in the second scenario.

We evaluate, taking into consideration the uncertainty induced by the stochastic nature of wireless networks, how noisy variations impact received signals. Finding out if the training data contains the received signal or any of its noisy variations is what this involves. Accuracy of the MIA decreases with increasing degree of noise variability when using the average score. The accuracy of the MIA, however, increases with the highest score when applied to member samples (authorized users) while decreasing with the number of noisy changes in non-member data (unauthorized users).

Noisy variations increase with the number of authorized users decreasing. In order to counter the MIA, we offer an active defense strategy. The service provider creates a shadow MIA model to carry out the defense strategy of employing controlled noise during the classification phase. This perturbation aims to maintain classification results while achieving poor accuracy for the MIA in the presence of defense. After a few variable adjustments and the application of a loss function to eliminate constraints, the defense strategy transitions from an optimization issue to an unconstrained optimization. Gradient search is then used to determine which perturbation is optimal. This defense strategy successfully thwarts the adversary-launched MIA, reducing accuracy from 97.88% to 50%.

4 Implementation

4.1 Navie Bayes

Naive Bayes: The Naive Bayes approach is a supervised learning technique based on the simple premise that a feature's presence or absence is independent of the presence or absence of any other feature in the class. This method has been shown to be reliable and effective, exhibiting comparable performance to other supervised learning techniques, despite its seemingly simple assumption. Its success is partly attributed by researchers to representation bias. Like linear discriminant analysis, logistic regression, or linear SVM, the Naive Bayes classifier is a linear classifier. Its simplicity in programming, straightforward parameter estimation, speedy learning on big databases, and passably good accuracy account for its popularity in the research domain. Revaluating learning outcomes is necessary for better comprehension and ease of implementation, though, due to its limited interpretability and difficulties in practice.

4.2 K Nearest Neighbour

K Nearest Neighbour is a simple yet effective classification algorithm utilizes a similarity metric to classify non-parametric and uses a lazy learning strategy, postponing learning until a test example is given entails classifying new data by determining K-nearest neighbors from the training set. As an example, the training dataset uses instances to determine learning and consists of the K-closest examples in feature space.

4.3 SVM

A discriminant machine learning technique in classification tasks looks for a discriminant function that, given an independent and identically distributed (ii d) training dataset, predicts labels for new instances. A data point is assigned to one of the several classes in the classification task by discriminant classification functions, as opposed to generative machine learning techniques, which call for the computation of conditional probability distributions. SVM, a discriminant technique, provides the same ideal hyperplane parameters every time it solves the convex optimization problem analytically. On the other hand, perceptron's and genetic algorithms (GAs) have the potential to produce distinct models with every training initialization. Perceptron's and GAs work to reduce error during training, which leads to a number of hyperplanes that satisfy the requirement (Fig. 3).

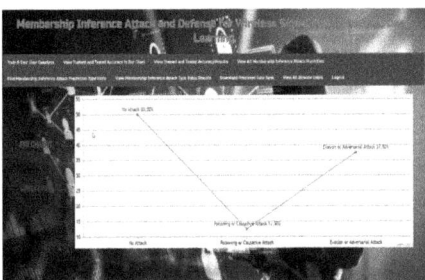

Fig. 3. Percentage of Attacks

4.4 Gradient Boosting

Gradient boosting is a machine learning technique composed primarily of weak prediction models, most frequently decision trees, that generates a prediction model in the form of an ensemble. It is used in regression and classification tasks [1, 2]. The algorithm that results from using decision trees as weak learners is called gradient-boosted trees, and it frequently performs better than random forests. Similar to other boosting techniques, the gradient-boosted trees model is developed step-by-step. However, it differs in that any differentiable loss function can be optimized, offering a more flexible and comprehensive capability.

5 Experimental Result

Accuracy: This parameter represents how well the attack model performs overall in identifying samples that belong to the training set and those that don't.

$$Accuracy = \frac{TP + TN}{TP + TN + FP + FN} \quad (2)$$

Precision: The fraction of samples classified as belonging to the training set that actually belong to the positive class is evaluated by precision.

$$Precision = \frac{TP}{TP + FP} \quad (3)$$

Recall: Recall is a metric that expresses how many real positive samples the model properly identified in the in training set.

$$Recall = \frac{TP}{TP + FN} \quad (4)$$

F1-Score: This score provides an impartial assessment of the overall performance of the model by combining precision and recall.

$$F1 = \frac{2 * Precision * Recall}{Precision + Recall} = \frac{2 * TP}{2 * TP + FP + FN} \quad (5)$$

Figure 4 describes the Ml model is trained on the attack in top k vector dataset. Table 1 shows the different performance metrics of MIA attack. Figure 5 describes MIA ROC Curve CIFAR10. Figure 6 represents MIA ROC Curve CIFAR100.

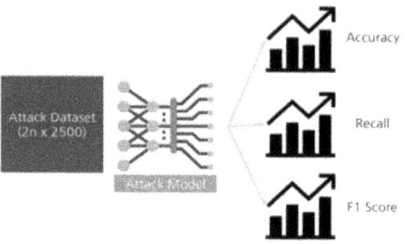

Fig. 4. Ml model is trained on the attack in top k vector dataset.

Table 1. Different performance metrics of MIA attack

MIA Attacks Metrices	Accuracy	Precision	Recall	F1 Score
CIFAR10	0.7761	0.7593	0.8071	0.7825
CIFAR100	0.9746	0.9627	0.9875	0.9749

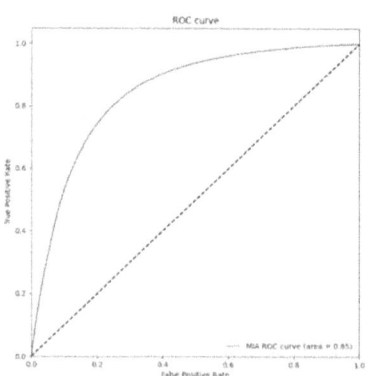

Fig. 5. MIA ROC Curve CIFAR10

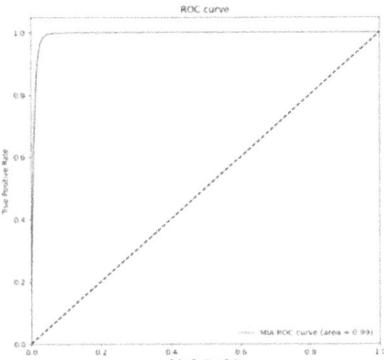

Fig. 6. MIA ROC Curve CIFAR100

6 Conclusions

Membership Inference Attacks (MIA), a fresh privacy problem in machine learning-driven wireless applications, were investigated in this paper. Our goal was to create a Deep Learning (DL) classifier that used radio frequency (RF) fingerprints to distinguish authorized users, which would be especially useful in 5G or Internet of Things (IoT) networks. As input features, the model makes use of phase shift and received power. The adversary uses MIA to scan for signals, build a surrogate classifier, and effectively identify whether a received signal matches the training set, attaining 77.01% accuracy for weak signals and 88.62% accuracy for strong signals increasing noisy variations reduce membership inference accuracy using average scores, particularly affecting non-member samples, where utilizing maximum scores results in decreased accuracy. In scenarios where non-member signals are from distinct devices, the Membership Inference Attack (MIA) excels, achieving 97.88% accuracy. This underscores MIA's threat to wireless privacy. A defensive tactic, involving deliberate perturbations in the categorization process, is devised. While reducing MIA accuracy by around 5% in the first scenario, it performs exceptionally in the second, lowering accuracy to 50%.

References

1. Davaslioglu, K., Soltani, S., Erpek, T., Sagduyu, Y.E.: DeepWiFi: cognitive WiFi with deep learning. IEEE Trans. Mob. Comput. (2021)
2. Hui, B., Yang, Y., Yuan, H., Burlina, P., Gong, N.Z., Cao, Y.: Practical blind membership inference attack via differential comparisons. In: Network and Distributed System Security Symposium (NDSS) (2021)
3. Song, L., Mittal, P.: Systematic evaluation of privacy risks of machine learning models. In: USENIX Security Symposium (2021)
4. Kim, B., Sagduyu, Y.E., Erpek, T., Davaslioglu, K., Ulukus, S.: Channel effects on surrogate models of adversarial attacks against wireless signal classifiers. In: IEEE International Conference on Communications (ICC) (2021)
5. Yi, J., El Gamal, A.: Gradient-based adversarial deep modulation classification with data-driven subsampling. arXiv preprint arXiv:2104.06375 (2021)

6. Erpek, T., Sagduyu, Y.E., Shi, Y.: Deep learning for launching and mitigating wireless jamming attacks. IEEE Trans. Cogn. Commun. Netw. (2019)
7. Shi, Y., Sagduyu, Y.E., Erpek, T., Gursoy, M.C.: How to attack and defend 5g radio access network slicing with reinforcement learning. arXiv preprint arXiv:2101.05768 (2021)
8. Sagduyu, Y.E., et al.: When wireless security meets machine learning: motivation, challenges, and research directions. arXiv preprint arXiv:2001.08883 (2020)
9. Sadeghi, M., Larsson, E.G.: Physical adversarial attacks against end-to-end autoencoder communication systems. IEEE Commun. Lett. (2019)
10. Kim, B., Sagduyu, Y.E., Davaslioglu, K., Erpek, T., Ulukus, S.: Over-the-air adversarial attacks on deep learning based modulation classifier over wireless channels. In: Conference on Information Sciences and Systems (CISS) (2020)
11. Kim, B., Sagduyu, Y.E., Davaslioglu, K., Erpek, T., Ulukus, S.: Channel-aware adversarial attacks against deep learning-based wireless signal classifiers. arXiv preprint arXiv:2005.05321
12. Lin, Y., Zhao, H., Tu, Y., Mao, S., Dou, Z.: Threats of adversarial attacks in DNN based modulation recognition. In: IEEE INFOCOM (2020)
13. Kim, B., Sagduyu, Y.E., Davaslioglu, K., Erpek, T., Ulukus, S.: Adversarial attacks with multiple antennas against deep learning based modulation classifiers. In: IEEE Global Communications Conference (GLOBECOM) (2020)
14. Rout, S.K., Rath, A.K., Bhagabati, C.: Energy efficient and cost effective secure node localization with key management in wireless sensor networks. In: 2016 5th International Conference on Reliability, Infocom Technologies and Optimization (Trends and Future Directions) (ICRITO), pp. 515–520. IEEE (2016)
15. Manoj, B., Sadeghi, M., Larsson, E.G.: Adversarial attacks on deep learning based power allocation in a massive MIMO network. arXiv preprint arXiv:2101.12090 (2021)
16. Kim, B., Sagduyu, Y.E., Erpek, T., Ulukus, S.: Adversarial attacks on deep learning based mmWave beam prediction in 5G and beyond. In: IEEE Statistical Signal Processing Workshop (2021)
17. Sahay, R., Brinton, C.G., Love, D.J.: Ensemble-based wireless receiver architecture for mitigating adversarial interference in automatic modulation classification. arXiv preprint arXiv:2104.03494 (2021)
18. Bahramali, A., Nasr, M., Houmansadr, A., Goeckel, D., Towsley, D.: Robust adversarial attacks against DNN-based wireless communication systems. arXiv preprint arXiv:2102.00918 (2021)
19. Shi, Y., Davaslioglu, K., Sagduyu, Y.E.: Over-the-air membership inference attacks as privacy threats for deep learning-based wireless signal classifiers. In: ACM Conference on Security and Privacy in Wireless and Mobile Networks (WiSec) Workshop on Wireless Security and Machine Learning (WiseML) (2020)
20. Chen, D., Yu, N., Zhang, Y., Fritz, M.: GAN-leaks: a taxonomy of membership inference attacks against generative models. In: ACM SIGSAC Conference on Computer and Communications Security (CCS) (2020)

Wearable Circularly Polarized MIMO Antenna: Design and Simulation for High-Data Biomedical Sensing Devices

Mallavarapu Sandhya[1](✉) and Lokam Anjaneyulu[2]

[1] IFHE-FST, ICFAI University, Dontanpally, Hyderabad 501203, India
sandhyamallavarapu@ifheindia.org
[2] National Institute of Technology Warangal, Warangal, Telangana, India

Abstract. This paper introduces a novel Multi-Input Multi-Output (MIMO) antenna tailored for high-data wearable applications, emphasizing circular polarization. The antenna design is meticulously crafted with two C-shaped patch components, both featuring a specialized ground structure aimed at enhancing circular polarization efficiency. Each component is equipped with 50Ω SMA connectors and integrates L-shaped stubs within the ground plane. One notable feature of the antenna is its remarkable bandwidth, reaching a maximum of 440 MHz (2.32 GHz–2.76 GHz), which effectively covers unlicensed frequencies from 2.4 GHz to 2.48 GHz. Additionally, the antenna showcases outstanding performance metrics: an envelope correlation coefficient below 0.169 signifies minimal correlation between antenna elements, while a diversity gain exceeding 9.46 dB indicates robust diversity performance. Furthermore, the antenna boasts a multiplexing efficiency surpassing −0.85 dB, suggesting efficient data transmission within the MIMO system. Additionally, the channel capacity loss remains below 0.32 bits/s/Hz, indicating minimal loss in communication capacity. With its elevated gain and robust MIMO characteristics, the proposed antenna emerges as a highly promising solution for high-data wearable biomedical devices, particularly in ISM band applications. Its performance metrics position it favourably for reliable and high-speed wireless communication in challenging wearable environments.

Keywords: Multi input-Multi output (MIMO) · Envelop Correlation Coefficient (ECC) · Directive Gain (DG) · Channel Capacity Loss (CCL) · Multiplexing Efficiency (ME) · Total Active Reflection Coefficient (TARC) · Wearable antennas · Defected ground structure · Circular polarization

1 Introduction

Wearable antennas have garnered significant attention from researchers and developers due to their versatile applications in the medical, tracking, and entertainment industries [1, 2]. Efficient operation in human environments, accommodating bending and dynamic movements, necessitates the use of wearable antennas. Wearable circularly polarized MIMO antennas, with their orientation flexibility and capability to suppress multi-path interference, emerge as the superior option for such requirements [3–6]. Moreover, employing a multi-element antenna with polarization diversity facilitates the establishment of reliable channel connections and enhances isolation between them. Crucially, there is a growing need to elevate data rates for biomedical devices, enabling the reception and transmission of data at higher speeds. For context, contemporary image sensors can transfer images at rates reaching 78 Mbps. The ISM band stands out as one of the suitable and promising frequency bands for achieving high-data-rate transfers.

In the realm of wearable devices, the operational environment is closely tied to human surroundings. The dynamic movements of individuals can lead to polarization mismatches. Consequently, circularly polarized antennas are favored for such applications due to their adaptability. However, it's worth noting that while circularly polarized antennas excel in adaptability, they may fall short in delivering the high data rates demanded by biomedical sensing applications [7]. Hence, the introduction of a Circularly Polarized (CP) MIMO antenna aims to address this challenge by simultaneously delivering high data rates and mitigating polarization mismatch issues in dynamic environments [6, 8, 9].

Therefore, the research gaps that have been identified encompass the requirement for wearable antennas adept at accommodating dynamic movements, ensuring high data rates in biomedical applications, and addressing polarization mismatches. The introduction of Circularly Polarized MIMO antennas emerges as a prospective solution to these challenges, underscoring the necessity for additional research and development in this domain.

In this work, a novel MIMO wearable antenna is designed specifically for high-data wearable applications. The antenna is constructed using textile materials and comprises two C-shaped patch components, each featuring a defective ground structure to enhance circular polarization. The antenna exhibits a broad bandwidth of 440 MHz. Notably, it attains outstanding performance metrics, featuring an Envelope Correlation Coefficient (ECC) below 0.169, Diversity Gain (DG) surpassing 9.46 dB, Multiplexing Efficiency (ME) exceeding −0.85 dB, and a Channel Capacity Loss (CCL) below 0.32 bits/s/Hz. These attributes render the proposed antenna exceptionally well-suited for high-data wearable biomedical devices, especially in ISM band applications.

2 Design Methodology of MIMO Antenna

Patients with chronic illnesses or those recovering from surgery can benefit from remote patient monitoring systems equipped with MIMO antennas. These antennas enable the transmission of health data from wearable sensors worn by patients to healthcare providers located remotely. This allows healthcare providers to monitor patients' health status without the need for frequent in-person visits. The antenna is constructed on a thin and flexible jeans material, characterized by a permittivity of 1.7 and a tangent loss of 0.025 [10]. The dimensions of the individual antenna element are specified as $0.308\lambda_0 \times 0.308\lambda_0 \times 0.02\lambda_0$, where λ_0 represents the free-space wavelength at 2.4 GHz. The design progression begins with a conventional rectangular radiator resonating at f_0, taking into account well-established equations [11]:

$$W_p = \frac{C}{f_0}\sqrt{\frac{1}{2(1+\varepsilon_r)}} \quad (1)$$

$$L_p = \frac{C}{2f_0\sqrt{\varepsilon_{\text{eff}}}} \quad (2)$$

$$\varepsilon_{\text{eff}} \approx \frac{\varepsilon_r + 1}{2} \quad (3)$$

where W_p and L_p are the width and length of the traditional patch radiator, ε_{eff} is the effective permittivity of the substrate.

The antenna, designed using these equations, takes on a C-shaped configuration [12–14], achieved by introducing a slot of length L3. This slot enhances the electrical length of the antenna, facilitating miniaturization for resonance at 2.4 GHz. To improve impedance matching, a rectangular-shaped defect is incorporated. Additionally, to support circular polarization, rectangular and L-shaped stubs are printed on the ground plane. Figure 1 illustrates the profile of the presented wearable MIMO antenna, comprising two identical elements arranged in a mirrored fashion. The radiators are excited with a 50Ω microstrip line, and their dimensions are optimized using CST MW Studio. A common ground plane with symmetrical L-shaped stub lines is implemented on the backside of the jeans surface. The mirrored arrangement of the radiating elements ensures stable S12 parameters without the need for external decoupling networks.

3 MIMO Antenna Simulation Explorations

The diversity performance of the MIMO antenna can be evaluated by examining MIMO parameters. All simulations are conducted using CST MW Studio.

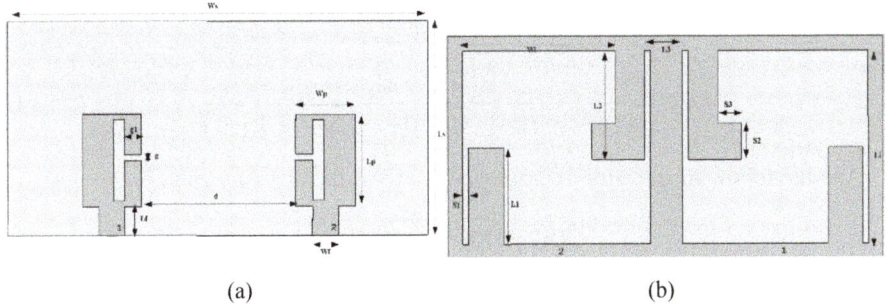

Fig. 1. Geometrical profile of the anticipated MIMO antenna (a) Radiator (b) Ground layer

The anticipated dimensions are: $W_s = 74.5$ mm, $L_s = 37$ mm, $W_P = 10.5$, $L_P = 16$, $W_f = 4.5$, $L_f = 5$ mm, $d = 27.5$ mm, $g_1 = 3$ mm, $g = 1$ mm, W_i, $L_i = 32$ mm, $L_1 = 16$ mm, $L_2 = 18$ mm, $L_3 = 5.5$ mm, $S_1 = 1$ mm, $S_2 = 6$ mm, $S_3 = 4$ mm.

3.1 S-Parameters and Radiation Pattern

The simulated S-parameters and radiation patterns are depicted in Fig. 2. As observed in Fig. 2(a), the 10 dB bandwidth spans from 2.32 GHz to 2.76 GHz, effectively covering the desired 2.4 GHz range. The isolation between ports 1 and port 2 exceeds 30 dB, ensuring significant decoupling between the two ports. The maximum gain of the system is 3.71 dBi at 2.4 GHz, and the normalized radiation patterns are illustrated in Fig. 2(b).

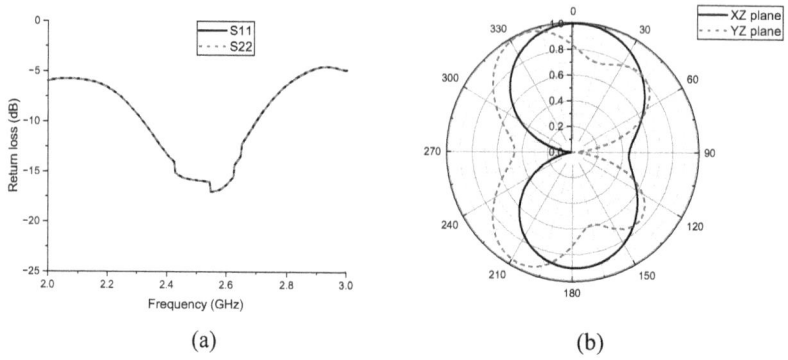

Fig. 2. Simulated (a) S_{11}, S_{22} curves (b) Normalized patterns on XZ and YZ planes

3.2 ECC and DG

Understanding the ECC helps in designing MIMO systems to maximize diversity gain or spatial multiplexing gain depending on the application specified. A low ECC implies better diversity and spatial multiplexing capabilities since the antennas are less correlated, while a high ECC suggests that the antennas are highly correlated, which might limit the system's performance. The ECC is the measure of the correlation between the antenna ports. Mathematically, it is expressed as

$$ECC = \frac{\left|s_{11}^* s_{12} - s_{21}^* s_{22}\right|}{\left(1 - |s_{11}|^2 - |s_{21}|^2\right)\left(1 - |s_{22}|^2 - |s_{12}|^2\right)} \quad (4)$$

And the following equation is employed to assess the diversity gain:

$$DG = 10\sqrt{1 - ECC^2} \quad (5)$$

Figures 3(a) and (b) depict the computed curves representing the Envelope Correlation Coefficient (ECC) and Diversity Gain (DG) for the proposed antenna. These metrics play a pivotal role in assessing antenna system performance. From Fig. 3, it is evident that the ECC is calculated to be 0.169, while the DG measures 9.46 dB. It is worth noting that in an ideal scenario, the ECC ideally approaches zero, signifying perfect orthogonality among antenna elements. However, in practical scenarios, a value below 0.5 is generally deemed acceptable. The ECC value of 0.169 falls within this acceptable range. On the other hand, Diversity Gain (DG) quantifies the enhancement in the received signal-to-noise ratio (SNR) attributable to multiple antenna elements. In this instance, the DG is determined to be 9.46 dB within the operational band. A higher DG value indicates superior diversity performance and improved signal quality.

Moreover, Fig. 3(c) presents the multiplexing efficiency, a critical parameter in antenna system evaluation. This metric evaluates the antenna system's ability to efficiently manage multiple signals or data streams simultaneously. Therefore, the assessment illustrated by Fig. 3 emphasizes the performance attributes of the proposed antenna design, showcasing its ability to attain acceptable Envelope Correlation Coefficient (ECC) levels, favorable Diversity Gain (DG), and efficient multiplexing within the operational band.

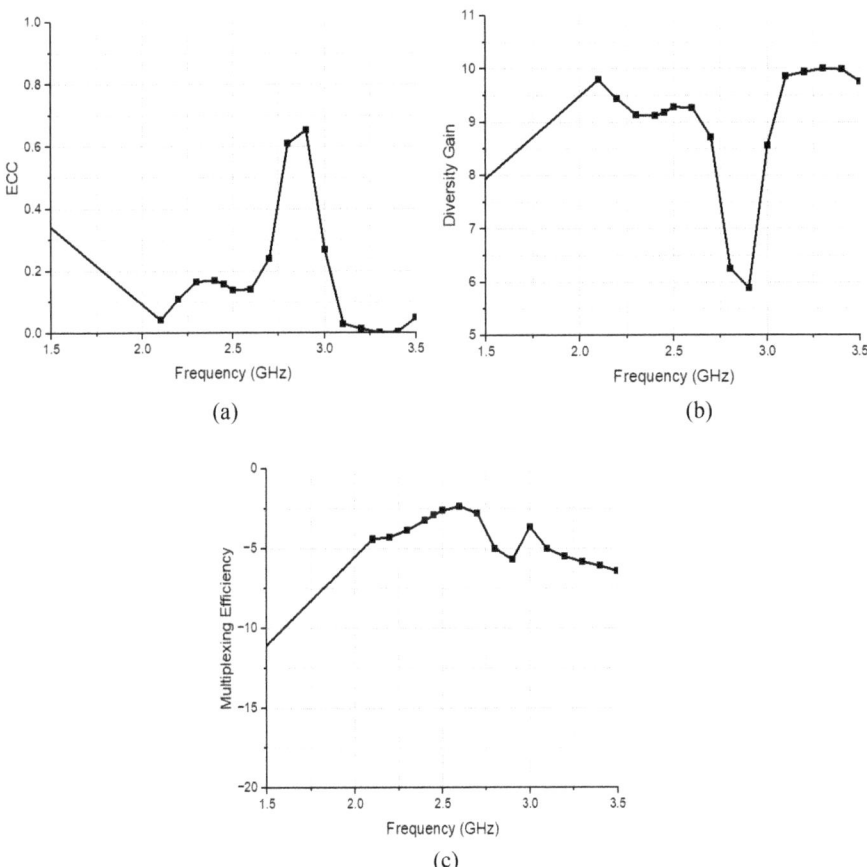

Fig. 3. Simulated (a) Envelope correlation coefficient (b) Directive gain (c) Multiplexing efficiency.

3.3 TARC and CCL

In MIMO (Multiple Input Multiple Output) systems, minimizing reflections from antenna elements is crucial to prevent interference, maintain signal quality, and uphold system performance. The TARC (Total Active Reflection Coefficient) parameter is instrumental in quantifying the total reflected power from all antenna elements in a MIMO array. It serves as a key consideration in antenna design and optimization, ensuring efficient power transmission and reception. The calculation of the TARC parameter typically involves measuring the reflected power from individual antenna elements and summing them to determine the total reflected power. By minimizing the TARC parameter, MIMO antenna systems can optimize signal transmission and reception, thereby enhancing overall efficiency and performance.

In a two-element MIMO antenna system, both elements operate simultaneously, necessitating consideration of the influence of each port on the other to effectively manage interference and maximize system performance. The TARC parameter measures this mutual influence and is given by

$$TARC = \frac{\sqrt{(s_{11} + s_{22})^2 + (s_{21} + s_{12})^2}}{\sqrt{2}} \tag{6}$$

For any MIMO system, the acceptable TARC is below −5 dB. For the proposed antenna, the simulated TARC is estimated as 0.874.

Moreover, the computation of channel capacity loss in a MIMO antenna system, based on S-parameters and radiation patterns, entails the evaluation of both the electrical attributes of the antennas (illustrated by S-parameters) and their spatial characteristics (illustrated by radiation patterns). By amalgamating information derived from S-parameters and radiation patterns, the optimization of the MIMO antenna is achievable. Nonetheless, the Channel Capacity Loss (CCL) represents the utmost channel capacity without any communication loss. The permissible threshold stands at less than 0.4 bits/s/Hz. Calculations are conducted employing the following mathematical equations:

$$CCL = -\log|\alpha| \tag{7}$$

where

$$\alpha = \begin{bmatrix} \alpha_{11} & \alpha_{12} \\ \alpha_{21} & \alpha_{22} \end{bmatrix}$$

$$\alpha_{ij} = 1 - \left(\sum_{j=1}^{2} |S_{ij}|^2 \right) \tag{8}$$

$$\alpha_{ij} = -\left| S_{ii}^* S_{ij} + S_{ji}^* S_{jj} \right| \tag{9}$$

where σ_{ii}, and σ_{ij} represent the correlation between the antenna elements of a MIMO system. For the proposed antenna, the estimated CCL appeared as below 0.32 bit/s/Hz.

3.4 Diversity and Isolation

In MIMO systems, it is vital to achieve a high degree of diversity and isolation between the individual antennas to minimize mutual interference and maximize the system's capacity. This requires careful consideration of the spacing and orientation of the antennas to ensure that they operate independently and effectively in tandem. Quantifying the impact of polarization on data rates and other relevant metrics of wearable MIMO antennas involves assessing signal strength, interference levels, and multipath effects. Polarization alignment enhances signal strength and data rates, mitigates interference, and improves overall communication performance. Table 1 provides a comparative analysis between the present work and existing literature. Upon reviewing Table 1, it becomes evident that the proposed antenna exhibits superior performance compared to the published literature.

Table 1. Comparison with Published Literature

Ref	F_0 (GHz)	Size (λ_0^3)	No. of Elements	ECC	DG	TARC (dB)	CCL (bits/s/Hz)	Substrate
[15]	2.4	0.24 × 0.24 × 0.004	2	<0.1	NA	NA	NA	FR-4
[16]	2.52	0.04 × 0.03 × 0.001	2	<0.11	>9.9	NA	NA	RT 6010
[17]	2.4	0.19 × 0.59 × 0.05	2	<0.01	>9.8	NA	NA	Jeans
Proposed	**2.4**	**0.596 × 0.29 × 0.02**	**2**	**<0.169**	**>9.46**	**<−5**	**0.32**	**Jeans**

4 Conclusions

An efficient circularly polarized MIMO antenna is successfully built and simulated for high-data wearable devices. The MIMO system has achieved an impedance bandwidth of 440 MHz, and the MIMO wearable antenna displays a diversity performance in terms of MIMO parameters. The predicted antenna was a promising contender for the high data wearable biomedical device at ISM band applications because to its high gain and good MIMO features.

References

1. Hariprasad, S., Anusree, S., Sreedevi, R., Anoop, A., Kishor, K.K., Balamurugan, V.: A compact flexible two-port textile antenna. In: 2022 IEEE 19th India Council International Conference, INDICON 2022, pp. 8–11 (2022)

2. Mallavarapu, S., Lokam, A.: A critical survey on fractal wearable antennas with enhanced gain and bandwidth for wban. Lect. Notes Netw. Syst. **145**, 737–745 (2021)
3. Te Liao, C., Yang, Z.K., Chen, H.M.: Multiple integrated antennas for wearable fifth-generation communication and internet of things applications. IEEE Access **9**, 120328–120346 (2021)
4. Shankar Singh, H.: Investigations of MIMO antenna for smart mobile handsets and their user proximity. Med. Internet Things Enabling Technol. Emerg. Appl. (2019)
5. Govindan, T., Palaniswamy, S.K., Kanagasabai, M., Kumar, S.: Design and analysis of UWB MIMO antenna for smart fabric communications, vol. 2022 (2022)
6. Kumar, S., et al.: Wideband circularly polarized textile MIMO antenna for wearable applications. IEEE Access **9**, 108601–108613 (2021)
7. Mallavarapu, S., Lokam, A., Farooq, U.: A small, flexible, circularly polarized wearable antenna for wireless applications. In: Proceedings of 2022 IEEE International Symposium on Smart Electronic Systems, iSES 2022, pp. 175–179 (2022)
8. Babu, B.A., Pokkunuri, P.S., Boddapati, M., Srigakolapu, S.S., Chintha, M., Donepudi, T.S.C.: Design and analysis of a compact textile MIMO antenna for ISM band wearable applications. In: IEEE Delhi Section Conference, DELCON 2022, pp. 6–10 (2022)
9. Noghanian, S.: A dual-band wearable MIMO WiFi antenna. In: Proceedings of 2022 International Symposium on Antennas and Propagation and USNC-URSI Radio Science Meeting, pp. 1170–1171 (2022)
10. Mallavarapu, S., Lokam, A.: Circuit modeling and analysis of wearable antennas on the effect of bending for various feeds. Eng. Technol. Appl. Sci. Res. **12**(1), 8180–8187 (2022)
11. Balanis, C.A.: Antenna Theory: Analysis and Design (1996)
12. Mahfuz, M.M.H., Islam, M.R., Sakib, N., Habaebi, M.H., Raad, R., Tayab Sakib, M.A.: Design of wearable textile patch antenna using C-shape etching slot for Wi-MAX and 5G lower band applications, pp. 168–172 (2021)
13. Sran, S.S., Sivia, J.S.: Design of C shape modified Sierpinski carpet fractal antenna for wireless applications. In: International Conference on Electrical, Electronics, and Optimization Techniques, ICEEOT 2016, pp. 821–824 (2016)
14. Patil, S., Singh, A.K., Kanaujia, B.K., Yadava, R.L.: Design of dual band dual sense circularly polarized wide slot antenna with c-shaped radiator for wireless applications. Frequenz **72**(7–8), 343–351 (2018)
15. Qu, L., Piao, H., Qu, Y., Kim, H.H., Kim, H.: Circularly polarised MIMO ground radiation antennas for wearable devices. Electron. Lett. **54**(4), 189–190 (2018)
16. Alazemi, A.J., Iqbal, A.: A compact and wideband MIMO antenna for high-data-rate biomedical ingestible capsules. Sci. Rep. **12**(1), 14290 (2022)
17. Pathan, T.U., Kakde, B.: A compact circular polarized MIMO fabric antenna with AMC backing for WBAN applications. Adv. Electromagn. **11**(3), 26–33 (2022)

Implementation of Antenna in Satellite Ground Station for Cubesat

Kummari Harshavardhini[✉], Vikas Kumar Ghanathey, SriSrujan Ryali, and Sulakshana Chilukuri

Department of ECE, Vardhaman College of Engineering,
Hyderabad, Telangana, India
`harshakummari56@gmail.com, sulakshana@vardhaman.org`

Abstract. The functionality of the Satellite depends on the payload, which contributes to the majority of work in extracting the data in a satellite. The purpose of the satellite payload is to support national security initiatives, advance space exploration, monitor the Earth, collect scientific data, or provide communication services, it is specifically designed to meet these goals. A transponder (Communication device) is responsible for establishing a communication link with the ground station. Ground Station is a basic communication element that receives data/signal transmitted by the transponder of the satellite. In the project, we proposed to build a student-level Ground Station to receive data from source Satellites such as Weather satellites and ISS (International Space Station). A Ground Station is a terrestrial radio station that is designed for extra-planetary and other Satellite communication purposes. The Ground Stations communicate with spacecraft by transmitting and receiving radio waves in VHF (30 to 300 MHz) and UHF (300 MHz to 3 GHz). The major components that are involved in building a Ground Station are SDR, Raspberry Pi, Antenna. There are many antennas used for receiving a signal such as the Yagi-Uda antenna, Patch antenna, Log-Periodic antenna, Helical antenna, and V-Dipole antenna. In this project, a Log periodic antenna that works at 100 MHz to 500 MHz is proposed to receive the signals from NOAA-15 (National Oceanic and Atmospheric Administration) [1] at the frequency of 162.400–162.550 MHz for broadcasting weather information.

Keywords: Ground Station Satellite · Antenna · Payload

1 Introduction

A Ground station is also known as an Earth station or tracking station. The Ground stations are the critical link between Earth and space, enabling seamless communication, data exchange, and control of spacecraft and satellites [1]. Ground stations receive data collected by satellites or spacecraft, such as scientific measurements, weather data, and other satellite-tracked data. The establishment of an intricate network of ground stations represents a remarkable feat in modern space communication technology. These ground stations serve as vital lifelines, enabling a continuous flow of data and information between Earth and distant spacecraft, no matter where they may be positioned within the vast expanse of space [2]. A central feature of these ground stations is their exceptional capability to receive data from a wide array of spacecraft, including compact and innovative Cubesat. These miniature satellites have ushered in a new era of space exploration, and the ground stations are adept at capturing the streams of data they transmit back to Earth. Satellite Ground Stations (SGS) are built for collecting and streaming remote sensing satellite data to a variety of users and applications. Ground stations are establishments situated on Earth with the purpose of facilitating instantaneous communication with satellites [3]. In addition to receiving data transmissions from the satellite (downlink) and sending radio signals to it (uplink), the crew at these stations occasionally acts as the satellite network's command and control center [17].

1.1 Hardware Design

A basic ground station can be constructed using off-the-shelf components that are commonly available such as a simple omnidirectional antenna to more complex multi-rotor antennas. The reference design contains a Raspberry Pi + RTL-SDR dongle + Antenna.

1. **Raspberry Pi:** Raspberry Pi is a credit-card-sized single-board computer design. Raspberry Pi is a versatile and affordable computer that can perform various tasks. Its compact size and low cost make it accessible to anyone. Using a Raspberry Pi imager installation of Raspberry OS is simple and easy.
2. **SDR:** SDR stands for Software-Defined Radio, which refers to a communication system where traditional hardware components in a radio system. It enables seamless integration of different wireless standards, dynamic spectrum allocation, and improved spectrum efficiency.

In the realm of weather satellite communications, the choice of an optimal frequency range is crucial to ensure reliable and efficient data transmission between satellites and ground stations. In this context, a frequency range spanning from 100 MHz to 500 MHz has emerged as a particularly suitable option. This choice takes into account the specific transmission frequencies employed by weather satellites, as well as the availability of radio spectrum for ground-based communication systems. Weather satellites commonly utilize frequencies within the UHF (Ultra High Frequency) and VHF (Very High Frequency) bands due to their advantageous propagation characteristics, which facilitate communication through various atmospheric conditions.

1.2 Related Work

Atharva College Ground Station: One of the receiving stations used to receive and process Pratham's data is Atharva Ground Station. The satellite weighs close to 10 kg and is made to fit inside a cube with 30-cm sides. Pratham will help with tsunami warnings, scientific research, and fixing GPS communication issues. The team's shared enthusiasm for satellite communication and space technology has motivated them to conduct research on satellite tracking and to share their knowledge on everything from antenna design to signal decoding [15]. The Ground Station innovative student team at Atharva College of Engineering has successfully established a functional receiving Ground Station for the PRATHAM satellite of IIT Bombay, marking a significant accomplishment (Fig. 1).

Fig. 1. On September 26, 2016, at 9:00 a.m., the student satellite Pratham was successfully launched by ISRO's four-stage Polar Satellite Launch Vehicle (PSLV) at Sriharikota's Satish Dhawan Space Centre [15]. The satellites known as Pratham were launched. As part of the project, Atharva College students worked with project guides Prof. Samuel Jacob and Prof. Archana Chaudhary to develop a fully functional satellite tracking system, with ongoing support from Atharva College Management.

Norway, Design of Low-Cost Ground Stations for Satellite Communications: The ongoing investigation in Norway is centered around the ambitious goal of crafting an uncomplicated and cost-effective ground station. This facility is envisioned to serve as a dynamic laboratory, catering to the needs of both researchers and aspiring students interested in the intricate domains of satellite communication advancements and space technology. The scope of the system design is impressively comprehensive, encompassing several vital aspects [9]. The ground station is primed to undertake the pivotal task of tracking signals emitted by an array of satellites, spanning low earth orbit satellites and diminutive nano-satellites. Additionally, the ground station will provide an invaluable platform for error correction methodologies, frame synchronization techniques, and digital signal processing [14]. This venture in Norway aspires to catalyze significant advancements in these cutting-edge fields while nurturing the minds that will shape their future trajectories.

2 Design Flow of Antenna

The ground station's antenna is designed to receive signals from the satellite. As the satellite orbits the Earth, the antenna needs to be able to capture signals coming from various directions. These signals may contain information such as telemetry data, images, or other types of data transmitted by the satellite. A ground station is a point of contact between the spacecraft and the earth [7]. The design of antennas and their working environment will decide the effectiveness of any provided ground station.

Ground stations use radar, telescopes, and other tracking instruments to continuously track the satellite's trajectory. This information is crucial for maintaining communication with the satellite and ensuring collision avoidance with other space objects. This information helps operators assess the satellite's health and performance, diagnose issues, and make informed decisions about its operation.

Software Defined Radio (SDR) is a technology that allows for the flexible and reconfigurable reception and processing of radio signals using software. SDR is responsible for receiving the signals captured by the antenna and tracking the received signals' characteristics. The decoding ratio is a metric that indicates how many of the transmitted data packets from the satellite are successfully decoded and received by the ground station. The SDR processes the received signal to decode these packets.

Once the SDR decodes the packets, a Raspberry Pi (a small computer) starts processing the data. This processing might involve various tasks, such as error correction, data formatting, or extracting useful information from the received packets.

Processed data from the Raspberry Pi is sent to a server via similar communication system. The server will be hosted locally or remotely and act as a central repository for collecting data from various ground stations.

Data retrieval involves collecting the processed data from the server [8]. This data could be raw telemetry, images, scientific measurements, or any other type of information transmitted by the satellite [13]. Different satellites may operate in different modes to accommodate varying communication requirements, data rates, and interference considerations.

For a ground station to successfully communicate with a satellite, its communication equipment must be compatible with the satellite's designated modes. This means that the ground station's antenna, SDR hardware and software must be capable of receiving and decoding signals transmitted by the satellite using the specified frequencies and modulation schemes [16]. The ground station needs to be equipped to send and receive signals within the specified parameters for effective communication with satellites orbiting the Earth.

3 Results and Analysis

To receive pictorial data from NOAA APT Signals and SSTV Signals [10], the weather satellites. Ground stations are necessary for mission control and data communication in satellite space missions. Satellite technology facilitates telecommunications, security, and technological development [11]. During the constellation design process, at least one satellite can be connected at all times for the transmission between the source node satellite and the source node ground station, and the ground-to-satellite link is always connected.

The final results obtained are (Fig. 2):

Fig. 2. Result of NOAA-15 (National Oceanic Atmospheric Administration) satellite which was tracked on 17th of June 2023. The process begins with capturing raw images from the NOAA-15 satellite. These images may contain various types of noise, such as electronic noise, and atmospheric interference.

A V-dipole antenna, often referred to as a V-dipole or simply a dipole antenna, is a type of antenna commonly used for receiving signals from satellites and other sources in space. A V-dipole antenna consists of two straight elements arranged in a V shape. The two arms of the V are typically equal in length, and they are oriented in opposite directions. The angle between the arms of the V is often around 120 to 150°, although variations exist (Fig. 3).

Fig. 3. V-dipole antenna is used to track the satellite. This antenna design is popular for satellite tracking due to its simplicity, omnidirectional properties, and effectiveness in receiving signals from various directions.

Denoising is a technique used to remove noise or unwanted artifacts from an image, enhancing its quality and making it more suitable for analysis or

Fig. 4. The Raw image is preprocessed to correct any inherent issues, such as geometric distortions, radiometric corrections, and noise occurrence. This step aims to ensure that the data is in a standardized and accurate form for further analysis.

interpretation. In the context of satellite imagery, denoising can be crucial for obtaining accurate and clear information from the captured data (Figs. 4 and 5).

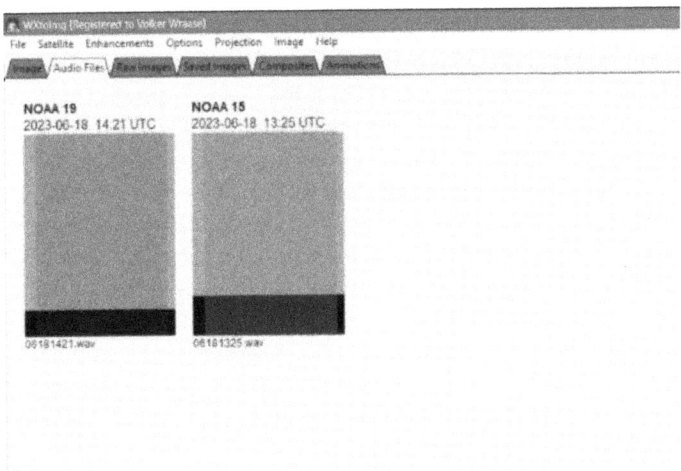

Fig. 5. The different satellites of NOAA-15, NOAA-19 are tracked.

Tracking involves identifying the satellite's position over time, predicting its future location, and possibly correlating this information with other data sources (Fig. 6).

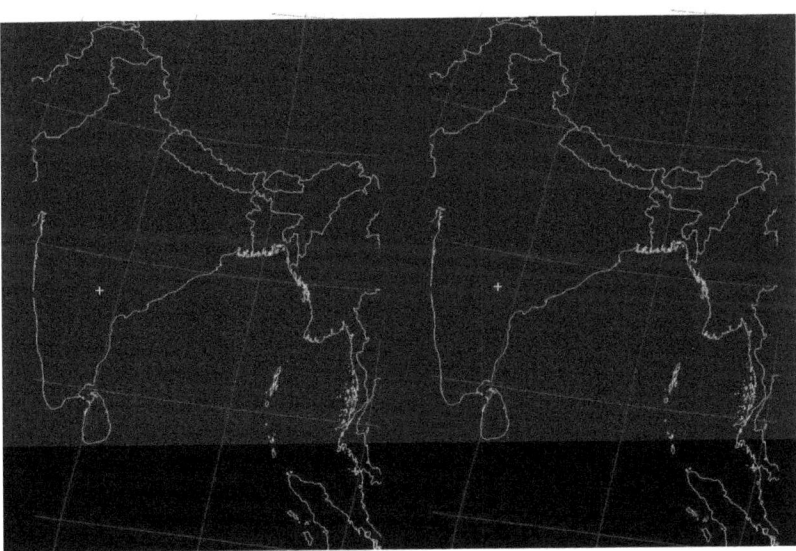

Fig. 6. The above figure shows the target and reduces the noise while preserving important features. The final output of the denoising process is a set of clear, noise-reduced images of the NOAA-15 satellite. This image is more suitable for accurate performance, analysis, and interpretation. This tracked image is used for weather monitoring, and also environmental studies.

4 Conclusion

Low earth orbit (LEO) satellite systems, with their low launch, satellite, and transmission latency costs, are a key component of the next generation of global communication systems [5]. The present system used for ground stations is satisfying the industry need but is lacking in a few sectors due to the current trend in CubeSat and small satellite advancement there is a great need for a ground station for data processing [6]. Data processing should be done fast and accurately, so switching to a hybrid model where IoT helps to swift the process and is very cost-efficient compared to a traditional setup. This model helps to track the Satellite information easily and it is completely student-based level. Every student can access the tracked data from Satellites at different locations [12]. Research is being done on a basic, reasonably priced satellite ground station system for satellite communication and space technology development. The goal of the project is to create a satellite ground station system that can serve as a learning environment and a testing ground for novel wireless technologies with potential applications.

References

1. Fuchs, C., Moll, F.: Ground station network optimization for space-to-ground optical communication links. J. Opt. Commun. Netw. **7**(12), 1148–1159 (2015). https://doi.org/10.1364/JOCN.7.001148
2. Muri, P., Challa, O., McNair, J.: Enhancing small satellite communication through effective antenna system design. In: MILCOM 2010 Military Communications Conference, San Jose, CA, USA, pp. 347–352 (2010). https://doi.org/10.1109/MILCOM.2010.5680405
3. Zhang, J., Zhu, S., Bai, H., Li, C.: Optimization strategy to solve transmission interruption caused by satellite-ground link switching. IEEE Access **8**, 32975–32988 (2020). https://doi.org/10.1109/ACCESS.2020.2973698
4. Jones, T.R., Grey, J.P., Daneshmand, M.: Solar panel integrated circular polarized aperture-coupled patch antenna for CubeSat applications. IEEE Antennas Wirel. Propag. Lett. **17**(10), 1895–1899 (2018). https://doi.org/10.1109/LAWP.2018.2869321
5. Cakaj, S.: The low noise amplifier isolation and linearity measurement at double antenna LEO satellite ground station. In: 2013 Science and Information Conference, London, UK, pp. 875–878 (2013)
6. Popescu, O.: Power budgets for CubeSat radios to support ground communications and inter-satellite links. IEEE Access **5**, 12618–12625 (2017). https://doi.org/10.1109/ACCESS.2017.2721948
7. Vazquez-Alvarez, A.J., Tubio-Pardavila, R., Gonzalez-Muino, A., Aguado-Agelet, F., Arias-Acuna, M., Vilan-Vilan, J.A.: Design of a polarization diversity system for ground stations of CubeSat space systems. IEEE Antennas Wirel. Propag. Lett. **11**, 917–920 (2012). https://doi.org/10.1109/LAWP.2012.2211854
8. Liu, Y., Chen, Y., Jiao, Y., Ma, H., Wu, T.: A shared satellite ground station using user-oriented virtualization technology. IEEE Access **8**, 63923–63934 (2020). https://doi.org/10.1109/ACCESS.2020.2984485

9. Abulgasem, S., Tubbal, F., Raad, R., Theoharis, P.I., Lu, S., Iranmanesh, S.: Antenna designs for CubeSats: a review. IEEE Access **9**, 45289–45324 (2021). https://doi.org/10.1109/ACCESS.2021.3066632
10. Lance, V.P., Abecassis, M., Soracco, M., Neely, M.B., Trinaues, J., Goni, G.: NOAA CoastWatch, Ocean Watch, PolarWatch: ocean satellite data and services for US Gulf Coast, Central Pacific, and global applications and information. In: Global Oceans 2020: Singapore - U.S. Gulf Coast, Biloxi, MS, USA, pp. 1–6 (2020). https://doi.org/10.1109/IEEECONF38699.2020.9389194
11. Fischer, M., Scholtz, A.L.: Design of a multi-mission satellite ground station for education and research. In: 2010 Second International Conference on Advances in Satellite and Space Communications, Athens, Greece, pp. 58–63 (2010). https://doi.org/10.1109/SPACOMM.2010.13
12. Yu, P., et al.: Self-organized and distributed green resource allocation for space-air-ground IoT networks. IEEE Internet Things J. **10**(11), 9385–9397 (2023). https://doi.org/10.1109/JIOT.2022.3222238
13. Ryan, W.E., Han, L., Quintana, P.A.: Design of a low-orbit-to-geostationary satellite link for maximal throughput. IEEE Trans. Commun. **45**(8), 988–996 (1997). https://doi.org/10.1109/26.618315
14. Sandalidis, H.: Performance analysis of a laser ground-station-to-satellite link with modulated gamma-distributed irradiance fluctuations. J. Opt. Commun. Netw. **2**(11), 938–943 (2010). https://doi.org/10.1364/JOCN.2.000938
15. Johannsen, K.G.: Ground station tracking of dual linearly polarized satellites. IEEE Trans. Aerosp. Electron. Syst. **AES-11**(6), 1333–1345 (1975). https://doi.org/10.1109/TAES.1975.308190
16. Rastinasab, V., Weidong, H.: Implementation and design of RF-front-end telemetry tracking and command subsystem of a CubeSat with 500-km altitude. IEEE J. Miniaturization Air Space Syst. **2**(1), 43–47 (2020). https://doi.org/10.1109/JMASS.2020.3026705
17. Lopez-Salamanca, J.J., Seman, L.O., Berejuck, M.D., Bezerra, E.A.: Finite-state Markov chains channel model for CubeSats communication uplink. IEEE Trans. Aerosp. Electron. Syst. **56**(1), 142–152 (2019). https://doi.org/10.1109/TAES.2019.2911769

AESHA3: Efficient and Secure Sub-Key Generation for AES Using SHA-3

Ankush Soni, Sanjay K. Sahay[✉], and Parit Mehta

Department of Computer Science and Information Systems, BITS, Pilani, K. K. Birla Goa Campus, Zuarinagar, India
{p20180413,ssahay,h20210036}@goa.bits-pilani.ac.in

Abstract. Advanced Encryption Standard (AES) is one of the most widely used symmetric cipher for the confidentiality of data. Also it is used for other security services, viz. integrity, authentication and key establishment. However, recently, authors have shown some weakness in the generation of sub-keys in AES, e.g. bit leakage attack, etc. Also, AES sub-keys are generated sequentially, which is an overhead, especially for resource-constrained devices. Therefore, we propose and investigate a novel encryption AESHA3, which uses sub-keys generated by Secure Hash Algorithm-3 (SHA3). The output of SHA3 is one-way and highly non-linear, and random. The experimental analysis shows that the average time taken for generating the sub-keys to be used for encrypting the data using our approach i.e. AESHA3 is ~1300 times faster than the sub-key generated by the standard AES. Accordingly, we find that AESHA3 will be very relevant not only in terms of security but also it will save the resources in IoT devices. We investigated AESHA3 in Intel Core i7, 6th Generation processor and Raspberry Pi 4B and found that up to two MB data encryption is very significant, and lesser the data size, more the resource saving compared to AES.

Keywords: Advanced Encryption Standard · Sub-keys · Secure Hash Algorithm-3 · IoT Devices

1 Introduction

Advanced Encryption Standard (AES) is the most widely used symmetric key cipher, basically for data confidentiality. However it can provide other security services viz. integrity, authentication and key establishment in several real-life applications, including financial services, data centres, web security, etc. The AES has three variant based on the key size i.e. AES-128, AES-192 and AES-256. The design of AES is cryptographically strong [7], and to date, no attack better than brute force has been found. Additionally, because of the 256-bit key variant, it might even cope with the offing quantum computations for the next two decades. However, the sub-key generation process of AES from the master key is arguably frail [10]. Also, with the advent of smart devices and the Internet of Things (IoT) over the last few years, there is a high demand for an efficient and secure algorithm for these resource and energy-constrained devices. Therefore in this paper we propose a novel efficient and secure sub-key generation for AES using Secure Hash Algorithm-3 (SHA-3) for security services, and named AESHA3. We use the same three fundamental layers of AES (Key Addition, Shift Rows and Mix Columns) approved by the National Institute of Standards and Technology (NIST) [7]. However the sub-keys are generated from SHA3, Which is highly random, non-linear and one-way (i.e. the key cannot be generated in the reverse order) [8] i.e., it has all the properties that the NIST-approved AES sub-keys posses. Hence, we have used it to generate the sub-keys of all rounds of AES for the encryption of the data.

The remainder of the paper is divided as follows: Sect. 2 briefly discusses the related work. Section 3 gives the brief description of AES and SHA3. While Sect. 4 discusses the problem overview and our approach for sub-key generation for AESHA3. Sections 5 and 6 describes the experimental setup and analysis of our results respectively. Finally, the Sect. 7 contains the conclusion of the paper.

2 Related Work

According to Kerckhoff's Principles [13], a cipher or cryptosystem should be secure even if the attacker knows all details about the system, except the secret key i.e. the system should be secure even if the attacker knows the encryption and decryption processes. Therefore, the keys used for any cipher are the most important aspect of achieving the desired security level. In symmetric cipher, generally sub-keys are generated from the selected key so that even if the selected key is weak, the sub-key generation process makes the sub-keys highly random so that security of the cipher entirely lies on the sub-keys. Therefore, time-to-time researchers investigated one of the widely used AES sub-keys generation processes. The first weakness in the AES key schedule was discovered by Lauren and Matt in 2002 [10]. According to them, the key schedule of the AES is vulnerable to bit leakage i.e. even with partial knowledge of the previous sub-key, all the other sub-keys can be generated. They proposed a rectified key schedule in which every subkey depends on every bit of the original key. Their proposed key schedule secures the keys from bit leakage. However, the computational resources required for generating the sub-keys remain more or less the same as the original AES sub-key generation processes. Later in 2008, Bahrak et al. [2] proposed a differential attack which exploits differences at the intermediate state of the AES algorithm and time-memory trade off. They have shown that the best differential attack requires $2^{115.5}$ chosen plain-texts, 2^{109} bytes of memory and seven rounds only to attack AES-128. However, it is almost impossible to get $2^{115.5}$ of plain-texts.

In 2010, Biryukov et al. [3] show that AES-192 and AES-256 security level can be 176 and 199 bits respectively. However, still, it is completely impractical to find the key. The reason for their reduced security level may be due to generating 1.5 and 2 sub-keys with the standard AES key schedule. Therefore, their attack is not applicable to AES-128 because one sub-key is generated in each iteration in AES-128. Also, their attack depends on how the keys are related.

Understanding the importance of light weight cipher for IoT devices, Bogdanov et al. [5] in 2014 proposed a light weight encryption scheme which uses AES-128 key schedule. The cipher is an online, single-pass authenticated encryption algorithm that supports optional associated data, and its security relies on nonces. Later in 2019 Alasaad et al. [1] claimed that as the S-box used in AES is a static and fixed matrix, therefore, a backdoor can be built into the cipher to exploit the AES. Hence, they proposed a simple key dependent S-box scheme which generates a dynamic S-box for each round of encryption. Their approach uses some bits of the primary key to directly manipulate the standard S-box in such a way that its content is changed but its cryptographic properties are preserved. They have shown that their proposed method strengthens the cipher against certain attacks at the expense of a relatively modest one-time computational procedure during the set-up phase.

In 2020, Leurent et al. [9], proposed a key schedule in which all the sub-keys of the rounds are generated independently of each other, unlike the original AES key schedule, where the sub-keys are generated from a single master key. Their proposed approach security level remains the same as that of the original AES. Also, the number of steps for generating the sub-keys was exactly same. Later in 2021, G. Leurent et al. [9] proposed a modified AES key schedule in which all the sub-keys of the rounds are generated independently, unlike the original AES key schedule, where the sub-keys are generated sequentially from the master key. Their basic idea is to parallelise the computation of the key schedule. They generate an equivalent representation of the AES key schedule using invariant subspace attacks. However, the number of computations for the variants of AES are the same as the original AES.

Recently, Sawka et al. [16] proposed a scheme to create key expansion algorithms for modern block ciphers. Their approach uses the sponge construction for creating the key expansion algorithm. Further, their method uses the key expansion algorithm on a specifically designed block cipher, IJON. As their approach was specific to the custom block cipher, its scalability is not guaranteed.

3 Brief Description of Advanced Encryption Standard and Secure Hash Algorithm-3

3.1 Advanced Encryption Standard

The first approved block cipher was Data Encryption Standard (DES) [11], which is still secure as per its design, i.e. no attack better than brute force attack has been found yet. However, due to its small key size (56 bits), DES is no longer recommended; instead, one can use 3DES, which is three times slower than DES and provides 112-bit security only. Therefore, to have an efficient and more secure symmetric cipher, NIST approved AES in 2002 [7]. In general, symmetric block cipher processes n bits of plain text and m bits of the key to generate n bits of random cipher text. The security of the modern symmetric cipher is achieved by applying two characteristics, i.e. confusion and diffusion, introduced by Claude Shannon [17] in multiple rounds (in AES, the number of rounds depends on the key size to produce a completely random ciphertext). The confusion property obscures the relationship between the key and cipher text, while diffusion obscures the relationship between plain text and cipher text to resist cryptanalysis. AES transforms the input data into three layers, i.e. substitution layer for confusion property, diffusion layer for diffusion property and in key addition layer, data state is XORed with the generated non-linear sub-keys to make the cipher random.

The AES operates on bytes rather than bits, and its input (plaintext) of 128 bits is represented as 16 bytes, arranged in a 4×4 matrix. This plaintext of the matrix is known as the initial state and is modified as the algorithm progresses. AES comes in three different variants viz. 128, 192, and 256 input key bits. Each of these is arranged in a $4 \times 4/6/8$ matrix, each column representing a word of 4 bytes. However, in encryption processes, only 128 bits are used to XOR the data state irrespective of the main key size. Therefore, the number of rounds of encryption processes increases with key size and are 10, 12 and 14 rounds for 128, 192 and 256-bit key sizes, respectively. Table 1 shows the number of rounds, number of sub-keys and total number of bits generated to get the ciphertext. The number of sub-keys is one more than the number of rounds because before the start of the encryption processes, the original plaintext is initially XORed with the first subkey (master-key), and this XORing of plaintext before the start of the actual encryption processes is known as key whitening.

Table 1. Number of rounds and sub-keys in the variants of AES

AES Version	AES-128	AES-192	AES-256
Number of bits in the sub-key	128	192	256
Number of rounds	10	12	14
Number of sub-keys	11	13	15
Total number of bits required	1408	1664	1920

3.2 Secure Hash Algorithm-3

A cryptographic hash function (CHF) is a one-way function which takes arbitrary size input and provides a highly compressed fixed-size output. It is key-less but plays a very important role in digital security, viz., checks the integrity of the data because it is deterministic and highly sensitive (on average, when a single bit in the data is changed, approximately half of the bits in the hash output will be modified), and it is computationally impossible to find another message for the known hash value. Therefore, it is also known as checksum, message digest and fingerprint. The security level of a hash function is determined by computationally in-feasibility to find two different inputs that generate the same hash, i.e. collision resistance, and to find the original input from the hash value, i.e. preimage-resistance. Generally, if n is the size of the hash value, then a good hash function shall have $n/2$ bits security level.

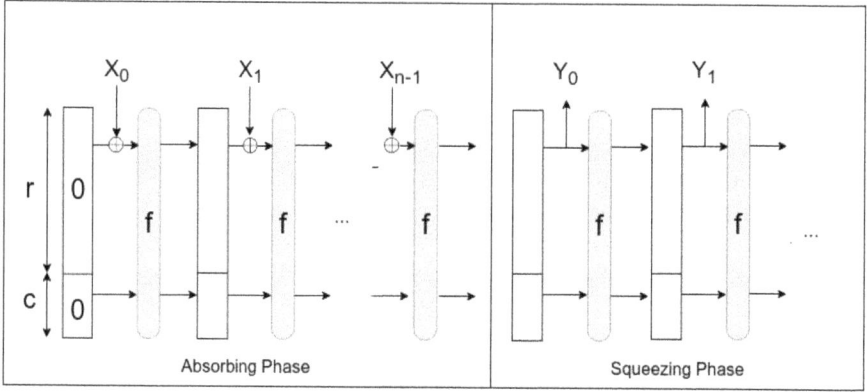

Fig. 1. A schematic of SHA-3

The first CHF was designed by Rabin in the late 70s. He proposed a 64-bit hash function using DES block cipher [14]. Later, in the 80s, more hash functions were proposed, and in 90s, MD5 and SHA-1 were used in several applications [15]. However, in 2004, it was shown that finding the collision in Message Digest-5 (MD5) is easy, and the security level of SHA-1 is significantly less than the standard required security [4,18]. Hence SHA-2 series (SHA-256, SHA-384, SHA-512) has been approved, and to date, no collision has been found in SHA-2. However, understanding the significance of CHF for security services, in 2012, NIST approved SHA-3 [8] to meet out the digital security requirements. The design of SHA-3 is very different from earlier hash functions. A schematic of the SHA-3 is shown in Fig. 1, which is based on sponge construction. It has two phases: in the first phase, the message is absorbed into the sponge, and in the second phase, the result is squeezed. In the absorbing phase, message blocks (x_i) are XORed into a subset of the state and the output blocks are read from the same subset of the state and alternated with the state transformation function (f). The size of the part of the message that is written and read is known as the *rate* (r), and the size of the part that is untouched by input/output is known as the *capacity* (c). The capacity determines the security of the SHA-3 and is $c/2$, and the security level does not changes even one take more than the double the bit of the desired security level from the output of the SHA-3. The message transformation is done by the f-function in five steps called θ, ρ, π, χ and ι

in which computation of the parity, bit-wise rotation, permutation of 25 words, bit-wise combination along rows and exclusive-OR are done respectively. To get the hash, after the absorption is completed, the function f of the state is taken until the required length is obtained, i.e. Hash(x) = $Y_0||Y_1||...$

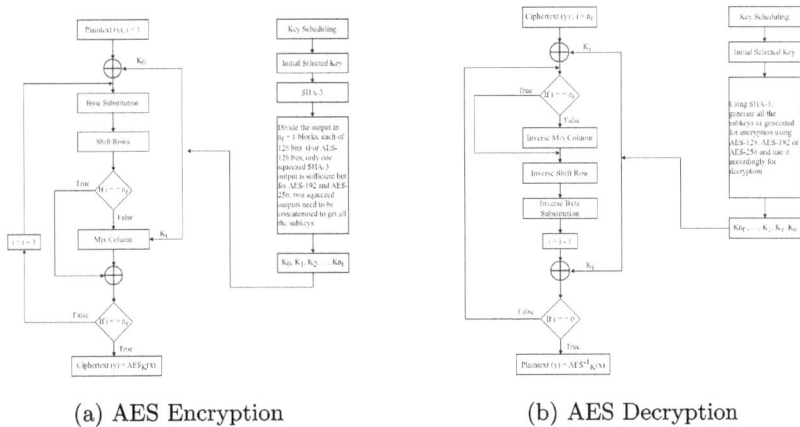

(a) AES Encryption (b) AES Decryption

Fig. 2. Flowchart for AES

4 Problem Overview and Proposed Approach

4.1 Problem Overview

In AES, the round sub-keys are generated sequentially from the master key using a non-linear g-function, which uses the same S-box that is used in the byte substitution layer [7]. Depending on key size, the number of words (32 bits) are generated. This sequential generation of keys creates additional computational overhead, resulting in more resource utilisation, especially in resource-constrained IoT devices. Also, the authors [6,9,10,12] pointed out the weakness in the key generation process of the AES. Therefore, we investigate SHA-3 for efficient and secure sub-key generation processes for data encryption and decryption.

4.2 Proposed Approach

We propose and investigate a novel and efficient approach for generating the sub-keys using SHA-3. The output of the squeezed phase in SHA-3 provides a non-linear one-way 1600-bit output and can be used as sub-keys in the encryption of data in AES. The required number of bits for encrypting data in different variant of AES is shown in Table 1. For AES-128, just first output of the squeezing phase is sufficient to have all the 11 sub-keys. However, in case of AES-192 and AES-256, one more iteration of the squeezing phase had to run to get all the sub-keys to encrypt the data, i.e. one can have 3200 bits of non-linear bits to make 13 or 15 sub-keys, i.e.

$$\text{Hash}(x) = Y_o || Y_1$$

where x denotes the input string, Y_o and Y_1 are the output of SHA-3 squeezing phase, which is of 1600 bits. The processes of squeezing phase in such that from Y_1 it is computationally infeasible to find Y_o and taking any sequence of 128 bits from Hash(x) does not effect the security of the sub-keys. Figures 2a and 2b show the flowchart of AES encryption and decryption processes of AESHA3.

5 Experimental Setup

To investigate the proposed novel approach, we implemented it on Intel Core i7 6th generation, 12 GB RAM, in Ubuntu 22.04 LTS OS and Raspberry Pi 4, 8 GB RAM with Raspbian OS using Python 3.10. First, we run the SHA-3 10,000 times with random inputs strings and found the average time taken for generating the sub-keys to be used for encrypting the data using the AES three layer is ~1300 times faster then sub-key generated by he standard AES. The detail results are shown in Table 2. Then we used Electronic Code Book modes of operations i.e. encrypting data of 128 bits or more independently to find how much time can be saved for data encryption for IoT devices, which are generally resource constrained.

Table 2. Time taken in milliseconds for the sub-key generation by AES and AESHA3

System Specifications	Operating System	AES-128	AESHA3-128	AES-192	AESHA3-192	AES-256	AESHA3-256
Intel Core i7 6th generation CPU	Ubuntu 22.04 LTS	1334.31	1.21	1403.26	1.231	1442.18	1.237
Raspberry Pi 4B 8GB RAM	Raspbian OS	5996.36	4.55	6084.61	4.74	6205.45	4.69

6 Results Analysis

As we find that sub-key generated by SHA-3 takes ~ 1300 less time than the sub-key generated by AES. Therefore for IoT devices we investigated that how much it will be efficient if data is encrypted by AESHA3. For the purpose first we implemented AESHA3 and AES to encrypt data in intel core i7, 6th generation processor and then we implemented in Raspberry Pi 4B because it has limited computational power and can be considered as IoT device. We encrypted the data in both operating systems starting from 1 KB and doubling the data till

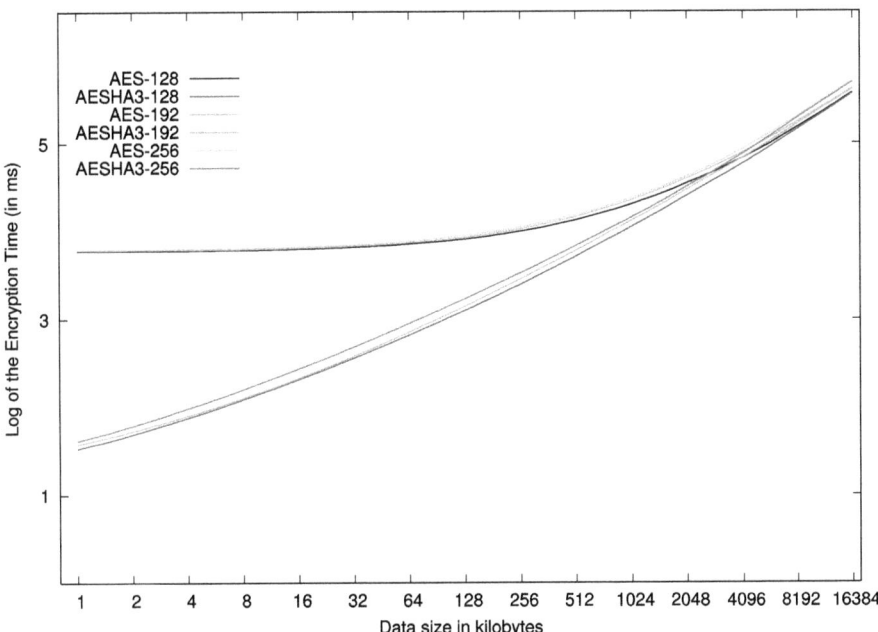

Fig. 3. Comparison of the time taken to encrypt the data by AES and AESHA3 by intel core i7, 6th generation processor.

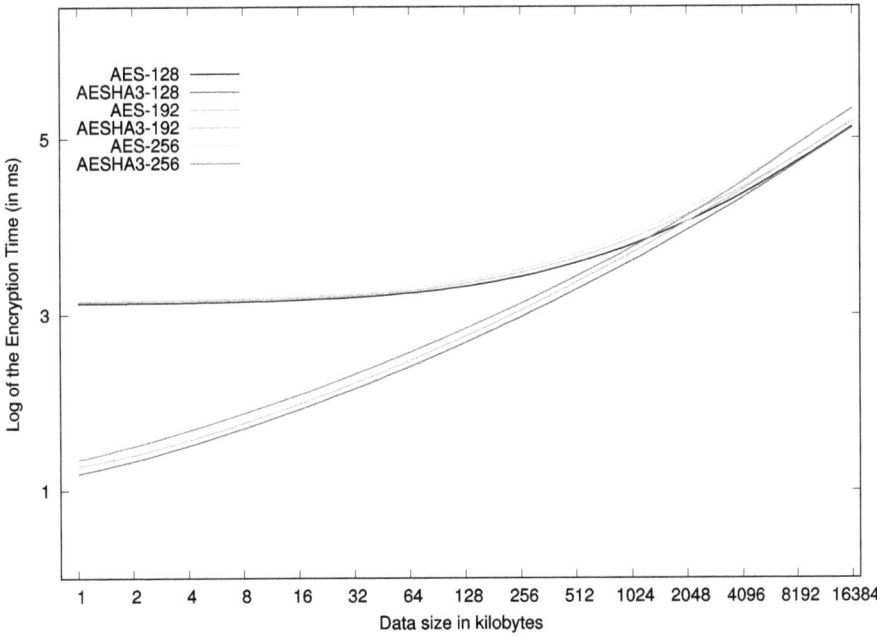

Fig. 4. Comparison of the time taken to encrypt the data by AES and AESHA3 by Raspberry Pi 4B.

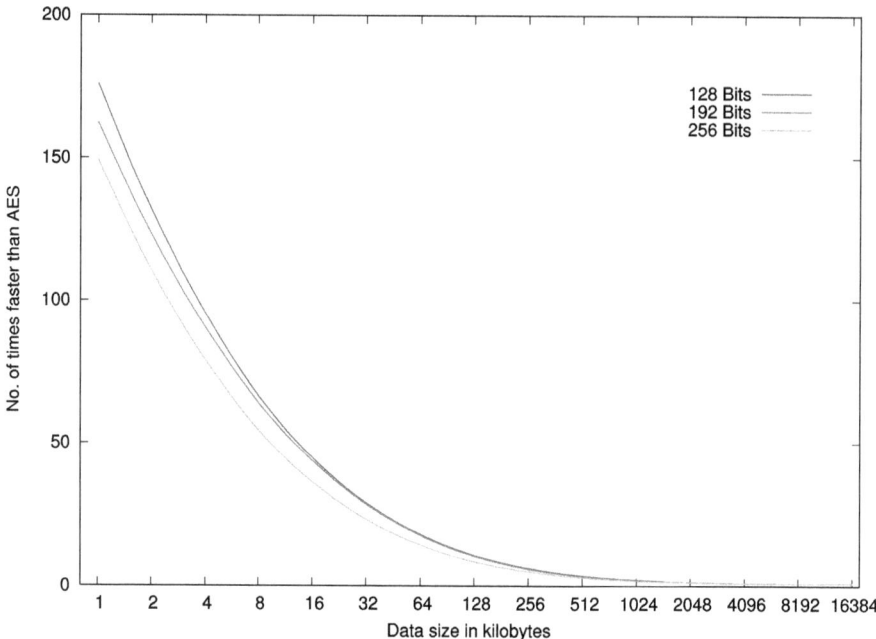

Fig. 5. Number of times AESHA3 faster then AES to encrypt data by Raspberry Pi 4B.

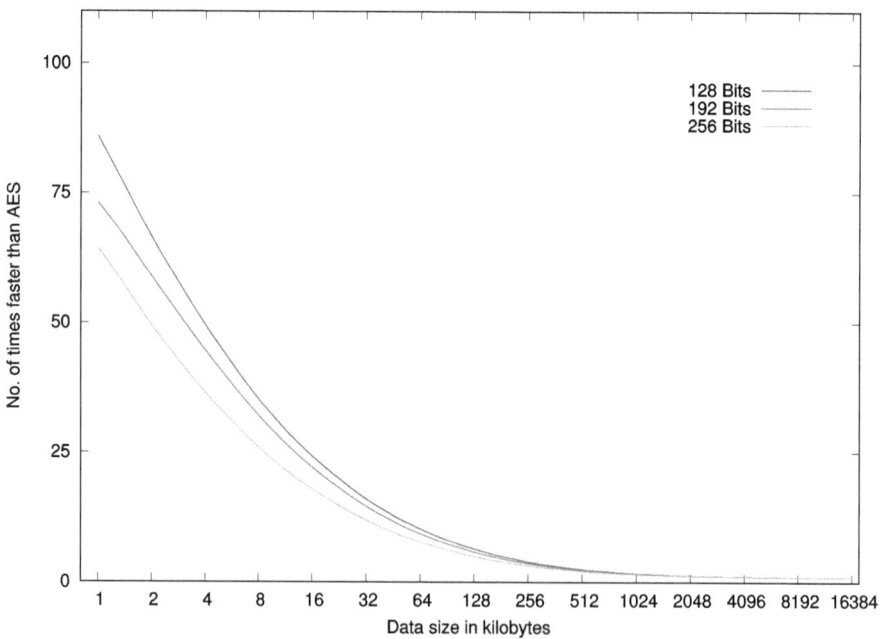

Fig. 6. Number of times AESHA3 faster then AES to encrypt data by intel core i7, 6th generation processor.

Table 3. Time taken and efficiency to encrypt the data up to 16 MB using AES and AESHA3 in Intel Core i7 6th Generation processor.

File Size	Total Time AES-128 (ms)	Total Time AESHA3-128 (ms)	Efficiency of AESHA3-128 (X)	Total Time AES-192 (ms)	Total Time AESHA3-192 (ms)	Efficiency of AESHA3-192 (X)	Total Time AES-256 (ms)	Total Time AESHA3-256 (ms)	Efficiency of AESHA3-256 (X)
1 KB	1347.24	15.68	85.92	1417.22	19.38	73.12	1464.15	22.70	64.5
2 KB	1355.44	23.69	57.21	1424.68	26.26	54.25	1476.69	34.88	42.33
4 KB	1373.93	42.29	32.49	1448.18	49.99	28.97	1509.12	68.89	21.91
8 KB	1413.34	81.60	17.32	1491.14	92.22	16.17	1548.31	106.64	14.52
16 KB	1473.12	141.49	10.41	1566.51	168.31	9.31	1665.26	222.89	7.47
32 KB	1604.57	272.77	5.88	1729.70	330.97	5.22	1861.00	418.86	4.44
64 KB	1881.59	550.00	3.42	2044.98	646.93	3.16	2225.71	783.58	2.84
128 KB	2402.95	1071.30	2.24	2656.92	1257.83	2.43	2903.74	1462.38	1.98
256 KB	3388.58	2056.83	1.65	3892.48	2493.95	1.56	4358.85	2917.59	1.49
512 KB	5461.41	4129.83	1.32	6398.85	4999.23	1.28	7278.61	5836.77	1.25
1 MB	9649.51	8317.80	1.16	12831.64	11432.31	1.12	13094.25	11653.24	1.12
2 MB	17779.87	16448.04	1.08	22338.69	20939.92	1.06	24701.81	23259.94	1.062
4 MB	35315.09	33984.14	1.04	40327.12	38924.27	1.03	57461.65	56015.52	1.025
8 MB	67805.52	66472.24	1.02	80735.64	79330.45	1.02	114207.08	112728.99	1.013
16 MB	134256.81	132920.93	1.01	160978.36	159569.76	1.01	219933.49	218440.19	1.006

Table 4. Time taken and efficiency to encrypt the data up to 16 MB using AES and AESHA3 in Raspberry Pi 4B.

File Size	Total Time AES-128 (ms)	Total Time AESHA3-128 (ms)	Efficiency of AESHA3-128 (X)	Total Time AES-192 (ms)	Total Time AESHA3-192 (ms)	Efficiency of AESHA3-192 (X)	Total Time AES-256 (ms)	Total Time AESHA3-256 (ms)	Efficiency of AESHA3-256 (X)
1 KB	6,021.61	34.22	175.97	6,109.35	37.62	162.40	6,230.05	41.73	149.29
2 KB	6,044.45	56.67	106.66	6,131.04	60.83	100.79	6,258.88	71.06	88.08
4 KB	6,088.72	101.13	60.21	6,174.92	103.58	59.61	6,319.90	131.98	47.89
8 KB	6,185.17	197.83	31.27	6,263.59	190.93	32.81	6,445.41	256.86	25.09
16 KB	6,351.80	364.67	17.42	6,445.58	373.80	17.24	6,685.70	497.24	13.45
32 KB	6,700.51	713.00	9.40	6,853.98	782.73	8.76	7,158.61	970.84	7.37
64 KB	7,393.14	1,406.06	5.26	7,722.23	1,651.22	4.68	8,126.02	1,938.22	4.19
128 KB	8,790.51	2,803.58	3.14	9,437.66	3,366.87	2.80	10,078.41	3,891.07	2.59
256 KB	11,656.09	5,668.24	2.06	12,743.25	6,675.07	1.91	13,874.86	7,689.83	1.80
512 KB	17,375.71	11,388.39	1.53	19,583.15	13,510.26	1.45	21,684.56	15,499.15	1.40
1 MB	28,641.21	22,653.57	1.26	32,821.73	26,749.37	1.23	28,572.75	22,384.93	1.28
2 MB	51,266.41	45,279.09	1.13	59,780.93	53,657.67	1.11	67,857.84	61,664.73	1.10
4 MB	98,149.74	92,156.76	1.07	111,105.16	104,965.89	1.06	129,221.49	123,033.96	1.05
8 MB	187,024.09	180,998.08	1.03	218,761.47	212,593.99	1.03	255,063.21	248,797.29	1.03
16 MB	368,645.63	362,567.91	1.02	415,755.80	409,473.02	1.02	499,292.89	493,065.41	1.01

16 MB. We find that up to 2 MB data encryption it is significant, and lesser the data size more the resource saving (Table 3 and 4). This is basically due to fact that sub-key generation is one time job. The Fig. 3 and 4 shows the time taken to encrypt the data with AESHA3 and AES upto 16 MB, and Fig. 5 and 6 shows the number of times AESHA3 is faster then AES in intel core i7, 6th generation processor and Rasberry Pi 4B respectively.

7 Conclusion

In symmetric cipher, AES is the most widely used cipher for the confidentiality of the data and is also used for the security services viz. integrity, authentication and key establishment. According to Kerckhoff's Principles, a cipher or cryptosystem should be secure even if the attacker knows all details about the system, except the secret key, i.e. the system should be secure even if the attacker knows the encryption/decryption algorithms. However, recently authors have shown some weakness in the generation of sub-keys in AES, hence a threat to the AES cipher. Therefore, we proposed and investigated a novel encryption AESHA3, which uses sub-key generated by SHA3, which provides a one way and highly non-linear output i.e. the overall security will not change. However, our analysis shows that the average time taken for generating the sub-keys to be used for encrypting the data using the three layers of AES is $\sim$ 1300 times faster than sub-key generated by the AES. Therefore, AESHA3 will be very relevant not only in terms of security but also it will save the resources in IoT devices. We implemented AESHA3 in intel core i7, 6th generation processor and Raspberry Pi 4B and find that up to 2 MB data encryption is very significant, and lesser the data size, more the resource saving compared to AES. In this we have made some initial analysis to compare the randomness (i.e. uniformity and independence) of the sub-keys generated by SHA-3 with AES generated sub-keys. The results are encouraging and the detail analysis will be published elsewhere.

References

1. Alasaad, A., Alghafis, A.: Key-dependent s-box scheme for enhancing the security of block ciphers. In: 2019 2nd International Conference on Signal Processing and Information Security (ICSPIS). pp. 1–4 (2019). https://doi.org/10.1109/ICSPIS48135.2019.9045900
2. Bahrak, B., Aref, M.R.: Impossible differential attack on seven-round AES-128. IET Inf. Secur. **2**(2), 28–32 (2008)
3. Biryukov, A., Dunkelman, O., Keller, N., Khovratovich, D., Shamir, A.: Key recovery attacks of practical complexity on AES-256 variants with up to 10 rounds. In: Advances in Cryptology–EUROCRYPT 2010: 29th Annual International Conference on the Theory and Applications of Cryptographic Techniques, French Riviera, 30 May–3 June 2010, Proceedings 29, pp. 299–319. Springer (2010)
4. Black, J., Cochran, M., Highland, T.: A study of the MD5 attacks: insights and improvements. In: Robshaw, M. (ed.) Fast Software Encryption, pp. 262–277. Springer, Heidelberg (2006)
5. Bogdanov, A., Mendel, F., Regazzoni, F., Rijmen, V., Tischhauser, E.: ALE: AES-based lightweight authenticated encryption. In: Fast Software Encryption: 20th International Workshop, FSE 2013, Singapore, 11–13 March 2013, Revised Selected Papers 20, pp. 447–466. Springer (2014)
6. De Los Reyes, E.M., Sison, A.M., Medina, R.: Modified AES cipher round and key schedule. Indonesian J. Electr. Eng. Inform. (IJEEI) **7**(1), 29–36 (2019)
7. Dworkin, M., et al.: Advanced encryption standard (AES) (2001). https://doi.org/10.6028/NIST.FIPS.197
8. Dworkin, M.J.: SHA-3 standard: permutation-based hash and extendable-output functions (2015)
9. Leurent, G., Pernot, C.: New representations of the AES key schedule. In: Advances in Cryptology – EUROCRYPT 2021, pp. 54–84 (2021)
10. May, L., Henricksen, M., Millan, W., Carter, G., Dawson, E.: Strengthening the key schedule of the AES (2002)

11. National Institute of Standards and Technology: Data encryption standard (DES). FIPS Publication 46-3 (1999)
12. Nikolić, I.: Tweaking AES. In: Biryukov, A., Gong, G., Stinson, D.R. (eds.) Selected Areas in Cryptography, pp. 198–210. Springer, Heidelberg (2011)
13. Petitcolas, F.A.P.: Kerckhoffs' principle, pp. 675–675. Springer, Boston (2011). https://doi.org/10.1007/978-1-4419-5906-5_487
14. Preneel, B.: The first 30 years of cryptographic hash functions and the NIST SHA-3 competition. In: Pieprzyk, J. (ed.) Topics in Cryptology - CT-RSA 2010, pp. 1–14. Springer, Heidelberg (2010)
15. FIPS PUB: Secure hash standard (SHS). FIPS PUB 180-4 (2012)
16. Sawka, M., Niemiec, M.: A sponge-based key expansion scheme for modern block ciphers. Energies **15**(19), 6864 (2022)
17. Shannon, C.E.: Communication theory of secrecy systems. Bell Syst. Tech. J. **28**(4), 656–715 (1949). https://doi.org/10.1002/j.1538-7305.1949.tb00928.x
18. Wang, X., Yin, Y.L., Yu, H.: Finding collisions in the full SHA-1. In: Shoup, V. (ed.) Advances in Cryptology - CRYPTO 2005, pp. 17–36. Springer, Heidelberg (2005)

UWB Antenna with Integrated Quadruple Notch Bands

Nallanagula Sanjana[✉], Yellavula Jaswanth, Perumandla Sai Sushumna, and Sulakshana Chilukuri

Department of ECE, Vardhaman College of Engineering, Hyderabad, Telangana, India
sanjanachary2002@gmail.com, Yellavulajaswanth21ec@student.vardhaman.org, sulakshana@vardhaman.org

Abstract. Ultra-Wideband (UWB) communications have inherently very wide bandwidth and the frequency range for UWB communication can vary, but it often falls within the range of 3.1 GHz to 10.6 GHz. Microstrip antenna is widely used in UWB antenna design and can be used in an various applications, including aircraft, spacecraft, satellite, missile, mobile radio, and wireless communications. A quadruple notch band planar UWB antenna for wireless body area networks (WBANs) is proposed to solve the interference problem between UWB and narrowband communications, such as WiMAX (3.30–3.70 GHz), C band (3.7–4.2 GHz), WBAN (2.4 GHz), WLAN (5.47–5.725 GHz, 5.725–5.825 GHz), ISM band (5.725–5.875 GHz), Xband Satellite communication application (7.9–8.4 GHz). Thus the performance of antenna is improved by reducing the interference of other signals. The gain of the proposed antenna is -3.0 to -1.2 dBi.

Keywords: UWB · notch band · Microstrip antenna

1 Introduction

Ultra-Wideband (UWB) antennas are a type of wireless communication antenna designed to transmit and receive signals over a broad frequency range, covering a vast spectrum of frequencies. These notches are intentional gaps in the antenna's frequency response, where the antenna does not efficiently radiate or receive signals. Wireless Body Area Network (WBAN) systems are gaining attention as a promising field of study due to their extensive use in medical, health monitoring, entertainment, and remote sensing applications. Nonetheless, to function effectively, WBAN systems necessitate high data transfer rates while consuming minimal power. Ultra-Wideband (UWB) technology offers fast data transmission, minimal power spectral density, wide bandwidth, and resilience to multipath fading. These features contribute to fulfilling the demands of WBAN systems.

1.1 Related Works

Over the past few years, several methods have been introduced for integrating notch bands into UWB antennas. In the work presented by reference [1], an intricately designed compact Ultra-Wideband (UWB) extended gap ridge horn (EGRH) antenna, manufactured using 3D printing, is elaborated upon for its application in biological measurements on the human body. In [2], a miniaturized MIMO antenna tailored for UWB applications, which incorporates triple band-notched characteristics to reduce interference from specific frequency bands. The compact design and experimental validation make it a promising candidate for use in modern wireless communication systems. The design aims to provide a wide frequency bandwidth, enhanced performance, and interference rejection capabilities by the incorporation of SRR and CSRR structures [3–7]. A CPW-fed Circular-Like Slot Antenna designed for wideband performance and dual band-notched characteristics. The antenna's ability to operate across a broad frequency range while rejecting signals in specific bands [8–14]. A compact frequency-reconfigurable UWB antenna with 8 different operating states [15], allowing it to cover a wide range of frequency bands while maintaining compatibility with UWB communication standards. In [16], novel compact UWB planar monopole antenna is designed that incorporates a ribbonshaped slot for improved performance. The antenna's compact design and enhanced characteristics make it a promising choice for modern wireless communication systems requiring wide bandwidth and efficient signal. A recently developed and constructed Vivaldi antenna, designed for ultra-wideband (UWB) multiple-input multiple-output (MIMO) applications, incorporates distinctive dual band-notched features as detailed in references [17–23]. The antenna offers UWB performance while providing the ability to customize its interference rejection capabilities to address specific frequency bands [24–30]. In this article, we have proposed a UWB antenna with integrated quadruple notch bands for Wireless Body Area Network (WBAN) applications in the medical and healthcare domains. By integrating quadruple notch bands, the antenna will mitigate interference issues and comply with regulatory requirements, ensuring interference-free communication within the WBAN environment. The goal is to achieve a compact, low-profile design that can be seamlessly integrated into small, wearable medical devices, without compromising performance or biocompatibility. The use of four notch bands enhances the overall radio performance of the UWB antenna. It helps in achieving a cleaner and more robust signal, reducing bit error rates, and increasing the overall communication range and reliability.

2 Antenna Configuration and Design

The design of the antenna under consideration is depicted in Fig. 1, outlining the specific design parameters. This antenna features a printed elliptical radiator incorporating two inverted L-shaped stubs aimed at introducing two notch bands and enhancing the lower operating frequency. Inverted L-shaped stubs in the antenna design serve to optimize impedance matching, control the radiation pattern, tune frequencies, and reduce the antenna's overall size. Various methodologies have been proposed to integrate these notch bands into UWB antennas. One common technique involves etching suitable structures onto either the patch or the ground plane. Figure 1 illustrates the fundamental structure of the proposed antenna. In a UWB antenna fed through a coplanar waveguide (CPW) and integrated with a stub-loaded meander line resonator, a triple-notch band configuration is suggested. This is achieved by incorporating stubs and slots in the radiating patch and introducing parasitic stubs in the ground plane. Alternatively, another approach involves inserting resonator structures, such as split ring resonators, to create the desired notch bands. To obtain four notch bands the structure is modified by adding a slot on the ground plane as shown in Fig. 1. Adding a slot on the ground plane of an antenna can create a notch band, also known as a stop band or frequency notch. A notch band refers to a specific frequency range where the antenna's response is significantly attenuated, causing a dip or "notch" in its frequency response. This can be a useful feature for suppressing interference from certain frequency bands or for avoiding specific frequency regions. The refined design parameters for the proposed antenna structure are outlined as follows: W = 12 mm, L = 19 mm, d1 = 10.8 mm, P1 = 4.5 mm, d2 = 7.7 mm, P2 = 1 mm, d3 = 3.9 mm, P3 = 3.5 mm, S = 0.5 mm, Wf = 1.9 mm, Lf = 7.39 mm.

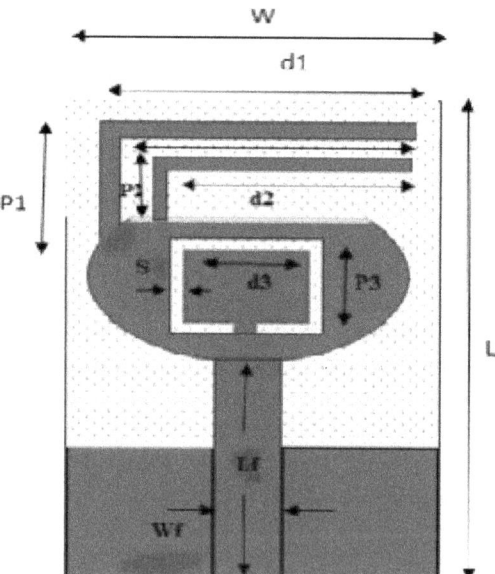

Fig. 1. Structure of proposed antenna

3 Simulated Results and Analysis

The Fig. 2 shows the reflection coefficient plot of the final structure. The reflection coefficient plot provides valuable insights into the impedance matching and reflection characteristics of the UWB antenna. The observed reflection coefficient aligns well with the simulated counterpart, indicating a consistent agreement between measurement and simulation. Minor discrepancies at higher frequencies could be attributed to substrate losses, as well as potential errors during measurement and fabrication processes. Parametric results of an antenna refer to the specific measurable characteristics and performance metrics obtained from analysis, simulation, or measurement of the antenna's behavior. These results provide quantitative information about how the antenna performs in its intended operating environment and under specific conditions.

Table 1. Parametric analysis

	Radius	Bandwidth	dimension change
1	4.9 mm	6.4 GHz	L = 19 mm, Lf = 7 mm
2	5 mm	5.7 GHz	L = 17 mm, d1 = 9.5 mm
3	5.2 mm	5.6 GHz	L = 16.7 mm, P2 = 0.7 mm
4	5.5 mm	5.2 GHz	L = 14 mm, Wf = 1.5 mm

Changing the length of the antenna structure, specifically the radiating element, can have a significant impact on the antenna's performance and characteristics. The Table 1 shows the changes in lengths we have made. Parametric results of an antenna refer to the specific measurable characteristics and performance metrics obtained from analysis, simulation, or measurement of the antenna's behavior. Parametric results of an antenna refer to the specific measurable characteristics and performance metrics obtained from analysis, simulation, or measurement of the antenna's behavior. Optimizing the design parameters of an antenna structure involves balancing factors like frequency range, radiation pattern, polarization, impedance matching, environmental conditions, size, manufacturability, and regulatory compliance to achieve desired performance goals. It requires iterative design, simulation, prototyping, and testing processes to fine-tune the antenna for efficient operation in real-world scenarios.

The Fig. 2 shows the analysis the results which indicates the range of frequencies over which the antenna operates efficiently. The accurate results were not obtained at first but after changing the lengths randomly the desired results are obtained as per given range.

The Fig. 3 shows the parametric results obtained when changes in dimensions are done as per the given table in accordance to attain the perfect notch bands at required frequencies.

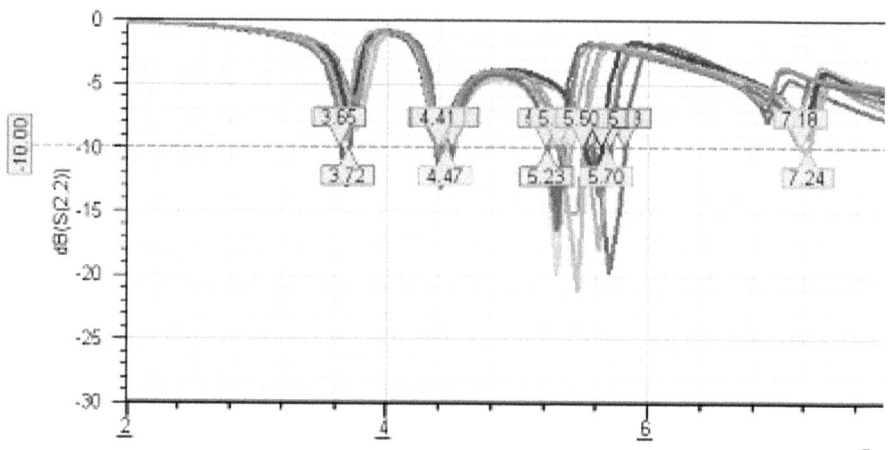

Fig. 2. Parametric analysis by the change of lengths

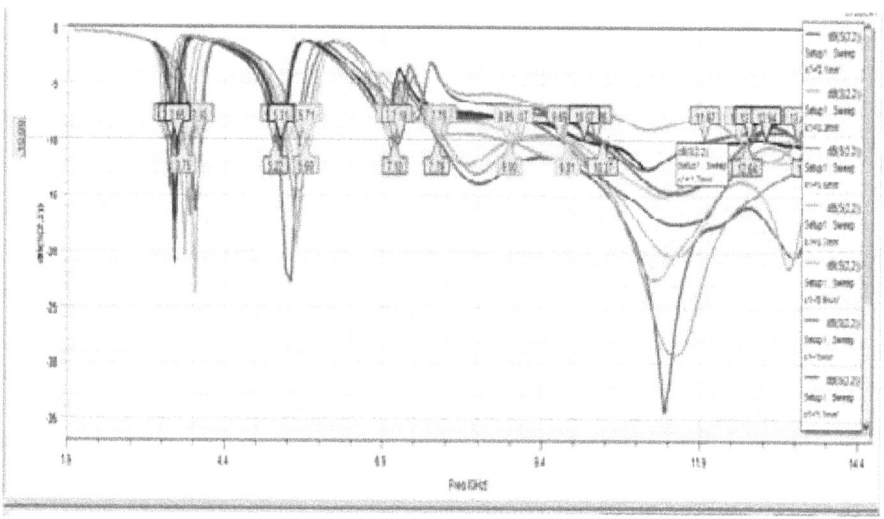

Fig. 3. Parametric analysis by the change of position of slots

The Fig. 4 shows the reflection coefficient plot of the final structure. The reflection coefficient plot provides valuable insights into the impedance matching and reflection characteristics of the UWB antenna. The obtained reflection coefficient findings closely align with the simulated results, indicating a

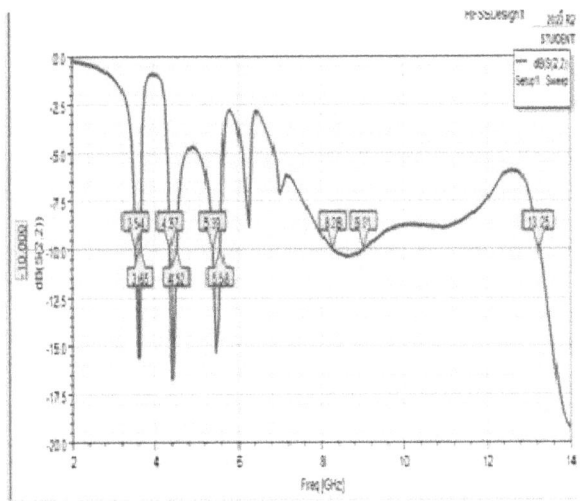

Fig. 4. Reflection Coefficient plot of the final antenna design

satisfactory agreement between the measured and simulated reflection coefficients. Minor discrepancies at higher frequencies could potentially be attributed to substrate losses, as well as errors during the measurement and fabrication processes.

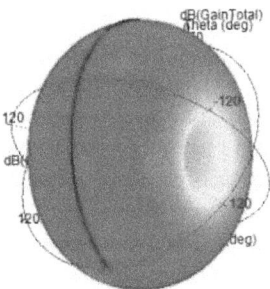

Fig. 5. Gain plot

The Fig. 5 shows the gain plot at 5.6 GHz. The gain of an antenna is a critical parameter that quantifies its ability to radiate electromagnetic energy in a specific direction. It represents the amplification or concentration of power in the direction of interest compared to an ideal isotropic radiator. In this report, we analyze the gain characteristics of the UWB antenna at a frequency of 5.6 GHz. The analysis focused on determining the antenna's gain at a specific frequency of interest This frequency was chosen due to its significance in WLAN applications.

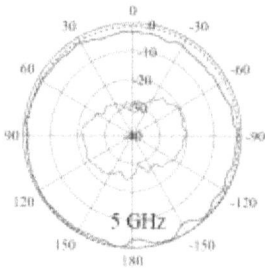

Fig. 6. Azimuth Pattern

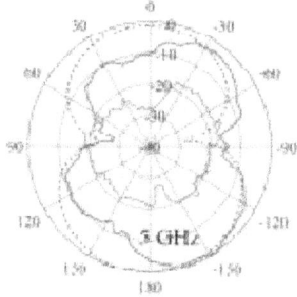

Fig. 7. Elevation Pattern

The Fig. 6 shows the H plane or Azimuth pattern. The azimuth pattern is also known as the azimuthal radiation pattern or the horizontal radiation pattern. It represents the radiation characteristics of an antenna in the horizontal plane, which is typically the plane parallel to the ground. The H-plane, or horizontal plane, is often considered parallel to the ground because it helps optimize antenna performance in certain applications, particularly those where horizontal coverage is more critical than vertical coverage.

The Fig. 7 shows the E plane or Elevation pattern. The elevation pattern, also called the elevation radiation pattern or the vertical radiation pattern, represents the radiation characteristics of an antenna in the vertical plane, which is typically the plane perpendicular to the ground.

4 Conclusion

The UWB antenna with integrated quadruple notch bands presented in this report presents an innovative solution for achieving wideband performance with the added benefit of interference mitigation. The ability to suppress specific frequencies provides a valuable advantage in crowded wireless environments, ensuring high-quality communication and reliable signal transmission. While the antenna's performance and characteristics have been extensively evaluated through simulation, real-world testing and validation will be necessary to confirm its suitability for specific practical applications. Overall, this UWB antenna design holds great promise for addressing the challenges of modern wireless communication, and it paves the way for further advancements in the field of antenna technology. Some areas of interest for further studies on UWB antennas with notches may include investigating different techniques to optimize notch designs, such as the use of different materials, shapes, or geometries to achieve desired notch characteristics while maintaining UWB performance, exploring methods to enhance the bandwidth of UWB antennas with notches while ensuring efficient rejection of unwanted frequency bands.

4.1 Applications

- Remote Health Monitoring
- Telemedicine
- Body Area Communication

References

1. Rashid, S., et al.: 3-D printed UWB microwave bodyscope for biomedical measurements. IEEE Antennas Wirel. Propag. Lett. **18**(4), 626–630 (2019). https://doi.org/10.1109/LAWP.2019.2899591
2. Chen, Z., Zhou, W., Hong, J.: A miniaturized MIMO antenna with triple band-notched characteristics for UWB applications. IEEE Access **9**, 63646–63655 (2021). https://doi.org/10.1109/ACCESS.2021.3074511
3. Paul, P.M., Kandasamy, K., Sharawi, M.S.: A triband circularly polarized strip and SRR-loaded slot antenna. IEEE Trans. Antennas Propag. **66**(10), 5569–5573 (2018). https://doi.org/10.1109/TAP.2018.2854911.LAWP.2009.2021286
4. Zamora, G., Zuffanelli, S., Paredes, F., Herraiz-Martínez, F.J., Martín, F., Bonache, J.: Fundamental-mode leaky-wave antenna (LWA) using slotline and split-ring-resonator (SRR)-based metamaterials. IEEE Antennas Wirel. Propag. Lett. **12**, 1424–1427 (2013). https://doi.org/10.1109/LAWP.2013.2287525
5. Khan, M.S., Capobianco, A.-D., Asif, S.M., Anagnostou, D.E., Shubair, R.M., Braaten, B.D.: A compact CSRR-enabled UWB diversity antenna. IEEE Antennas Wirel. Propag. Lett. **16**, 808–812 (2017). https://doi.org/10.1109/LAWP.2016.2604843
6. Liu, X.Y., Wu, Z.T., Fan, Y., Tentzeris, E.M.: A miniaturized CSRR loaded wide-beamwidth circularly polarized implantable antenna for subcutaneous real-time glucose monitoring. IEEE Antennas Wirel. Propag. Lett. **16**, 577–580 (2017). https://doi.org/10.1109/LAWP.2016.2590477
7. Ramachandran, A., Valiyaveettil Pushpakaran, S., Pezholil, M., Kesavath, V.: A four-port MIMO antenna using concentric square-ring patches loaded with CSRR for high isolation. IEEE Antennas Wirel. Propag. Lett. **15**, 1196–1199 (2016). https://doi.org/10.1109/LAWP.2015.2499322
8. Lin, X.-C., Yu, C.-C.: A dual-band CPW-fed inductive slot-monopole hybrid antenna. IEEE Trans. Antennas Propag. **56**(1), 282–285 (2008). https://doi.org/10.1109/TAP.2007.905978

9. Yu, C.-C., Lin, X.-C.: A wideband single chip inductor-loaded CPW-fed inductive slot antenna. IEEE Trans. Antennas Propag. **56**(5), 1498–1501 (2008). https://doi.org/10.1109/TAP.2008.919224
10. Angelopoulos, E.S., Anastopoulos, A.Z., Kaklamani, D.I., Alexandridis, A.A., Lazarakis, F., Dangakis, K.: Circular and elliptical CPW-fed slot and microstrip-fed antennas for ultrawideband applications. IEEE Antennas Wirel. Propag. Lett. **5**, 294–297 (2006). https://doi.org/10.1109/LAWP.2006.878882
11. Nourinia, J., Mirmozafari, M.H., Emadian, S.R., Ghobadi, C., Pourahmadazar, J.: Bandwidth enhancement of CPW-fed circle-like slot antenna with dual band-notched characteristic. IEEE Antennas Wirel. Propag. Lett. **11**, 543–546 (2012). https://doi.org/10.1109/LAWP.2012.2199274
12. Chen, C., Yung, E.K.N.: Dual-band dual-sense circularly-polarized CPW-fed slot antenna with two spiral slots loaded. IEEE Trans. Antennas Propag. **57**(6), 1829–1833 (2009). https://doi.org/10.1109/TAP.2009.2019990
13. Fu, S., Fang, S., Wang, Z., Li, X.: Broadband circularly polarized slot antenna array fed by asymmetric CPW for L-band applications. IEEE Antennas Wirel. Propag. Lett. **8**, 1014–1016 (2009). https://doi.org/10.1109/LAWP.2009.2031662
14. Chang, D.-C., Zeng, B.-H., Liu, J.-C.: CPW-fed circular fractal slot antenna design for dual-band applications. IEEE Trans. Antennas Propag. **56**(12), 3630–3636 (2008). https://doi.org/10.1109/TAP.2008.2007279
15. Nan, J., Zhao, J., Gao, M., Yang, W., Wang, M., Xie, H.: A compact 8-states frequency reconfigurable UWB antenna. IEEE Access **9**, 144257–144263 (2021). https://doi.org/10.1109/ACCESS.2021.3122250
16. Tomar, S., Kumar, A.: Design of a novel compact planar monopole UWB antenna with triple band-notched characteristics. In: 2015 2nd International Conference on Signal Processing and Integrated Networks (SPIN), Noida, India, pp. 56–59 (2015). https://doi.org/10.1109/SPIN.2015.7095346
17. Li, Z., Yin, C., Zhu, X.: Compact UWB MIMO Vivaldi antenna with dual band-notched characteristics. IEEE Access **7**, 38696–38701 (2019). https://doi.org/10.1109/ACCESS.2019.2906338
18. Yang, C., Kim, J., Kim, H., Wee, J., Kim, B., Jung, C.: Quad-band antenna with high isolation MIMO and broadband SCS for broadcasting and telecommunication services. IEEE Antennas Wirel. Propag. Lett. **9**, 584–587 (2010). https://doi.org/10.1109/LAWP.2010.2053515
19. Kang, L., Li, H., Wang, X., Shi, X.: Compact offset microstrip-fed MIMO antenna for band-notched UWB applications. IEEE Antennas Wirel. Propag. Lett. **14**, 1754–1757 (2015). https://doi.org/10.1109/LAWP.2015.2422571
20. Hussain, R., Sharawi, M.S.: An integrated slot-based frequency-agile and UWB multifunction MIMO antenna system. IEEE Antennas Wirel. Propag. Lett. **18**(10), 2150–2154 (2019). https://doi.org/10.1109/LAWP.2019.2939112
21. Pan, Y., Cui, Y., Li, R.: Investigation of a triple-band multibeam MIMO antenna for wireless access points. IEEE Trans. Antennas Propag. **64**(4), 1234–1241 (2016). https://doi.org/10.1109/TAP.2016.2526082
22. Rhee, C., et al.: Pattern-reconfigurable MIMO antenna for high isolation and low correlation. IEEE Antennas Wirel. Propag. Lett. **13**, 1373–1376 (2014). https://doi.org/10.1109/LAWP.2014.2339012
23. Li, J.-F., Chu, Q.-X., Li, Z.-H., Xia, X.-X.: Compact dual band-notched UWB MIMO antenna with high isolation. IEEE Trans. Antennas Propag. **61**(9), 4759–4766 (2013). https://doi.org/10.1109/TAP.2013.2267653

24. Sun, C.: A design of compact ultrawideband circularly polarized microstrip patch antenna. IEEE Trans. Antennas Propag. **67**(9), 6170–6175 (2019). https://doi.org/10.1109/TAP.2019.2922759
25. Ghaderi, M.R., Mohajeri, F.: A compact hexagonal wide-slot antenna with microstrip-fed monopole for UWB application. IEEE Antennas Wirel. Propag. Lett. **10**, 682–685 (2011). https://doi.org/10.1109/LAWP.2011.2158629
26. Foroutan, F., Nikolova, N.K.: UWB active antenna for microwave breast imaging sensing arrays. IEEE Antennas Wirel. Propag. Lett. **18**(10), 1951–1955 (2019). https://doi.org/10.1109/LAWP.2019.2929016
27. Lee, C.-H., Wu, J.-H., Hsu, C.-I.G., Chan, H.-L., Chen, H.-H.: Balanced band-notched UWB filtering circular patch antenna with common-mode suppression. IEEE Antennas Wirel. Propag. Lett. **16**, 2812–2815 (2017). https://doi.org/10.1109/LAWP.2017.2748279
28. Elsheakh, D.N., Elsadek, H.A., Abdallah, E.A., Elhenawy, H., Iskander, M.F.: Enhancement of microstrip monopole antenna bandwidth by using EBG structures. IEEE Antennas Wirel. Propag. Lett. **8**, 959–962 (2009). https://doi.org/10.1109/LAWP.2009.2030375
29. Sarkar, D., Srivastava, K.V., Saurav, K.: A compact microstrip-fed triple band-notched UWB monopole antenna. IEEE Antennas Wirel. Propag. Lett. **13**, 396–399 (2014). https://doi.org/10.1109/LAWP.2014.2306812
30. Moosazadeh, M., Ghobadi, C., Dousti, M.: Small monopole antenna with checkered-shaped patch for UWB application. IEEE Antennas Wirel. Propag. Lett. **9**, 1014–1017 (2010). https://doi.org/10.1109/LAWP.2010.2088375
31. Cai, Y.-Z., Yang, H.-C., Cai, L.-Y.: Wideband monopole antenna with three band-notched characteristics. IEEE Antennas Wirel. Propag. Lett. **13**, 607–610 (2014). https://doi.org/10.1109/LAWP.2014.2313178

Framework for Brute-Force Attack Detection Using Federated Learning

J. Chethana Datta[✉], S. Ananya, Mukund Deepak, Nishanth Mungara, and V. Sarasvathi

PES University, Bengaluru 560100, India
chethandatta2@gmail.com, sarsvathiv@pes.edu

Abstract. Intrusion Detection and Prevention Systems (IDPS) play a pivotal role in safeguarding computer networks by identifying and responding to potential threats. This paper focuses on the implementation of a Federated Learning-based Intrusion Detection and Prevention System which mainly focuses on detecting brute-force attacks. The IDPS captures network packets, predicts anomalies using a Decision Tree model and logs malicious flows for further analysis. The Federated Server holds a pre-trained machine learning model, it also communicates with the IDPS to send and receive model updates facilitating collaborative learning. Additionally, the malicious traffic is redirected to the honeypot service employed in the system. The paper aims to enhance realtime brute-force detection for specific services, such as SSH and FTP, through the federated learning paradigm. By harnessing the collaborative power of multiple nodes in a network, our system showcases improved detection capabilities with minimized communication overhead. Detailed design and experimentation reveals that the IDPS is capable of predicting the nature of interaction while ensuring that data privacy is preserved. The success of this experiment is evident with it's remarkable 99.997% accuracy rate. The system's capacity to provide smooth communication between the various intrusion detection components highlights how effective it is at defending computer networks against a variety of dynamic cyber threats.

Keywords: Federated Learning · IDPS · Decision Tree · SSH · FTP

1 Introduction

The implementation of Intrusion Detection and Prevention Systems (IDPS) remains a key defence mechanism against the rapidly expanding types of sophisticated cyber threats, in this exponentially growing area of cybersecurity. Traditional IDPS systems perform the necessary tasks of monitoring network traffic with the use of predefined attack signatures and heuristics. They also make use of anomaly detection methods to identify potential security breaches in the system. IDPSs thoroughly monitor the communication between the devices, mainly searching for known patterns of hostile behaviour in the interactions and also looking for any indicators of unusual activity. Therefore, IDPSs serve as a crucial line of defence in digital environments by actively identifying and mitigating security threats in this ever-evolving domain of cyber threats.

The Verizon DBIR 2023 [11] report emphasises that the Small and Medium Businesses (SMBs) are the most vulnerable to brute-force attacks. These attacks can have a devastating impact on their day-to-day operations and overall finances. These attacks can result in the theft of sensitive data like customer records and financial records as well. This can lead to loss of trust among the customers which will eventually lead to loss of business. These businesses may not have the necessary resources to detect and respond to such attacks resulting in prolonged downtime and loss in productivity. The report also states that the average loss occurred during a data breach for SMBs is $149,000, which can be a significant financial burden for the small and mid-size organizations making it crucial for them to employ effective security measures.

However, there is an immediate need for innovative security systems which can dynamically adapt to the emerging diversity and complexity of cyber threats. Machine Learning (ML) has proved to be a revolutionary contributor in the enhancement of the capabilities of a traditional IDPS system. An ML based IDPS systems can categorise and identify patterns in network traffic by using various ML algorithms which significantly improves their efficiency and accuracy. These systems unlike the rule-based systems, enable the detection of new unseen cyber threats and progressively develop the system's defence against them. Recently, Federated Learning has emerged as a ground breaking technique within the ML domain. It proposes a decentralised approach of collective learning which keeps in mind principles of privacy preservation as well. Federated Learning uses power of collaboration among the edge devices to train machine learning models without the need to centralise sensitive data. This concept is highly relevant in the context of an IDPS as well, where maintaining the privacy of network traffic data is of utmost importance.

Threats are becoming more frequent and varied in the rapidly evolving domain of cybersecurity. Therefore, real-time threat detection and protection of user privacy are undoubtedly required. This paper presents an efficient IDPS framework based on the Federated Learning approach to address these issues. By fusing the advantages of a classic IDPS with the benefits of Federated Learning, this proposed innovative solution presents a paradigm shift in the Intrusion Detection space.

In the proposed framework, the collective effort of the Intrusion Detection and Prevention System, the Federated Server which oversees the global machine learning model and a Honeypot dedicated for further in-depth threat analysis is required to secure users' access to critical resources on the End Server. This federated approach facilitates adaptive learning across distributed components, ensuring the system's resilience in the face of evolving threats. Positioned at the forefront of the evolving cybersecurity landscape, this Federated Learning-based IDPS system aligns with the contemporary requirements for real-time threat detection, adaptability, and privacy preservation in modern network security.

2 Related Works

The field of intrusion detection has witnessed significant advancements, with notable works contributing to the enhancement of security measures. For instance S. Krishnaveni et al.'s research on Classification through Ensemble Method for Network Intrusion Detection on Cloud Computing [6] addresses the challenges of precise intrusion detection in cloud environments. Their ensemble-based approach demonstrates efficiency in recognizing and categorizing network intrusions, offering a promising solution to reduce false positives and false negatives. Nevertheless, the limited evaluation on real-world datasets and the lack of comparison with state-of-the-art methods highlight areas for improvement.

In the survey by Joffrey L et al. [7], the focus is on analyzing intrusion detection research utilizing the CSE-CIC-IDS2018 dataset. The survey identifies gaps in current research and sheds light on performance metrics used in curated works, offering valuable insights for future directions in intrusion detection. However, it lacked sufficient information for a comprehensive evaluation, and the survey does not provide an exhaustive analysis of the performance of different intrusion detection models.

Laurens Hellemons et al.'s flow-based SSH Intrusion Detection System [5] presents SSHCure, a flow-based intrusion detection system designed to efficiently detect brute-force SSH attacks in real-time. The system operates solely on flow data and offers an effective algorithm for real-time detection, contributing to network security. However the limitations include its focus on detecting specific types of attacks and reliance on flow data, which may not be available in all network environments.

Li Yang et al.'s Open Source Code for Intrusion Detection System Development Using Machine Learning [12] introduces IDS-ML, an open-source code facilitating the development of intrusion detection systems using machine learning. This code offers automated procedures for various aspects of IDS development, enhancing network security through the application of traditional and advanced machine learning techniques. However the limitations include need for further evaluation on real-world datasets and the sensitivity of the code to feature selection.

László Göcs and Zsolt Csaba Johanyák [4] propose a comprehensive workflow for feature identification in the development of intrusion detection systems. Their work evaluates different feature selection methods, providing valuable insights into feature relevance. However, the focus on filter-based feature selection methods and lack of a detailed analysis of computational complexity pose considerations for broader applicability.

Yang Qin and Masaaki Kondo introduced Federated Learning-Based Network Intrusion Detection with a Feature Selection Approach [10]. This work employs federated learning and a feature selection approach to enhance network intrusion detection, showcasing a novel application of machine learning in security. However, challenges such as need for robust federated learning models and potential communication overhead pose considerations for practical implementation. Jonathas A. de Oliveira et al. [8] introduce F-NIDS, a network intrusion detection system leveraging federated learning. The system aims to address privacy concerns while achieving excellent detection performance with a low network communication overhead. Challenges include the detection performance's sensitivity to specific attack types, such as SQL injection attacks, and potential organizational reluctance to share network traffic data due to privacy concerns.

Dasu et al.'s recent contribution on a Risk-Based Authentication [3] explores risk-based authentication as an innovative strategy to fortify security measures against identity threats. Their study complements our emphasis on intrusion detection and brings an important perspective to the current discussion on preventive security measures. Their findings add to the larger field of cybersecurity by highlighting the significance of dynamic risk assessment in verifying identity and adopting risk-based authentication solutions.

These varied contributions offer insight on how intrusion detection is changing and combining cutting-edge methods and tools to tackle new cybersecurity issues. Even if each study offers insightful information, the shortcomings and difficulties that have been noted emphasize the necessity of continued investigation and improvement in the quest for more reliable and efficient intrusion detection systems.

This study, among others, sets the context for our work on a Federated Learning-based Intrusion Detection and Prevention System (FL-IDPS). Our focus lies in real-time analysis, federated learning, and an adaptable, scalable architecture to provide an effective solution for network security.

3 Proposed Methodology

In our proposed methodology, we have adopted a systematic approach, encompassing pre-processing, federated learning setup, Intrusion Detection and Prevention System (IDPS) implementation, and virtual machine (VM) configuration for the Federated Learning-based Intrusion Detection and Prevention System. The research began with an in-depth exploration of the CICIDS2018 dataset, laying the foundation for subsequent analyses. Feature extraction was crucial, and after evaluating various techniques, we opted for information gain, ensuring a robust set of features for model training. This stepwise process, from data exploration to feature extraction and model training, facilitated the construction of a resilient predictive model. The establishment of the Federated Learning setup involved configuring the Federated Server with a pretrained model, enabling collaborative machine learning across multiple IDPSs. Socket API communication facilitated the exchange of model parameters between the Federated Server and individual IDPSs, ensuring synchronization and iterative model improvement. The IDPS component was designed to classify network packets as benign or malicious, leveraging the global federated model hosted on the Federated Server. Predicted benign packets were directed to the End Server, while malicious packets underwent further analysis in a Honeypot – a decoy system designed to lure and log information about potential attackers.

3.1 System Design

The architecture illustrated in Fig. 1 shows an advanced system for intrusion detection and prevention which prioritises the availability of a secure and efficient environment for resource access from the End Server. This unified system mainly relies on key components of the system collectively working together to maintain the overall integrity of the system and to ensure that the system can adapt quickly to emerging cyber threats. The heart of the system is the Intrusion Detection and Prevention System (IDPS) which is entrusted with the crucial task of monitoring network traffic packets in real time. This is done using a Machine Learning (ML) model such as Decision Trees to classify the packets as benign or malicious, and if malicious, the type of attack being conducted is also detected. In this framework, we focus on identifying threats like SSH and FTP Brute-force attacks and the model has been trained accordingly. The IDPS smoothly handles the redirecting of packets by directing the legitimate users' benign requests to the End Server for uninterrupted resource access. On the other hand, the attackers, detected due to the malicious packets are routed to a Honeypot for further in depth analysis of the attack patterns which will help in enhancing the overall security posture of the system.

The Federated Server plays a pivotal role in this framework by facilitating the distribution of the global machine learning model and by managing the updates to the model based on communication with various IDPS' present in the network. This further ensures an adaptive resilience to evolving threat landscapes. This architectural approach highlights the system's effectiveness in the face of a dynamic threat scenario by considering the periodic retraining.

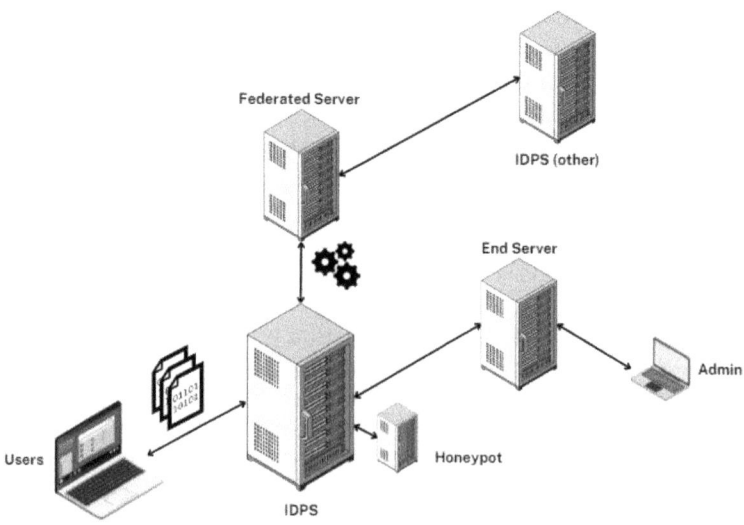

Fig. 1. Architecture Diagram

3.2 Algorithm

The collaborative machine learning process in the intrusion detection system is coordinated by the Federated Server code. The code was implemented using Python with Scapy [1] and Scikit-learn [9] libraries, and it creates a channel of communication with IDPS devices through a Socket API. A global decision tree model, which was pre-trained on the CICIDS 2018 [2] dataset at first, is managed by the server [2]. The decision tree was chosen for its simplicity, speed of training, and ability to handle categorical data well. The model is continuously improved by being updated on a regular basis using real-time data through iterative exchanges with IDPS units. Communication overhead is reduced through a federated approach, exchanging only model parameters via a Socket API between the server and IDPS units. Privacy is preserved by keeping sensitive data on IDPS devices and using a simple yet secure Socket API for communication, despite potential constraints on more complex protocols like gRPC. This federated approach leverages the strengths of collaborative machine learning, providing adaptability to evolving threats while preserving privacy in network security. The model will be refreshed with the latest anomalous flows, enabling the detection of dynamic attacks through the utilization of specific environmental metrics.

Algorithm 1. Federated Learning Algorithm

1: **Initialize:** Federated Server, Local IDPS, Pretrained Global Model
2: **Load:** CICIDS2018 dataset, preprocess, and extract features
3: **for each communication round do**
4:     **Send Global Model to IDPS:** Federated Server sends global model to each IDPS
5:     **for each IDPS do**
6:         **Receive Local Model at Server:** Federated Server receives local model from IDPS
7:         **Aggregate Models:** Federated Server aggregates models from all IDPS
8:     **end for**
9:     **Update Global Model:** Federated Server updates global model based on aggregated models
10: **end for**

The IDPS module is a critical component of the system, responsible for real-time packet analysis and intrusion detection. It was developed using Scapy [1] and Scikit-learn [9] in Python, the IDPS module also incorporates the global machine learning model hosted on the Federated Server. Upon receiving network packets, it leverages the model to classify them as benign or malicious, specifically identifying SSH and FTP brute-force attacks. Benign packets proceed to the End Server for normal resource access, while malicious packets are redirected to a Honeypot for detailed analysis. The implementation includes a routing mechanism within the IDPS, ensuring proper packet redirection based on the model's predictions. This module, operating on a distinct virtual machine, adheres to the principles of isolation and security.

Algorithm 2. Intrusion Detection and Prevention System (IDPS) Algorithm

1: **Initialize:** IDPS Components, Real-time Packet Capture, Communication Module
2: **while system is active do**
3:    **Receive Global Model:** IDPS receives global model from Federated Server
4:    **Capture Packet:** Capture real-time network packet
5:    **Local Model Prediction:** Use local model to classify packet as benign or malicious
6:    **if malicious then**
7:       **Send to Honeypot:** Route malicious packet to Honeypot for analysis
8:    **else**
9:       **Send to End Server:** Route benign packet to End Server for normal processing
10:    **end if**
11:    **Send Local Model to Server:** IDPS sends updated local model to Federated Server
12: **end while**

The flow-based analysis for SSH and FTP Brute-force prediction involves the IDPS module examining specific features extracted from network packets in real-time. Parameters such as Flow Inter Arrival Time (IAT) Mean, Flow Duration, Destination Port are evaluated to classify sessions as either benign or indicative of a brute-force attack. Benign sessions seamlessly proceed to the End Server for regular resource access, while sessions identified as potentially malicious are rerouted to the Honeypot for detailed analysis. This flow-based approach supported by machines learning models assures the swift and accurate identification of SSH and FTP Brute-force attacks which enhances the overall security of the system.

4 Implementation and Results

The implementation phase consisted of the deployment of separate Virtual Machines (VMs) to emulate various components of the system. This approach was adopted as it can closely simulate real-world scenarios while ensuring a controlled and secure environment.

The virtual machines were interconnected through a NAT (Network Address Translation) network to ensure isolation and security of the system. The VMs were allocated 2 GB of RAM and 20 GB of storage each to run the Ubuntu OS. The interconnected VMs formed a unified subnet with IP addresses that ranged from 10.0.3.X band. The above network configuration allowed controlled communication and interaction between the different components of the system.

In this simulated environment, the attacks were carried out using Hydra, which is an open source password brute-forcing tool generally used to emulate malicious activities. Hydra supports various network protocols including SSH and FTP. The attacker module in the system aims to replicate a malicious user attempting to obtain unauthorised access through brute-force attacks.

The attacker module utilised Hydra, specifically targeting SSH and FTP services to systematically and exhaustively try different combinations of usernames and passwords until a valid set of credentials were identified, essentially exploiting we ak or easily guessable login credentials. This type of attack, known as a brute-force attack, is a common method employed by attackers to compromise systems by repeatedly attempting different login credentials until a correct combination is found (Figs. 2 and 3).

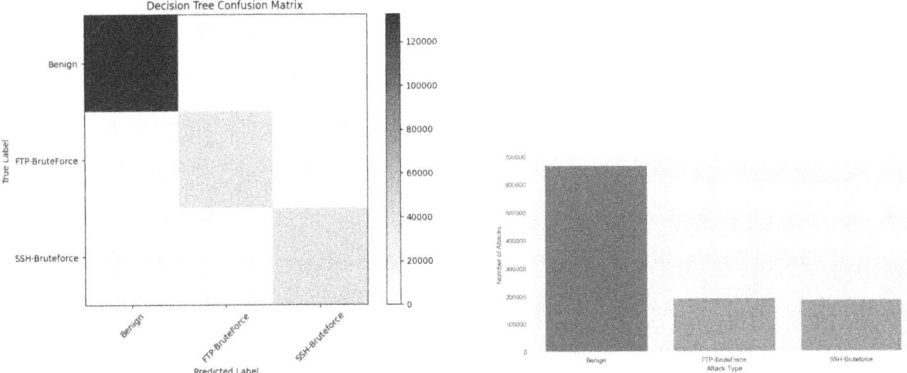

Fig. 2. Confusion Matrix   **Fig. 3.** Attack Type Plot

We used a Decision Tree for model training and Information Gain for feature selection in our study technique. A metric called Information Gain assesses how well a feature classifies data. As indicated in Table 2, we carefully examined the CICIDS2018 dataset, choosing suitable variables and used Information Gain to evaluate their importance. Upon conducting extensive pre-processing and exploratory data analysis, we determined that Information Gain was the most suitable feature extraction method for our analysis.

Subsequently, we used the selected features to train our model, opting for a Decision Tree due to its interpretability and effectiveness with categorical features. The training process involved fitting the model with the training data, evaluating its performance metrics (such as accuracy, precision, recall, and F1 score), and extracting feature importance using Gini indices. This step-by-step approach, from feature extraction to model training, enabled the development of a robust predictive model for intrusion detection. Despite limitations such as resource constraints and dataset usability, we could enhance our approach by considering a packet-based approach over a flow-based one, potentially mitigating these challenges while refining our intrusion detection model.

When tested using performance criteria such as accuracy, precision, recall, and F-score, the Decision Tree model exceeds 99.99% as shown in Table 1, demonstrating its excellent results in accurately categorizing network packets as benign

Table 1. Feature Importance

Feature	Importance
Flow IAT Mean	0.0
Bwd IAT Tot	0.0
Bwd Pkts/s	1.70×10^{-10}
Flow Duration	9.31×10^{-10}
Flow Pkts/s	3.47×10^{-9}
Dst Port	9.03×10^{-6}
Bwd IAT Mean	4.52×10^{-5}
Flow IAT Max	1.03×10^{-3}
Init Fwd Win Byts	0.35
Fwd Seg Size Min	0.65

Table 2. Performance Metrics

Metric	Value
Accuracy	0.9999714776705814
Precision	0.9999714806204552
Recall	0.9999714776705814
F-Score	0.9999714776477965

or malicious. The model's remarkable precision and recall indicate its ability to reliably identify positive occurrences and relevant examples, respectively, while its high accuracy demonstrates its precision in making accurate predictions. Recall highlights the model's capacity to catch all real positive events, whereas precision highlights the accuracy of positive predictions. When combined, precision, recall, and the F-score give a detailed assessment of the Decision Tree model's effectiveness and a thorough grasp of how well it can differentiate between legitimate and malicious network packets.

5 Conclusion

In this paper, we have proposed a highly efficient brute-force detection setup which takes into account the need for a better Federated Network framework with minimal overhead and of a real time threat detection system which we have achieved using Hydra to simulate real world attacks and breach scenarios. This system was designed keeping in mind the salient features of using the collective power of multiple IDPS' for more accurate classification and results of ever-evolving brute-force attacks. The Decision Tree model was trained using the CICIDS 2018 dataset with a test accuracy of 99.997%. We were able to establish communication between the IDPS modules by enabling the exchange of the updated parameters of the locally retrained machine learning model in an IDPS with the Federated Server to further update the global ML model, which aligns with the principles of a traditional Federated Learning setup.

The aspects we would like to work on in the future include identifying and mitigating diverse attacks. By comprehensively understanding and addressing a broader spectrum of threats, our goal is to enhance the currently existing intrusion detection and prevention mechanisms. Incorporating real-world datasets can enhance the model's robustness and applicability to diverse scenarios. Additionally, focusing on a lower level approach will significantly enhance the operational efficiency in terms of speed. Enhancing defenses at the foundational level help us fine-tune and streamline our security mechanisms. Considering scalability in terms of handling larger datasets or increasing system demands will contribute to the effectiveness of the system in practical environments.

References

1. Biondi, P.: Scapy. The Scapy Development Community (2022). https://scapy.net/
2. Canadian Institute for Cybersecurity, N.: CIC-IDS 2018 dataset (2018). https://www.unb.ca/cic/datasets/ids-2018.html
3. Dasu, L.S., Dhamija, M., Dishitha, G., Vivekanandan, A., Sarasvathi, V.: Defending against identity threats using risk-based authentication. Commun. Appl. Ind. Math. **23**(2), 105–123 (2023). https://doi.org/10.2478/cait-2023-0016. Received 08 Dec 2022. Accepted 12 May 2023
4. Göcs, L., Johanyák, Z.C.: Identifying relevant features of CSE-CIC-IDS2018 dataset for the development of an intrusion detection system. J. Big Data **7** (2023). https://doi.org/10.1186/s40537-023-00523-0
5. Hellemons, L., Hendriks, L., Hofstede, R., Sperotto, A., Sadre, R., Pras, A.: SSHCure: a flow-based SSH intrusion detection system. In: Proceedings of the 6th IFIP WG 6.6 International Autonomous Infrastructure, Management, and Security Conference on Dependable Networks and Services (2012). https://doi.org/10.1109/DSN.2012.6263955
6. Krishnaveni, S., Sivamohan, S., Sridhar, S.S., Prabakaran, S.: Efficient feature selection and classification through ensemble method for network intrusion detection on cloud computing. Clust. Comput. **24**, 1–13 (2021). https://doi.org/10.1007/s10586-021-03450-8
7. Leevy, J.L., Khoshgoftaar, T.M.: A survey and analysis of intrusion detection models based on CSE-CIC-IDS2018 big data. J. Big Data **7**, 104 (2020). https://doi.org/10.1186/s40537-020-00379-5
8. de Oliveira, J.A., et al.: F-NIDS - a network intrusion detection system based on federated learning. Comput. Netw. **236**, 110010 (2023). https://doi.org/10.1016/j.comnet.2023.110010
9. Pedregosa, F., et al.: Scikit-learn: machine learning in Python. J. Mach. Learn. Res. **12**, 2825–2830 (2011)
10. Qin, Y., Kondo, M.: Federated learning-based network intrusion detection with a feature selection approach. In: Proceedings of the 3rd International Conference on Electrical, Communication and Computer Engineering (ICECCE), Kuala Lumpur, Malaysia, pp. 12–13 (2021). https://doi.org/10.1109/ICECCE51249.2021.9483204
11. Verizon, C.: DBIR report 2023 - Master's guide (2023). https://www.verizon.com/business/resources/reports/dbir/2023/master-guide/. Accessed 30 Dec 2023
12. Yang, L., Shami, A.: IDS-ML: an open source code for intrusion detection system development using machine learning. Softw. Impacts **14**, 100446 (2022). https://doi.org/10.1016/j.simpa.2021.100446

Differential Cascode Voltage Switch Logic (DCVSL) Level Shifter with Logic Error Detection

Azmath Noorain[✉], G. Sanjeeva Reddy, Srimanthula Manish Goud, and Sangeeta Singh

Department of ECE, Vardhaman College of Engineering, Hyderabad, Telangana, India
noorainazmath@gmail.com, {srimanthulamanishgoud20ece, sangeethasingh}@vardhaman.org

Abstract. Lowering the supply voltage proves highly effective in reducing dynamic power consumption within system-on-chip architectures, given its direct proportionality to VDD^2. A Level Shifter, also referred to as a Voltage Level Translator, is an electronic circuit specialized in converting signals between different voltage levels. The suggested LS design adopts the Cross-Coupled pFET Level Shifter approach. However, CPLS encounters contention issues during transitions due to its cross-coupled pFET structure. In this configuration, an nFET powered by VDDL needs to surpass a pFET powered by VDDH for positive feedback to trigger the operation. Consequently, as the voltage difference (VDDH–VDDL) increases, contention intensifies, potentially leading to operational failures. To mitigate this challenge, Differential Cascode Voltage Switch Logic (DCVSL) serves as an alternative to the single cross-coupled flip-flop. The circuit design, implemented using the Cadence Virtuoso tool, underwent comprehensive comparative analysis against existing level shifters. The utilization of DCVSL notably improved noise immunity, speed, and robustness while resulting in a 50% reduction in Static Power consumption.

Keywords: Level Shifter (LS) · System-on-chip (SoC) · Cross-Coupled pFET LS (CPLS) · DCVSL · Logic Error Detection

1 Introduction

In response to the growing demand for energy-efficient technologies, there is a critical imperative to design electronic systems that minimize power consumption, particularly in battery-powered devices and Internet of Things (IoT) applications. This imperative arises from the need to prolong battery life, reduce environmental impact, and optimize resource usage. As electronic devices become increasingly pervasive in various aspects of daily life, the drive toward energy efficiency becomes paramount for sustainable and cost-effective technological solutions.

The significance of ensuring the accuracy and reliability of Level Shifter (LS) systems cannot be overstated, especially in applications where errors in logic operations could have severe consequences. Critical domains such as aerospace, medical devices and automotive safety systems demand flawless performance to guarantee the safety and functionality of the overall system. By integrating advanced logic error detection mechanisms into LS systems, the reliability of these systems is significantly enhanced. This proactive approach to error detection not only safeguards against potential malfunctions but also reinforces the integrity of electronic systems operating in mission-critical environments.

Reducing the supply voltage stands as an immensely effective strategy for mitigating dynamic power consumption in system-on-chip designs [14, 15]. Dynamic power consumption, which is associated with transistor switching, decreases significantly as the VDD2 decreases. Operating circuits near the threshold voltage of transistors, known as near-threshold operation, offers particular advantages, potentially resulting in a nearly tenfold reduction in dynamic power consumption compared to standard operation at nominal voltage levels.

For a deeper exploration of the technical details, there exist two traditional forms of low-swing (LS) architectures—the cross-coupled pFET and the current mirror-based LS. These structures are recognized elements within integrated circuit design. Their specific characteristics and configurations are pivotal in optimizing power consumption, mainly for near-threshold operation. But these two conventional LS structures are having limitations which were further solved by various schemes refer to papers [5–13]. By employing these conventional LS structures, engineers can further enhance the efficiency of the system, ensuring that the reduction in supply voltage translates into a substantial reduction in dynamic power consumption for the overall system-on-chip.

With the proliferation of electronic devices across industries and households, the cumulative energy usage of these systems has become a significant contributor to overall energy consumption. By prioritizing energy-efficient design principles, we not only address immediate concerns such as battery life but also contribute to the long-term sustainability of our planet.

Moreover, the optimization of power consumption in electronic systems goes hand in hand with advancements in renewable energy technologies. As the world shifts towards renewable sources of energy such as solar and wind power, the importance of energy efficiency in electronic devices becomes even more pronounced. By minimizing power consumption, we can maximize the efficiency of renewable energy systems and further reduce reliance on fossil fuels, thereby accelerating the transition to a cleaner and more sustainable energy future.

2 Literature Survey

The [1] introduces an innovative level shifter design boasting a wide conversion range and emphasizing both speed and energy efficiency. It employs a unique architecture utilizing the multi-threshold CMOS technique, alongside a mixed-threshold current mirror circuit to address swing issues and auxiliary bias circuits to reduce power consumption during idle states.

[2] Presents an energy-efficient level shifter (LS) with a wide conversion range, featuring a logic error detection circuit (LEDC). Based on a current mirror-based design (CMLS), it addresses static current limitations by integrating a feedback pFET, unlike Wilson's CMLS (WCMLS) which struggles with low-to-high voltage conversion. The proposed LS utilize the LEDC to achieve full conversion from VDDL to VDDH. Post-layout simulation using a 7-nm finFET model demonstrates a propagation delay of 0.21 ns and energy consumption of 20.43 fJ at 0.4/1.2 V and 1 MHz, showcasing its effectiveness in reducing delay and energy usage under specific conditions.

[3] Presents a voltage level shifter, also referred to as a voltage level translator, tailored for analog and digital integrated circuits (ICs). This shifter effectively transforms voltage levels from the sub-threshold range to the super-threshold domain, all while minimizing propagation delay. Simulations conducted across various CMOS technologies, including 45 nm, 65 nm, 90 nm, and 180 nm, highlight significant enhancements over recent designs. Particularly in the context of 90 nm CMOS technology, the proposed shifter demonstrates a remarkable 69.12% reduction in propagation delay, while 45 nm technology shows a 67.07% improvement. Corner analysis consistently indicates superior performance compared to recent techniques, suggesting promising advancements in key performance metrics like propagation delay across diverse CMOS technologies.

The paper [4] delves into the critical concern of energy efficiency in modern System-on-a-Chip (SoC) designs. While reducing power supply voltage effectively minimizes power consumption, it can detrimentally affect speed performance. Time-sensitive sections operate at VDDH for optimal performance, while less critical areas function at VDDL to enhance power efficiency. In scenarios demanding low power, sub-threshold operation is considered for certain sections. Utilizing multiple-supply circuits requires the optimization of costs associated with voltage domain conversion, achieved through the implementation of level shifter (LS) circuits.

3 Design and Implementation

The objective encompasses several key components aimed at enhancing the performance and versatility of the Differential Cascoded Voltage-Switched Logic (DCVSL) Level Shifters.

Firstly, the focus is on designing and implementing a DCVSL Level Shifter that prioritizes energy efficiency. This involves careful consideration of voltage-switching mechanisms and circuit configurations to optimize power consumption, aligning with contemporary standards for energy-conscious design [1–4].

Secondly, an emphasis is placed on integrating advanced logic error detection mechanisms within the Level Shifter (LS) system [2]. This addition serves the crucial role of promptly identifying and rectifying errors, contributing to the overall accuracy and reliability of the system's output. By incorporating error detection at the logic level, the system becomes more robust and resilient, minimizing the impact of potential errors on its performance.

Furthermore, the designing of the LS system was done in a scalable manner [3]. This scalability aspect ensures that the Level Shifter can be seamlessly integrated with other systems or modules. This adaptability is vital for accommodating diverse applications and varying requirements, facilitating easy expansion and enhancing the overall flexibility of the system.

The basic elements were implemented on the cadence virtuoso tool using 90 nm technology and were verified by their transient response. Figure 1 below illustrates the schematic diagram of the Existing Project incorporates mixed-threshold current mirror, as well as auxiliary bias circuits. However, the convention problem arose due to the current mirrors.

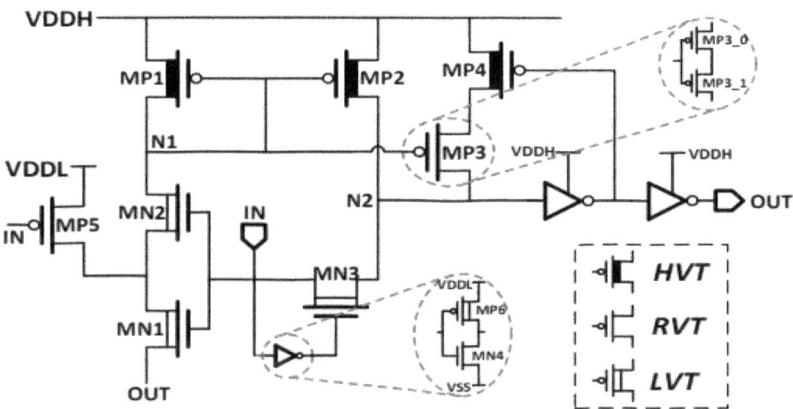

Fig. 1. Diagram of Existing project Level Shifter (LS)

4 Results and Discussions

4.1 Schematic Diagram of Proposed LS

Figure 2 is the implementation of a Schematic Diagram of the proposed Level Shifter in the cadence virtuoso tool using 90 nm technology.

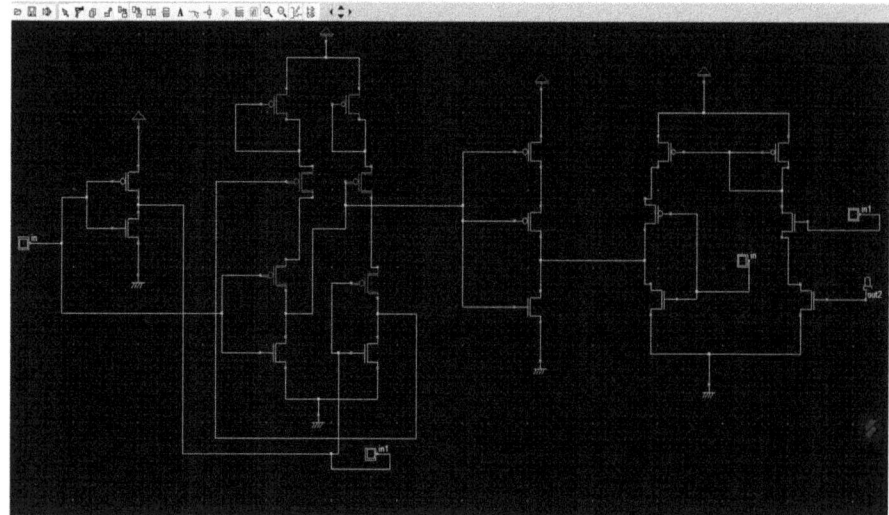

Fig. 2. Proposed project Level Shifter schematic diagram

4.2 Proposed Level Sifter Layout Implementation

Figure 3 is the implementation of proposed project layout in the cadence virtuoso tool using 90 nm technology.

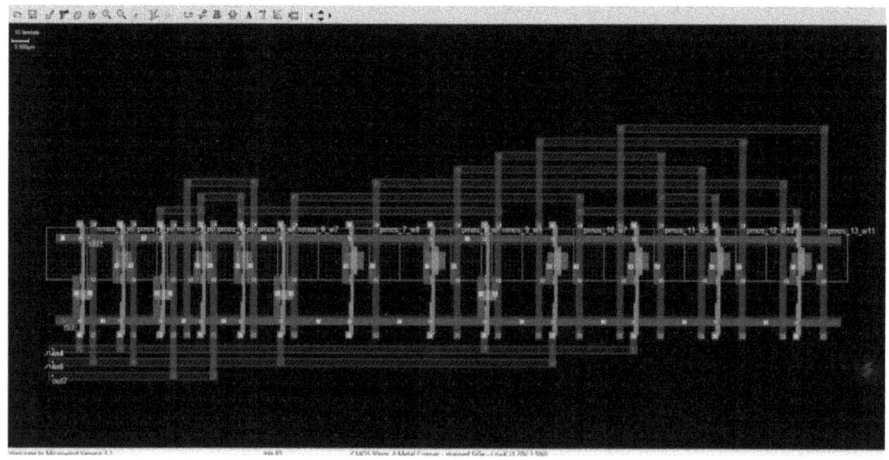

Fig. 3. Layout of proposed project Level Shifter

4.3 Various Combination of Input Diagrams

Figure 4 is the Proposed Level Shifter Schematic diagram implementation having Low Input.

Differential Cascode Voltage Switch Logic (DCVSL) 79

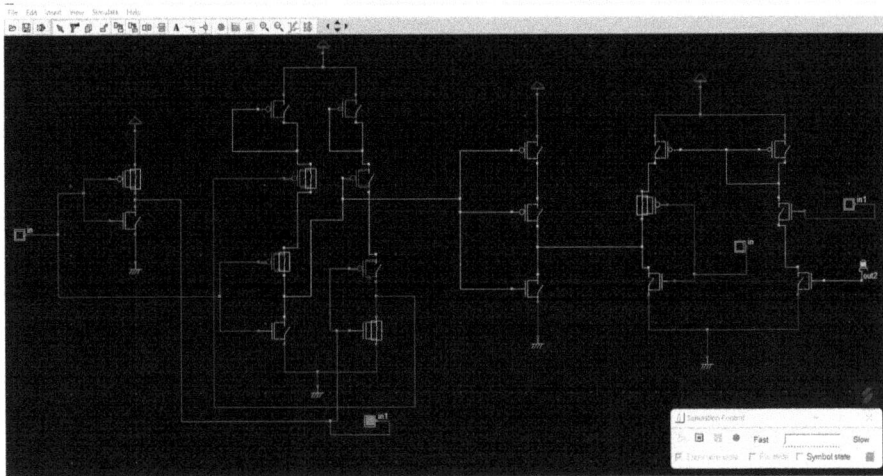

Fig. 4. The Low Input

Figure 5 is the Proposed Level Shifter Schematic diagram implementation having High Input.

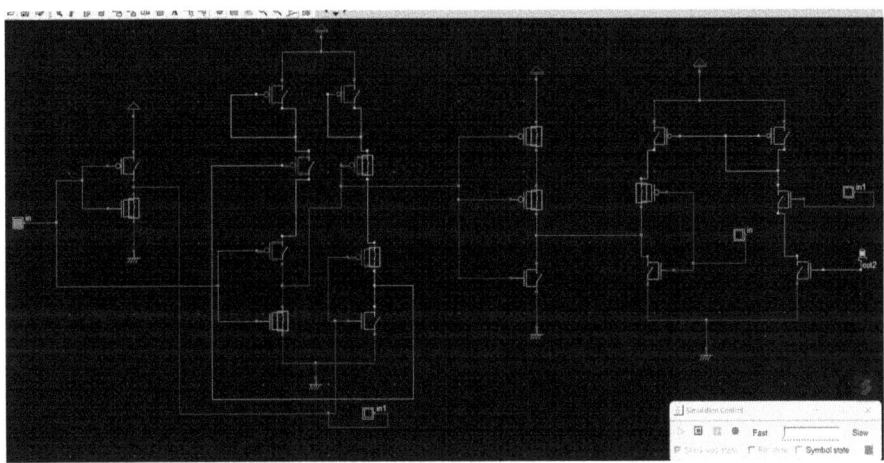

Fig. 5. The High Input

4.4 Transient Response

Figure 6 is the Transient response of the proposed project in the cadence virtuoso tool using 90 nm technology.

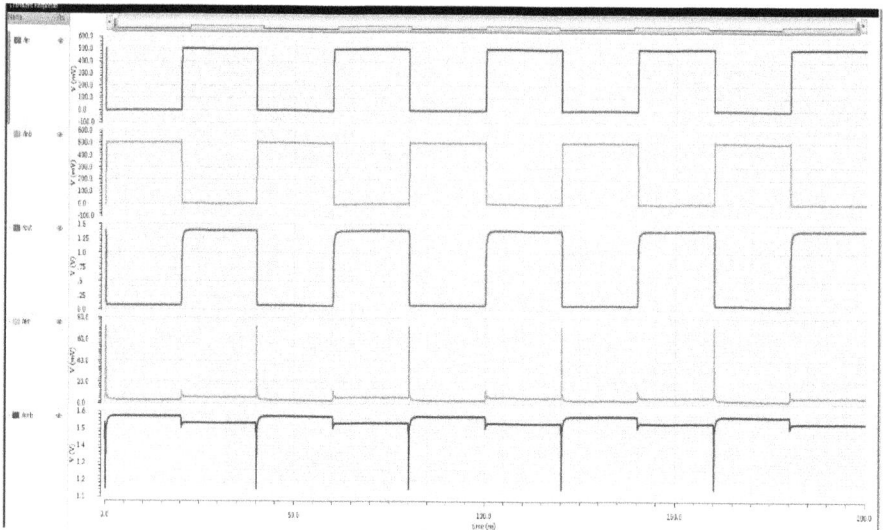

Fig. 6. Output Transient Waveform

4.5 Comparison of Parameters

Table 1 displays a comparative analysis of specific parameters between the existing project and the proposed one.

Table 1. Parameter Comparison

Parameters	Existing Project	Proposed Project
Technology used	90 nm	90 nm
Time/Duration of signal	0–200 ns	0–200 ns
VDDL	300 m V	375 m V
No. of Transistors used	14	19
Delay of o/p w.r.t i/p	17.86 ns	25 ns
Static Power	4.37 n W	2.15 n W
No. of stages used energy	26.59 f J	30 f J

The comparison between the existing and proposed projects, both utilizing a 90 nm technology, reveals nuanced differences. While the proposed project boasts a higher supply voltage (VDDL) at 375 mV compared to the existing project's 300 mV, it also incorporates a more intricate design with 19 transistors, surpassing the 14 transistors in the existing project. Despite exhibiting a longer processing time with a 25 ns delay in comparison to the existing project's 17.86 ns, the proposed project showcases notable improvements in static power consumption, recording a lower 2.15 nW compared to the existing project's 4.37 nW. Furthermore, the proposed project achieves enhanced energy efficiency with 30 fJ per stage, compared to the existing project's 26.59 fJ. These tradeoffs underscore the need for a comprehensive assessment considering specific project goals and constraints.

5 Conclusions

In conclusion, the reduction of supply voltage emerges as a highly effective strategy for mitigating dynamic power consumption in system-on-chip architectures. This is particularly significant given the direct proportionality between dynamic power consumption and VDD^2. The focus of this paper has been on the design and optimization of a Level Shifter (LS), specifically addressing the contention issue associated with the Cross-Coupled pFET LS (CPLS). The proposed solution leverages a Differential Cascode Voltage Switch Logic (DCVSL) as an alternative, effectively enhancing noise immunity, speed, and robustness. The implementation of this design, analyzed through the Cadence Virtuoso tool, demonstrated notable improvements, including a 50% reduction in Static Power, marking a substantial advancement in the efficiency of level shifting within SoC architectures.

References

1. You, H., Yuan, J., Tang, W., Qiao, S., Hei, Y.: An energy-efficient level shifter for ultra low-voltage digital LSIs. IEEE Trans. Circuits Syst. II Express Briefs **67**(12), 3357–3361 (2020). https://doi.org/10.1109/TCSII.2020.2980681
2. Park, J., Jeong, H.: Energy-efficient wide range level-shifter with a logic error detection circuit. IEEE Trans. Very Large Scale Integr. (VLSI) Syst. **32**, 701–705 (2023)
3. Kapoor, A., Jha, C.S., Thapar, A., Kumar, C.I.: High performance CMOS voltage level shifters design for low voltage applications. In: 2023 International Conference for Advancement in Technology (ICONAT), Goa, India, pp. 1–6 (2023). https://doi.org/10.1109/ICONAT57137.2023.10079972
4. Sinthuja, S., Saravaran, S.V.: Design of level shifter with wide voltage conversion range for system on chip applications. J. Emerg. Technol. Innov. Res. (JETIR) **5**(11), 1811486 (2018)
5. Kabirpour, S., Jalali, M.: A low-power and high-speed voltage level shifter based on a regulated cross-coupled pull-up network. IEEE Trans. Circuits Syst. II Exp. Briefs **66**(6), 909–913 (2019)
6. Chen, T.-H., Chen, J., Clark, L.T.: Subthreshold to above threshold level shifter design. J. Low Power Electron. **2**(2), 251–258 (2006)
7. Hosseini, S.R., Saberi, M., Lotfi, R.: A low-power subthreshold to above-threshold voltage level shifter. IEEE Trans. Circuits Syst. II Exp. Briefs **61**(10), 753–757 (2014)
8. Matsuzuka, R., Hirose, T., Shizuku, Y., Kuroki, N., Numa, M.: A 0.19-V minimum input low energy level shifter for extremely low-voltage VLSIs. In: Proceedings of the International Symposium on Circuits and Systems (ISCAS), pp. 2948–2951 (2015)
9. Lütkemeier, S., Ruckert, U.: A subthreshold to above-threshold level shifter comprising a Wilson current mirror. IEEE Trans. Circuits Syst. II Exp. Briefs **57**(9), 721–724 (2010)
10. Osaki, Y., Hirose, T., Kuroki, N., Numa, M.: A low-power level shifter with logic error correction for extremely low-voltage digital CMOS LSIs. IEEE J. Solid-State Circuits **47**(7), 1776–1783 (2012)

11. Hosseini, S.R., Saberi, M., Lotfi, R.: A high-speed and power-efficient voltage level shifter for dual-supply applications. IEEE Trans. Very Large Scale Integr. (VLSI) Syst. **25**(3), 1154–1158 (2017)
12. Lotfi, R., Saberi, M., Hosseini, S.R., Ahmadi-Mehr, A.R., Staszewski, R.B.: Energy-efficient wide-range voltage level shifters reaching 4.2 fJ/transition. IEEE Solid-State Circuits Lett. **1**(2), 34–37 (2018)
13. Le, V.L., Kim, T.T.-H.: An area and energy efficient ultra-low voltage level shifter with pass transistor and reduced-swing output buffer in 65-nm CMOS. IEEE Trans. Circuits Syst. II Exp. Briefs **65**(5), 607–611 (2018)
14. Gosatwar, P., Ghodeswar, U.: Design of voltage level shifter for multi-supply voltage design. In: 2016 International Conference on Communication and Signal Processing (ICCSP), pp. 0853–0857 (2016)
15. Moghaddam, M., Moaiyeri, M.H., Eshghi, M.: A low-voltage level shifter based on double-gate MOSFET. In: 2015 18th CSI International Symposium on Computer Architecture and Digital Systems (CADS), pp. 1–5 (2015)

Smart City Smart Grid

Robot for Transportation with an SMS Alert

Pavani Arra[(✉)], Ganesh Reddy, Santhosh Reddy, and V. Harini

Department of ECE, Vardhaman College of Engineering, Shamshabad, India
{pavaniarra20ece,langatiganeshreddy20ece,sidduloorisanthoshreddy20ece,
v.harini}@vardhaman.org

Abstract. Most of the imports in India are done by people. Robotic systems have an advantage over other distribution systems because of the large transport environment that can transport jumbo products in long lengths. Automation, like driverless cars, is the result of technological development. The proposed model describes a controlled robot that moves from point A to point B with load on it. It is a robotic vehicle which is an electrical machine controlled by batteries and smartphone application. Bluetooth is connected to the controller via UART. It uses ATmega32 microcontroller for transmitter and receiver. In the receiver, the microcontroller receives the radio frequency signal and controls the robot according to the instructions. The robot's motion is controlled by two DC motors connected to each wheel. The main objective is to deliver the goods within hospital premises or physically aided people can make use of it without directly being involved in transporting.

Keywords: Automation · bluetooth · ATmega32Microcontroller

1 Introduction

Smart phones are getting more sophisticated today thanks to upgraded computers, larger storage capabilities, and more communication options. Nowadays, Bluetooth is frequently utilized to distribute data and give smartphones additional capabilities. The integration of Bluetooth technology with mobile phones, developed in 1994 by Telecom supplier Ericsson, reveals its advantages [2]. Old school wired digital gadgets have been converted to wireless ones as a result of changes in how people use them at home and at work. Up to seven Bluetooth modules can talk to a host Bluetooth system simultaneously over a single connection. In the 1960s, the first industrial robot was made available in the United States. Since then, their program has made great strides, greatly advancing robotics. Robots are now more common in variety of industries, including construction and healthcare. Robots are known as intelligent machines that may be created and employed [3]. These robots carry out heavy, dangerous, and precise labors because they can work continuously for 24 h without rest and can perform human tasks more effectively and quickly [4]. Introducing robots for physically aided people allows them to walk less and rest at a place. Controlling a robot with supplies by being at one place can make things more easier and reduces some amount of work. The goal of this research is to employ robots to reach their destination and later alert the user about the result.

2 Literature Survey

A track-following robot created by Roman Osorio C. in 2006 [5] uses magnetic sensors to guide its movement. They have chosen infrared sensors because it is not easy to detect this sensor. Comparator circuitry was utilised to increase the system's sensitivity. A line-following robot with the ability to avoid collision if an object crosses its path of motion has been the subject of various design studies. Dr. Bindu A. Thomas and colleagues (2013) [6] created an industrial based robotic arm that can lift loads and identify obstacles. If there are any hurdles in between the path it would wait for a while and make buzzer sound or any other sound by which it can alert the user so that the hurdle can be cleared or the path is made safe for transporting, later on the robotic arm continues its work. Al-Taharwa et al. (2008) [7] described how a robot that follows a predetermined path functions. His work is completely based on using genetic algorithms to find an optimal path or a easy way to travel for a robot from the initial point to its desired destination, because there may be may paths in which a robot can be moved but it will be more optimal to find a path which takes lesser time then required and also which is obstacle free. He used genetic algorithm method because it has successfully been able to solve the old traditional problems and find new methods. To get to any store location, the robot navigates queues. The work of Abrar M. Alajlan and others [8,15] have given collision avoidance algorithm for robotic system. There study has helped further works to achieve a system which tackles any objects in their path and provide a clear way.

2.1 Types of Robots

In recent years, a wide variety of robots with various jobs have arisen in numerous industries. These various robot types are developing steadily and providing many occupations that assist people in various facets of their lives [6]. According to their intended uses, robots can be categorised into the following types:

- Industrial robots: They use articulated arms designed for a variety of industrial operations, including painting, welding etc.
- Domestic or home robots: These are employed in the houses for variety of jobs, including robotic pool cleaners, vacuum cleaners and sweepers.
- Medical robots: These devices are utilised in hospitals and the medical field. Surgery, automated guided vehicles, and possibly lifting aids are just a few of the various duties that a medical robot can carry out in this profession.
- Service robots: These can perform a variety of tasks, including data collection, technology demonstration, research, and others.

3 Motivation

The inspiration behind our work comes from a number of sources:

- Growing Need for Automation: Traditional manual ways of transporting goods may not be sufficient given the growing need for faster and more dependable transportation.
- Labour Shortages and Increasing Labour Costs: The use of robots in the delivery of goods can serve to lighten the load on the workforce and decrease the need for costly physical labour.
- Increased Productivity and Efficiency: An autonomous robot can work continuously without getting tired, taking breaks, or needing to rest, which dramatically boosts productivity and efficiency in the movement of goods [9].
- Increased Safety and Risk Mitigation: By giving complicated activities to robots, we can reduce the possibility of mishaps and occupational injuries, making the workplace safer.

4 Problem Statement

Our goal is to create an autonomous robot that can move objects with efficiency in enclosed spaces like warehouses, hospitals, or distribution centres. It can reduce work load and increase the efficieny of work.

5 System Architecture

5.1 A Robot

As described in Fig. 1 In general, robots have three roles: line monitor, collision detection, and heavy load loading and unloading. From the figure shown below the arrows indicate signal transmission between different components. The main component and central unit of the system is Arduino Uno. It is powered by a DC motor, a motor driver and a rechargeable battery.

5.2 Servo Motor Controlled Function

The destination Selector used to choose a favourite destination is shown in the below block diagram Fig. 2. Used to load bulk onto the robot is the loading unit. Unloading device used to remove mass from robot. The path is changed to follow the intended path by a servo motor. The system is fed with power supply.

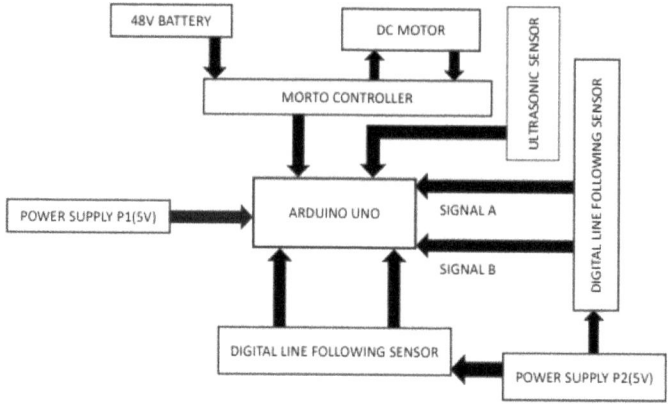

Fig. 1. Robot Block Diagram

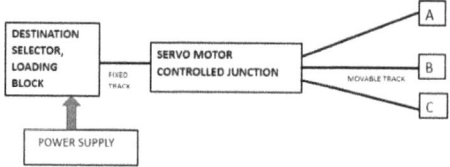

Fig. 2. Servo Motor Controlled Function

5.3 Controller

Central Controller is shown in the Fig. 3, where Bluetooth technology is used to connect the robot unit to the central unit. Through a channel, the track unit communicates with the central unit. The robot and track's entire movement is controlled by a central unit.

Fig. 3. Central Controller

5.4 Components

In the beginning, we have to connect all the components accordingly. Second, we require a phone, we should download a mobile app from the playstore called as serial bluetooth terminal, and we need to modify settings accordingly in the application to connect to the robot and we can operate according to the way we need for performing activity.

1. Arduino Uno: Arduino Uno which is displayed in Fig. 1, is a microcontroller which is used for the purpose of doing main calculation it can be easily used by connecting the device with a USB cable to support the microcontroller. Arduino stands out among microcontroller platforms due to its unique combination of open-source accessibility, user-friendliness, and a vast, supportive community. Its open-source nature fosters collaboration and innovation, allowing anyone to freely access and modify its hardware and software designs. The platform's cross-platform compatibility, cost-effectiveness, and integration capabilities make it a versatile choice for everything from educational endeavors to advanced IoT projects (Fig. 4).

Fig. 4. Arduino UNO

2. Motor Controller: It is called a stepper motor as shown in Fig. 2. it divides the full rotation into several equal steps. Stepper motor can easily be operated with Arduino Microcontroller. Can control Arduino Uno [6] using a USB cable. Power is given to the Ardunio using an A/D converter or any other external power source. Plug in 1mm positive plug into the power jack on the connection board to which adapter is attached. You must plug the battery lead into the ground pin and Vin pin (Fig. 5).

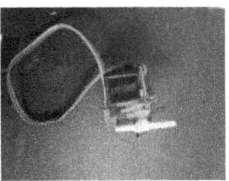

Fig. 5. Servo Motor

3. Bluetooth HC-06: The HC-06, which is depicted in Fig. 3, defines a serial port from which data can be sent and received. REsearchers utilised Teraterm as the serial terminal. Before uploading the code to the Arduino, the HC-06 module must be unplugged. Once the code has been successfully submitted, it is linked once more (Fig. 6).

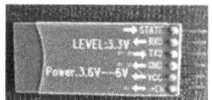 

Fig. 6. Bluetooth Module

4. Motor Driver Board: The motor driver acts as the interface between the Arduino and controllers. The motor is responsible for propelling or controlling the robot's movements. Whether it's DC motors for wheels, stepper motors for precise control, or servo motors for specific applications, the motor driver is compatible with the motor type, voltage, and current requirements. It Ensures that the chosen motor driver can handle these parameters and is compatible with Arduino model, allowing seamless integration and precise control for the robot's mobility (Fig. 7).

Fig. 7. Motor Driver Board

5. GSM Module: Compact electronic devices known as GSM (Global System for Mobile Communications) modules allow for communication between devices and mobile networks. These modules are essential for enabling wireless communication for a variety of applications, including robots, embedded systems, mobile phones, and the Internet of Things (IoT). A microprocessor, a GSM modem, and other parts including SIM card readers and antenna connectors are the standard components of a GSM module. It works with a SIM (Subscriber Identity Module) card, which enables voice and data services and authenticates the device with the mobile network [7].

5.5 Circuit Diagram

Connections to all the components is shown below using Tinkercad software which gives clear view on the connections to each components. The components are arranged on a support. The suitable code has be dumped into Arduino for its better working and functionality. Which makes the motor work and GSM module function. Vehicle starts moving to the required directions and directed and stops when reaches (Fig. 8).

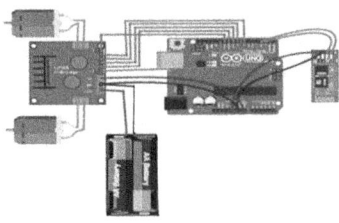

Fig. 8. Connection diagram

6 Results

6.1 Prototype

The figure shown below is of the output model (Fig. 9).

Fig. 9. Output model

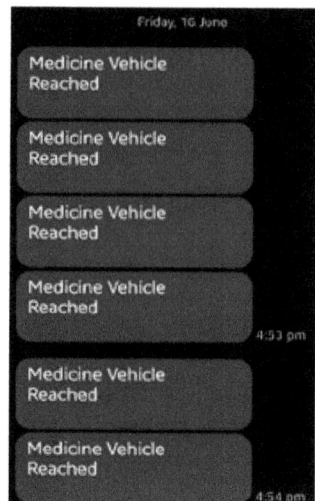

Fig. 10. App Interface and SMS alert

The application which we are using called "Serial Bluetooth Terminal" in the beginning looks like as shown in Fig. 10. After initializing the setup the terminal gets activated and it starts taking and giving responses accordingly.

Efficiency of model: A person who is enable to walk or is physically disabled and has to transport some items to other place in home then that person has to take some support to reach destiny or some other person has to come to take those things. But if the disabled person has access to this robot he can call it whenever required and supply items to its destiny.

7 Applications

1. Autonomous Vehicles: Self-driving cars and trucks are a significant area of development in transportation. These robots use sensors, cameras, and advanced AI algorithms to navigate roads and transport passengers or goods without human intervention [13].
2. Delivery Robots: Smaller robots designed for last-mile delivery can transport packages and goods from a distribution center or store directly to a customer's doorstep. These robots can navigate sidewalks and pedestrian pathways safely. [12]
3. Warehouse Robots: Automated guided vehicles (AGVs) or autonomous mobile robots (AMRs) are used in warehouses to transport goods, pallets, and containers between storage locations and picking stations. They optimize order fulfillment and reduce manual labor [9].
4. Public Transportation: Robots can be used in public transportation systems to assist passengers, provide information, and maintain cleanliness in stations and vehicles [15].

8 Conclusions

8.1 Conclusion

The main goal has been is to create an autonomous robot that can be utilised to move loads more quickly. When compared to the time needed for humans to complete the jobs, less time is needed in case of robots. As a result, efficiency is higher because it requires less time. The safe transportation in limited time is the primary goal. Additionally, the robot successfully avoids running into any roadblocks and is effective at moving objects quickly to alleviate human pain.

8.2 Limitations

1. This robot is being run on Batteries, and long lasting batteries is quite pricey.
2. Since The mobile application is connected through Bluetooth so, the connectivity is upto limited range. These two things can be considered for better performance of the current running model.

8.3 Future Scope

1. Autonomous Delivery Robots: Delivery robots have the potential to revolutionize last-mile logistics. These robots can navigate sidewalks and streets to deliver packages, groceries, or food orders autonomously. They can reduce delivery costs, increase efficiency, and minimize the need for human drivers.
2. Warehouse Automation: Robots can be employed in warehouses for tasks such as picking, sorting, and organizing inventory [9].
3. Agriculture: Autonomous tractors are set to revolutionize farming. These driverless tractors allow farmers to control them via an app on their phone or computer, freeing them from long hours of driving [10,11].
4. Autonomous Robots in Construction and Mining: They can handle repetitive tasks, hazardous environments and heavy lifting without risking human lives [12].

References

1. Farrugia, J.L., Fabri, S.G.: Swarm robotics for object transportation. In: 2018 UKACC 12th International Conference on Control (CONTROL), pp. 353–358 (2018). https://doi.org/10.1109/CONTROL.2018.8516829
2. Nasereddin, H.H.: Smartphone control robots through Bluetooth. Int. J. Res. Rev. Appl. Sci. **4**, 399–404 (2010)
3. Kashiwazaki, K., et al.: A car transportation system using multiple mobile robots: iCART II. In: 2011 IEEE/RSJ International Conference on Intelligent Robots and Systems, pp. 4593–4600 (2011). https://doi.org/10.1109/IROS.2011.6094889
4. Inglett, J.E., Rodríguez-Seda, E.J.: Object transportation by cooperative robots. In: SoutheastCon 2017, pp. 1–6. (2017). https://doi.org/10.1109/SECON.2017.7925348

5. Pakdaman, M., Sanaatiyan, M.M.: Design and implementation of line follower robot. In: 2009 Second International Conference on Computer and Electrical Engineering, Dubai, United Arab Emirates, pp. 585–590 (2009). https://doi.org/10.1109/ICCEE.2009.43
6. Bindu, T., Stafford, M.: Industry based automatic robotic arm. Int. J. Eng. Innovative Technol. **2** (2008)
7. AL-Taharwa: A mobile robot path planning using genetic algorithm in static environment. J. Comput. Sci. **4**, 341–344 (2008). https://doi.org/10.3844/jcssp.2008.341.344
8. Almasri, M.M., Alajlan, A.M., Elleithy, K.M.: Trajectory planning and collision avoidance algorithm for mobile robotics system. In: IEEE Sens. J. **16**(12), 5021–5028 (2016). https://doi.org/10.1109/JSEN.2016.2553126
9. Plaksina, I.G., Chistokhina, G.I., Topolskiy, D.V.: Development of a transport robot for automated warehouses. In: 2018 International Multi-Conference on Industrial Engineering and Modern Technologies (FarEastCon), pp. 1–4 (2018). https://doi.org/10.1109/FarEastCon.2018.8602651
10. Sudipto, K., Ifthakhar, H., Ragib, M.: Autonomous agriculture robot (2023). https://doi.org/10.13140/RG.2.2.32024.37122
11. Rupali, P.: Design and development of a multi-tasking autonomous agriculture robot using ESP32 microcontroller (2023)
12. Kumar, V., Balasubramanian, M., Raj, S.: Robotics in construction industry. Indian J. Sci. Technol. **9** (2016). https://doi.org/10.17485/ijst/2016/v9i23/95974
13. Koung, D., Kermorgant, O., Fantoni, I., Belouaer, L.: Cooperative multi-robot object transportation system based on hierarchical quadratic programming. IEEE Robot. Autom. Lett. **6**(4), 6466–6472 (2021). https://doi.org/10.1109/LRA.2021.3092305
14. Hossain, M.: Autonomous delivery robots: a literature review. IEEE Eng. Manage. Rev. **51**(4), 77–89. Fourthquarter (2023). https://doi.org/10.1109/EMR.2023.3304848. keywords: Robots;Codes;Business;Companies;Urban areas;Robot sensing systems;Navigation;Autonomous delivery robots;delivery service;healthcare;hospitality;retail
15. Gumus, O., Topaloglu, M., Ozcelik, D.: The use of computer controlled line follower robots in public transport. Procedia Comput. Sci. **102C**, 202–208 (2016). https://doi.org/10.1016/j.procs.2016.09.390
16. Teixeira, F.M., Silva, M.F.: Simulation of a robotic co-transport system. In: 2021 IEEE International Conference on Autonomous Robot Systems and Competitions (ICARSC), Santa Maria da Feira, Portugal, pp. 179–184 (2021). https://doi.org/10.1109/ICARSC52212.2021.9429776
17. Min, T.W., Zhe, L., Yin, H.K., Hiang, G.C., Yong, L.K.: A rules and communication based multiple robots transportation system. In: Proceedings,: IEEE International Symposium on Computational Intelligence in Robotics and Automation, CIRA 1999 (Cat. No.99EX375), pp. 180–186. Monterey, CA, USA (1999). https://doi.org/10.1109/CIRA.1999.810046

Joint Design of User Association, Caching and Power Allocation for Delay Optimization in UAV-Enabled Networks

Gezahegn Abdissa Bayessa[1], Rong Chai[1(✉)], Yetmwork Gutema Lemu[2], and Qianbin Chen[1]

[1] Chongqing University of Posts and Telecommunications, Chongqing 400065, China
L202010006@stu.cqupt.edu.cn, {chairong,cqb}@cqupt.edu.cn
[2] Adama Science and Technology University, Adama, Ethiopia

Abstract. The rapid surge of multimedia and video applications poses challenges to the content-delivering service in wireless networks. In this paper, we study the proactive caching problem in unmanned aerial vehicle (UAV)-enabled networks, where a number of UAVs are deployed to offer content delivery service for user equipments (UEs). In order to acquire user request information, we first propose a bidirectional long short-term memory-based user request prediction algorithm. Then, based on the obtained user content requests, we examine the content fetching delay of users and formulate UAV deployment, content caching, and power allocation problems as an overall content fetching delay minimization problem. To solve the formulated optimization problem, we decouple it into two subproblems, namely, the UAV deployment and content caching subproblem, and the power allocation subproblem, and solve the two subproblems by using an alternate iteration-based algorithm. Specifically, we first design a modified K-means-based clustering scheme to group UEs into various clusters, and then develop a UAV deployment strategy for individual clusters by applying quadratic transformation and first-order Taylor expansion. A heuristic proactive content caching algorithm is further proposed for individual UAVs. Finally, the Lagrangian dual method is employed to solve the power allocation subproblem. Simulation results demonstrate the effectiveness of the proposed algorithms.

Keywords: Unmanned aerial vehicles (UAVs) · user clustering · UAV deployment · proactive content caching · power allocation

1 Introduction

The proliferation of multimedia and video applications brought rapid growth of data traffic, which in turn poses formidable challenges to the transmission performance of the traditional cellular systems [1]. In response, proactive caching technology which stores popular files at network edge has been proposed as a promising solution [2]. Recently, unmanned aerial vehicles (UAVs) have garnered significant attention as a potential platform for proactive caching. Leveraging the flexible deployment and scalability of UAVs, UAV-aided caching is capable of improving the efficiency of the content delivery [3].

In recent years, content delivery problem has been widely studied for UAV-enabled networks [4–10]. The research works in [4,5] investigate a content caching algorithm to maximize content availability [4] or to minimize energy consumption [5]. In [6], the authors propose a long short-term memory (LSTM)-based caching algorithm to minimize the weighted delivery cost. To address the challenges associated with LSTM in capturing dependencies and adapting to patterns of sequential input data in both forward and backward directions, bidirectional long short-term memory (BiLSTM) have been employed in [7]. By considering UAV deployment, the research works in [8–10] propose a joint content placement scheme and UAV deployment strategy to minimize storage cost [8], maximize throughput [9] and maximize mean opinion score [10].

The research works in [11,12] jointly consider UAV deployment, cache placement and power allocation issues to minimize the average outage probability [11] or to maximize the hit probability [12]. User clustering and resource allocation are considered along with UAV deployment and cache placement strategy in [13–17]. The authors propose a K-means algorithm for user clusters to deploy UAVs, and design a resource allocation strategy to fulfill users' QoS requirements. The authors in [13] design a quality of experience (QoE) based user grouping scheme that finds optimal positions of UAVs and stores popular contents to maximize content delay index. In [14] the authors propose joint optimization of UAV deployment and resource allocation for UAV-aided relay systems to maximize the energy efficiency. The research work in [15] introduces joint UAV deployment and communication resource allocation to maximize the total long-term QoE of users in multiuser video streaming in UAV relay networks. The authors in [16] design joint deployment of aerial base stations (ABSs), user associations, and corresponding bandwidth allocations to minimize total downlink transmit power in cache-enabled wireless networks. Research work in [17] presents joint user clustering, UAV deployment, and resource allocation algorithms to minimize transmit power and improve overall spectral efficiency (SE).

Although content caching in UAV-enabled networks have been exploited in aforementioned research works, yet the existing research mainly design joint UAV deployment and caching strategy based on user locations and rarely considers the impact of user request distribution on the UAV deployment. On the other hand, recent studies assume perfect knowledge of users' content requests [4,5], which may not be practical. As the content caching strategy is designed proactively, the difficulty of acquiring explicit user demand information in advance poses a significant challenge in designing a joint strategy. Few existing solutions for unknown content popularity are mostly based on conventional predict-then-optimize schemes (predict the content popularity first and then optimize the cache policy) [6,8]. While it can achieve good performance when user demand follows clear patterns, it is far less effective when explicit user demand information is not available. In this context, the existing content prediction schemes are not well-suited for addressing the challenges posed by unknown content request patterns. Thus, the problem of joint UAV deployment, content placement and power allocation with unknown user requests remains open for multi-UAV-assisted wireless networks.

In this paper, we consider the content delivery problem in a UAV-enabled network and jointly design UAV deployment, content caching, and power allocation strategy. Specifically, we first propose a bidirectional long short-term memory (BiLSTM)-based content request prediction algorithm. Then, based on the obtained user request information, we examine the overall delay incurred for content fetching in the network and formulate the joint UAV deployment, content caching, and power allocation problem as an overall delay minimization problem. To solve the formulated problem, we transform it into two subproblems and solve them respectively. Specifically, we first design a UAV deployment strategy through utilizing quadratic transformation and first-order Taylor expansion. Then, we design a heuristic proactive content caching algorithm for the UAVs. Based on the obtained local UAV deployment and content caching strategy, we then design a power allocation strategy by means of the Lagrangian dual method (Fig. 1).

2 System Model

2.1 Network Model

In this paper, we consider the content delivery service of UEs in a wireless network. Suppose that UEs have some content fetching requirements. As the content server is in general deployed at the core network which is far from the UEs, resulting in undesired transmission performance. To tackle this problem, we deploy a number of UAVs, which are equipped with certain cache capacity. The UAVs are capable of retrieving contents requested by users and store the contents locally in their own storage. By accessing the UAVs, UEs are able to fetching their requested contents directly from the UAVs instead of interacting with the core network. We denote the number of UAVs to be deployed as J and the number of UEs as I. Let UAV_j denote the j-th UAV, and UE_i denote the i-th UE, $1 \leq i \leq I$, $1 \leq j \leq J$.

To enable multi-user accessing on an individual UAV, we apply orthogonal frequency division multiple access (OFDMA) scheme which allows multiple UEs to access one UAV using orthogonal subcarriers. We denote B as subcarrier bandwidth.

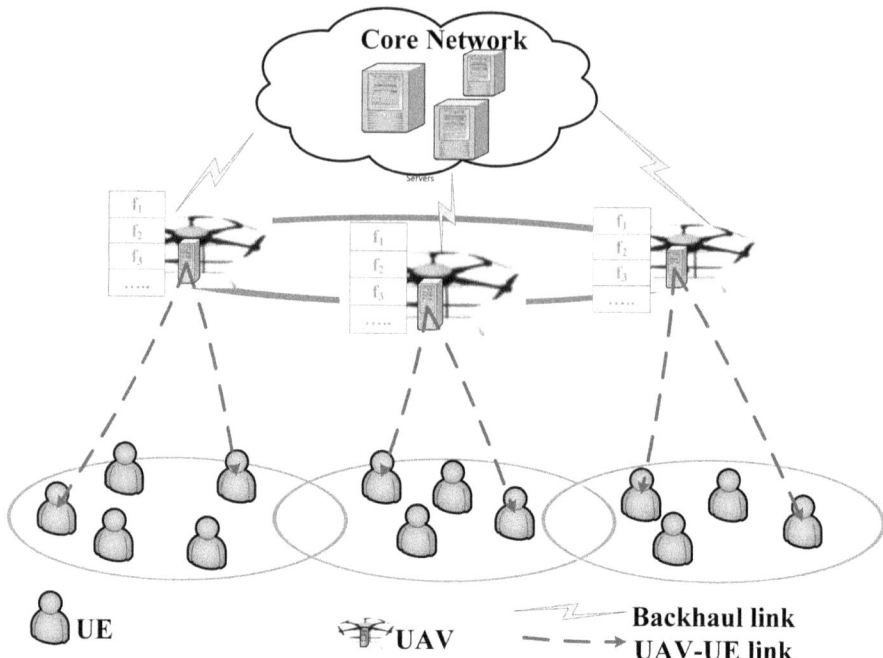

Fig. 1. The UAV-enabled network: a number of UAVs and several UEs.

Suppose that all the files are stored at the remote content server and each UAV may cache certain contents. Let F denote the total number of content files that UEs request, η_f denote the size of file f and ρ_j denote the cache capacity of UAV_j. We assume that each UE is allowed to associate with one UAV and denote UE association variable as $\xi_{i,j}$. If UE_i is associated with UAV_j, $\xi_{i,j} = 1$, otherwise $\xi_{i,j} = 0$.

Without loss of generality, we assume that the UAVs are deployed at a constant hovering altitude z. Let $\mathbf{q}_j = (x_j, y_j)$ denote the two-dimensional coordinate of UAV_j and $\mathbf{n}_i = (\bar{x}_i, \bar{y}_i)$ denote the coordinate of UE_i.

2.2 Communication Model

In this subsection, we discuss the channel model of UAV-UE links and then formulate the data rate of the transmission links. Assuming the UAV-UE links experience free-space path-loss. Let $h_{i,j}$ denote the channel coefficient of the link from UAV_j to UE_i, which can be expressed as

$$h_{i,j} = \frac{c}{4\pi f_0(\|\mathbf{q}_j - \mathbf{n}_i\|^2 + z^2)}, \tag{1}$$

where c is the speed of light and f_0 denotes the carrier frequency.

Let P_j denote the total transmit power of UAV$_j$, $\alpha_{i,j}$ denote the fraction of power allocated to UE$_i$ when accessing UAV$_j$, $0 \leq \alpha_{i,j} \leq 1$. Denote R_i as the achievable data rate of UE$_i$, which can be computed as

$$R_{i,j} = B \log_2 \left(1 + \frac{\alpha_{i,j} P_j |h_{i,j}|}{\sigma^2}\right). \tag{2}$$

3 Content Request Prediction

In the UAV-enabled content delivery system, the content fetching performance is expected to be improved by caching user requests. However, user content requests may vary over time, thus posing challenges to content caching in UAVs. To resolve this problem, we first predict user requests based on their historical request information. Specifically, for each user, we propose a BiLSTM-based algorithm to predict the probabilities for requesting all the files.

In a BiLSTM network, two hidden layers are connected to the same output layer and pass the learned prediction history forward and backward. We denote $\mathbf{h}_t^f$ and $\mathbf{h}_t^b$ respectively as the forward and backward hidden states of the BiLSTM architecture at time slot t. The final output of the BiLSTM model is a concatenation of the forward and backward hidden state sequences. Let $\hat{\mathbf{y}}_t$ denote the output of the BiLSTM model, which can be given as

$$\hat{\mathbf{y}}_t = \phi \left(\mathbf{W}_{hy} \left[\mathbf{h}_t^f ; \mathbf{h}_t^b \right] + \mathbf{b}_y \right), \tag{3}$$

where $[\mathbf{h}_t^f; \mathbf{h}_t^b]$ denotes the concatenation of forward and backward hidden states, $\mathbf{W}_{hy}$ is the weight matrix for the output layer, $\mathbf{b}_y$ is the bias vector for the output layer, and $\phi(\cdot)$ is the activation function.

Let $\gamma_{i,f,t}$ denote the content request identifier of UE$_i$ at time slot t. We set $\gamma_{i,f,t} = 1$, if UE$_i$ requires content f at time slot t, otherwise, $\gamma_{i,f,t} = 0$, $1 \leq i \leq I$, $1 \leq f \leq F$. Let $x_{i,f,t}$ denote the number of requests of UE$_i$ for content f until time slot t, we obtain $x_{i,f,t} = \sum_{t_1=1}^{t} \gamma_{i,f,t_1}$. Denote $\mathbf{x}_{i,t}$ as the content request vector of UE$_i$ at time slot t, which can be expressed as

$$\mathbf{x}_{i,t} = \left[x_{i,1,t}, \cdots, x_{i,f,t}, \cdots, x_{i,F,t} \right]. \tag{4}$$

We set the input of the BiLSTM-based prediction model of UE$_i$ at time slot t as $\mathbf{x}_{i,t}$. Given input sequence $\mathbf{x}_{i,t}$, we train the BiLSTM model based on the historical request data of UE$_i$. Then, the output of the BiLSTM model at $t+1$ which is the predicted request of UE$_i$, can be expressed as

$$\hat{\mathbf{y}}_{i,t+1} = \left[\hat{y}_{i,1,t+1}, \cdots, \hat{y}_{i,f,t+1}, \cdots, \hat{y}_{i,F,t+1} \right], \tag{5}$$

where $\hat{y}_{i,f,t+1}$ is the probability that UE$_i$ requests content f at time slot $t+1$. To describe user content request we introduce $\gamma_{i,f}$. Based on $\hat{\mathbf{y}}_{i,t+1}$, we obtain $\gamma_{i,f}$. Specifically, if $f^* = \arg\max_{\forall f} \hat{y}_{i,f,t+1}$, we set $\gamma_{i,f^*} = 1$, otherwise, $\gamma_{i,f^*} = 0$.

4 Problem Formulation

In this paper, we jointly design the UAV deployment, content caching and power allocation strategy so as to minimize overall delay.

4.1 Objective Function Formulation

Considering that content requests at UAVs follow a Poisson distribution and request processing at the UAVs follows an exponential distribution, we model the content request processing at UAVs using an M/G/1 queuing model. Let λ_j^q and μ_j^q denote the request rate and service rate at UAV_j, respectively, D is the overall delay incurred for fetching requested contents, which can be given by,

$$D = \sum_{i=1}^{I}\sum_{j=1}^{J}\sum_{f=1}^{F} \xi_{i,j}\gamma_{i,f}\left(\frac{\eta_f}{R_{i,j}} + \frac{1}{\mu_j^q - \lambda_j^q}\right)$$
$$+ \sum_{j=1}^{J}\sum_{f=1}^{F}(1-\delta_{j,f})\eta_f D_j^s, \qquad (6)$$

$\delta_{j,f}$ is the content caching variable of UAV_j. We set $\delta_{j,f} = 1$, if UAV_j caches content f, otherwise, $\delta_{j,f} = 0$. D_j^s is the backhaul delay of UAV_j for fetching unit content from the content server. Without loss of generality, we consider D_j^s as a constant.

4.2 Optimization Problem Formulation

We formulate the joint UAV deployment, content caching and power allocation as a delay minimization problem, which is given as follows

$$P1: \min_{\{\xi_{i,j}\},\{\mathbf{q}_j\},\{\delta_{j,f}\},\{\alpha_{i,j}\}} D$$

$$\text{s.t. } C1: \sum_{j=1}^{J}\xi_{i,j} \leq 1, \forall i,$$

$$C2: \sum_{i=1}^{I}\xi_{i,j} \leq N_0, \forall j,$$

$$C3: 0 \leq x_j \leq x_{\max}, \forall j,$$

$$C4: 0 \leq y_j \leq y_{\max}, \forall j,$$

$$C5: \sum_{f=1}^{F}\eta_f \delta_{j,f} \leq \rho_j, \forall j,$$

$$C6: \sum_{i=1}^{I}\alpha_{i,j} \leq 1, \forall j,$$

$$C7: R_{i,j} \geq \xi_{i,j} R^{\min}, \qquad (7)$$

where constraint C1 indicates that each UE can only be associated to one UAV, constraint C2 limits the maximum number of UEs associated with one UAV, where N_0 denotes the maximum number of UEs associated with UAVs. Constraint C3 and C4 are for the UAV deployment, where $x_{\max} = \max\{\bar{x}_i\}$, and $y_{\max} = \max\{\bar{y}_i\}$ denote the maximum values of the positions of users in x and y coordinates, respectively. C5 is the constraint for the available cache capacity of UAVs, C6 and C7 are the constraint for power allocation and UEs minimum required data rate, respectively.

5 UE Clustering, UAV Deployment and Content Caching Strategy

The aim of problem P1 is to minimize overall delay by jointly optimizing UAV deployment, content caching and power allocation strategy. However, the coupling of UAV deployment, content caching, power allocation in (7) makes the optimization problem very challenging to solve directly. To solve this problem, we decompose P1 into tractable sub-problems. In particular, under the assumptions on power allocation, we first formulate and solve UAV deployment and content caching problem in this section. In the next section, we tackle power allocation problem.

5.1 Modified K-Means-Based UE Clustering Algorithm

In this subsection, we design a modified K-means clustering algorithm. In particular, we first define the similarity metrics and discuss the algorithm in detail.

Similarity Metrics. In our considered system model, users may have different content requests. To jointly consider the similarity of users in terms of geographical positions and content requests, we define similarity metrics.

Let $\psi_{d,i,\hat{i}}$ and $\psi_{i,\hat{i},f}$ respectively denote the position similarity between UE$_i$ and UE$_{\hat{i}}$ and the content similarity of UE$_i$ and UE$_{\hat{i}}$ on content f, which are expressed as follows

$$\psi_{d,i,\hat{i}} = 1 - \frac{d_{i,\hat{i}}}{\max\limits_{i,\hat{i}}\{d_{i,\hat{i}}\}},$$

$$\psi_{i,\hat{i},f} = \begin{cases} \zeta, & \text{if } \gamma_{i,f} = \gamma_{\hat{i},f}, \forall f, i \neq \hat{i} \\ 1, & \text{otherwise,} \end{cases} \qquad (8)$$

where $d_{i,\hat{i}}$ is the distance between UE$_i$ and UE$_{\hat{i}}$. Users may have similar content requests. To describe the similarity of users on contents, we define content similarity between users. Where ζ is a constant defined to indicate the level of importance of the content similarity, we set $\zeta > 1$.

Accordingly, we define the similarity matrix, $\psi = [\psi_{i,\hat{i}}, \forall i \neq \hat{i}]$, where $\psi_{i,\hat{i}}$ denotes the similarity between UE_i and $UE_{\hat{i}}$, which is computed as

$$\psi_{i,\hat{i}} = \frac{1}{F} \psi_{i,\hat{i},d} \sum_{f=1}^{F} \psi_{i,\hat{i},f}. \tag{9}$$

Steps of the Proposed Algorithm. Based on the similarity metric between UEs expressed in (9), we define identifier matrix and select the UE with the highest neighborhood degree as a cluster head to initialize clustering. Then, neighboring users are added to the candidate cluster. Subsequently, distance and cluster size constraints are examined. This process continues until all the remaining users are checked.

The steps of the proposed user clustering algorithm is summarized as follows.

a) Initialization: Let Ω_j, Ω_j^c and Ω^u denote the set of UEs in the j-th cluster, the j-th candidate cluster and the set of unclustered UEs, respectively. N_j denotes the number of UEs in Ω_j, $d^{\max}$ denotes the maximum radius of the cluster, N_0 stand for the maximum limit of each cluster. We set $\Omega_j = \Omega_j^c = \Omega^u = \emptyset, 1 \leq j \leq J$, $\Omega^u = \Omega^u \cup \{UE_i, \forall 1 \leq i \leq I\}$, and $j = 1$, where $\emptyset$ denotes the empty set. Let F_i denote the clustering flag of UE_i, we set $F_i = 0, 1 \leq i \leq I$.

b) Compute similarity metric and identifier index: Compute $\psi_{i,\hat{i}}$ based on (8)-(9), and denote $a_{i,\hat{i}}$ as the identifier index between UE_i and $UE_{\hat{i}}$. If $\psi_{i,\hat{i}} \geq \psi^{th}$, we set $a_{i,\hat{i}} = 1$, otherwise, $a_{i,\hat{i}} = 0$, $\forall i \neq \hat{i}$, where ψ^{th} denotes the threshold for similarity.

c) Select the UE with the highest neighborhood degree: Let μ_i denote the neighborhood degree of UE_i, we define μ_i as $\mu_i = \sum_{\hat{i}=1}^{I} a_{i,\hat{i}}, i \neq \hat{i}$. If $\mu_{i^*} = \arg\max_i \{\mu_i\}$, we select UE_{i^*} as the initial user to start clustering and update user sets, i.e., put we put UE_{i^*} in Ω_j^c and remove UE_{i^*} from Ω^u, i.e., $\Omega_j^c = \Omega_j^c \cup \{UE_{i^*}\}$, and $\Omega^u = \Omega^u / \{UE_{i^*}\}$. If $\mu_{i^*} = 1$, jump to Step f).

d) Form candidate cluster Ω_j^c: If $\mu_{i^*} \neq 1$, update the candidate cluster Ω_j^c. Specifically, randomly select one UE, say $UE_{\hat{i}}$, if $a_{i^*,\hat{i}} = 1$ and $F_{\hat{i}} = 0$, we check the maximum distance constraint. If $d_{i^*,\hat{i}} \leq d^{\max}$, we put $UE_{\hat{i}}$ in Ω_j^c. i.e., $\Omega_j^c = \Omega_j^c \cup \{UE_{\hat{i}}\}$, and $\Omega^u = \Omega^u / \{UE_{\hat{i}}\}$. We set $F_{\hat{i}} = 1$ and $a_{i^*,\hat{i}} = 0$. Repeat this step, until all the remaining UEs are checked.

e) Check the cluster size condition: Compute the size of Ω_j^c, i.e., $N_j = |\Omega_j^c|$. If $N_j \leq N_0$, we set $\Omega_j = \Omega_j^c$, jump to Step f). If $N_j > N_0$, remove the farthest UE from the candidate cluster. That is, if $\hat{i} = \arg\max_{\hat{i}} \{d_{i^*,\hat{i}}\}$, remove $UE_{\hat{i}}$ from the candidate cluster, i.e., $\Omega_j^c = \Omega_j^c / \{UE_{\hat{i}}\}$ and $\Omega^u = \Omega^u \cup \{UE_{\hat{i}}\}$, we set $F_i = 0$. Repeat this process, until the cluster size condition holds. We set $\Omega_j = \Omega_j^c$.

f) Check algorithm termination: If $\Omega^u = \emptyset$, the algorithm terminates, otherwise, we set $j = j + 1$, return to Step c).

5.2 UAV Deployment Subproblem Formulation and Solution

In this subsection, based on user clustering strategy, we design UAV deployment strategy for individual clusters. Under the assumption that the data transmission in different clusters can be considered independently, we may design the UAV deployment strategy for various clusters individually. Hence, the UAV deployment problem in the system is reduced to the deployment problem for one specific cluster. For convenience, we consider cluster j and design the corresponding UAV deployment strategy, where UAV$_j$ is deployed above cluster j.

Since power allocation strategy may affect the transmission performance between UAVs and UEs, resulting the difficulty in designing UAV deployment. For simplicity, we first apply equal power allocation strategy for cluster j. Specifically, we divide the transmit power equally, i.e., $\alpha_{i,j}^* = 1/N_j, \forall \text{UE}_i \in \Omega_j$.

$$\bar{D}_j = \sum_{i=1}^{N_j} \xi_{i,j} \frac{\sum_{f=1}^{F} \gamma_{i,f} \eta_f}{B \log_2 \left(1 + \frac{P_j c}{N_j 4\pi f_0 (\|\mathbf{q}_j - \mathbf{n}_i\|^2 + z^2) \sigma^2}\right)}. \tag{10}$$

UAV deployment subproblem for cluster j can be formulated as

$$\text{P2}: \min_{\mathbf{q}_j} \bar{D}_j \tag{11}$$
$$\text{s.t. C3} - \text{C4 in (7)}.$$

To solve the problem in (11), we employ the quadratic transformation technique on the objective function in $\bar{D}_j$. Specifically, the fractional term X/Y is transformed to the form of $2\kappa\sqrt{X} - \kappa^2 Y$, where $\kappa = \sqrt{X}/Y$. By defining X, Y and κ respectively as $X = \Upsilon_{i,j}$. We denote, $\Upsilon_{i,j}$, ν_j, and $\chi_{i,j}$ by $\xi_{i,j} \sum_{f=1}^{F} \gamma_{i,f} \eta_f$, $\frac{P_j c}{N_j 4\pi f_{m^*} \sigma^2}$, and $\|\mathbf{q}_j - \mathbf{n}_i\|^2$, respectively. Let $\chi_{i,j}^t$ is the value of $\chi_{i,j}$ at the t-th iteration, the content fetching delay at t-th iteration, $\bar{D}_j^t$ can be given as

$$\bar{D}_j^t = \sum_{i=1}^{N_j} \frac{\Upsilon_{i,j}}{B \log_2 \left(1 + \frac{\nu_j}{\chi_{i,j}^t + z^2}\right)}. \tag{12}$$

We then transform (12) to the form of $2\kappa\sqrt{X} - \kappa^2 Y$, where $\kappa = \sqrt{X}/Y$, and X and Y are respectively the numerator and denominator of the ratio of polynomial expressions.

As $\Upsilon_{i,j}$ and ν_j are both constants, it can be demonstrated that $\lambda_{i,j}^t$ is concave with respect to $\chi_{i,j}^t$. Therefore, $\bar{D}_j^t$ is also a concave function with respect to $\chi_{i,j}^t$. Due to the fact that any concave function is globally upper bounded by its first-order Taylor expansion [18], we apply the first-order Taylor expansion formula on $\bar{D}_j^t$. Let $\hat{\mathbf{q}}_j^t$ denote the local point of $\hat{\mathbf{q}}_j^t$ at the t-th iteration, applying the first-order Taylor expansion of $\bar{D}_j^t$ with respect to $\chi_{i,j}^t$, we obtain

$$\bar{D}_j^t \leq \sum_{i=1}^{N_j} 2\lambda_{i,j}^t \sqrt{\Upsilon_{i,j}}$$
$$+ \sum_{i=1}^{N_j} B(\lambda_{i,j}^t)^2 H_{i,j}^t (\|\mathbf{q}_j^t - \mathbf{n}_i\|^2 - \|\hat{\mathbf{q}}_j^t - \mathbf{n}_i\|^2)$$
$$- \sum_{i=1}^{N_j} (\lambda_{i,j}^t)^2 G_{i,j}^t = \hat{D}_j^t \tag{13}$$

where $\hat{D}_j^t$ denotes the upper bound of $\bar{D}_j^t$, $\lambda_{i,j}^t$, H_i^t and $G_{i,j}^t$ are given by

$$\lambda_{i,j}^t = \frac{\sqrt{\Upsilon_{i,j}}}{B \log_2\left(1 + \frac{\nu_j}{\chi_{i,j}^t + z^2}\right)}, H_{i,j}^t = \frac{\frac{\nu_j}{\|\mathbf{q}_j^t - \mathbf{n}_i\|^2} \log_2(e)}{1 + \frac{\nu_j}{\|\mathbf{q}_j^t - \mathbf{n}_i\|^2}},$$
$$G_{i,j}^t = \log_2\left(1 + \frac{\nu_j}{\|\mathbf{q}_j^t - \mathbf{n}_i\|^2}\right) \tag{14}$$

At the t-th iteration, given local point $\hat{\mathbf{q}}_j^t$, the optimization problem (11) can be reformulated as

$$\begin{array}{c} \text{P3}: \min_{\{\mathbf{q}_j^t\}} \hat{D}_j^t \\ \text{s.t. C3} - \text{C4 in (7)}. \end{array} \tag{15}$$

Problem (15) is a convex optimization problem that can be efficiently solved by standard convex optimization solvers such as CVX. Let $\mathbf{q}_j^*$ represent the obtained deployment position of UAV$_j$.

5.3 UAV Content Caching Subproblem Formulation and Solution

The UAV deployment strategy $\mathbf{q}_j^*$ is obtained under the assumption that users' requested contents are cached at the UAVs. However, this assumption may not hold due to the limited storage capacity of the UAVs. Therefore, efficiently caching the most requested contents and utilizing the limited storage of UAVs become a crucial problem. Since the caching strategy for different UAVs can be designed independently, for simplicity, we formulate and solve content caching problem for UAV$_j$ in this subsection.

Following similar assumptions on transmit power and subchannel allocation strategy in Subsect. 5.2, we compute the content fetching delay of UEs associated with UAV$_j$. Let $\check{D}_j$ denote the content fetching delay for cluster j, which can be expressed as

$$\check{D}_j = \sum_{i=1}^{I} \xi_{i,j} \left(\frac{\sum_{f=1}^{F} \gamma_{i,f} \eta_f}{B \log_2(1 + \frac{\nu_j}{\|\mathbf{q}_j^* - \mathbf{n}_i\|^2 + z^2})} \right.$$
$$\left. + \sum_{f=1}^{F} (1 - \delta_{j,f}) \gamma_{i,f} \eta_f D_j^s \right), \forall \text{UE}_i \in \Omega_j. \tag{16}$$

Then, we formulate the content caching subproblem for UAV$_j$ as follows

$$P4: \min_{\{\delta_{j,f}\}} \check{D}_j \qquad (17)$$
$$\text{s.t. C5 in (7)}.$$

To solve P4, we propose a heuristic algorithm that places popular contents in the UAVs. Specifically, we examine the required fetching delay from the content server to UAV$_j$ for various contents. To this end, we denote $\epsilon_f = \sum_{i=1}^{I} \xi_{i,j} \eta_f D_j^s$ as the overall delay incurred to fetch content f from content server. Then, we sort ϵ_f in a descending order. For convenience, we set $\epsilon_{f_1} \geq \epsilon_{f_2} \geq \cdots \geq \epsilon_{f_F}$. In order to reduce the backhaul delay, the highest ranking contents should be cached in UAV$_j$ by fulfilling constraint C5. Specifically, if $\eta_{f_1} \leq \rho_j$, we cache content f_1 in UAV$_j$ and we set $\delta^*_{j,f_1} = 1$, otherwise $\delta^*_{j,f_1} = 0$. We then check whether content f_2 can be cached in UAV$_j$. The above process repeats until no content can be cached in UAV$_j$ under constraint C5 in (7). We use $\delta^*_{j,f}$ to represent the obtained content fetching strategy.

6 Power Allocation Formulation and Solution

Given user clustering, UAV deployment and content caching strategy, which is obtained from Sect. 5, the optimization problem P1 in (7) is reduced to a joint power allocation subproblem. Let $\widetilde{D}$ denote the content fetching delay based on the obtained strategy. The power allocation subproblem can be formulated as

$$P5: \min_{\{\alpha_{i,j}\}} \widetilde{D} \qquad (18)$$
$$\text{s.t. C6 − C7 in (7)}.$$

To solve problem (18), we assume that optimal subcarrier allocation strategy is obtained based on the assumptions made in Subsect. 5.2. Therefore, given user clustering strategy, UAV deployment and content caching strategy for individual clusters, we design power control strategy for users in cluster j, i.e., UE$_i \in \Omega_j$.

It can be shown that problem P5 is convex which can be solved by using Lagrange dual method. Hence, the corresponding Lagrange function of the problem P5 can be expressed as

$$L\left(\alpha_{i,j^*}, \lambda_1, \Omega_i\right)$$

$$= \sum_{i=1}^{I} \sum_{f=1}^{F} \left(\frac{\xi_{i,j} \delta_{j,f}^* \gamma_{i,f} \eta_f}{B \log_2 \left(1 + \frac{\alpha_{i,j^*} P_j |h_{i,j^*}|}{\sigma^2}\right)} \right)$$

$$+ \lambda_1 \left(\sum_{i=1}^{I} \xi_{i,j} \alpha_{i,j^*} - 1 \right) + \sum_{i=1}^{I} \xi_{i,j} \Omega_i \left(R^{\min} - R_{i,j^*} \right), \quad (19)$$

where λ_1 and Ω_i are non-negative Lagrange multipliers. Then, (18) can be reformulated as

$$\text{P6}: \max_{\lambda_1, \{\Omega_i\}} \min_{\{\alpha_{i,j^*}\}} L\left(\alpha_{i,j^*}, \lambda_1, \Omega_i\right)$$

$$\text{s.t. } \lambda_1, \Omega_i \geq 0. \quad (20)$$

For a given set of Lagrange multipliers λ_1 and Ω_i, the allocated power α_{i,j^*} can be obtained by calculating the derivative of $L\left(\alpha_{i,j^*}, \lambda_1, \Omega_i\right)$ with respect to α_{i,j^*} and setting it to zero. We set $\alpha_{i,j}^*$ as the obtained power control strategy.

7 Simulation Results

In this section, we evaluate the performance of the proposed BiLSTM-based user request prediction algorithm, user clustering, UAV deployment, content caching, and power allocation strategies. In Table 1, we present the detailed simulation parameters.

We conduct the simulation using the MovieLens dataset [19]. The dataset comprises movie information, such as movie ID and genres, recorded from January 9, 1995, to September 26, 2018. To accurately simulate users' content requests, we selected the eighteen most viewed movie genres based on their view counts. These genres encompass Action, Adventure, Animation, Children, Comedy, Crime, Documentary, Drama, Fantasy, Horror, IMAX, Musical, Mystery, Romance, Science Fiction (Sci-Fi), Thriller, War, and Western.

To simulate user requests, we first pre-process the dataset, which involves cleaning the dataset by removing rows with missing values and unnecessary columns. In this simulation, we consider the view counts for each particular genre as requests received from the UEs. We record the request counts for each genre to obtain the request history information for the UEs, as described in (4). Then, we train our model using the request history of the UEs.

Table 1. Simulation parameters.

Simulation Parameters	Notations	Values
Simulation Area		1000 m × 1000 m
Total number of UEs	I	60
Carrier frequency	f_0	2.4 GHz
Bandwidth	B	4 MHz
Noise power	σ^2	-174 dB
Total number of files	F	18
File size	η_f	[5, 6] Mbits
Request rate	λ_j^q	[9, 14] b/s
Service rate	μ_j^q	[15, 20]
Maximum number of UEs in clusters	N_0	10
Content similarity	ζ	{1, 1.6}
Threshold for similarity	ψ^{th}	0.7
Maximum radius of clusters	d^{max}	200 m
UAV hovering altitude	z	100 m
Total power of UAV	P_j	1 W
Cache capacity of UAV	ρ_j	36 Mbits
Minimum data rate	R_{min}	0.1 Mbps
Learning rate	λ	0.1

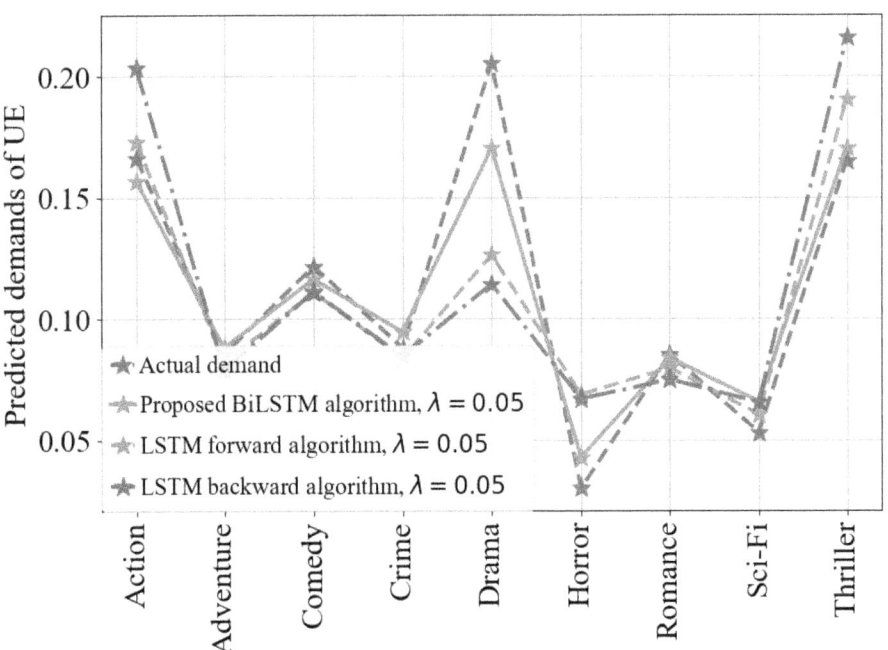

Fig. 2. User content request prediction vs learning rate ($\lambda = 0.05$).

In Figs. 2 and 3, we plot the predicted request of one UE for nine genres. To investigate the prediction accuracy of the proposed BiLSTM-based algorithm versus baseline algorithms, we evaluate the predicted user request versus the actual demand for different learning rates, $\lambda = 0.05$ in Fig. 2, and $\lambda = 0.1$ in Fig. 3. As observed from the figures, the prediction accuracy of the proposed BiLSTM-based algorithm surpasses the baseline algorithms due to its effective learning of UE request history. Thereby indicating the potential advantage that our proposed content caching algorithm achieves compared to the LSTM forward and LSTM backward-based algorithms. The figure demonstrates that for $\lambda = 0.1$ the error difference between the predicted and the actual demands is relatively small compared with $\lambda = 0.05$, which highlights the critical role of the learning rate in enhancing the accuracy of user request prediction.

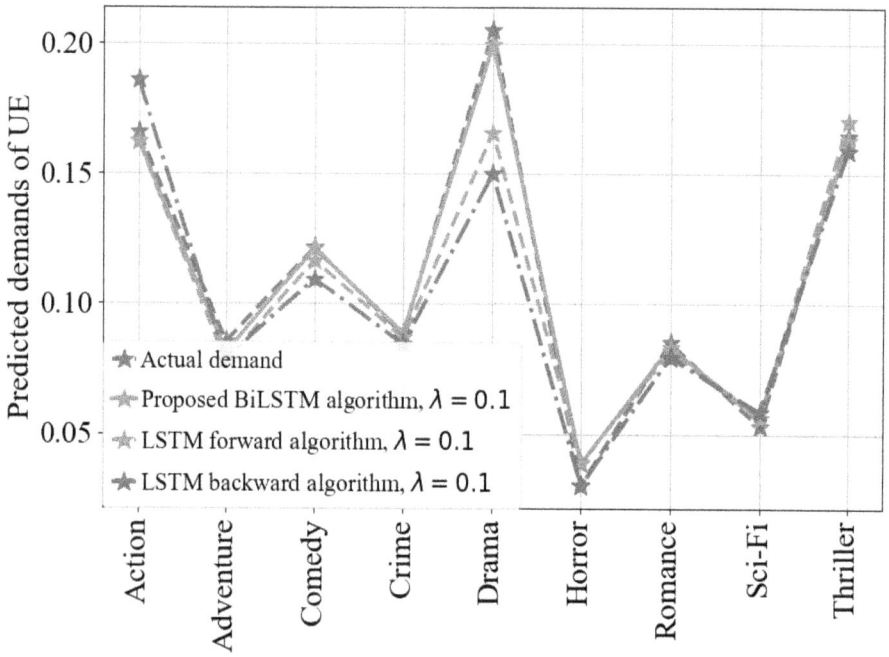

Fig. 3. User content request prediction vs learning rate ($\lambda = 0.1$).

Figure 4, compares UE cluster results with values of $\zeta = 1$ and $\zeta = 1.6$. In the figure, the two numbers in the bracket represent the user ID and request content ID of the user. For instance, Fig. $(40, 12)$ represents that, the content demand of UE_{40} is file $f = 12$. In Fig. 4(a), UE_{40} is clustered with $(7, 14)$ and $(2, 3)$, indicating that UE_2, UE_7, and UE_{40} are grouped based on their geographical location despite differences in their requested content. However, in Fig. 4(b), UE_{40} is clustered with UEs that are both geographically close and have similar content demands, such as $(15, 12)$, $(30, 12)$, $(31, 12)$, and $(51, 12)$. Generally, in

4(b) more UEs with similar content requests are grouped into clusters, emphasizing the influence of user content requests on clustering. The black stars in the figures indicate the positions of the deployed UAVs.

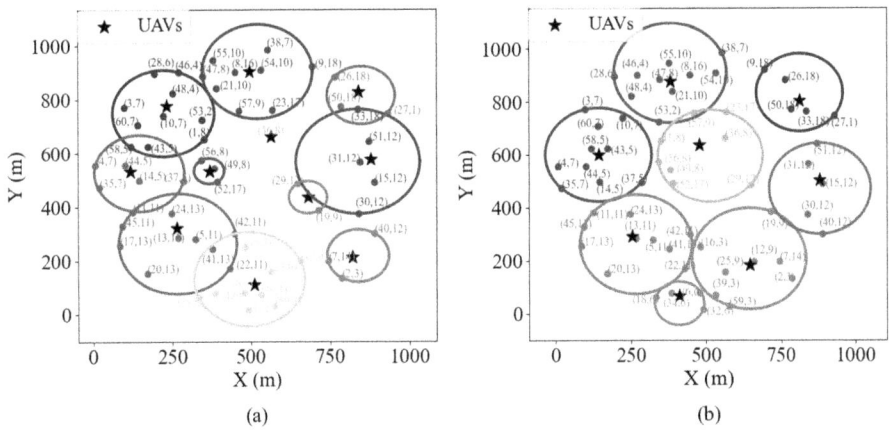

Fig. 4. UE clustering result ((a) $\zeta = 1$ and (b) $\zeta = 1.6$).

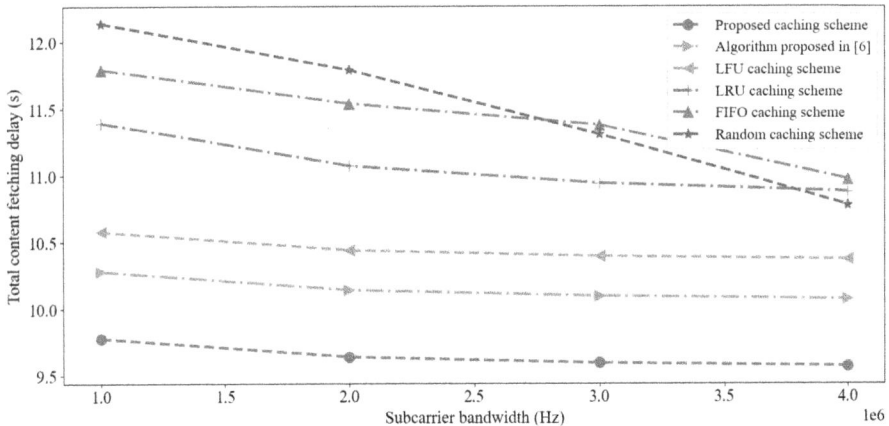

Fig. 5. Total content fetching delay vs subcarrier bandwidth.

Figure 5, plots the total content fetching delay versus bandwidth. The figure presents a comparison of the proposed BiLSTM algorithm against the baseline algorithms, namely, the caching scheme proposed in [6], least frequently used (LFU), least recently used (LRU), first-out (FIFO), and random caching schemes. To evaluate the performance we use the cluster result $\zeta = 1.6$, and utilize the predicted user requests based on the proposed BiLSTM algorithm. It can be observed that the total content fetching delay decreases as bandwidth increases. Moreover, in comparison to the baseline algorithms, our proposed algorithm achieves the lowest overall content caching delay. This outcome indicates that our proposed algorithms offer the most efficient caching performance. The reason is that our proposed content caching algorithm caches contents that reduce backhaul delay, resulting in an overall reduction of content fetching delay.

In Fig. 6, we evaluate the performance of our proposed algorithms for various UAV cache sizes. The figure plots the total content fetching delay versus the total power of the UAVs. As can be seen from the figure, the total content fetching delay decreases as power increases. Similarly, as the cache size of the UAV increases the overall content fetching delay decreases.

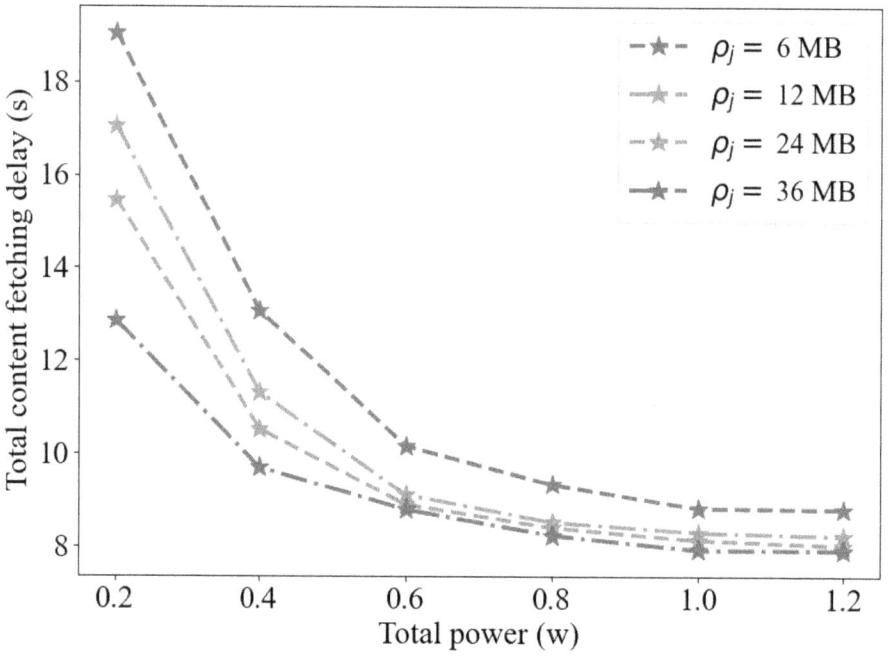

Fig. 6. Total content fetching delay vs UAVs cache sizes.

Figure 7 plots content fetching delay versus cache sizes of the UAVs for various minimum data rates of UEs. As can be seen from the figure, the total content fetching delay decreases as UAV cache size increases. Similarly, as the cache size required minimum data rate of UEs increases the overall content fetching delay of UEs decreases. This is because as the minimum required data rate for each UE increases our proposed power allocation strategy efficiently allocate transmission power for the UEs. This, in turn, lead to reduced overall content fetching delay.

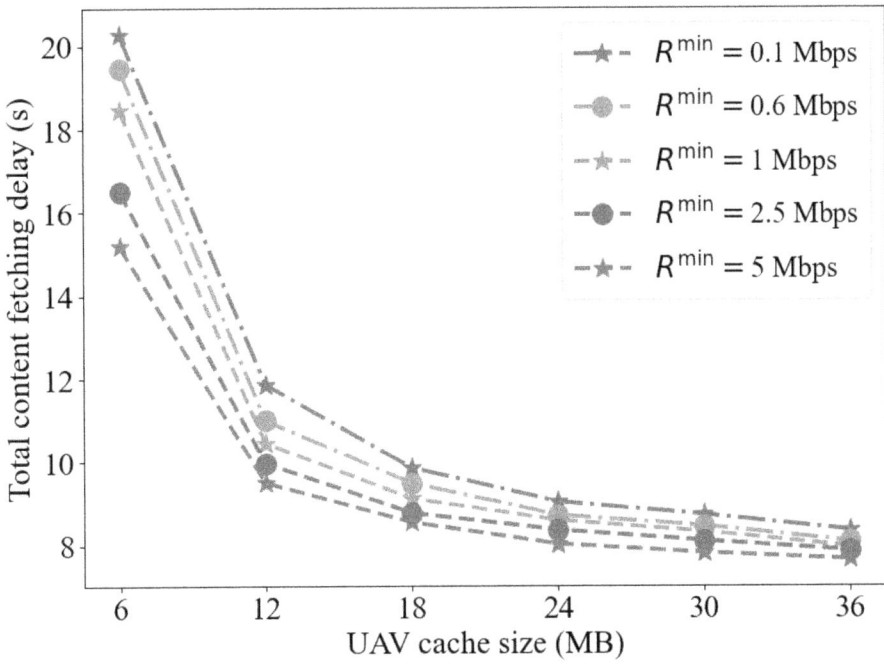

Fig. 7. Total content fetching delay vs UAVs cache sizes.

8 Conclusions

In this paper, we have studied UAV deployment, proactive content caching, and power allocation problems in UAV-enabled networks. Considering the scenario where user content requests are unknown, we developed a BiLSTM-based user request prediction algorithm. Based on the obtained user request prediction and by introducing a content fetching delay function, the joint UE clustering, UAV deployment, content caching, and power allocation problem is formulated as a delay minimization optimization problem, which is solved by applying a heuristic algorithm. Simulation results have shown the effectiveness of the UE clustering, UAV deployment, and content caching strategies in reducing the overall content fetching delay and improving caching performance. In future work, we may extend our current work to a scenario where UAV mobility is considered, and their trajectory is optimized to enhance content-fetching services for UEs. As BiLSTM models rely on fixed-size hidden states, which might not effectively capture variable-length dependencies in sequences, the BiLSTM-based user request prediction can be further studied by considering the request history of users that spans different lengths.

References

1. Khan, M.A., et al.: A survey on mobile edge computing for video streaming: opportunities and challenges. IEEE Access **10**, 120514–120550 (2022). https://doi.org/10.1109/ACCESS.2022.3220694
2. Li, L., Zhao, G., Blum, R.S.: A survey of caching techniques in cellular networks: research issues and challenges in content placement and delivery strategies. IEEE Commun. Surv. Tuts. **20**(3), 1710–1732 (2018). https://doi.org/10.1109/COMST.2018.2820021
3. Li, B., Fei, Z., Zhang, Y.: UAV communications for 5G and beyond: recent advances and future trends. IEEE Internet Things J. **6**(2), 2241–2263 (2019). https://doi.org/10.1109/JIOT.2018.2887086
4. Bhuyan, A.K., Dutta, H., Biswas, S.: Towards a UAV-centric content caching architecture for communication-challenged environments. In: IEEE Global Communications Conference, pp. 468-473, Rio de Janeiro, Brazil, (2022). https://doi.org/10.1109/GLOBECOM48099.2022.10001616
5. Khuwaja, A.A., Zhu, Y., Zheng, G., Chen, Y., Liu, W.: Performance analysis of hybrid UAV networks for probabilistic content caching. IEEE Syst. J. **15**(3), 4013–4024 (2021). https://doi.org/10.1109/JSYST.2020.3013786
6. Kang, M.W., Chung, Y.W.: Content caching based on popularity and priority of content using seq2seq LSTM in ICN. IEEE Access **11**, 16831–16842 (2023). https://doi.org/10.1109/ACCESS.2023.3245803. https://doi.org/10.1109/LWC.2021.3124943
7. Li, D., Zhang, H., Li, T., Ding, H., Yuan, D.: Community detection and attention-weighted federated learning based proactive edge caching for D2D-assisted wireless networks. IEEE Trans. Wirel. Commun. **22**, 7287–7303 (2023). https://doi.org/10.1109/TWC.2023.3249756
8. Wang, E., Dong, Q., Li, Y., Zhang, Y.: Content placement considering the temporal and spatial attributes of content popularity in cache-enabled UAV networks. IEEE Wirel. Commun. **11**(2), 250–253 (2022). https://doi.org/10.1109/LWC.2021.3124943
9. Jiang, B., Yang, J., Xu, H., Song, H., Zheng, G.: Multimedia data throughput maximization in internet-of-things system based on optimization of cache-enabled UAV. IEEE Internet Things J. **6**(2), 3525–3532 (2019). https://doi.org/10.1109/JIOT.2018.2886964
10. Wang, Y., Feng, C., Zhang, T., Liu, Y., Nallanathan, A.: QoE based network deployment and caching placement for cache-enabling UAV networks. In IEEE International Conference on Communications (ICC), pp. 1-6, Dublin, Ireland (2020). https://doi.org/10.1109/ICC40277.2020.9149163
11. Zhang, H., Tang W., Peng, J.: Performance analysis of cooperative caching and transmission diversity in cache-enabled UAV networks. IEEE Trans. Wirel. Commun., 1-1 (2023). https://doi.org/10.1109/TWC.2023.3318110
12. Yin, Y., Liu, M., Gui, G., Gacanin, H., Sari, H., Adachi, F.: Cross-layer resource allocation for UAV-assisted wireless caching networks with NOMA. IEEE Trans. Veh. Technol. **70**(4), 3428–3438 (2021). https://doi.org/10.1109/TVT.2021.3064032
13. Bera, A., Misra, S., Chatterjee, C.: QoE analysis in cache-enabled multi-UAV networks. IEEE Trans. Veh. Technol. **69**(6), 6680–6687 (2020). https://doi.org/10.1109/TVT.2020.2985933

14. Do-Duy, T., Nguyen, L.D., Duong, T.Q., Khosravirad, S.R., Claussen, H.: Joint optimization of real-time deployment and resource allocation for UAV-aided disaster emergency communications. IEEE J. Sel. Areas Commun. **39**(11), 3411–3424 (2021). https://doi.org/10.1109/JSAC.2021.3088662
15. Chen, Y., Zhang, H., Hu, Y.: Optimal power and bandwidth allocation for multiuser video streaming in UAV relay networks. IEEE Trans. Veh. Technol. **69**(6), 6644–6655 (2020). https://doi.org/10.1109/TVT.2020.2985061
16. Kalantari, E., Yanikomeroglu, H., Yongacoglu, A.: Wireless networks with cache-enabled and backhaul-limited aerial base stations. IEEE Trans. Wirel. Commun. **19**(11), 7363–7376 (2020). https://doi.org/10.1109/TWC.2020.3010845
17. Zhou, F., Wang, N., Luo, G., Fan, L., Chen, W.: Edge caching in multi-UAV-enabled radio access networks: 3D modeling and spectral efficiency optimization. IEEE Trans. Signal Inf. Process. Netw. **6**, 329–341 (2020). https://doi.org/10.1109/TSIPN.2020.2986360
18. Duistermaat, J.J., Kolk, J.A.C.: Taylor expansion in several variables. Distributions: Theory and applications. Birkhäuser Boston, Boston (2010)
19. Harper, F.M., Konstan, J.A.: The MovieLens datasets: history and context. ACM Trans. Interact. Intell. Syst **5**, 2160–6455 (2016)

Low Power VLSI Architecture for Rail To Rail Dynamic Voltage Comparator

S. Karunakaran[(✉)][iD], S. Srivardhan[iD], M. Harshith[iD], and K. SaiManish[iD]

Vardhaman College of Engineering, Hyderabad 501218, India
{s.karunakaran,samalasrivardhan20ece,moredddyharshithreddy20ece,
kawlaskarsaimanish20ece}@vardhaman.org

Abstract. Rail to Rail Dynamic Voltage Comparator (RRDVC) works on very low voltages which is constructed and developed using cadence virtuoso tool. Here 90nm technology was used to construct and analyse the 3 different architectures of Rail to Rail Dynamic Voltage Comparators.Here Three different architectures are made by varying the stages with NOT of AND and NOT of OR. The power dissipation, delay and the power delay products(PDP) are compared for the three different architectures developed by varying the inputs. Comparator circuit takes the analog signal , reference voltage and the clock signal as input and gives the outputs as digital signals with 0's and 1's. not operation of AND and not operation of OR based stages are arranged as per requirement to obtain the three different architectures and the outputs of these stages are combined using latch circuits. The outputs are obtained for different frequencies of input analog signals with the different reference voltage. All these architectures are implemented using basic CMOS transistors. The power dissipations obtained here are 1.9×10^{-6}W , 19×10^{-12}W and 1.7×10^{-6}W for the RRDVC with NOT of AND and OR , NOT of NAND, and NOT of OR based stages respectively. The architecture with NOT of AND stages provides less power when compared to the other architectures.

Keywords: Dynamic comparator · low voltage · RR-DVC · CMOS · low power · PUN-Pull Up Network · PDN-Pull Down network · VGS-Gate to Source Voltage · Cadence Virtuoso

1 Introduction

A Rail-to-Rail Dynamic Voltage Comparator is a specialized type of comparator that overcomes some of the limitations of standard comparators. As the name suggests, it operates with a rail-to-rail input and output voltage range, meaning it can accept and provide output signals that are close to the power supply rails. This feature makes them highly desirable in applications where the input voltage can vary across the full range of the power supply voltage. Using NOT of AND and NOT of OR gates is cost-effective and simpler to manufacture, making them the preferred building blocks for digital logic circuits in integrated circuits (ICs).

2 Fully-Synthesizable Dynamic Voltage Comparators

It has been noted that transistor current contention affects fully synthesizable dynamic voltage comparators. Lower voltages improperly force NAND gates' outputs in NAND-based stages at the circuit power supply, regardless of the input (the comparator stops working as a result). Hence the project is designed to overcome the current contention and which works at low power, at last use of low power increases the speed of the circuit and gives good outcome.

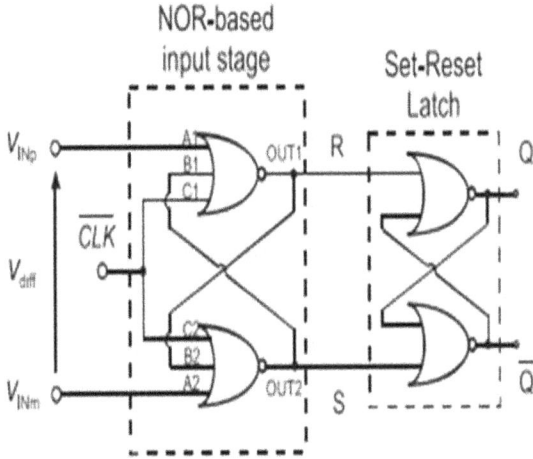

Fig. 1. Fully Synthesizable DVC with not operation of AND using set reset latch.

The DVC in Fig. 1 receives the digital output during the rising edge of the clock signal. The not operation of OR-based stage is created so that the digital output is accessible during the rising edge.

The logic switching and the differential voltage at the analogue input are used to determine the polarity. Reducing the voltage levels of OUT1 and OUT2 within the DVC could lead to a diminished driving capacity and logic levels. The driving by the analogue inputs causes the current in the transistor load terminals of 1st PUN and 2nd PUN to counteract. For the purpose of lowering the common mode input voltage, the Vsg of 1st PUN transistor and 2nd PUN transistor is raised. The current opposes the dropping transients of OUT1 and OUT2.

2.1 Limitations of Dynamic Voltage Comparators:

- Noise Sensitivity
- Propagation Delay
- Offset Voltage
- Limited Input Range
- Power Consumption
- Current Contentions

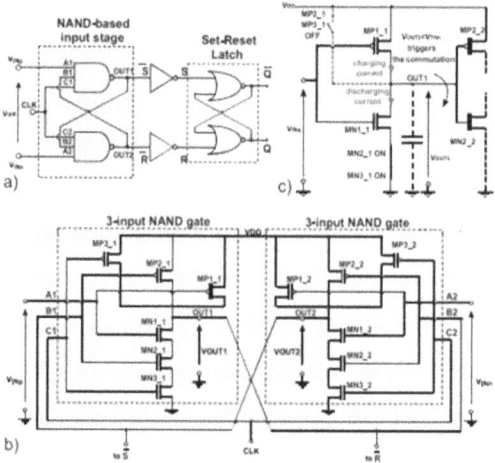

Fig. 2. DVC with not operation of AND based stages a) logic-level and b) transistor-level implementation, c) same circuit during output switching.

2.2 Related Works

Standard-Cell Based: Utilize digital standard cells, enabling design automation and integration with digital circuits. Offer low power and scalability but may suffer from process variations and limited performance.

Analog Based: Employ traditional analog design techniques, achieving higher performance but with larger area and increased design complexity.

3 Existing Architecture of Rail to Rail Dynamic Voltage Comparators:

The RR-DVC in Fig. 3a overrides the circuits of completely synthesizable DV Comparators given in Figs. 1 and 2a half-swing common-mode constraints. According to this picture, the RR-DVC combines the digital outputs of the not operation of AND3 and not operation of OR3-based DVCs in a similar way as traditional rail-to-rail analogue operational amplifiers combine an CMOS transistors differential pair into push-pull differential pair.

Outputs of the not operation of AND Based stage and the not operation of OR based Stage are combined using set-rest latch, a bistable multivibrator. The first stable condition is high output, whereas the second is low production. A Latch has a feedback route that allows information to be maintained by any device.

The Existing Architecture will result in higher power consumption hence new architectures are formed by changing both the input stages with the NOT of AND stages. Usually NOT of AND consumes less power than the NOT of OR because power supplied to NOT of AND pmos transistors are connected parallel consumes less power whereas NOT of OR consumes more power as pmos transistors connected in series.

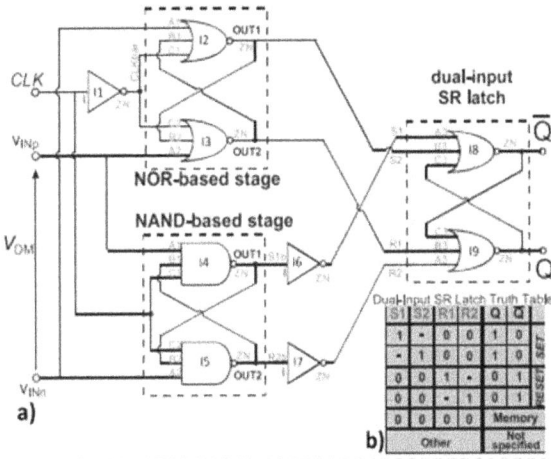

Fig. 3. Existing fully-synthesizable RR-DVC with not operation of AND3 and not operation of OR3 based stages a) logic-level implementation b) logic table of the Set-Reset latch

3.1 Limitations of the Existing RR-DVC:

Higher Power Consumption: RR-DVCs generally consume more power compared to standard DVCs due to the additional circuitry required for railto-rail operation. The extended input and output voltage range necessitates more complex design and increased power dissipation.

Increased Complexity: RR-DVCs have a more intricate design to achieve rail-to-rail functionality, which can make them more challenging to implement and potentially increase the risk of design errors.

Higher Cost: Due to their increased complexity and specialized functionality, RR-DVCs are generally more expensive than standard DVCs.

4 Proposed Architecture of the Rail to Rail Dynamic Voltage Comparator:

It is almost similar to the existing architecture, in the proposed architecture, not operation of AND3 and not operation of OR3 based stages are replaced with the not operation of AND3 based Stages. RR-DVC sum up or merges the digital results of the two not operation of AND3-based stages. Set-Reset latch is used to mix the outputs of these stages as shown in Fig. 4. Set-Reset Latch is a bistable multivibrator. The first stable condition is high output, whereas the second is low production. A Latch has a feedback route that allows information to be maintained by any device. This circuit is implemented in the cadence virtuoso tool in the 90nm technology. Then the Comparator outputs are obtained. Power can also be calculated using cadence virtuoso tool.

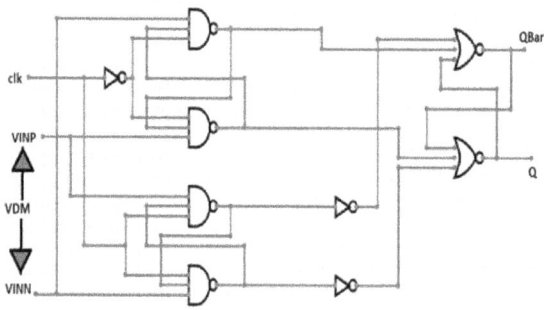

Fig. 4. Block Diagram of Proposed RR-DVC with not operation of AND3- based stages.

Table 1. Truth Table of Proposed Architecture

Clk	Vinp	S1	S2	R1	R2	Q	Qbar
0	x	0	0	0	0	Memory	Memory
1	>vinn	1	x	0	0	1	0
1	>vinn	x	1	0	0	1	0
1	<vinn	0	0	1	x	1	0
1	<vinn	0	0	x	1	1	0

The next proposed architecture is also similar to the existing RR-DVC. Here not operation of AND3 and not operation of OR3-based stages from the existing architecture are replaced with the NOR based stages and these outputs are combined using Set-Reset Latch as shown in the Fig. 5. Set-Reset Latch, a Bistable Multivibrator used to combine the NOR based stages. The Results of the Set-Reset bistable multivibrator are Q and Qbar and the inputs are the outputs of the not operation of OR3-based stages (Table 1).

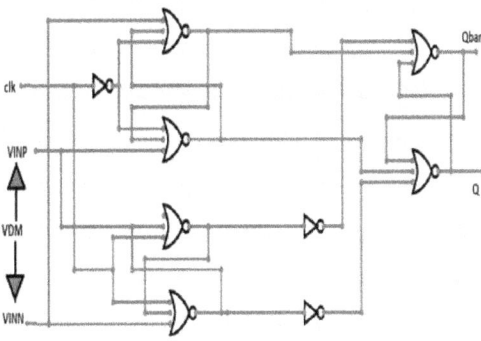

Fig. 5. Block Diagram of Proposed RR-DVC with not operation of OR3-based stages.

The cadence virtuoso tool with 90nm technology was used to develop completely synthesizable dynamic voltage comparators with not operation of AND3-based input stages (NAND-DVC) and completely synthesizable dynamic voltage comparators with not operation of OR3-based stages. The crucial elements of analog-to-digital converters can operate across a wide span of supply voltage values, primarily influenced by the sensor's maximum input voltage.

The sensor input used to determine the step size changes determines the reference voltage. The circuit's high speed operating in the 1GHz band makes it appropriate for flash ADC. The supply voltage ranges from 0.6 to 1.2 V. If the supply voltage falls, the driving capacity drops.

The driving power of the circuit is also impacted by the leakage current. As a result, the suggested design is tailored, and a digital standard cell-based module is made as part of the ADC integration process. When using a speed greater than 5GHz, several restrictions are observed. Power grows, yet at little sacrifice. This circuit is executed in its entirety with a very small footprint and under full synthesizability. When compared to CMOS, the switching speed of FinFET is faster. Therefore, by raising the Vgs of the PUN transistor gates, the common-mode input voltage is decreased (Table 2).

5 Results and Outputs

Existing RR-DVC produces power dissipation of $1.927 \times 10\text{-}6W$ While the Rail to Rail Dynamic Voltage Comparator with NAND Based stages produces power dissipation of $19.08 \times 10\text{-}12W$ and RR-DVC with NOR based stages produces a power dissipation of $1.796 \times 10\text{-}6W$. The NAND-based DVC is quite effective when compared to the NAND, NOR, and RR-DVC performance. The suggested NAND logic work base performs better (Fig. 6).

High output occurs when the voltage at the non-inverting input surpasses that at the inverting input. Conversely, low output is observed when the voltage

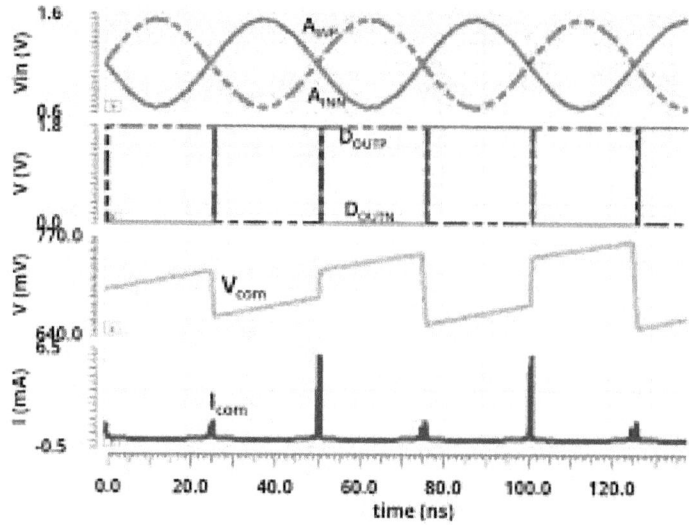

Fig. 6. Output of RR-DVC with NAND Based Stages

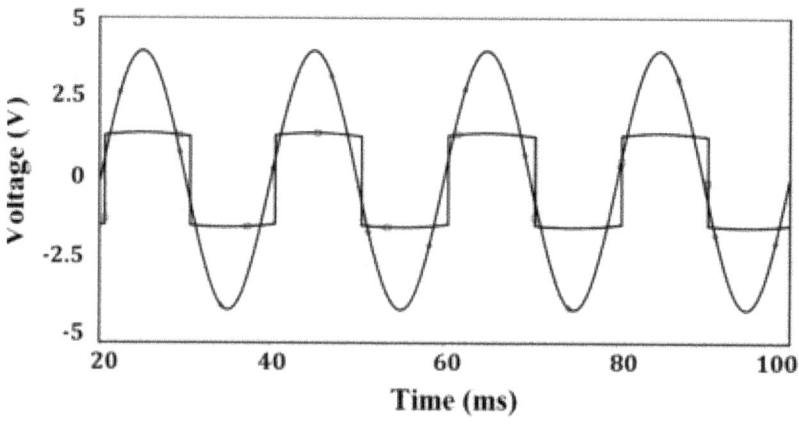

Fig. 7. Output of RR-DVC with NOR Based Stages

at the inverting input equals or exceeds that at the non-inverting input. Certain designs may feature a variable threshold voltage instead of a direct reference to VDD or VSS (Fig. 7).

Table 2. Comparative Analysis of three circuits

$Existing RRDVC$	$Proposed RRDVC1$	$Proposed RRDVC2$
power = 1.927×10^{-6} W	power = 19.08×10^{-12} W	power = 1.796×10^{-6} W
Delay = 103 ps	Delay = 115 ps	Delay = 107 ps
PDP = 198.481×10^{-18}	PDP = 1984.32×10^{-24}	PDP = 192.172×10^{-18}
Dual SR latch is used.	Dual SR latch is used.	Dual SR latch is used.
Consumes more power	Consumes less power	Consumes same power as the existing one.
Both NAND and NOR based Stages are used.	Only NAND Based stage is used.	Only NOR Based stage is used.

6 Conclusion

Hence both existing and proposed Rail to Rail Dynamic Voltage Comparators are designed. Hence it is observed from the obtained graphs that, Rail to Rail Dynamic Voltage Comparator (i.e., proposed model) dissipates less power when compared to existing method. Hence Proposed RR-DVC gives around 80% lesser power when compared to Existing Rail to RR-DVC. In circuits with low amplitude signals, the design of the comparator becomes critically important. ADCs use comparators at the input step of the transformation process. To achieve faster operation and lower power consumption, data converters require efficient circuit designs.

References

1. O. Aiello, P. Crovetti, L. Lin, and M. Alioto, "Rail-to-Rail Dynamic Voltage Comparator Scalable Down to pW-Range Power and 0.15-V Supply," IEEE TRANSACTIONS ON CIRCUITS AND SYSTEMS-II: EXPRESS BRIEFS, VOL. 68, NO. 7, JULY 2021
2. Chevella, S., O'Hare, D., O'Connell, I.: A low-power 1-V supply dynamic comparator. IEEE Solid State Circuits Lett. **3**, 154–157 (2020)
3. Weaver, S., Hershberg, B., Moon, U.-K.: Digitally synthesized stochastic flash ADC using only standard digital cells. IEEE Trans. Circuits Syst. I, Reg. Pap. **61**(1), 84-91 (2014)
4. Gao, J., Li, G., Li, Q.: High-speed low-power common-mode insensitive dynamic comparator. Electron. Lett. **51**(2), 134–136 (2015)

Enhanced Semantic Communication in 6G Networks Using DCGAN

Sowmya Sri Nalluri[✉], G. A. E. Satish Kumar, Dileep Kumar Arumulla, and Vinod Kumar Auti

Department of ECE, Vardhaman College of Engineering,
Hyderabad, Telangana, India
sowmyasn2003@gmail.com, gaesathi@vardhaman.org

Abstract. Semantic communication diverges from Shannon's communication theory by prioritizing the semantic essence of data over its step-by-step reconstruction at the receiver's end, signifying its potential to shape the future of mobile communication. This approach aims to address the limitations posed by finite bandwidth in transmitting information for modern, high-volume multimedia applications. Leveraging the integration of AI technology with 6G networks, it provides complete communication systems built on semantic communication concepts. This research focuses on creating an end-to-end picture transmission system based on semantic communication by investigating important design factors that are linked with physical channel features.

To achieve transmission of realistic images from semantically segmented inputs, previously trained DCGAN (Deep Convolutional Generative Adversarial Network) model is used at the target end., trained using COCO-Stuff dataset for both receiver DCGAN (decoder) and transmitter semantic segmentation (encoder). Notably, the study unveils that broadcasting semantic segmentation maps, rather than actual images, across the physical channel yields substantial resource gains, particularly in bandwidth conservation compared to conventional communication methods. Additionally, the research delves into examining the effects of quantization noise and physical channel irregularities on multimedia content transfer facilitated by semantic communication.

Keywords: Semantic Communications · Deep Convolutional Generative Adversarial Network (DCGAN) · Encoder and Decoder

1 Introduction

The progress in wireless sensor networks (WSNs), Internet of Things (IoT), and the increasing volume of multimedia traffic pose sustainability challenges in the administration of communication networks. The complexity amplifies bandwidth and energy demands, urging integration of sustainability measures. Semantic communication emerges as a solution, aiming to [9] convey information meaningfully, reducing physical bandwidth. While beneficial for high-bandwidth applications like video streaming, its cost-effectiveness the situation with machine-to-machine (M2M) communication is less clear. However, incorporating semantic communication promises longer operational periods for battery-powered gadgets and less complexity [22].

Traditional communication focused on minimal error transmission based on Shannon's capacity limit. Semantic communication prioritizes conveying intended meaning, [18]often overlooked in traditional systems. For instance, a system proposed for image transmission through mobile channels extracts a semantic map, transmitting only essential information rather than the entire image, thus reducing data volume without compromising quality [3].

DCGAN-Based Semantic Communication System: A DCGAN-based semantic communication system for picture transmission was created employing Polar codes as the channel coding in order to overcome sustainability concerns. [20] Evaluation in various noisy scenarios showed its superior performance over JPEG compression, promising in both human perception and technical efficiency. These findings support its real-world implementation.

The escalating demands on communication networks necessitate sustainable solutions. [1] Semantic communication offers a promising approach by focusing on conveying meaning, not just data, showcasing potential for reducing bandwidth and energy consumption in various applications, with implications for future network designs and sustainability measures.

Polar Codes for Channel Coding: One kind of linear block error-correcting code is the polar code. The code creation process converts the physical channel into virtual outer channels by means of numerous recursive concatenation of a brief kernel code. They are used in the DCGAN-based semantic communication system for channel coding.

2 Objectives

- Create advanced semantic communication systems that prioritize the transmission of data's inherent semantic essence over traditional methods, revolutionizing the way information is exchanged in mobile communication networks.
- Address the urgent bandwidth limitations faced by contemporary high-volume multimedia applications by developing efficient and bandwidth-friendly techniques for data transmission and reconstruction [1].
- Incorporate cutting-edge artificial intelligence technologies into 6G communication networks to enhance the understanding of data semantics and context, enabling more intelligent and context-aware communication.

3 Literature Review

In 2016, the Journal of Circuits and Systems published "Binary phase shift keying digital modulation technique for noiseless and noisy transmission," volume 5, number 3, pages 24–30.

This research investigates Binary Phase Shift Keying (BPSK) Digital Modulation for Noiseless and Noisy Transmission, with an emphasis on (i) constructing a BPSK system, (ii) proving modulation/demodulation using noiseless channels, and (iii) demonstrating the same approach in noisy channels. The study and simulations use a model-based method in Matlab/Simulink to assess the system's efficacy and requirements. However, in noisy transmission channels, mistakes might arise in the demodulated bits, showing the influence of channel noise on the operation [2].

6G white paper on machine learning in wireless communication networks," released in 2020

This white paper investigates the integration of machine learning (ML) into wireless communications, specifically in the context of 6G networks. These networks are set to power societal digital changes by providing ubiquitous, stable, and ultra-fast wireless access for both humans and machines. Recent advances in ML research have sparked new innovations like driverless vehicles and voice assistants, powered by powerful ML models, enormous datasets, and strong computational capabilities.

As the demand for connectivity escalates, innovation within 6G wireless networks becomes imperative. ML tools emerge as pivotal solutions in addressing wireless domain challenges. The paper outlines the envisioned impact of ML on wireless communication systems, highlighting key ML methodologies applicable to wireless networks. It delves into problem-solving aspects across network layers-physical, medium access, and application-using ML techniques. Notably, it explores zero-touch optimization of wireless networks, a compelling facet. Each section concludes by posing crucial research questions pertinent to its scope [13].

I. Goodfellow, J. Pouget-Abadie, M. Mirza, B. Xu, D. Warde-Farley, S. Ozair, A. Courville, and Y. Bengio, "Generative adversarial networks," Commun. ACM, vol. 63, no. 11, pp. 139–144, 2020:

We can outline a novel approach to training generative models that involves employing an adversarial setup consisting of two models working simultaneously: A generative model, labeled as G, is intended to understand the intrinsic data distribution, whereas a discriminative model, denoted as D, is constructed for the same reason. Tasked with distinguishing between samples originating from the training data and those generated by G. G's training focuses on maximizing D's mistake rate, which results in a minimax game. In the realm of potential functions represented by G and D, a unique solution arises: G replicates the data distribution, while D consistently approaches an output of 1/2. By utilizing multilayer perceptrons to define G and D, the complete system may be trained with backpropagation, eliminating the requirement for Markov chains or approximation inference networks.

Summary: Studied about the Generative adversarial networks

The Mathematical Theory of Communication was published in 1949 by the University of Illinois Press in Champaign.

During the Manhattan Project in the 1940s, rural Anderson County, Tennessee, transformed into Oak Ridge. A research project conducted in Oak Ridge investigated how transitioning from rural to urban land use impacts street tree diversity, soil characteristics, and nutrient dynamics. Of 607 street trees across five main roads, Acer rubrum (21.91%) and Pyrus calleryana (19.93%) were predominant. Chemical soil properties notably influenced tree performance, while soil characteristics varied between streets but not due to traffic. Seasonal differences in soil microbial biomass and nutrient levels were observed.

4 Proposed Method

Shannon's theory served as the inspiration for the three-layered theoretical model that forms the foundation of the Semantic Communication-Based Image Transmission System's design. Positioned within the semantic layer are the semantic encoder and decoder components. [10]managing semantic feature extraction and interpretation using a shared knowledge base. The encoder interprets the message's intent, while the decoder extracts meaning from received semantic symbols through mutual knowledge [14].

The physical layer, below the semantic layer, handles bit-level transmission and channel data optimization. Above, the application layer manages task-specific aspects of incoming messages, involving classification, object detection, and scene prediction [21].

The system leverages the COCO dataset as its shared knowledge base, while the COCOStuff subset aids in pre-training the DCGAN. This repository encompasses images for object detection and captioning, featuring 20 pre-trained semantic object classes for the experiment's GAN [15] (Fig. 1).

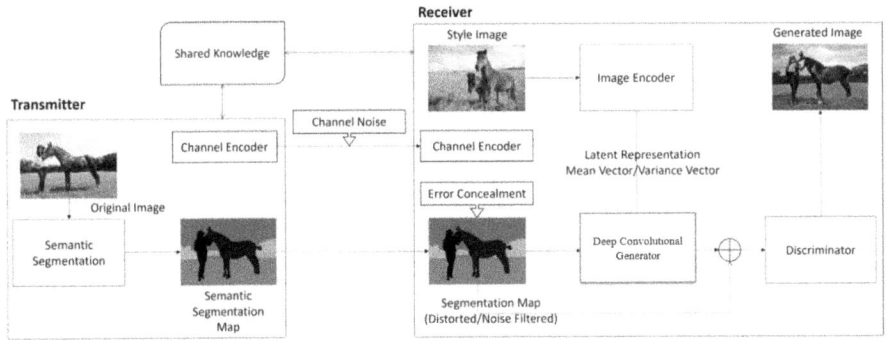

Fig. 1. Proposed Method.

Employing data from the aforementioned dataset, the study generates segmented semantic maps, focusing on ten representative images showcasing diverse subjects. [11] Classification at the receiver is a task within the application layer, categorizing objects based on the GAN's training.

Losses are computed and fed back through the system during the learning process, with each epoch improving both the generator and discriminator more. [12] The discriminator's goal is to improve the value function V(D,G) by accurately categorizing actual pictures (where D(s) approaches 1) and decreasing the classification of fraudulent images. [16] The generator aims to deceive the discriminator into thinking that the images are real, so that there is a lower chance that the discriminator will accurately identify them as created (Table 1).

Table 1. Channel Decoding Specifications

S.No	Parameter	Value
1.	Channel n/Decoder	Polar Codes
2.	Information Bits	2048
3.	Codeword Bits	4096
4.	Code Rate	1/2
5.	Modulation	BPSK
6.	Bits per symbol	2
7.	Demaping Method	Log-liklihood ratios
8.	Channel	AWGN

Polar codes, indicated as PC(M, L), have the power to convert physical channels into dependable or unreliable virtual channels, especially as the code length approaches infinity. For example, a polar code with parameters M = 8192 and L = 4096 is modulated with Binary Phase Shift Keying (BPSK) over an Additive White Gaussian Noise (AWGN) channel to achieve a required Eb/No ratio of 2.5 dB. The receiver's decoder then uses the received noisy Log-Likelihood Ratios (LLRs) to construct approximation codewords, using the suggested practical code validation processes included into the semantic communication system.

4.1 Advantages

– In line with semantic communication principles, the project focuses on conveying the semantic substance of data rather than step-by-step reconstruction. [17] Transferring more significant information is made possible by this prioritizing, particularly when dealing with high-volume multimedia applications [7].
– Significant resource savings are achieved by the initiative, especially in terms of bandwidth conservation, by broadcasting semantic segmentation maps across the physical channel rather than real pictures. [4] This is a significant benefit for resolving the issues caused by current communication networks' limited capacity [19].

– To facilitate the transmission of realistic images from semantically segmented inputs, a pre-trained DCGAN network is used on both the transmitter encoder and the receiver decoder. This method efficiently reduces data consumption while retaining the quality of delivered photographs [6].

5 Results

Fig. 2. The input picture refers to the original image intended for transmission, which serves as the starting point for future processing processes.

The project effectively illustrates the efficient use of DCGAN-enabled enhanced semantic communication in 6G communications networks. [8] Semantically segmenting the input image, which generates a semantically segmented image displaying important features. Using a pre-trained DCGAN network, the system leverages semantic segmentation to generate a realistic output image, demonstrating the potential for communicating important information with less input. The project's success is attributed to the integrated three-layer model, which is in accordance with Shannon's theory and efficiently handles bit-level transmission, task-specific components, and semantic essence prioritizing. [5] Overall, these results emphasize the advantages of semantic communication, especially its ability to minimize bandwidth, and incorporate AI technology, making it a viable option for the next-generation mobile communication networks (see Figs. 2, 3, 4, 5).

Fig. 3. Semantic Segmented Image. This image is the output of the semantic segmentation, which involves creating a semantic map and extracting the features which are essential.

Fig. 4. Generated Output Image. The DCGAN network tries to produce an image which is close to the actual image that has to be transmitted.

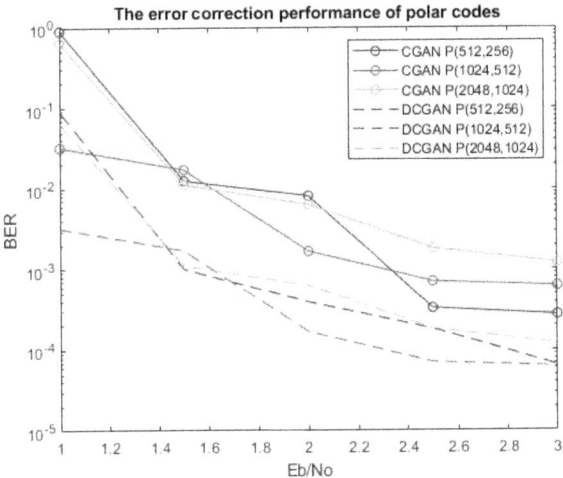

Fig. 5. The Polar codes error correction capability demonstrates the relationship between signal-to-noise ratio and capacity to repair mistakes.

6 Conclusion

In conclusion, by implementing semantic essence prior to step-by-step reconstruction, the proposed Enhanced Semantic Communication in 6G Networks Using DCGAN presents an extensive approach to transform mobile communication networks. Using a three-layer paradigm built around Shannon's theory, the system employs an application layer for handling task-specific characteristics, a physical layer that transmits information at the bit-level, and a semantic encoder and decoder for feature extraction. The integration of pre-training DCGAN with the COCO dataset and COCOStuff subset demonstrates an excellent foundation for object detection and captioning. The system's efficiency is demonstrated by the generation of segmented semantic maps and the classification that follows at the application layer's receiver. Polar Codes for channel encoding/decoding are a viable and optimal solution for both dependable and unreliable virtual channels. Through each epoch, the system is refined by learning, which is powered by the min-max formulation for the discriminator and generator. The discriminator attempts to correctly classify genuine images, whereas the generator attempts to fool by producing convincing images. Robustness, great efficiency, and the possibility of deep-level implementation are some benefits of the suggested approach.

According to the research, by fusing technology and artificial intelligence, semantic communication in 6G networks has the ability to completely transform the transmission of multimedia material. Semantic segmentation maps are an effective way to conserve resources, especially bandwidth. This is demonstrated by their adoption. An in-depth understanding of how semantic communication affects multimedia material transfer is made possible by examining issues like quantization noise.

References

1. Ali, S., et al.: 6G white paper on machine learning in wireless communication networks. arXiv preprint: arXiv:2004.13875 (2020)
2. Creswell, A., White, T., Dumoulin, V., Arulkumaran, K., Sengupta, B., Bharath, A.A.: Generative adversarial networks: an overview. IEEE Sig. Process. Mag. **35**(1), 53–65 (2018)
3. Dong, P., Qihui, W., Zhang, X., Ding, G.: Edge semantic cognitive intelligence for 6G networks: novel theoretical models, enabling framework, and typical applications. China Commun. **19**(8), 1–14 (2022)
4. Hu, H., Zhu, X., Zhou, F., Wu, W., Hu, R.Q., Zhu, H.: One-to-many semantic communication systems: design, implementation, performance evaluation. IEEE Commun. Lett. **26**(12), 2959–2963 (2022)
5. Huang, D., Gao, F., Tao, X., Qiyuan, D., Jianhua, L.: Toward semantic communications: Deep learning-based image semantic coding. IEEE J. Sel. Areas Commun. **41**(1), 55–71 (2022)
6. Huang, D., Tao, X., Gao, F., Lu, J.: Deep learning-based image semantic coding for semantic communications. In: 2021 IEEE Global Communications Conference (GLOBECOM), pp. 1–6. IEEE (2021)
7. Iyer, S., et al.: A survey on semantic communications for intelligent wireless networks. Wireless Pers. Commun. **129**(1), 569–611 (2023)
8. Jiang, P., Wen, C.K., Jin, S., Li, G.Y.: Wireless semantic communications for video conferencing. IEEE J. Sel. Areas Commun. **41**(1), 230–244 (2022)
9. Omijeh, B., Oteheri, T.: Binary phase shift keying digital modulation technique for noiseless and noisy transmission. Sci. J. Circuits, Syst. Sig. Process. **5**(3), 24–30 (2016)
10. Pokhrel, S.R., Choi, J.: Understand-before-talk (UBT): a semantic communication approach to 6g networks. IEEE Trans. Veh. Technol. **72**(3), 3544–3556 (2022)
11. Rezaei, H., Rajatheva, N., Latva-aho, M.: A combinational multi-kernel decoder for polar codes. arXiv preprint: arXiv:2211.08778 (2022)
12. Rezaei, H., Ranasinghe, V., Rajatheva, N., Latva-aho, M., Park, G., Park, O.S.: Implementation of ultra-fast polar decoders. In: 2022 IEEE International Conference on Communications Workshops (ICC Workshops), pp. 235–241. IEEE (2022)
13. Rogers: Claude shannon's cryptography research during world war ii and the mathematical theory of communication. In: 1994 Proceedings of IEEE International Carnahan Conference on Security Technology, pp. 1–5. IEEE (1994)
14. Sana, M., Strinati, E.C.: Learning semantics: an opportunity for effective 6G communications. In: 2022 IEEE 19th Annual Consumer Communications & Networking Conference (CCNC), pp. 631–636. IEEE (2022)
15. Shocher, A., et al.: Semantic pyramid for image generation. In: Proceedings of the IEEE/CVF Conference on Computer Vision and Pattern Recognition, pp. 7457–7466 (2020)
16. Strinati, E.C., Barbarossa, S.: 6G networks: beyond Shannon towards semantic and goal-oriented communications. Comput. Netw. **190**, 107930 (2021)
17. Uysal, E., et al.: Semantic communications in networked systems: a data significance perspective. IEEE Netw. **36**(4), 233–240 (2022)
18. Wang, Y., Gao, Z., Zheng, D., Chen, S., Gunduz, D., Poor, H.V.: Transformer-empowered 6G intelligent networks: from massive MIMO processing to semantic communication. IEEE Wirel. Commun. (2022)

19. Xie, H., Qin, Z., Li, G. Y., Juang, B.H.: Deep learning based semantic communications: an initial investigation. In: GLOBECOM 2020-2020 IEEE Global Communications Conference, pp. 1–6. IEEE (2020)
20. Yang, W., et al.: Fundamentals, applications, and challenges. IEEE Commun. Surv. Tutorials, Semant. Commun. Fut. Internet (2022)
21. Zhang, H., Shao, S., Tao, M., Bi, X., Letaief, K.B.: Deep learning-enabled semantic communication systems with task-unaware transmitter and dynamic data. IEEE J. Sel. Areas Commun. **41**(1), 170–185 (2022)
22. Zhang, P., Wenjun, X., Gao, H., Niu, K., Xiaodong, X., Qin, X., Yuan, C., Qin, Z., Zhao, H., Wei, J., et al.: Toward wisdom-evolutionary and primitive-concise 6g: A new paradigm of semantic communication networks. Engineering **8**, 60–73 (2022)

An Efficient FR-1 MIMO Antenna for N78/77/48 Bands with Enhanced Isolation Using DGS

Manumula Srinubabu[✉] and Nuthakki Venkata Rajasekhar

School of Electronics Engineering (SENSE), VIT-AP University, Amaravati,
Vijayawada 522237, Andhra Pradesh, India
{srinubabu.21phd7112,rajasekhar.venkata}@vitap.ac.in

Abstract. A high-efficiency, single-band microstrip patch antenna designed for the 5G-sub-6 GHz spectrum is introduced in this research. The antenna incorporates a unique defective ground structure (DGS) by integrating a rectangular cut strip to enhance its characteristics. Constructed on an FR-4 epoxy substrate using the inset feed method, the single antenna measures $15.5 \times 19.4\,\text{mm}^2$, while the proposed two-port MIMO antenna spans $52.8 \times 52.8\,\text{mm}^2$. With a moderate maximum gain of 4.1 dBi, isolation above 15 dB and radiation efficiency of 97%, this antenna operates within the frequency range of 2.5 GHz to 4.2 GHz, covering the isolation above 15 dB in the sub-6 GHz section of the N78/77/48 band in the 5G spectrum. The antenna's anticipated and observed properties affirm its suitability for 5G-NR band applications below the 6 GHz frequency range.

Keywords: 5G MIMO Antenna · DGS · Isolation · Radiation efficiency · Gain · Bandwidth

1 Introduction

It is conceivable that the technology of the 5th Generation of Communication will be implemented into mobile communication networks in the not-too-distant future. Its frequency range begins with frequencies that are lower than 6 GHz and continues all the way up to millimetre waves. The frequency band below 6 GHz, which is used for 5G, has a number of advantages, including improved coverage, accelerated data transfer speeds, and less signal loss in humid environments. [1, 2]. The performance of antennas built for 5G operation in the sub-6 GHz frequency region has greatly increased, which has raised the bar for all forms of communication technology. A microstrip patch antenna is a candidate for use in 5G communication systems because of the advantages that are inherent to this kind of antenna. This is made possible by the use of a microstrip patch antenna.

N. V. Rajasekhar—Contributed equally to this work.

Microstrip antennas are advantageous owing to their cheap cost, low profile, flat design, conformability, lightweight, and appropriateness for arrays. In addition, they are flat and have a conformable design. In addition to that, their price is really reasonable. Microstrip antennas, which are used at low frequencies, are considered to have significant flaws in terms of gain, bandwidth, and size, all of which are considered to be significant disadvantages. [3–8]. Microstrip antennas are gaining popularity as a result of improvements in both their design and performance in recent years. Numerous strategies for boosting the performance of microstrip patch antennas have been published in [7,9–13]. These approaches may be found in a variety of different publications. These citations may be found at this location. Increases in antenna gain and bandwidth were achieved by the use of a frequency-selective surface (FSS), as described in [12]. The use of this invention resulted in the creation of a design that had a gain of 17.78 dBi at 28 GHz, a boost of 9% in bandwidth, and a radiation efficiency of 90 percent. In this article, the construction and modelling of a wideband antenna are discussed. Based on the observations, it seems that a bandwidth ranging from 5.50 to 7.25 GHz was successfully achieved. In [9], FSS was used to broaden the bandwidth of the antenna, which ultimately resulted in a gain of 9.4 dBi. The antenna has an extremely broad frequency range, spanning from 3.1 GHz all the way up to 18.6 GHz. In addition to that, the ratio of this antenna's front lobe to its rear lobe is a high 10 dB over the whole of the UWB (ultra-wideband) band. Following the use of DGS in antenna arrays in [10], the 22 array was designed with a 12 dB increase in radiation between the co-pole and cross-pole radiation. This step was taken after going through and looking at the arrays there. When the DGS and the reflecting plate were applied to the antenna, the results were reported in [13] as a four-element linear array with gains of 9.02 dB and directivities of 12.81 dB, respectively. This was accomplished. A single-layer, single-probe-fed wideband antenna is described in this [14]. The antenna has one layer. A rectangular patch with a parasitic pattern in the form of a U was developed first, before the construction of the radiating patch. The antenna that was created as a consequence emitted electromagnetic waves at frequencies ranging from 4.82 GHz to 6.26 GHz, 5.25 GHz to 5.35 GHz, and 5.725 GHz to 5.875 GHz. Slots have been thoughtfully cut out of the ground plane of the antenna in order to provide room for the DGS component of the design. These slots have an inductive influence on the circuit, and they also have a capacitive impact on the circuit. The total performance of the antenna may be improved by optimizing the circuit, which can be accomplished by adjusting both the size of the slot and its position [15]. To ensure that the circuit works as efficiently as it possibly can, the slot sizes and locations are given careful consideration. When it is adequately calibrated, the impedance that the DGS design contributes to the circuit may be used to reduce the size of the antenna, increase its bandwidth, and boost its gain [16–18]. This is only possible if the impedance is properly tuned for different scenarios. Thus, it can be observed that wide bandwidth antennas must be modelled to improve performance under real-time use cases. To perform this task, the next section proposes the design of a high bandwidth n78 band

FR-1 antenna with isolation enhancements via DGS. The model was simulated and results were compared with standard techniques, under real-time scenarios.

2 Antenna Design Details

The given N78/48/77 band FR (frequency range)-1 antenna uses a technique founded on a transmission model to calculate an approximate antenna size. The antenna operates at a frequency of 3.55 GHz and is constructed on a substrate made of FR-4 epoxy with a dielectric constant of 4.4.

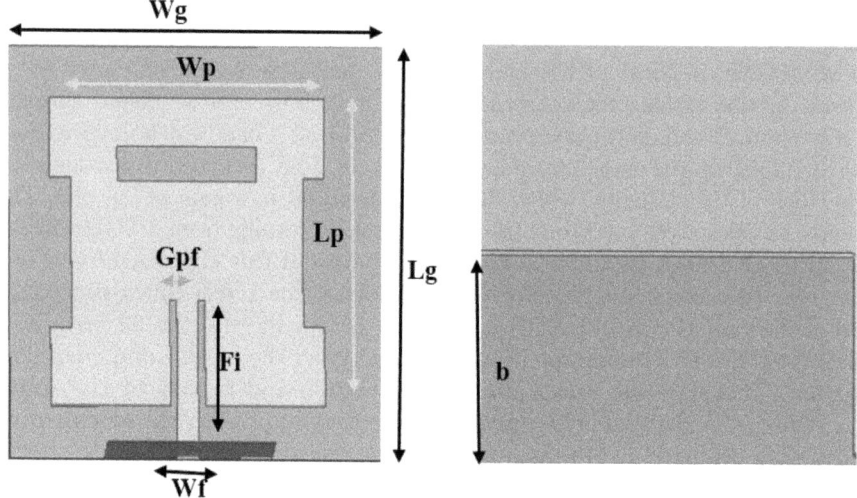

Fig. 1. Single monopole antenna front and rear view

The timing of its execution is also detailed. The recommended form of the FR1 antenna for the N78/48/77 band is seen in Figs. 1 and 2, which may be found here. This illustration clearly demonstrates the usage of DGS in the design of the provided antenna from above to enhance the antenna's qualities. You can tell by looking at the graph. The microstrip antenna, which does not use DGS, is responsible for the limited bandwidth. In order to permit broad operation in the sub-6 GHz frequency range, the ground plane of the FR-1 antenna has to be modified for the N78/48/77 band. As a means of improving the antenna's gain, a triangular strip was inserted into the ground plane. To do this, the strip was laid flat on the ground. The inset feed strategy, matched to a 50-ohm feeding impedance, has been chosen as the optimal feeding technique for the projected N78/48/77 band FR-1 antenna. This decision was made after much deliberation over other diet plans. After the antenna has been optimized, a reflective plate is attached to it and placed only two millimetres above the ground plane. This process is carried out to improve the antenna's radiation.

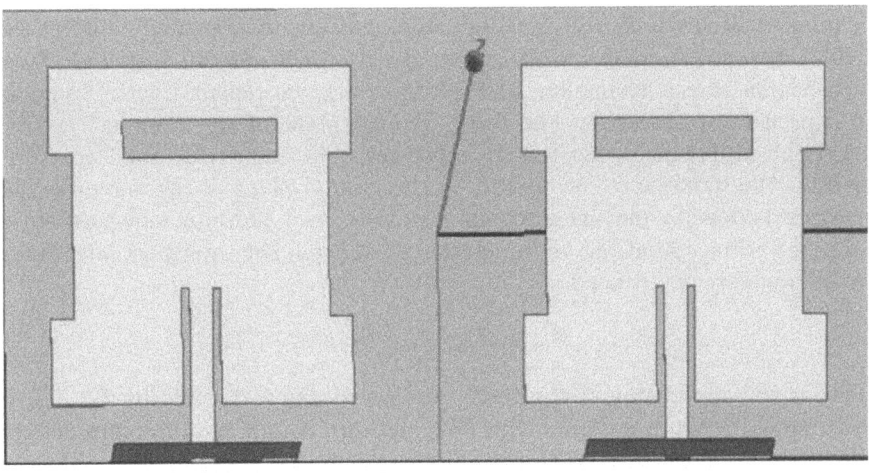

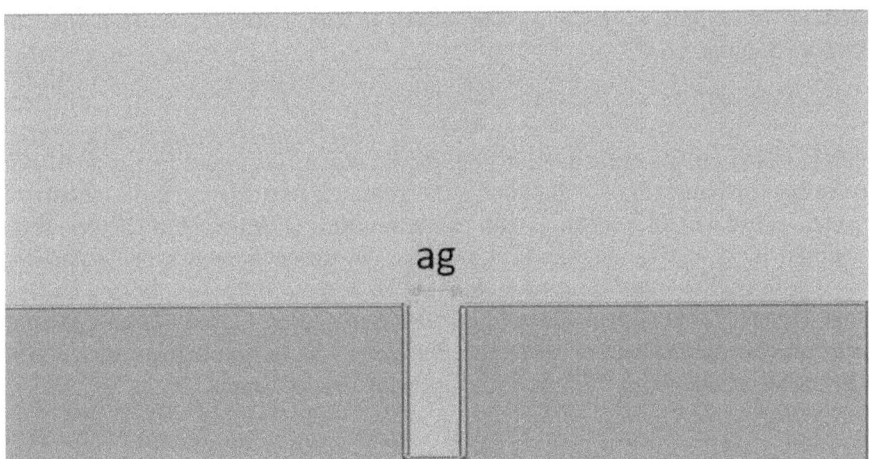

Fig. 2. Design of the proposed antenna front and rear view of the patch with element gap = 32.5 mm

The copper coating on top of the reflecting plate has been etched away (i.e., single layer sheet). The copper reflecting surface on the underside of the plate will remain in place and no copper will be added to the top. The antenna's side lobes may be focused and improved with the help of the reflecting plate, which acts as a reflector. The copper reflecting surface at the plate's underside is not removed since it serves an essential purpose in the reflector. The N78/48/77 band FR1 antenna has been proposed as an alternative since it operates in a frequency range appropriate for 5G communications while still being below 6 GHz. Research into the proposed FR-1 antenna was grounded on equations derived from the transmission model. The proposed antenna may be modelled as a lumped circuit, with resistors, inductors, and capacitors standing in for the patch's inherent impedance, respectively. However, the antenna's ground plane, which has an etched triangular DGS pattern, may be replaced with inductors and capacitors if necessary. The term "ground plane of the antenna" is used to describe inductance even though other resistors, inductors, and capacitors also show the inductance introduced by the ground plane of the antenna. The separation is done by placing antennas at a distance of 32.5 mm, which assists in dual port feeding operations. Through the use of Eq. 1, the equivalent impedance may be precisely determined.

$$Z_{in} = Z_{dgs\|}Z_p \| Z_{ref}. \tag{1}$$

Following the application of the patch, the impedance is denoted by Z_p. Z_{dgs} is used to describe the impedance that DGS induces. Z_{ref} is used to represent the impedance that is brought on by the reflecting plate. In this instance, isolation is accomplished via the use of both polarization diversity and straightforward DGS. Application of rectangular-shaped microstrip line feed configuration achieves impedance matching operations. The width of the rectangular patch may be determined using Eq. 2,

$$W = \frac{c}{2f_r}\sqrt{\frac{2}{\varepsilon_r + 1}}. \tag{2}$$

which is based on the transmission line model equations found in Eq. 3, In this expression, the constants c (light speed), f_r (resonant frequency), and r (substrate dielectric constant) all have their own characteristics. The height of the substrate is denoted by h in this context h is 1.6 mm, the dielectric constant, is denoted by $\varepsilon_r = 4.4$, and the loss tangent is denoted by $\tan\delta = 0.02$. In addition to this, we determined that the resonance frequency, denoted by f_r, is 3.55 GHz. We can figure out the dimensions of the patch by using the formulas from Eqs. 5, and we find that its length is 15.5 mm and its width is 19.4 mm.

$$\varepsilon_{reff} = \frac{\varepsilon_r + 1}{2} + \frac{\varepsilon_r - 1}{2\sqrt{1 + \frac{12h}{w}}}. \tag{3}$$

If you wish to maintain the square shape of the Patch while increasing the amount of rotation in the circular field, keep the width equal to the length. Because of this, the antenna will have a lower frequency at which it resonates.

$$L = L_{eff} - 2\Delta L = \frac{c}{2 * f_r\sqrt{\varepsilon_{eff}}} - 2\Delta L. \tag{4}$$

$$\Delta L = \frac{0.412 * h(\varepsilon_{reff} + 0.3)(\frac{w}{h} + 0.264)}{(\varepsilon_{reff} - 0.258)(\frac{w}{h} + 0.8)} \tag{5}$$

In order to achieve a frequency of 3.55 GHz, it was necessary to raise the length to 52.8 mm; conversely, decreasing the patch size led to an increase in operating frequency. Achieving the necessary axial ratio required some trial and error to identify the appropriate degree of chamfering to apply to the edges.

In order to make room for the printed circuit board (PCB), a hole was drilled through the middle of the board. The dimensions of the cut were also adjusted to ensure the lowest possible S_{21} between the antennas while they are both broadcasting and receiving on the same frequency. This is accomplished by fine-tuning the size of the cut. It is possible to get a decoupling of -15 dB in conditions when everything goes well. In the next section of this text, we are going to analyse the results that arise from following these designs.

3 Results and Comparative Analysis

The substrate of this antenna is made of FR-4, which has a significant loss (measured as a tangent, or tan), which comes in at 0.02. You may get some FR-4 at a minimal cost and acquire some with little to no work on your part. The lossy of the substrate has no effect on the performance of the antenna. The simulation is carried out with the help of an HFSS toolkit that is available for purchase.

The findings of the study on the design procedure of the N78/48/77 band FR-1 antenna are presented and spoken about in this article. When there is just the DGS present, the antenna is referred to as an antenna with DGS (ADGS), and when there is neither the DGS nor the reflecting plate present, the antenna is referred to as a plane antenna (PA). The dielectric ground plane and the reflecting plate are the components that make up the entire antenna, also known as the N78/48/77 band FR-1 antenna. When it comes to the radiation properties, the FR1 antenna for the n78 band performs superiorly to both ADGS and PA. The reflective plate that is secured to the rear of the n78 band FR1 antenna has been simulated, optimized, and fine-tuned to the point where it has been found that a distance of 1.6 mm is the most effective placement for it. A substrate made of FR-4 with just one side reflective is used for the reflecting surface The information on the plate's thickness may be found in Table 1,

Table 1. Design parameters for the given antenna configuration

Parameters	Dimensions (mm)
Wg	15.5
Lg	19.4
Wp	12.35
Lp	10.5
h	1.6
Fi	4.5
Wf	2.95
Gpf	0.8
ag	1.5
b	9.4

By minimizing both the antenna and the back lobe, the plate enables the antenna to radiate in a more focused manner. The antenna's gain is increased because of an inventive triangular plate that was placed on the ground plane. This plate also contributes to the design's already impressively broad bandwidth. A highly restricted antenna range would result in the absence of the triangular slot on the antenna. It's possible that we can increase the antenna's bandwidth even more if we cut a triangular slit in the ground plane and then optimize it. To ensure that the design produces a satisfactory response, the ideal dimensions of the antenna and the triangular plate utilized in the construction are detailed in Table 1. The computed reflection coefficients for the three different experimental settings are shown in Fig. 3,

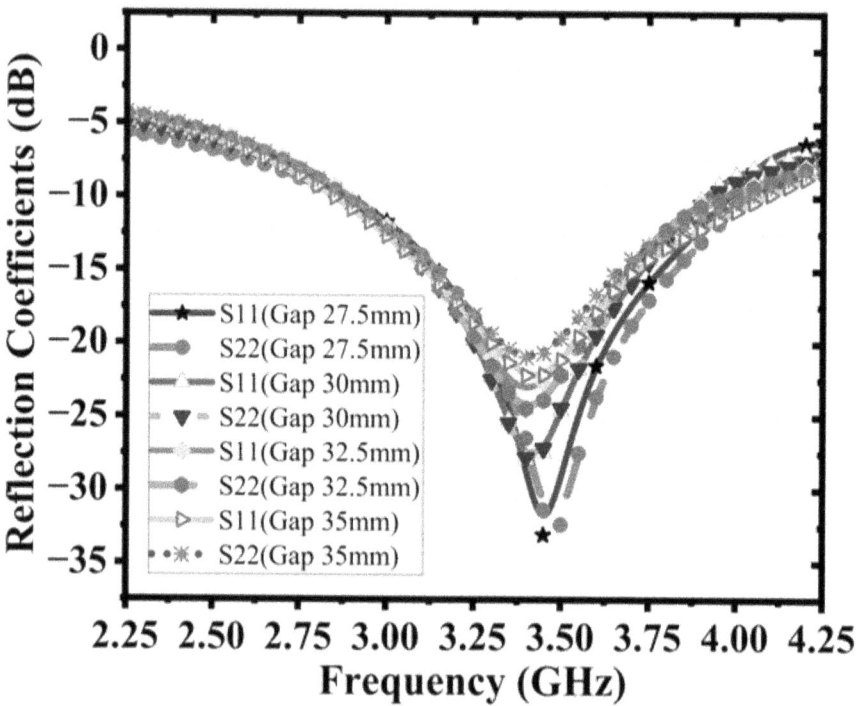

Fig. 3. Simulated results of the proposed 3-port MIMO antenna with different element gaps

In comparison, the PA and ADGS antennas have minimum values of S_{21} −15 dB and −22 dB, respectively, for their reflection coefficients, while the FR1 antenna is for the n78/48/77 band. The frequency range of the proposed n78 band FR1 antenna is 2.521 GHz to 4.2784 GHz, which proves without a reasonable doubt that it has a single band in the frequency that is lower than 6 GHz as observed from Figs. 3, 4 and 5 as follows,

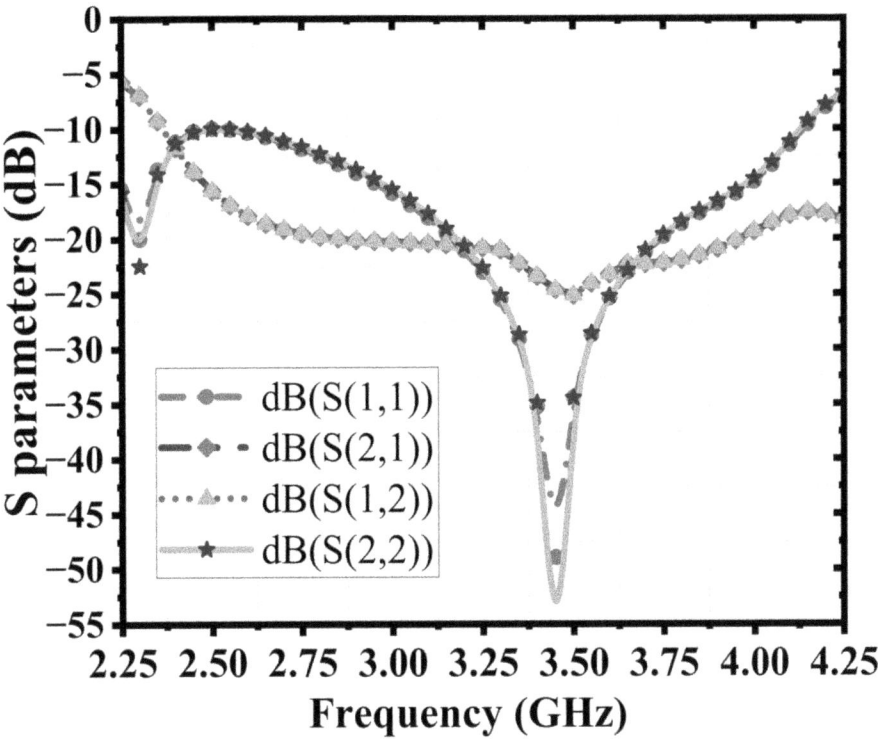

Fig. 4. Simulated S_{xx} results of the proposed MIMO designs

Table 2. Results of the proposed antenna

Ref.	Size	Op. Freq. (GHz)	BW Axial Ratio (%, Hz)	Gain (dBi)
[2]	175 × 47 × 1.7	1.75, 1.85, 1.95, 2.15, 2.6		2.1, −1.7, 1.9, 3.2, 4.8
[4]	58 × 40 × 1.6	1.51–3.69/4.67–5.25/5.78–5.96	83.8/11.69/3.06	5.2/4.8/5
[8]	R = 15 mm	4.74–6.79 GHz	35.55	4.2 dbi
[9]	70 × 30 × 1.6	770–1000 MHz/1.7–3.78 GHz	240 MHZ/2400 MHZ	3.54/5.89/3.52
[10]	51 × 52 × 1.6	1.17645 GHz/2.320–2.345 GHz/1.9 GHz	12–25 MHZ	3/6.5
[13]	87.5 × 61 × 1.6	1.8–2.9/3.4–4.6/5–5.6		2.58–3.34 dbi
[7]	75 × 75	1.575 /3.71/ 5.9 GHz	16.8 MHz/ 77 MHz/154 MHz	5.5 dbi/8 dbi/9 dbi
[1]	55 × 40 × 3	1.78–5.28/5.62–6.08	99.15/7.83	7
Our	52.8 × 52.8	2.5–4.278	2500–4278 MHz	Nearly 4.1 dBi

In the following table, the findings of the suggested model are contrasted with those of the methodologies that are currently in use. Similarly, isolation results can be observed in Fig. 4, which showcases DGS and without DGS outputs. Based on this, it can be observed that the proposed model is able to improve the isolation efficiency for different use cases. Thus, the proposed model of the antenna showcases good results and can be used for real-time use cases (Table 2).

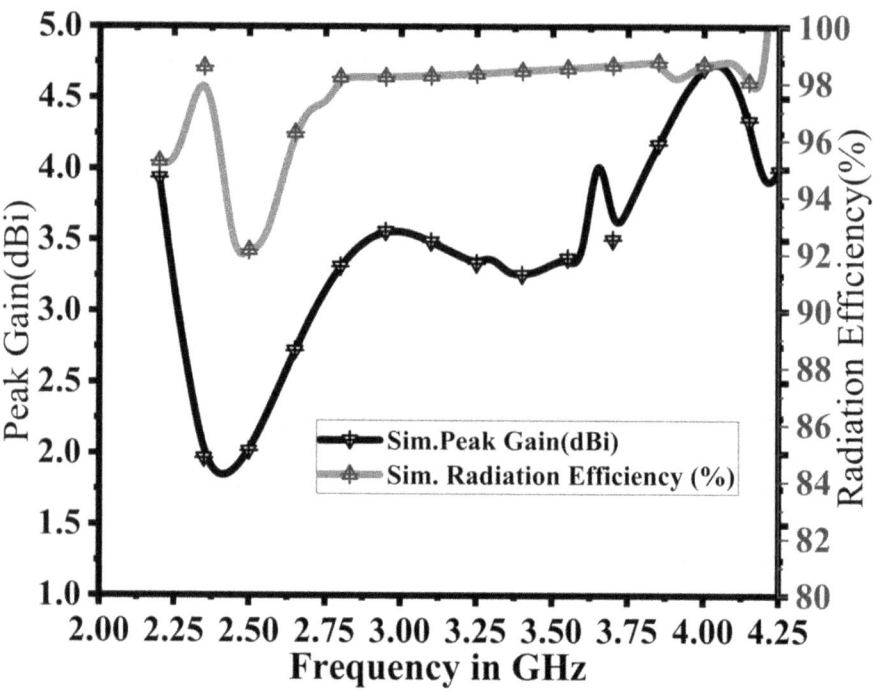

Fig. 5. Simulated radiation efficiency and gain results of the proposed MIMO designs

4 Conclusion and Future Scope

A small, rectangular microstrip patch antenna with high gain across a wide frequency range has been released, and it has been designed specifically for use in 5G applications operating at frequencies lower than 6 GHz. When running the simulations and trying to get the designs as good as they could be, we used a commercial EM tool called HFSS. The suggested single antenna has a substrate that is 15.4 mm by 19.4 mm, its best gain is just 4.1 dB, and its radiation efficiency is 97%. This effective antenna design, which has a frequency range that extends from 2.5 GHz to 4.2785 GHz and beyond, is able to cover the sub-6 GHz region of the 5G spectrum, which spans from 3 GHz to 4 GHz. A satisfactory fabrication and testing process has been completed for the FR-1 N78/48/77 band antenna. The findings obtained from both the simulation and the measurements are consistent with one another to a satisfactory degree. According to the technical specifications of the antenna, it has been shown that the proposed tiny N78/77/48 band FR-1 antenna is capable of handling 5G communications at frequencies lower than 6 GHz. Utilizing computer models that are biologically inspired will make it possible to simulate, in the future, the modelled antenna on a variety of substrates; this will allow for the adjustment of its size as well as the increase of its overall efficiency levels.

References

1. Satyanarayana, B., Srivastava, S.K., Meshram, M. K.: Compact 8-port coupled-fed MIMO antenna array for sub-6 GHz 5G smartphone terminals. In: IEEE MTT-S International Microwave and RF Conference (IMARC), pp. 1–4 (2021). https://doi.org/10.1109/IMaRC49196.2021.9714563
2. Kulkarni, J., Chitre, A., Kulkarni, N., Kulkarni, S., Talware, R.: Design and analysis of compact 2D MIMO sub-6 GHz 5G flexible antenna. In: 2021 IEEE Madras Section Conference (MASCON), pp. 1–5 (2021). https://doi.org/10.1109/MASCON51689.2021.9563492
3. Chaimool, S., Sangwijit, B., Pukna, P., Rakluea, C.: A dual-band dual-polarized MIMO antenna for 700 MHz and sub-6 GHz 5G systems. In: 2020 International Symposium on Antennas and Propagation (ISAP), pp. 103–104. IEEE (2021)
4. Kumari, P., Kumari, T., Suman, K.K., Gangwar, R.K., Chaudhary, R.K.: A circularly polarized sub-6 GHz MIMO antenna for 5G applications. In: 2022 IEEE International Symposium on Antennas and Propagation and USNC-URSI Radio Science Meeting (AP-S/URSI), pp. 1186–1187. IEEE (2022)
5. Zheng, Z., Ntawangaheza, J., Sun, L.: Wideband MIMO antenna system for sub-6 GHz cell phone. In: 2021 International Conference on Electronics, Circuits and Information Engineering (ECIE), pp. 1–5. IEEE (2021)
6. Rafique, U., et al.: Uni-planar MIMO antenna for sub-6 GHz 5G mobile phone applications. Appl. Sci. **12**(8), 3746 (2022)
7. Chen, Y.-R., Chen, W.-S.: Design of MIMO WLAN 2.4/5.2/5.8 and 5G sub-6 GHz antennas for laptop computer applications. In: 2020 International Workshop on Electromagnetics: Applications and Student Innovation Competition (iWEM), pp. 1–2. IEEE (2020)
8. Patnaik, P., Sarkar, D., Saha, C.: A multi-band 5G antenna for smart phones operating at sub-6 GHz frequencies. In: 2020 International Symposium on Antennas & Propagation (APSYM), pp. 32–35. IEEE (2020)
9. Supreeyatitikul, N., Phungasem, A., Aeimopas, P.: Design of wideband sub-6 GHz 5G MIMO antenna with isolation enhancement using an MTM-inspired resonators. In: 2021 Joint International Conference on Digital Arts, Media and Technology with ECTI Northern Section Conference on Electrical, Electronics, Computer and Telecommunication Engineering, pp. 206–209. IEEE (2021)
10. Shameena, V., Anila, P., Mohanan, P.: A compact four-element self decoupled MIMO antenna for sub-6 GHz 5D applications. In: 2021 IEEE International Symposium on Antennas and Propagation and USNC-URSI Radio Science Meeting (APS/URSI), pp. 1233–1234. IEEE (2021)
11. Manirathnam, C., Ghosh, S., Swati, M.: A compact, two-port MIMO antenna for mm-wave 5G application. In: 2022 IEEE 11th International Conference on Communication Systems and Network Technologies (CSNT), pp. 22–25. IEEE (2022)
12. Alam, T., Cheffena, M.: Four-port multiband MIMO filtenna with an isolation filter for sub-6 GHz 5G applications. In: 2021 IEEE MTT-S International Microwave Filter Workshop (IMFW), pp. 281–283. IEEE (2021)

13. Chandra, R., Sarkar, D., Ganguly, D., Saha, C., Siddiqui, J.Y., Antar, Y.M.: Design of NFRP based sir-loaded two element MIMO antenna system for 28/38 GHz sub mm-wave 5G applications. In: 2020 IEEE 3rd 5G World Forum (5GWF), pp. 514–518. IEEE (2020)
14. Saxena, S., Dwari, S., Kanaujia, B.K.: Design of 4 (n+ 1) element dual-CP massive MIMO antenna for 5G systems operating in sub-6 GHz band. In: 2020 Third International Conference on Advances in Electronics, Computers and Communications (ICAECC), pp. 1–4. IEEE (2020)
15. Parchin, N.O., Al-Yasir, Y.I., Abdulkhaleq, A.M., Basherlou, H.J., Ullah, A., Abd-Alhameed, R.A.: A new broadband MIMO antenna system for sub 6 GHz 5G cellular communications. In: 2020 14th European Conference on Antennas and Propagation (EuCAP), pp. 1–4. IEEE (2020)
16. Molins-Benlliure, J., Cabedo-Fabrés, M., Antonino-Daviu, E., Ferrando-Bataller, M.: Eight-port wideband MIMO antenna for sub-6 GHz 5G base stations. In: 2021 IEEE International Symposium on Antennas and Propagation and USNC-URSI Radio Science Meeting (APS/URSI), pp. 839–840. IEEE (2021)
17. Babu, S.S., Patre, S.R.: Meandered-line folded antenna for sub-6 GHz supported MIMO system. In: 2022 3rd International Conference for Emerging Technology (INCET), pp. 1–4. IEEE (2022)
18. Hussain, R., Khan, M.U., Almajali, E., Sharawi, M.S.: An integrated MIMO antenna for sub-6 GHz and millimeter-wave bands for 5G applications. In: 2020 IEEE International Symposium on Antennas and Propagation and North American Radio Science Meeting, pp. 1293–1294. IEEE (2020)

A Study on Efficient Approaches for Distributing Workloads Effectively in Edge Computing Systems

Kavya Lingutla, Vennela Priya Penumuchu, Hima Varsha Nagisetty, Niharika Nunna, and S. R. Reeja(✉)

VIT-AP University, Amaravati, India
{kavya.20bce7650,priya.20bce7645,himavarsha.20bce7279, niharika.20bcd7140,reeja.sr}@vitap.ac.in

Abstract. For the benefits of cloud computing, many enterprise companies have moved their services and apps to the cloud. The centralized cloud architecture experiences high workload, congestion, and delay bottlenecks resulting in high amounts of data and rapidly growing digits of connected devices that consume cloud services. Edge Computing (EC) is consequently presented as a new paradigm to increase cloud capabilities close to the end devices. Here, the task allocation is mentioned as the workload distribution amid innumerable nodes in an edge computing network. Major difficulties in workload distribution include locating each task optimally based on its needs for computing capacity, storing data, and bandwidth of the network, and adjusting to network's continuously changing nature. Algorithms for workload allocation can be centralized, decentralized, hybrid, or based on machine learning. The selection of technique relies on the particular application's pre-requisites. Each approach has advantages and disadvantages. In greater detail, the choice of the best work distribution techniques depends on the configuration and architecture of the edge computing system, namely MEC, joint computing of edge, fog and cloud, P2P EC and much more. As a result, allotting the tasks in edge computing is an intricate, varied, as well as a difficult challenge which calls for delicate balancing act amidst multiple potentially competing goals, inclusive of resource-aware, energy efficiency, machine learning with latency, safety and quality of Experience (QoE). Recent years have seen a rise in the amount of research studies on edge devices' work allocation optimization and performance evaluation. This paper compares and contrasts several methods for work load distribution, algorithms which are much optimized, and the communication network types which are often employed in edge computing systems.

Keywords: Artificial Intelligence-Based Task Allocation · Resource Aware · Energy and Delay Reduction

1 Introduction

A new paradigm known as edge computing (EC) appeared after cloud technology had matured. The availability of processing power as well as the high-bandwidth, low-latency communication links among edge nodes place it in the centre of network research's focus. According to Gartner, there will be 20 times as many smart devices on networks' edges by 2023, and by 2025, 75% of the data produced by businesses will be stored outside of traditional data centres and the cloud. The term "edge computing" mentions a decentralized computational model which enables data processing to take place near the storage alternative to depending on centralized data centres. Aforementioned method is especially beneficial to edge-of-the-network augmented reality applications, Internet of Things systems, and autonomous vehicles that require high bandwidth and low latency. The Edge-Fog-Cloud (EFC) architecture which is shown in Fig. 1, is a distributed computing platform created to enhance the effectiveness IoT, 5G, and other latency-sensitive applications. Edge computing, fog computing, and cloud computing are the three main layers that make up the multi-tiered strategy that is used to achieve this. Each layer has a specific function and manages various parts of computing and data processing.

The workload distribution practices used by edge devices today are examined in this article. To determine which important strategies would be most beneficial for future study and effectiveness of every strategy, we examine the major approaches presented in the literature review. We review and assess the body of recent research on the distribution of workload on edge computing devices. The article offers complete analysis including primary approaches and edge computing techniques for effectively handling challenging workloads.

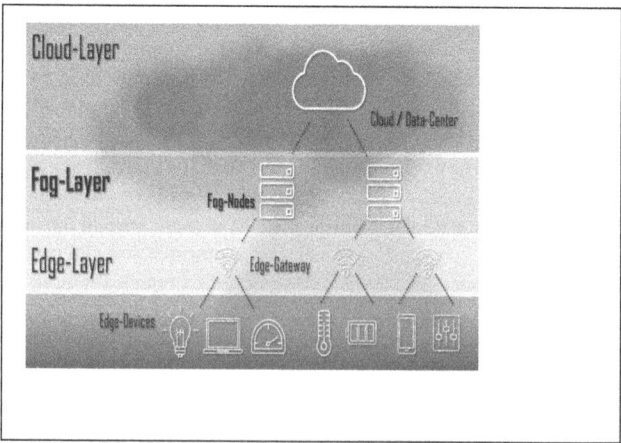

Fig. 1. An edge-fog-cloud computing system's Architecture.

This paper's primary contribution is an overview of contemporary task distribution techniques. This paper specifically stands out on the popular workload distribution techniques and algorithms which are much optimized along with the communication network types incorporated in various edge computing systems, and it only draws on research that has been published within the last three years. In order to improve the present perception of decision-making while coming to selecting the best workload distribution technique, optimized algorithms, and communication network types based on situation, the paper demonstrates the workload distribution as well as all algorithms that are optimized and techniques which have been recently, most frequently used.

2 Literature Review

The categorization of the job allocation techniques that are used in the latest works and literatures are presented in this section. Each job allocation technique, when combined with the kind of computer network and the deep learning compression techniques, have certain advantages and are used to achieve various goals, including minimizing processing power, energy use, and network delay. The following methods are used to categorize task allocation techniques:

AI/ML: Used some of the algorithms of machine learning for forecasting resource usage and assign work appropriately.

Resource-Aware: distributing tasks is done according to the capabilities of edge devices, such as their battery life, processing speed, and memory capacity.

Distributed: A framework of edge devices are used for distributing jobs in order to improve performance and reduce latency.

Energy-Efficient: Dividing up the work so that edge devices use the least amount of energy possible.

QoS: Task distribution depending on the various tasks needed QoS levels.

An overview of all the workload distribution techniques from all the considered papers is given in Table 1.

2.1 Machine-Learning/Artificial Intelligence-Based Task Allocation

Edge computing with AI and ML enables devices to make choices in real time, minimize data transmission to the cloud, improve security, and offer individualized experiences. This technology ensures the best performance in decentralized contexts for applications like autonomous cars, predictive maintenance, and effective resource allocation. The goal of this research study [9] Using a (DRL) method based on the DQN algorithm, scheduling of the various tasks in edge computing has been optimized. This strategy's main goals are to balance workload distribution, shorten service times, and lower the proportion of tasks that fail to complete. DQN succeeds in attaining these objectives, having been selected for its capability to manage the complex and high-dimensional nature of workload scheduling problems. It is noteworthy that it functions without the requirement for a mathematical model of the environment, instead relying on learnt information from previous actions. DQN outperforms both PPO and DDPG in terms of performance, having the shortest average service time of 0.7 s. Even though the number of devices have been growing, DQN continuously outperforms its competitors with an average VM utilization rate of about 24%. The most promising option for workload scheduling in edge computing scenarios, especially as the complexity and size of the environment increase, is DQN due to its extraordinary resilience in minimizing the failed task rate, achieving an incredibly low rate of only 3%.

The goal of the research study [10] is to apply a Coalitional Game-Based Service Migration (CGSM) approach that takes into account mobile user reallocation in crowded environments to address the problem of workload balancing in edge computing. The program uses a modified k-means clustering technique to group MEC servers into alliances, locate hotspots, and cooperatively schedule services. In order to improve utilization and load equality across coalition members, it also migrates services to suitable edge servers. Performance analysis shows that, in comparison to other methods, CGSM greatly lowers the number of service migrations and significantly increases user fairness. This method makes use of MEC to process data at mobile edge network and shows future potential for integrating device-to-device technology with service migration for handling large-scale user equipment requirements in crowded circumstances. Research's [13] main goal is to reduce the net cost spent by each individual edge server while offering edge computing services. A brand-new cooperative queueing game strategy is put forth to accomplish this goal. With the help of this strategy, each server's queueing game will have multiple dimensions. These tactics include how much labor is to be done, how much money peers will accept, and how fast computers will be used. The ultimate goal is to determine the judgement of a durable, ideal task distribution for every server on the EC system, and to obtain balance in contexts of costing approaches as well as regulate processing rate to reduce overall performance of the system.

In this study [15], we suggest a container scheduling system and an automatic parameter alteration method to boost serverless computing effectiveness in edge contexts. It introduces the Skippy algorithm, a complex method for placing serverless edge functions for maximum efficiency. It utilizes various kind of priority functions, metadata to allot resources precisely. It illustrates Skippy's usefulness in raising the effectiveness of edge computing deployments through performance comparisons and thorough experimentation. The research highlights the necessity of improving serverless function placement methodologies and the possibility for improvements in dynamic workload distribution as future directions for enhancing performance in edge computing. In this study [18], the positioning of application modules in the edge network is optimized using the BMOPSO algorithm. Results from experiment, which makes use of the Fog simulator, show that BMOPSO performs better than Edge wards and Popularity-based algorithms in matter of implementation time and placement time. The main objective of project was to improve workload placement using swarm intelligence, consequently improving processing times in a variety of areas, such as computation, data propagation, and service deployment in IoT and Edge computing. To sum up, the suggested BMOPSO strategy for workload placement in Edge computing offers a beneficial trade-off across the cloud, edge, and IoT layers. BMOPSO is a great tool for increasing resource utilization and reducing resource waste since experimental results show its effectiveness in maximizing task placement.

This study [1] discusses service pricing, task distribution, and incentive design for the practical use of CVEC in order to keep up with the computing needs of vehicular networks, CVEC integrates MEC into parked automobiles. This results in a new computing paradigm. In CVEC, MEC server is being deployed by an offloading service supplier and plans parked vehicles as required to manage offloading activities. In order to achieve the best service pricing and workload distribution, the study employs ideal contract layout in light of prospect theory. Comparison of performance shows that, for the lowest PV type, the solution based on Prospect Theory (PT) is almost 90% of the solution based on Expected Utility Theory (EUT). The scope for the future suggests using centralized/distributed machine learning, deep reinforcement learning, and other methods to further optimize. Dividing up the workload. In order to allocate tasks in the most effective way, the study [5] proposes a hierarchical control system to address load balancing issues in edge computing environments using evolutionary algorithms, hidden Markov models, and game theory. This paradigm optimizes task distribution by taking important aspects like service quality, resource efficiency, cost, and energy use into account. A comparison shows this technique is more effective in regards of make span, performance, and cost-effectiveness. In conclusion, this research gives an extensive and priceless answer to the complex work allocation problems in edge computing, promising improved efficiency, cost savings, and service quality, coinciding with the growing significance of edge computing in contemporary IT ecosystems.

2.2 Distributed Based Task Allocation

Caroline Rublein et al. [20] suggested a task allocation approach which is distributed where server works alone and doesn't interact with one another to decide on allocation. Clustering and a two-round bidding technique were suggested. Users post job requests with the necessary resources, a deadline, and utility. To increase the overall usefulness of jobs which are served, servers make decisions about which task to allocate based on the status inside as well as the features of requests that are incoming. An problem to enhance an online workload distribution system which authorizes for pre-emption while taking elastic resource requirements and deadlines into consideration was officially specified by the author. To increase the system's scalability, they also provided details on a clustering heuristic. A workload distribution mechanism for Enhanced Efficiency Across Multiple Devices and Base Stations for Minimizing Delay was suggested by the author in [16]. In intersecting domains of MEC, the goal is to propose an effective multidevice and multi-BS task offloading strategy to reduce time in job completion for Internet of Things devices. The article introduces the "DOLA" distributed work offloading method, which is based on the noncooperative game theory. In order to achieve a Nash equilibrium, DOLA seeks to decentralized task offloading decision-making optimization, making sure that no participant has an incentive to unilaterally modify its approach. The primary performance metric considered in this study is the reduction of work completion delay. The abstract emphasizes that these trials show the effectiveness of DOLA, with a focus on its greater performance as compared to alternative offloading techniques.

An Edge Computing method for distributed workload distribution in Smart Cities depending on the Internet of Things was also proposed by Omar Abdulkareem Mahmood et al. [19] to look at a multi-criteria optimization problem of a connected city which is based upon IOT, paying close attention to reducing the energy used and latency. In this study, a multi-layer consisting of 3 layers network topology was employed for connected cities. The first layer was the Internet of things and the second one was edge devices. Clouds made up the third stratum. With regard to range of virtual machines versus the latency, the suggested model on average outperformed existing approaches by 3.1% with 90 VMs and 9.2% with 30 VMs. Additionally, with 200 jobs, advancement with regard to the quantity of jobs compared to the computational delay was 7%. Additionally, the average improvement in energy usage compared to the jobs was 157% assigned to 200 tasks, while the gains in energy usage compared to count of virtual machines were 188% with 30 VMs and 565% with 90 VMs. Kaige Tan et al. [7] suggested an optimized technique for jointly offloading the tasks and allocating the resources which is decentralized for Vehicular Edge Computing Systems. It was for systems that used mobile edge computing. Here, the issue is broken down into two smaller divisions, such as offloading of jobs and workload distribution at the RSU and vehicle levels. Roadside units, or RSU, are used here. Dual decomposition makes the resource allocation problem simpler and more amenable to decentralized solutions. A probability-based method converts the discrete task offloading problem into a continuous convex problem. On a 1-km roadway, they stimulated that. Due to its benefit, decentralized offloading performs load balancing at the highest level.

2.3 QoS Based Task Allocation

In [14], the author develops an QoS based DEP technique. With regards of EC for IoV, DEP seeks to strike a compromise between the quantity and QoS, as well as reconstruction cost of existing ES deployments. Comparative studies utilizing actual traffic data are used to demonstrate the efficacy of DEP. According to comparative studies using actual traffic data, DEP delivers a lower latency and a smaller workload standard deviation than the clustering technique by a margin of 17.64% and 25.82%, respectively. Using the current placement as a benchmark, the performance of the ES placement is evaluated in terms of average latency and load balancing. The outcomes show how DEP may effectively boost edge computing's functionality in the IoV. For CEC-IoV, here the author of the research [17] proposes a levelled design to ensure QoS and low power consumption workload distribution, and latency and how efficiently the energy is used at Mobile edge computing systems are optimized, correspondingly. The assignment problem is resolved using a combinatorial optimization strategy in a polynomial amount of time. A suitable reaction time threshold is used to detect underloaded and overloaded MECSs, and load-balancing is then carried out among them. Additionally, VMs at a MECS have workload redistribution and computing resource reconfiguration integrated.

Additionally, the paper [3] intended to raise EC's level of service quality by using a game theoretic technique to handle load imbalance problems in linked IEC. A learning algorithm which was decentralized was suggested. Each IES initially chooses scheduling actions based on their strategies, which they then review and update to attain Nash equilibrium. This iterative process continues over many phases, dynamically adjusting task allocation. The suggested state-based gaming strategy outperforms the FMBRID technique and provides load balancing that is comparable to the optimization approach, especially in settings with bursts of task arrivals. The authors' goal was to maximize user Quality of experience by concurrently enhancing the selection of service, distributing the workload and offloading the tasks decisions by proposing a method which is distributed namely Lagrangian-dual based decomposition theory [8]. It demonstrated NP-hardness for the assignment by formulating it as a combined-integer nonlinear programming issue. It provided resource-efficiency based heuristic after reformulating the issue as a NUM problem in order to solve it effectively. Finally, it tested our methods using several simulations, and the outcomes showed how effective they were. It has been found that under real-world task demands, the cost-aware online algorithm outperforms the Highest Allocation of Rate method by more than 50% while requiring fewer service changes.

2.4 Energy Efficient Based Task Allocation

Tomaso Erseghe's [2] aims to make edge computing more energy-efficient and sustainable in the era of connected devices. It emphasizes workload distribution, reduced non-renewable energy use, load balancing, and server consolidation. The aim is to enhance sustainability, cut costs, and reduce grid dependency. Renewable energy for edge servers is encouraged while ensuring timely task completion. To predict arrivals, correlated Markov Chains with ON-OFF behavior are used. Three prediction methods, including the Genie Predictor (ideal), support Model Predictive Control (MPC). MPC leverages System State Equations for offloading and the Energy Consumption Model to optimize workload scheduling, energy management, and server decisions. It focuses on energy buffers. MPC uses two cost functions, quadratic and logarithmic, to minimize resource allocation costs, promoting server consolidation and load balancing. This leads to two optimization problems: one convex and one non-convex. In this paper, a decentralized MPC-based job allocation strategy for MEC networks is presented. It outperforms heuristics and myopic approaches, reduces grid dependency, and paves the way for GPU energy models and user mobility-aware workload distribution.

The objective of the research article [4] is to optimize mobile-edge computing for enhanced user experience and cost-efficiency by reducing energy consumption, task response delay, and cloudlet deployment. It introduces a powerful optimization algorithm. MGW, a multi-objective optimization technique, is used in Mobile Edge Computing (MEC) systems for job offloading and cloudlet distribution. In MGW, a collection of non-dominated solutions are discovered by combining a whale optimization algorithm with guided population archiving methods. The problem is NP-complete and has multiple objectives, and work on heuristic algorithm to get better solution. For enhancing discovery, MGW also uses opposition-based learning. According to simulation data, MGW acheives better solution when compared to other algorithms in contexts of solution quality and diversity as assessed by inverted generational distance (IGD) and hypervolume (HV), making it a useful tool for MECS service providers. MINP (Mixed-Integer Nonlinear Programming) is the method used to formulate the objectives. This NP-complete problem is addressed using a modified version of the GPAWOA (Gravitational Search Algorithm with Opposition-Based Learning), which improves position repair, initialization, and encoding techniques. The algorithm's performance is enhanced by incorporating a variety of optimization approaches, including GOBL, QOBL, and mutation/crossover from Differential Evolution. The suggested algorithm is more effective than existing metaheuristic algorithms at producing high-quality nondominated solutions quickly. Future work will entail applying multi-objective optimization to optimize channel bandwidth allocation.

The paper's [11] objective is to create a load-balancing group for container distribution synthesis, and migration in a SDE environment that uses little energy. Through simulation, this method is confirmed by looking at performance indicators such as energy usage, network, CPU deliver times, and the final retard time. Goal is to offer a SDE solution for delicate, CaaS for IoT applications that are latency-sensitive. In order to maximize performance and energy consumption, the suggested algorithm uses multi-layered system modeling, a multiple leader and follower game namely, Stackelberg and container-derived from virtualization. The results show decreased energy consumption in comparison to existing variations, regardless of changes in workload size.

2.5 Resource Aware

Resource-aware task allocation refers to the distribution of workloads according on the processor, memory, and battery life currently available on edge devices. The authors in [6] presented a messaging system for Artificial Internet of Things in edge computing (a distributed method) which concentrates on message ordering issues. DMSCO technique, which is dependent over DDPG, is also recommended in this study in order to enhance the efficiency of messaging system. The outcomes displays profound influence of the suggested DMSCO approach, delivering an exceptionally efficient output of 88.79 MB/s, which is an outstanding enhancement of 46.61% exceeding the messaging system (distributed) without any optimized configuration. Random searching, in contrast, shows a 22.17% improvement.

Table 1. An overview of edge computing task distribution techniques.

Ref.	Motto	Proposed Algorithm	Workload Distribution technique	Networks Utilized	Advantages	Disadvantages
[1]	Service pricing and workload allocation in cvec	Optimal contract design under prospect theory	AI	Vehicular	User-Centric Utility Maximization, Economic Benefits	Scalability Challenges, Resource Variability
[2]	Enhance energy-efficiency, reducing grid dependence, and optimizing edge task management	MPC Based Allocation of Processing Tasks	Energy-efficient	EC	Reduces the Transmission costs and renewable energy sold. Adapting to changing conditions	User Mobility is a challenge for handling of dynamic user movement. Can't address the complexity tasks
[3]	Improve QoS in EC by using game theory to balance IEC load	State-Based Decentralized Learning Algorithm	QoS	IEC	Enhance the Service Performance. Getting into optimal state for each reachable state	Couldn't address the load balancing issues with multiple types of servers under wireless connections

(*continued*)

Table 1. (*continued*)

Ref.	Motto	Proposed Algorithm	Workload Distribution technique	Networks Utilized	Advantages	Disadvantages
[4]	To reduce the amount of cloudlets deployed, task response time, and energy usage	Whale Optimization Algorithms 1. RFSCA 2. Sr Algorithm MGW algorithm	Energy-efficient	IOT	Energy and Delay Reduction, Multi-objective Optimization, Algorithm efficiency and quality for effective offloading	Fails to maximize channel bandwidth distribution, testing multi objective optimization algorithm
[5]	A method to boost serverless computing effectiveness in edge contexts	Genetic Algorithm (GA) Integer Linear Programming (ILP) Hidden Markov Model (HMM)	Ai	EC	Optimization Effective use has been made of factors like task costs, computational capacity, availability, and time restrictions	Lacks in improving of serverless function placement methodologies and improving in dynamic workload distribution
[6]	To address the challenges associated with message ordering	PSA, DMSCO	Resource Aware	IOT	Carries out distributed messaging system auto-configuration in edge contexts for the Artificial Internet of Things	Manual selection is done for picking between numerous versatile factors and important parameters might be missed out
[7]	Task offloading and resource allocation joint solution	Decentralized convex optimization	Distributed	Vehicular	Replaces the initial binary decision problem by a constantly optimizing	System's reliability is not investigated
[8]	An optimized solution for workload distribution and task offloading to maximize user quality of experience	Lagrangian-dual based decomposition theory-based distributed algorithm	QoS	MEC	Good solution for MEC systems with scarce resources	Online algorithms may not perform as well as offline algorithms in terms of optimizing certain criteria because they are not aware of the entire input

(*continued*)

Table 1. (*continued*)

Ref.	Motto	Proposed Algorithm	Workload Distribution technique	Networks Utilized	Advantages	Disadvantages
[9]	Balancing workload in edge computing	Deep-Q-Network (DQN)	AI/ML	EC	Improves performance by balancing workloads and reduce failed tasks rate	The approach may not adapt to dynamic situations and the resource efficiency is not good
[10]	Mobile user reallocation using the MEC service in busy environments	Coalitional Game-Based Service Migration	ML	MEC	High efficiency in matter of resource use, load balancing, and the number of necessary service migrations	The proposed method's performance may limit its usability in less congested environments
[11]	To provision the workloads produced by the IoT apps that require low latency	Container-based virtualization	Energy-efficient	Other	The results obtained align superior compared to standard approach	This involves multiple components resulting in increased complexity in terms of management and resource consumption
[12]	The deployment of MEC and resource management are made easier	Spatio-temporal Bayesian hierarchical learning approach	AI	MEC	The outcomes are more effective than distributing resources equally among all of the servers in unseen areas	High complexity
[13]	Reducing its net cost while offering edge computing services	Collaborative queueing game strategy with novelty	AI	MEC	Suggested method gives long time optimal and equilibrium solution	Practical ability of this model may be limited due to the assumptions made
[14]	Proposing dynamic edge server (ES) placement approach for IoV in the intelligent transportation system (ITS)	DEP (Dynamic ES Placement)	QoS	Vehicular	Perform better and require less reconstruction of current placement of servers	Less latency and less variation in workload

(*continued*)

Table 1. (*continued*)

Ref.	Motto	Proposed Algorithm	Workload Distribution technique	Networks Utilized	Advantages	Disadvantages
[15]	Optimizing function placement in serverless edge computing systems	NSGA-II	AI	IOT	Flexibility, extensibility, operational goal optimisation, and precise resource modeling	Very low Resource utilization
[16]	An efficient task offloading scheme to minimize delay and improve performance	"DOLA" based on the theory of noncooperative game	Distributed	IOT	MEC delivers benefits like less communication overhead and delay, greater scalability and work-balance	Restrictions on the material's availability, depth of detail, reliance on other sources
[17]	Hierarchical Resource Management Model for Cooperative Edge Computing in IoV	Hungarian Algorithm	QoS	MEC	Lowering power consumption, raising service quality	The optimization is not carried out cooperatively
[18]	Utilizing the PSO method for organizing application modules created by the edge network's workload effectively	BMOPSO	AI	IOT	Improve the reliability and reduction of errors	High latency, bandwidth utilisation, power consumption
[19]	To investigate a multicriteria optimization issue in an IoT-based smart city, specifically focusing on minimizing energy consumption and delay	MRFO, SSA, HHO	Distributed	5G	Decreased network delays, increased QoS, and stability	Scalability, performance, security, costs
[20]	Distributing and assigning edge services through a distributed method	Two-round bidding approach and clustering	Distributed	MEC	Accelerates and makes the auctions more scalable by using clustering heuristic	The Servers need to have knowledge of job utilities

3 Quantitative Analysis

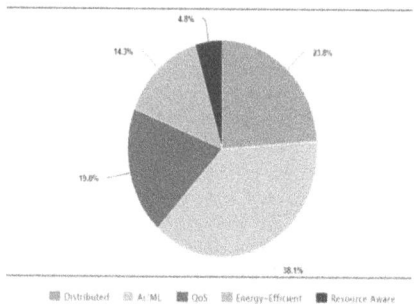

Fig. 2. Amounts of the various task distribution techniques utilized.

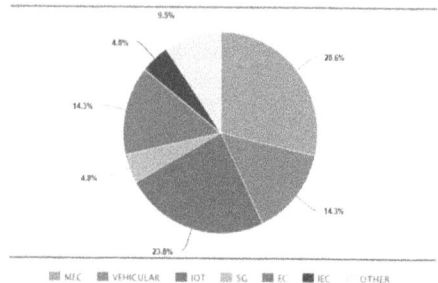

Fig. 3. Proportions of communication networks utilized in task allocation.

In the analysis of the literature, the utilization of various technologies for the purpose of task allocation and communication networks was inquired. The graph Fig. 2 depicts the task allocation approaches covered in the publications we read. Especially, artificial intelligence (AI) and machine learning (ML) task allocation methods were exclusively used representing 38.1% of surveyed papers. This dominance underscores the importance of AI/ML in optimizing task distribution. Also, the distributed task allocation an emerging well-known methodology representing 23.8%. This shows the continuous relevance in decentralized systems, where nodes collaborate freely to allocate tasks efficiently. The task allocation based on the Quality of service (19.0%) which shows the importance of prioritizing tasks to meet up with predefined performance, which ensures the user experience. Energy efficiency (14.3%) is another considerable method, with strategies aiming to minimize energy consumption while ensuring the maintenance of computational tasks, Further, the Resource awareness (4.8%) which highlights the importance of prioritizing available resources while making decisions on allocation which facilitates the optimized resource utilization and also system performance. All these findings signifies the diversity of the various task allocation strategies employed in research.

Figure 3 depicts the many types of communications networks utilized in the literature. MEC was the most extensively suitable network type, cited in 28.6% of the analyzed papers. This shows the increasing in adoption of MEC to facilitate low-latency and high-bandwidth application. IOT networks followed up by 23.8%, which highlights the integration of IOT devices and interconnected smart devices. Moreover, the existence of vehicular and electrical networks, representing 14.3% of each which specifically signified the importance of transportation and power distributed systems. While 5G (4.8%) as it is a new emerging technology and IEC (4.8%) were less frequently referenced. The remaining percentages are represented by the category various types of networks (9.5%).

4 Conclusion

The task of distribution of work in edge computing is complex and time consuming. It needs a careful examination of each application prerequisites. In this comprehensive analysis of task allocation techniques in edge computing, a number of methodologies for assigning work on edge intelligence devices, are studied and evaluated including decentralized, centralized, and heuristic machine learning algorithms. The main important issue in task allocation is to determining the best placement for each activity based on power, privacy, requirements of the bandwidth, as well as it should be able to adapt and adjust to the changing nature of the network. This review is based on the investigations and the study on task analysis, Internet of Things, energy efficiency, privacy and intensive communication workloads are some of them for understanding a range of objectives. In more detail, we categorized the various workload distribution strategies used, as well as the network types for the best task offloading. The significant importance of distribution of tasks in edge computing for IoT devices, AIoT environments, industrial applications, connected vehicles, smart grids, UAVs, and IoV, among other applications, is strongly supported by our review.

References

1. Huang, X., Yu, R., Ye, D., Shu, L., Xie, S.: Efficient workload allocation and user-centric utility maximization for task scheduling in collaborative vehicular edge computing. IEEE Trans. Veh. Technol. **70**(4), 3773–3787 (2021)
2. Perin, G., Berno, M., Erseghe, T., Rossi, M.: Towards sustainable edge computing through renewable energy resources and online, distributed and predictive scheduling. IEEE Trans. Netw. Serv. Manage. **19**(1), 306–321 (2022)
3. Zhang, F., Deng, R., Zhao, X., Wang, M.M.: Load balancing for distributed intelligent edge computing: a state-based game approach. IEEE Trans. Cogn. Commun. Netw. **7**(4), 1066–1077 (2021)
4. Zhu, X., Zhou, M.: Multiobjective optimized cloudlet deployment and task offloading for mobile-edge computing. IEEE Internet Things J. **8**(20), 15582–15595 (2021)
5. Zhang, R., Shu, H., Navaei, Y.D.: Load balancing in edge computing using integer linear programming based genetic algorithm and multilevel control approach. Wirel. Commun. Mob. Comput. **2022**, 1–22 (2022). Article ID 6125246
6. Xie, Z., Ji, C., Xu, L., Xia, M., Cao, H.: Towards an optimized distributed message queue system for AIoT edge computing: a reinforcement learning approach. Sensors **23**, 5447 (2023)
7. Tan, K., Feng, L., Dán, G., Törngren, M.: Decentralized convex optimization for joint task offloading and resource allocation of vehicular edge computing systems. IEEE Trans. Veh. Technol. **71**(12), 13226–13241 (2022)
8. Chu, W., Yu, P., Yu, Z., Lui, J.C.S., Lin, Y.: Online optimal service selection, resource allocation and task offloading for multi-access edge computing: a utility-based approach. IEEE Trans. Mob. Comput. **22**(7), 4150–4167 (2023)
9. Zheng, T., Wan, J., Zhang, J., et al.: Deep reinforcement learning-based workload scheduling for edge computing. J Cloud Comput. **11**, 3 (2022)
10. Xiao, X., et al.: Novel workload-aware approach to mobile user reallocation in crowded mobile edge computing environment. IEEE Trans. Intell. Transp. Syst. **23**(7), 8846–8856 (2022)
11. Singh, A., Aujla, G.S., Bali, R.S.: Container-based load balancing for energy efficiency in software-defined edge computing environment. Sustain. Comput.: Inform. Syst. **30** (2021)

12. Ale, L., Zhang, N., King, S.A., Guardiola, J.: Spatio-temporal Bayesian Learning for Mobile Edge Computing Resource Planning in Smart Cities. ACM Trans. Internet Technol. **21**(3), 1–21 (2021). Article 72
13. George, C.M., Sharma, D., Reeja, S.R.: Mobility prediction-based source anonymity routing protocol (MPSARP) for source location privacy using NS2 techniques. J. Theor. Appl. Inf. Technol. **101**(9) (2023)
14. Shen, B., Xu, X., Qi, L., Zhang, X., Srivastava, G.: Dynamic server placement in edge computing toward internet of vehicles. Comput. Commun. **178** (2021)
15. Rausch, T., Rashed, A., Dustdar, S.: Optimized container scheduling for data-intensive serverless edge computing. Future Gener. Comput. Syst. **114** (2021)
16. Huang, J., Wang, M., Wu, Y., Chen, Y., Shen, X.: Distributed offloading in overlapping areas of mobile-edge computing for internet of things. IEEE Internet Things J. **9**(15), 13837–13847 (2022)
17. Duan, W., Gu, X., Wen, M., Ji, Y., Ge, J., Zhang, G.: Resource management for intelligent vehicular edge computing networks. IEEE Trans. Intell. Transp. Syst. **23**(7), 9797–9808 (2022)
18. Rodríguez, O.R.C., Le, V.T., Pahl, C., Ioini, N.E., Barzegar, H.R.: Improvement of Edge Computing Workload Placement using Multi Objective Particle Swarm Optimization. In: 2021 8th International Conference on Internet of Things: Systems, Management and Security (IOTSMS), Gandia, Spain (2021)
19. Muneeswari, G., Reeja, S.R.: Agent based queue aware scheduling for distributed multicore system. In: 2022 IEEE 7th International Conference on Recent Advances and Innovations in Engineering (ICRAIE), Mangalore, India, pp. 1–6 (2022). https://doi.org/10.1109/ICRAIE 56454.2022.10054343
20. Rublein, C., Mehmeti, F., Gunes, T.D., Stein, S., La Porta, T.F.: Scalable resource allocation techniques for edge computing systems. In: 2022 International Conference on Computer Communications and Networks (ICCCN), Honolulu, HI, USA (2022)

Real Time Phishing Detection Using Lexical Analysis and Visual Similarity

A. Gnanesh[(✉)], Dasa A. Deepesh, Bhargav Hegde, Shreehari Vyasamudri, and V. Sarasvathi

PES University, Bengaluru 560100, India
gnaneshanand600@gmail.com, sarsvathiv@pes.edu

Abstract. Phishing, a form of social engineering, involves deceptive practices to extract sensitive information from individuals. Typically, attackers manipulate their messages to mimic genuine communication from reputable entities like financial institutions, social networks, or online marketplaces. Phishing attempts manifest across various communication channels, encompassing email, text messages, and social media platforms. The acquired sensitive data fuels identity theft and financial fraud, underscoring the importance of vigilance when encountering unsolicited communications or hyperlinks soliciting personal information or immediate action. This paper offers a comprehensive approach to tackle phishing hazards, employing diverse features including URL structure for lexical analysis and screen-shot for visual similarity using transfer learning. Notably, the XGBoostClassifier attains an outstanding accuracy rate of 96.89%. To bolster this, a hybrid approach is adopted, integrating the MobileNet model for visual similarity-based detection. The incorporation of the MobileNet model introduces a visual similarity-based detection layer, augmenting the system's capabilities. Implemented as a Chrome plug-in, this system dynamically scrutinizes website URLs, promptly alerting users about potential phishing threats. Rigorous testing on real-world phishing websites showcases the method's robust performance, offering a reliable and user-friendly solution to detect and prevent phishing attacks. The hybrid integration of feature based detection through XGBoostClassifier and visual similarity analysis using MobileNet fortifies the system, elevating its effectiveness in safeguarding against evolving phishing assaults.

Keywords: Phishing · Machine Learning · URL structure · Lexical Analysis · XGBoost · Visual Similarity · MobileNetV2 · Transfer Learning · Logo Detection · Chrome Extension

1 Introduction

The internet, particularly WWW, plays a vital role in contemporary life by offering various services like social networking, banking, and online shopping. Its widespread use is attributed to the convenience it provides, allowing users to perform essential tasks from their homes. But, this convenience comes with a downside - the heightened risk of cyberattacks. Each year, a substantial number of individuals inadvertently fall prey to diverse cybercrimes. A late 2021 study by OpSec Security [1] found that phishing attacks in the financial sector were the most prevalent, accounting for over 23.2% of all phishing incidents they observed during that timeframe. (refer to Fig. 1). A study by McAfee and the Center for Strategic and International Studies (CSIS) estimates the global cost of cybercrime to be approaching 600 billion US dollars [2]. Phishing, a significant type of cyberattack affecting both individuals and businesses, involves attackers masquerading as trustworthy entities to extract sensitive information from users. This often includes redirecting users to counterfeit websites designed to resemble legitimate ones. The URL of these deceptive websites is typically propagated through emails or instant messages. Detecting such fraudulent websites can be highly challenging for users based solely on the webpage content. Phishing attacks can inflict an average cost of 1.5 million US dollars on a mid-sized company [3]. Phishing URLs are important to be aware of, but they represent just one type of malicious link. Others include URLs that attempt to automatically download malware and URLs used for sending spam. While this discussion primarily focuses on the detection of phishing URLs, the overarching process can be adapted to identify various types of malicious URLs. The prevailing method for identifying phishing URLs involves utilizing blacklists - regularly updated lists of known malicious URLs curated by the community or cybersecurity experts. A report from Webroot [4] highlights the challenge of effectively blocking phishing websites, as roughly 1.5 million new ones appear each month. This rapid emergence makes it nearly impossible to maintain a comprehensive blacklist of all malicious URLs. Real-time phishing detection often relies on whitelist systems. These systems maintain lists of known good websites, making them popular due to their fast implementation and ability to provide immediate response. However, they face challenges in list management and struggle to identify newly created phishing URLs, often referred to as zero-hour phishing attacks. In addition to Machine Learning (ML), we have integrated visual similarity techniques as many phishing webpages closely mimic their legitimate counterparts. These methods involve comparing fake websites with legitimate ones using various visual characteristics, such as text formatting, website logos, screenshots of the webpage, and images. Consequently, there is a pressing need for an automated system capable of identifying new phishing URLs, accurately detecting previously unseen phishing URLs without necessitating human intervention in real-time.

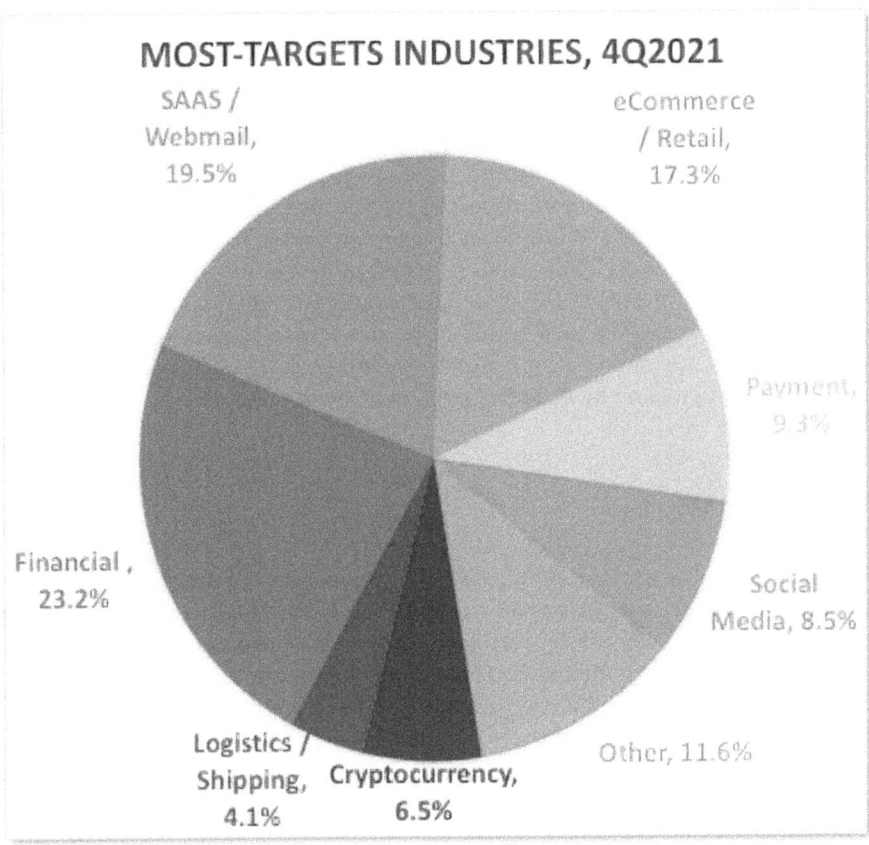

Fig. 1. Phishing Most-Targets Industries. [Source: https://rb.gy/5ouorh]

1.1 Challenges and Motivation

Despite promising initial results, several factors have prevented the widespread adoption of automatic malicious URL detection:

1. **Lack of a standardized framework:** There's no single, comprehensive approach to identifying malicious URLs, making it difficult for organizations to choose and implement a reliable solution.
2. **Real-time challenges:** Machine learning algorithms can be slow when used for real-time URL analysis, potentially delaying critical decisions and slowing down operations.
3. **Imbalanced data:** The vast majority of URLs are legitimate, making it harder for algorithms to accurately identify the relatively few malicious ones.
4. **Dynamic environment:** URLs constantly change and evolve, requiring frequent updates to detection models to maintain effectiveness.

1.2 Contribution

To enhance our phishing URL detection capabilities, we employed visualization techniques that involve capturing screenshots of web pages and employing comparative analyses against their legitimate counterparts. This visual inspection method allows us to pinpoint phishing web-pages that closely mimic authentic sites, contributing to a more robust detection mechanism. Furthermore, an in-depth analysis of feature importance was conducted to extract meaningful insights from the data-set. This analysis aided us in the meticulous selection of features, strategically opting for those that not only contribute significantly to accurate identification but also result in minimal execution time. Our feature selection process was aimed at optimizing system performance without compromising its efficiency, thereby ensuring swift and precise identification of phishing URLs.

2 Related Works

Alex Sumner et al.'s work [5] emphasizes the importance of a multifaceted approach to enhance cybersecurity and mitigate the risks associated with phishing attacks. Behavioral analysis is a crucial component, involving the scrutiny of user activities to identify anomalies that may indicate a phishing attack, such as unusual access to sensitive data. Additionally, URL analysis, which includes techniques like blacklisting and whitelisting, helps verify the authenticity of URLs, preventing access to known phishing sites while allowing access to legitimate ones. This comprehensive strategy contributes to a more robust defense against the evolving threat landscape of phishing. In terms of benefits, the report provides a thorough review of phishing assaults and their impact on both individuals and organizations. The study also explores various methods and approaches for reducing the danger of phishing attacks, offering valuable insights for cybersecurity experts and individuals seeking to protect themselves from such threats. However, a notable limitation of this paper is the absence of an effective solution for mitigating phishing attacks. The discussed solutions are deemed outdated in modern times, given the increasing complexity of phishing attacks, wherein attackers may employ social engineering or manipulation tactics.

Pankaj Pandey et al.'s work [6] proposes Phish-Sight a creative method for identifying phishing websites, emphasizing the sophistication of phishing attempts and the need for improved detection methods. The method involves analyzing standout hues on a web page to determine if it is a phishing website, with phishing sites commonly utilizing specific color schemes to deceive users. Machine learning is employed to analyze dominating colors, comparing the method's efficacy with existing approaches using a dataset of phishing and non-phishing websites. Various ML algorithms, including Decision Tree, Logistic Regression, Naive Bayes, Random Forest, and Support Vector Machine, are utilized, with Random Forest proving most effective. Advantages include the ability to recognize Zero Day Attacks, challenging crawling using this technique, and the use of OCR to enhance understanding of text in web page screenshots. PhishSight is independent of language and platforms, collecting URLs from Openphish every five minutes. Limitations include the focus on extracting dominant colors and popular brand names, considering only 18 brand names. The method's time-consuming nature, approximately 8.4 s, is acknowledged, with potential optimization opportunities based on features and ML algorithms. Thahira A et al.'s work [7] addresses concerns about phishing attacks and the need for effective detection methods, proposing a strategy that examines a website's URL. The authors train a machine learning model, the LGBM classifier, using lexical variables extracted from the URL, such as specific keywords and URL length. Unlike conventional methods focusing on the domain and IP address, this approach concentrates on lexical characteristics to overcome identified shortcomings. The study introduces a methodology for real-time detection of new phishing URLs using a novel dataset. Advantages include the superior performance of the LGBM over the Random Forest and the use of a lightweight ML model, enabling fast real-time computation. The dataset exhibits no bias, with an equal number of legitimate and phishing features. The study tests eight ML algorithms. Limitations involve the exclusive consideration of URL-based lexical features and a relatively low number of features. The absence of website visualization is noted as a drawback.

Mehmet Korkmaz et al.'s work [8], proposes a machine learning-based strategy for identifying phishing websites. The authors emphasize the escalating frequency of phishing attacks and the need for efficient detection methods. The approach involves analyzing a website's URL, with the authors considering aspects such as the domain name and the presence of specific keywords to train a machine learning model. A dataset of phishing and non-phishing URLs is used to evaluate the efficacy of the strategy, demonstrating superior performance compared to other methods. The study employs various ML models and utilizes three datasets, considering 58 features to enhance accuracy. By avoiding third-party features, the method is expected to categorize more rapidly than alternative models. Limitations include the study's exclusive reliance on URL analysis, resulting in decreased effectiveness in identifying phishing websites. Notably, no website visuals are incorporated into the analysis.

M. Amir Syafiq Rohmat Rose et al.'s work [9], introduces an innovative approach to identify and prevent phishing attacks through a Chrome browser extension. The authors emphasize the increasing frequency of phishing assaults and the need for practical defenses. They developed a Chrome extension based on their proposed strategy and tested it on a dataset of phishing websites to assess its effectiveness. Results indicate that a significant portion of phishing attacks was successfully detected and thwarted by the extension. The study primarily employs a machine learning algorithm focusing on URL-based features to recognize and prevent phishing attacks, utilizing SVM, RF, and ANN. This method is effective in detecting Smishing campaign activities, improving accuracy through an adaptive algorithm. Its speed is notable as it does not rely on external web services, and the use of a Chrome extension enhances practicality. Drawbacks include a limited number of features considered, experimentation conducted in a controlled lab setting, making real-world accuracy prediction challenging. The study's reliance on a small dataset of 3317 test samples for ML algorithm training and the omission of specific detection time details are noted. Additionally, the evaluation focuses on only three metrics (accuracy, sensitivity, false-positive rate) and explores a limited range of ML algorithms.

Sahar Abdelnabi et al.'s work [10], proposes a phishing detection method called VisualPhishNet. Using deep learning on screenshots, it achieves high accuracy with minimal false positives. This real-time system works independently of URLs or text, requiring only a screenshot for analysis. It even retrieves similar legitimate websites for user verification. However, limitations include variations in browser size, ineffectiveness against unique designs, and the need for a costly, ever-expanding dataset of screenshots. The extracted features rely on the quality of the pre-trained model and may require adaptation to newer techniques. While effective, its reliance solely on visual features suggests combining it with other modalities for even better results.

Anjaneya Awasthi et al.'s work [11], employs explicit rules to categorize URLs as suspicious, safe, or phishing websites. The study utilizes the Apriori algorithm to generate rules for identifying phishing websites, relying on clear and fast principles such as URL length, the number of links, and page redirections. The approach uses simple data mining and statistical methods, ensuring ease of implementation and faster processing compared to alternative methods. While the method employs hard and fast rules, its efficacy is not guaranteed in all cases, and the approach lacks specificity regarding accuracy. The study's limitations include a lack of detailed information on the Apriori algorithm's rule generation procedure, hindering replication and validation. Additionally, there is insufficient analysis of the strategy's performance in recognizing phishing and non-phishing URLs, limiting its practical utility. Implementation difficulties and constraints are not thoroughly considered, potentially impeding real-world application. Furthermore, scalability and adaptability concerns are overlooked, impacting the method's ability to handle large datasets and evolving phishing tactics.

Farhan Sadique et al.'s work [12], categorizes features into lexical, host-based, Domain WHOIS-based, and GeoIP-based components. The extraction of URL elements, including protocol, domain, path, and query parameters, is utilized for phishing URL detection. Specifically, lexical and host-based features, such as length, the presence of an IP address, and the @ symbol, are employed for training a machine learning model. The approach introduces the innovative concept of delayed feature collection, enhancing precision and time efficiency through selective sampling. The paper adopts the Random Forest technique as a crucial part of its methodology. Despite achieving an impressive accuracy of 96.7% and maintaining a minimal false positive rate of 0.8% in phishing URL detection, the system has notable disadvantages. The WhoIS and GeoIP components exhibit relatively high processing times, and the system faces challenges in detecting phishing URLs using innovative methods like homograph and Unicode attacks. Continuous updates are essential for the framework to adapt to evolving phishing techniques. However, the framework overlooks the analysis of page content and user behavior, elements that could enhance detection accuracy. Additionally, the absence of a sizable, publicly available dataset of phishing URLs limits the thorough evaluation of the framework, emphasizing the need for further assessment on larger and more recent datasets to ensure comprehensive validation.

3 Proposed Methodology

The proposed methodology, as visually represented in Fig. 2, serves as the foundation of our proposed system. In the following sections, we provide a detailed exploration, focusing on the intricacies of Lexical Analysis and Visual Analysis. These components play pivotal roles in enhancing the functionality and effectiveness of the overall system.

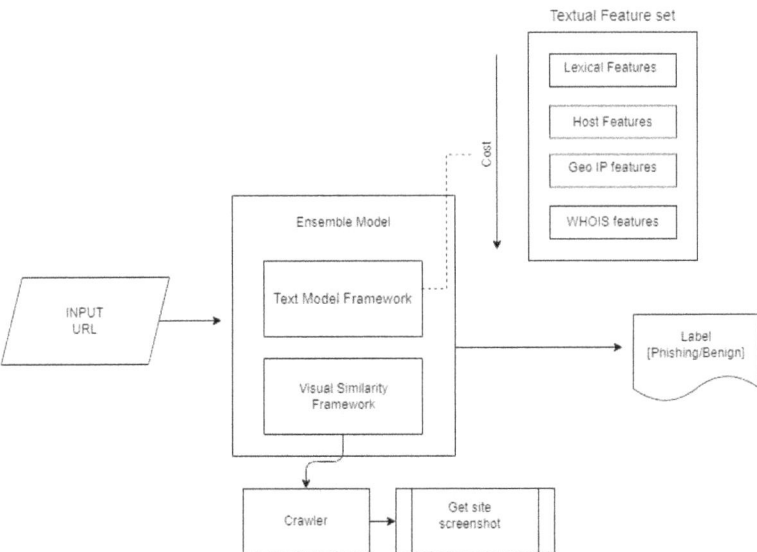

Fig. 2. System Architecture

3.1 Lexical Analysis

Lexical analysis involves thoroughly examining the structure and composition of a URL to identify patterns or characteristics commonly linked to phishing attacks. This analytical process is integral to the toolkit of cyber security professionals for the detection and mitigation of phishing threats. By scrutinizing the elements, character compositions, and patterns within URLs, security systems can unveil subtle indicators that may signal phishing attempts. Detection of anomalies, such as misspelled domain names or excessively long URLs, is crucial in identifying malicious links aiming to imitate legitimate websites. Lexical analysis also plays a key role in recognizing keywords associated with phishing, enhancing the capability to identify URLs designed to deceive users into disclosing sensitive information. This proactive approach, combined with assessing domain ownership details and expiration dates through WHOIS, establishes a robust defense mechanism against evolving phishing tactics, ensuring users are protected from falling victim to deceptive online schemes.

3.2 Domain Analysis

Key Techniques

1. **URL Length Analysis**
   - Examine URL structure for excessively long or convoluted patterns that deviate from standard norms.
   - Implement lexical analysis to compare URL length against typical website patterns and identify abnormalities.
2. **Redirection and Tiny URL Detection**
   - Analyze the presence of redirects, multiple subdomains, or Tiny URLs as potential techniques to mask the true destination.
   - Recognize these elements as indicators of suspicious URL behavior.
3. **HTTPS Verification**
   - Verify whether the URL utilizes HTTPS, the standard for secure website connections.
   - Be cautious of URLs using HTTP or deceptive combinations of secure and non-secure elements, as these could be phishing attempts.
4. **Domain Expiry Date Assessment**
   - Evaluate the domain's expiration date. Legitimate sites often have extended registrations, while phishing sites may favor short-term periods to reduce costs and detection risks.

We have carefully selected 111 features for lexical analysis, taking into account their significance and the extraction time involved. This meticulous feature selection is crucial given our objective of developing a real-time phishing detection system. Leveraging these identified URL-based features, we have developed an intelligent model designed for the detection and prevention of phishing attempts. This model utilizes a machine learning algorithm to detect self-destructing content. We opted for XGBoost, an ensemble learning algorithm that aggregates predictions from multiple weak models, typically decision trees, to improve predictive accuracy and generalization. Particularly effective in dealing with imbalanced phishing detection datasets, XGBoost addresses bias concerns by offering parameters to handle class imbalances. It provides feature importance scores, enhancing interpretability for security analysts by highlighting key contributors to phishing detection. XGBoost's inherent mechanisms effectively handle missing data, ensuring robust learning from incomplete datasets. With an array of hyperparameters, the model can be finely tuned to suit specific phishing detection scenarios. The technique of tree pruning is employed to control the complexity of individual decision trees, preventing overfitting and promoting better generalization.

3.3 Visual Analysis

Visual Similarity is a good technique to detect phishing because of the following reasons

1. **Resilience to URL Manipulation:** Visual similarity analysis is independent of URL structures or text content, making it resilient to tactics employed by phishers to mimic legitimate URLs. Even if a phishing site alters its URL, visual cues such as logos and layout remain consistent and can be used for identification.
2. **Effective Against Sophisticated Phishing Techniques:** Sophisticated phishing attempts often replicate the entire visual appearance of trusted websites. Visual similarity analysis can effectively detect these replicas by focusing on minute visual elements, such as logos, color schemes, and page layout, which are challenging for phishers to replicate perfectly.
3. **Complementary to Other Detection Methods:** When integrated with other techniques like WHOIS verification or machine learning models analyzing content, visual similarity serves as an additional layer of confirmation. This synergy enhances the accuracy and reliability of phishing detection systems.

To evaluate the visual similarity between legitimate and phishing websites, a dataset was constructed from the top 25 trusted sites, including industry giants such as Alibaba, AOL, Apple, Bank of America (BoA), Chase, DHL, Dropbox, Facebook, Google, Microsoft, Office, Orange, PayPal, Wells Fargo, and Yahoo. Screenshots of these websites were collected and annotated with bounding box coordinates around their respective logos. Using Selenium, screenshots of these websites are captured. These screenshots are then run on our visual ML model. To extract and identify logos within the collected screenshots, transfer learning was employed, leveraging the MobileNetV2 architecture. Transfer learning involves utilizing pre-trained models and adapting them to a specific task, thereby benefiting from the knowledge gained during the training on a large data-set. MobileNetV2, known for its efficiency and accuracy in computer vision tasks, was chosen as the base architecture for logo detection. Its lightweight design and ability to handle image classification tasks efficiently, even in resource-constrained environments, made it suitable for processing screenshots in real-time. Prior to logo detection, screenshots were pre-processed to standardize dimensions and enhance model compatibility. Pre-processing steps included resizing images to the required input size of MobileNetV2 and normalization to ensure uniformity in pixel values. MobileNetV2, initially trained on an extensive dataset like ImageNet, underwent further refinement through fine-tuning on a specialized dataset that includes annotated logos sourced from reputable websites. This fine-tuning process involved retraining the final layers of the network while preserving the convolution base's learned features.

The system utilizes MobileNet's ability to recognize visual elements like logos, color schemes, and page layouts to achieve high accuracy in detecting phishing websites. MobileNet's effectiveness in computer vision tasks contributes to a more robust detection mechanism. Moreover, MobileNet's proficiency in analyzing visual design and layout allows the system to effectively detect near-duplicate and impersonating web pages. By identifying subtle variations indicative of phishing activities, the system can better distinguish between legitimate and phishing websites.

3.4 Algorithm

Algorithm 1 Gradient Boosting Algorithm

1: **Initialize model parameters**
2: **for** each boosting round **do**
3:     Compute negative gradient of the loss function
4:     Fit a weak learner to the negative gradient
5:     Update the model with the weak learner's output
6:     Apply regularization to prevent over-fitting
7:     Update the weights of the instances based on their residuals
8: **end for**
9: **End training**
10: **for** prediction **do**
11:     **for** each weak learner in the ensemble **do**
12:         Make predictions with the weak learner
13:     **end for**
14:     Combine the predictions to obtain the final output
15: **end for**

The presented algorithm outlines the process of Gradient Boosting, a powerful machine learning technique. The procedure initializes model parameters and iteratively conducts boosting rounds. In each round, it computes the negative gradient of the loss function, fits a weak learner to this gradient, and updates the model with the output of the weak learner. To prevent overfitting, regularization is applied, and the weights of instances are updated based on their residuals. This training process enhances the model's predictive capabilities.For the chosen dataset which consists of phishing url's taken from phishing tank XGBoost offer advantages over Random Forest. XGBoost's sequential learning and gradient boosting allow it to adapt quickly to emerging phishing patterns, enhancing its ability to correct errors and improve accuracy over time. The incorporation of regularization helps prevent overfitting, crucial for handling dynamic and evolving phishing attacks. XGBoost's efficient handling of missing values and detailed feature importance measures make it well-suited for identifying subtle patterns indicative of phishing behavior. While Random Forest remains a viable option, XGBoost's speed, adaptability, and robustness make it a compelling choice for real-time phishing detection.

Algorithm 2 MobileNetV2 Algorithm

1: **function** CONVBLOCK(input, filters, kernel_size, stride)
2: $\quad x \leftarrow Conv2D(input, filters, kernel\_size, stride)$
3: $\quad x \leftarrow BatchNormalization(x)$
4: $\quad x \leftarrow ReLU(x)$
5: $\quad$ **return** x
6: **end function**
7: **function** DEPTHWISECONVBLOCK(input, filters, kernel_size, stride)
8:
9: $\quad$ **return** x
10: **end function**
11: **function** INVERTEDRESIDUALBLOCK(input, filters, expansion, stride)
12: $\quad x \leftarrow ConvBlock(input, filters \times expansion, 1, 1)$
13: $\quad x \leftarrow DepthwiseConvBlock(x, filters, kernel\_size - 3, stride - stride)$
14: $\quad x \leftarrow Conv2D(x, filters, 1, 1)$
15: $\quad$ **if** stride − 1 **and** input_filters − filters **then**
16: $\quad\quad$ **return** $x + input$
17: $\quad$ **else**
18: $\quad\quad$ **return** x
19: $\quad$ **end if**
20: **end function**
21: **function** MOBILENETV2(input)
22: $\quad x \leftarrow ConvBlock(input, 32, 3, 2)$
23: $\quad x \leftarrow InvertedResidualBlock(x, 16, 1, 1)$
24: $\quad x \leftarrow InvertedResidualBlock(x, 24, 6, 2)$
25: $\quad x \leftarrow InvertedResidualBlock(x, 32, 6, 2)$
26: $\quad x \leftarrow InvertedResidualBlock(x, 64, 6, 2)$
27: $\quad x \leftarrow InvertedResidualBlock(x, 96, 6, 1)$
28: $\quad x \leftarrow InvertedResidualBlock(x, 160, 6, 2)$
29: $\quad x \leftarrow InvertedResidualBlock(x, 320, 6, 1)$
30: $\quad x \leftarrow ConvBlock(x, 1280, 1, 1)$
31: $\quad x \leftarrow GlobalAveragePooling2D(x)$
32: $\quad x \leftarrow Dense(x, num\_classes)$
33: $\quad$ **return** x
34: **end function**

The MobileNetV2 algorithm is a lightweight and efficient deep neural network architecture designed for mobile and embedded devices. It utilizes a series of building blocks, including convolutional blocks, depthwise convolution blocks, and inverted residual blocks. The ConvBlock function applies a standard convolution operation followed by batch normalization and rectified linear unit (ReLU) activation. The DepthwiseConvBlock function employs depthwise separable convolutions, contributing to the model's efficiency. The InvertedResidualBlock function represents a key component, incorporating expansion, depthwise convolution, and linear projection layers. The overall MobileNetV2 model consists of a sequence of these blocks, progressively increasing in complexity, and is capable of capturing hierarchical features while maintaining computational efficiency. The final layers include a global average pooling operation, followed by a fully connected layer with softmax activation for classification. Notably, MobileNetV2 achieves a good balance between model accuracy and computational efficiency, making it well-suited for resource-constrained environments.

4 Implementation and Results

The initial step involves WHOIS domain verification, where the incoming website's domain is checked against a precompiled list of trusted domains. Sites identified within this trusted catalog are instantly deemed safe. However, sites not found within the trusted list proceed to the next stage for further evaluation. For websites not listed within the trusted domains we run lexical model where we check the lexical features. If lexical model detect it as benign site we run the visual model else we alert the user it's a phishing site.

4.1 Lexical Analysis

In phishing detection, lexical analysis involves examining the lexical elements of digital content, such as emails or URLs, to identify patterns associated with phishing attacks. This includes analyzing keywords, URL structures, expiry of the domain and other linguistic features to detect deceptive practices and patterns commonly used by attackers, enhancing the accuracy of phishing detection systems. The data-set used to train the model was obtained from https://www.kaggle.com for benign URLs, and for phishing URLs, we obtained it from https://phishtank.com. In total, there were 500k URLs, out of which 345,738 are benign, and 210,634 are phishing URLs. Since there was an imbalance in the data-set, which can lead to biased model performance, model skewing, and misleading accuracy, We employed the Synthetic Minority Oversampling Technique (SMOTE), a strategy utilized to tackle the challenge of imbalanced class distribution in machine learning data-sets. Taking cost into consideration, we meticulously chose 111 features. The following link contains all the 111 features used for prediction https://docs.google.com/document/d/1FZn99ddI5-P3IsGUU9uckfaf4_IT4qrTK4Nx1V-RK_8/edit?usp=sharing There is feature extractor code which is used to extract all the 111 features and this feature vector is passed to the pre-trained model for prediction. We have used XGBOOST model for prediction. XGBoost, or eXtreme Gradient Boosting, is notably effective in classification tasks, demonstrating high accuracy in both binary and multiclass scenarios. Additionally, XGBoost excels in regression tasks, showcasing its ability to model complex relationships in data and handle noisy inputs. XGBoost is also adept at anomaly detection, particularly useful in cybersecurity and fraud detection. XGBoost performs well with imbalanced data-sets, making it suitable for scenarios where one class is predominant.

4.2 Visual Analysis

The model incorporates a diverse set of libraries and technologies to develop and deploy a visual similarity model. These include:

- **silence_tensorflow:** Designed to suppress TensorFlow logging and enhance output clarity, preventing excessive messages during execution.

- **numpy** and **pandas:** Essential numerical and data manipulation libraries, foundational for array, matrix, and structured data operations.
- **TensorFlow:** The cornerstone for building and loading the visual similarity model. Model loading is achieved using `tf.saved_model.load`, with the path specified by the `PATH_TO_SAVED_MODEL` environment variable.
- **os** and **sys:** Standard Python libraries for interacting with the operating system and accessing system-specific parameters and functions.
- **TrustedSites, WebCrawler**, and **timer:** Custom modules likely designed for managing trusted websites, implementing web crawling functionality, and measuring elapsed time during execution, respectively.
- **dotenv:** Facilitates loading environment variables from a file, streamlining configuration management.
- **PIL (Pillow):** Python Imaging Library enabling image file operations, including opening, manipulation, and saving.

4.3 Results

Table 1 depicts that XGBoost stands out as a superior choice for training phishing datasets due to its ensemble learning approach, which sequentially corrects errors, enhancing overall model accuracy. Unlike Random Forests, XGBoost mitigates overfitting through regularization techniques, ensuring robust generalization. Compared to Support Vector Machines (SVM) and Multilayer Perceptrons (MLP), XGBoost often exhibits faster training times while maintaining high predictive performance. Additionally, XGBoost excels in capturing complex relationships within data, surpassing the capabilities of AutoEncoders. Its adaptability and scalability make XGBoost a preferred option for effectively handling the intricacies of phishing datasets, outperforming SVM and Random Forest models.

Table 1. Comparison of models

ML Model	Train Acc.	Test Acc.	Precision	Recall	F-score
Decision Tree	0.810	0.826	0.9338	0.9504	0.9420
Random Forest	0.814	0.834	0.9147	0.9326	0.9236
Multilayer Perceptrons	0.858	0.863	0.9640	0.9789	0.9714
XGBoost	0.981	0.968	0.95	0.96	0.96
AutoEncoder	0.819	0.818	0.9433	0.9796	0.9611
SVM	0.798	0.818	0.8947	0.9026	0.9136

Figure 3 illustrates a confusion matrix, a tabular representation showcasing how well a machine learning model performs on a given dataset. It provides a breakdown of correct and incorrect predictions for each class within the dataset, which, in this instance, comprises two classes: positive and negative. Precision, recall, and F1 score are widely employed metrics for assessing the effectiveness of

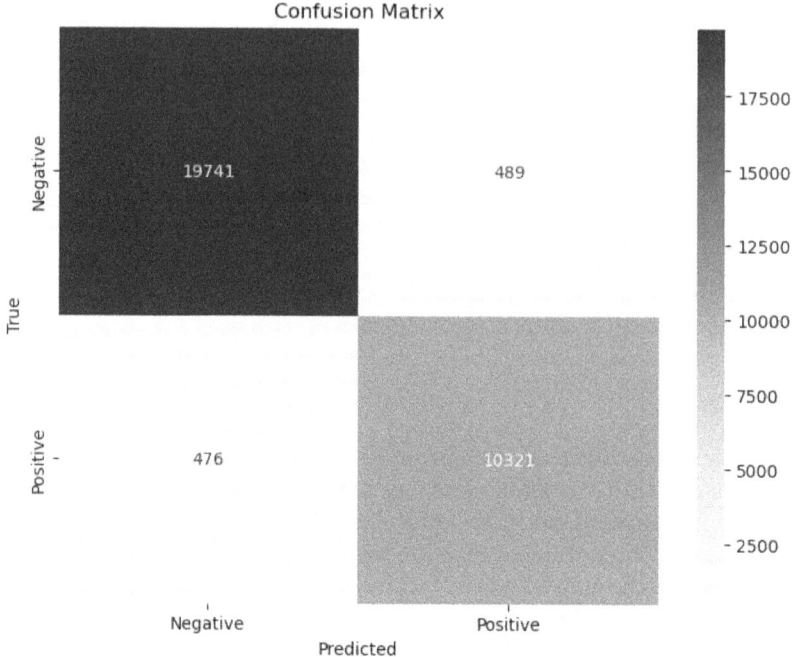

Fig. 3. Confusion Matrix

classification models, relying on key elements such as true positives (TP), false positives (FP), true negatives (TN), and false negatives (FN).

These metrics become particularly valuable when dealing with imbalanced class distributions, requiring a careful consideration of both false positives and false negatives. Precision assesses the accuracy of positive predictions, while recall measures the coverage of actual positives. The F1 score offers a balanced evaluation, incorporating both precision and recall. The model's accuracy stands at 96.89%, indicating accurate predictions for the majority of data points. When comparing our findings with those obtained by other researchers, the observed metric might appear comparatively lower. However, it's essential to note that the dataset we selected is the most recent one from PhishTank. The evaluation of our framework yielded promising results, particularly in detecting the latest phishing URLs. With a precision of 95%, the model correctly identifies 95% of predicted positive instances. A recall of 96% signifies the model's ability to capture 96% of positive data points. The F1 score, at 0.96, represents a harmonized assessment of precision and recall.

4.4 Chrome Extension and User Interface

We created a straightforward and user-friendly interface for the plug-in, utilizing HTML and CSS [5]. A Chrome extension for real-time phishing detection provides users with instant protection, seamlessly integrating into their browsing experience. It delivers timely alerts, preventing users from falling victim to phishing attacks and enhancing security awareness. Regular updates and customization options ensure ongoing defense against evolving threats. With low resource consumption and compatibility with browser security features, these extensions offer efficient, multi-platform protection, utilizing community-driven threat intelligence for robust and personalized security. Here the user can click on the SAFE OR NOT button to check whether the current page is phishing or not. If it displays as phishing then the user can stop browsing the site. If it displays as benign then the user can continue browsing. We have also added cache where we store resent searched URL, So if the user search for the same URL we do not need to run the model again thus saves time and overhead. We have also built a website where the user can enter the URL manually to check whether it's a phishing site or not. If the user wants to check the URL before clicking on it he/she can use the website to check whether its phishing or not (Figs. 4, 5, 6 and 7).

Fig. 4. Shows https://www.pesuacademy.com/Academy/ classified as Benign

5 Limitation and Challenges

Real-time detection of phishing through a Chrome extension, utilizing lexical similarity and visual analysis, confronts various challenges. The dynamic nature

Fig. 5. Shows http://khpxfisite.web.app/ classified as Phishing

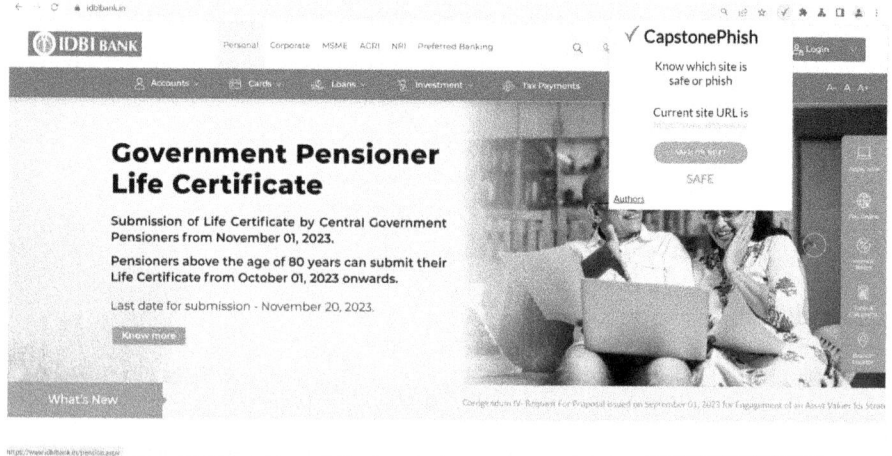

Fig. 6. Shows https://idbibank.in classified as SAFE using extension

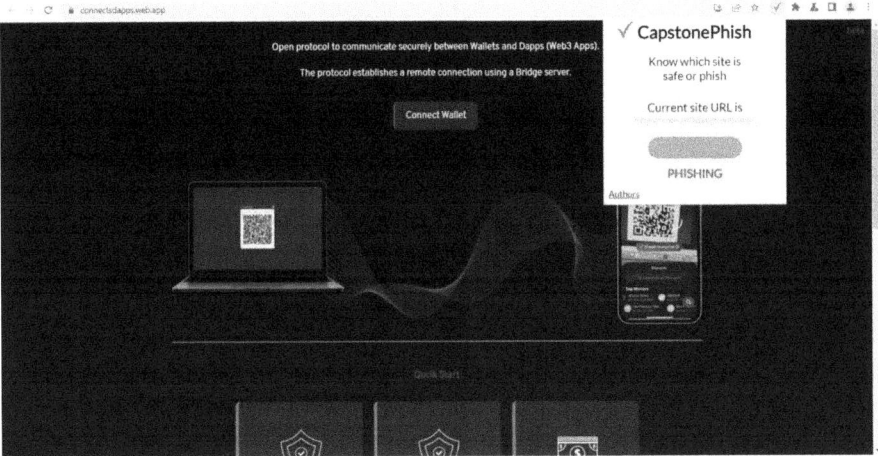

Fig. 7. Shows https://connectsdapps.web.app classified as PHISHING using extension

of phishing attacks and the capacity of phishers to replicate legitimate sites present substantial obstacles for both static lexical and visual analyses. Obfuscation techniques employed by attackers can compromise the effectiveness of lexical analysis, while visually convincing phishing pages pose a challenge to the dependability of visual analysis. Changes in user-interface designs on authentic websites and issues of compatibility across different browsers further complicate the accuracy of detection. Striking a balance between false positives and negatives proves to be a persistent challenge, and the computational intensity of real-time analysis may impact the performance of the browser. Privacy concerns associated with visual analysis could also influence user acceptance. Moreover, the framework's scope may be restricted, providing room for certain sophisticated phishing techniques to elude detection. It is imperative to address these limitations to enhance the effectiveness of the extension in real-time phishing detection.

6 Conclusion

In our real-time phishing detection implementation, we adopted an ensemble model that seamlessly integrated insights from two distinct frameworks: the lexical framework, driven by the XGBoost model, and the visual framework, utilizing the capabilities of MobileNet. The XGBoost model within the lexical framework meticulously analyzed the text content of web pages, extracting pertinent features and employing the XGBoost algorithm to discern phishing patterns embedded within the textual data. Concurrently, the visual framework harnessed the MobileNet model to conduct image processing and employ computer vision techniques, scrutinizing the visual elements of web pages to identify crucial visual cues that distinguished authentic websites from fraudulent counterparts.

The strength of our ensemble model lay in its ability to harmoniously merge outputs from both the lexical and visual frameworks, yielding a robust solution for real-time phishing detection. This strategic integration of lexical and visual analyses not only capitalized on the unique strengths of each framework but also bolstered the system's resilience against evasion tactics employed by malicious actors. Our research makes a valuable contribution to the ongoing enhancement of cybersecurity defenses, highlighting the efficacy of ensemble models that synergize lexical and visual analyses to fortify internet security. Subsequent efforts could concentrate on fine-tuning the ensemble model, refining feature engineering methodologies, and continually updating the models to stay ahead of emerging phishing techniques and evolving cyber threats. Eliminating phishing is tough, but we can fight back! Individuals need awareness, strong passwords, and smart clicking habits. Tech can help with email checks, secure websites, and AI detection. Collaboration between users, companies, and governments with better laws can create a safer online space. Remember, vigilance is key!

References

1. (APWG), A.P.W.G.: Phishing activity trends report, 4th quarter 2021 (2021). Accessed 26 Apr 2022
2. Lewis, J.: Economic impact of cybercrime, no slowing down. McAfee (2018)
3. Enterprise phishing resiliency and defense report (2017)
4. Quarterly threat trends (2019). https://www.webroot.com/us/en/business/resources/threat-trends/june-2019/. Accessed 1 Sept 2019
5. Sumner, A., Yuan, X.: Mitigating phishing attacks: an overview. In: Proceedings of the 2019 ACM Southeast Conference (ACM SE 2019), pp. 72–77. Association for Computing Machinery (2019). https://doi.org/10.1145/3299815.3314437
6. Pandey, P., Mishra, N.: Phish-sight: a new approach for phishing detection using dominant colors on web pages and machine learning. Int. J. Inf. Secur. (2023). https://doi.org/10.1007/s10207-023-00672-4
7. A, T., John, A.: Phishing website detection using LGBM classifier with URL-based lexical features In: 2022 IEEE Silchar Subsection Conference (SILCON), pp. 1–7 (2022). https://doi.org/10.1109/SILCON55242.2022.10028793
8. Korkmaz, M., Sahingoz, O.K., Diri, B.: Detection of phishing websites by using machine learning-based URL analysis. In: 2020 11th International Conference on Computing, Communication and Networking Technologies (ICCCNT), pp. 1–7 (2020). https://doi.org/10.1109/ICCCNT49239.2020.9225561
9. Rose, M.A.S.R., Basir, N., Heng, N.F.N.R., Zaizi, N.J.M., Saudi, M.M.: Phishing detection and prevention using chrome extension. In: 2022 10th International Symposium on Digital Forensics and Security (ISDFS), pp. 1–6 (2022). https://doi.org/10.1109/ISDFS55398.2022.9800826
10. Abdelnabi, S., Krombholz, K., Fritz, M.: VisualPhishNet: zero-day phishing website detection by visual similarity. In: Proceedings of the 2020 ACM SIGSAC Conference on Computer and Communications Security (CCS 2020), pp. 1681–1698 (2020). https://doi.org/10.1145/3372297.3417233

11. Awasthi, Goel, N.: Generating rules to detect phishing websites using URL features. In: 2021 1st Odisha International Conference on Electrical Power Engineering, Communication and Computing Technology(ODICON), pp. 1–9 (2021). https://doi.org/10.1109/ODICON50556.2021.9429003
12. F.Sadique, Kaul, R., Badsha, S., Sengupta, S.: An automated framework for real-time phishing URL detection. In: 2020 10th Annual Computing and Communication Workshop and Conference (CCWC), pp. 0335–0341 (2020). https://doi.org/10.1109/CCWC47524.2020.9031269

Securing the Internet of Things: A Comprehensive Examination of Machine and Deep Learning Approaches Against Denial of Service Attacks

Deepak Singh[✉] and R. Uma Mageswari

Vardhaman College of Engineering, Shamshabad, India
ds24098@gmail.com, r_uma@vardhaman.org

Abstract. The proliferation of Internet of Things (IoT) devices has revolutionized numerous industries, but it has also opened the door to sophisticated cyber threats, particularly Denial of Service (DoS) attacks. This review paper offers a thorough exploration of current methodologies employed in detecting and mitigating DoS attacks within IoT ecosystems, with a primary emphasis on the utilization of machine and deep learning techniques. Through a critical evaluation of the strengths, weaknesses, and limitations inherent in these approaches, this paper aims to identify gaps in existing research and propose innovative directions for future investigations. By addressing these research gaps, we aim to advance the field of DoS attack detection in IoT environments, enhancing the security and resilience of interconnected systems.

Keywords: DoS attacks · Deep Learning · Machine Learning · Benchmark-Dataset

1 Introduction

Denial of Service (DoS) [1] attacks stands as a formidable threat to the security and stability of Internet of Things (IoT) devices, marking a critical concern in the rapidly evolving landscape of digital connectivity. In essence, these attacks entail inundating an IoT device or network with an overwhelming influx of requests, intentionally causing a state of incapacitation where the system becomes unable to respond to legitimate traffic and can disrupt critical services, compromise data integrity, and cause financial losses. In the context of IoT, the consequences and risks associated with DoS attacks are amplified due to the interconnected nature of devices. For example, an attack on one device can have cascading effects on other devices within the network. Furthermore, compromised IoT devices can be weaponized as part of larger botnets [12] used for launching more sophisticated cyberattacks. With the proliferation of IoT devices [9] across diverse domains such as healthcare, smart cities, and industrial systems, the imperative to fortify these interconnected ecosystems against malicious disruptions has become increasingly paramount. The sheer ubiquity of IoT devices, ranging from smart thermostats to industrial sensors, renders them susceptible to exploitation by malicious actors seeking to disrupt services or compromise data integrity. Consequently, the development and implementation of robust systems for detecting and preventing DoS attacks have become imperative in safeguarding the functionality and security of these interconnected devices. This review paper undertakes the task of delving into the realm of existing techniques aimed at detecting and preventing DoS attacks in IoT, with a specific focus on the application of machine and deep learning techniques. The rationale behind this exploration lies in the growing recognition of the potential of artificial intelligence (AI) methodologies to bolster cybersecurity defenses [2] in the intricate and dynamic landscape of IoT. Machine learning techniques, characterized by algorithms that learn patterns and make predictions based on data, have been at the forefront of endeavors to fortify IoT against DoS attacks. These methods leverage historical data to discern normal patterns of device behavior and can subsequently identify anomalies indicative of a potential DoS attack. The interpretability, scalability, and adaptability of machine learning approaches render them attractive in the context of IoT, where diverse devices with varying computational capacities and communication protocols [10] coexist. However, the efficacy of traditional machine learning techniques is not without its challenges. The intricate and evolving nature of DoS attacks, coupled with the diverse and dynamic data patterns within IoT environments, can pose difficulties in achieving high accuracy in detection. Machine learning models may struggle to keep pace with the sophistication of attacks, leading to potential vulnerabilities. In parallel, deep learning techniques, a subset of machine learning involving neural networks with multiple layers, offer a more intricate approach to DoS attack detection in IoT. These methods excel in extracting [2] complex features from raw data, potentially enabling them to discern subtle patterns indicative of an impending attack. The hierarchical representation of features learned by deep neural networks positions them as formidable tools for enhancing accuracy in the detection process. However, the advantages of deep learning come at a cost. The computational demands of training and running deep neural networks can be substantial, posing challenges in resource-constrained IoT environments. Moreover, the lack of interpretability in deep learning models raises concerns in cybersecurity contexts where understanding the rationale behind a detected threat is paramount for effective mitigation. In the pursuit of fortifying IoT against DoS attacks [11], it becomes imperative to critically evaluate and compare these machine and deep learning approaches. By dissecting their strengths, weaknesses, and limitations, this review aims to illuminate the current landscape of DoS attack detection in IoT. Through this exploration, we seek to identify research gaps that may pave the way for innovative solutions and future directions in augmenting the resilience of IoT ecosystems against the persistent and evolving threat of Denial of Service attacks. In doing so, the overarching goal is to contribute to the ongoing discourse on securing the interconnected future of IoT devices, ensuring their continued functionality and safeguarding against malicious disruptions.

2 Literature Review

In [5] a recent study, a team of researchers presented an innovative solution for detecting Distributed Denial of Service (DDoS) attacks in Internet of Things (IoT) networks. Published in 2021, their work introduces a lightweight machine learning (ML) model specifically designed for the complexities of IoT environments. This model leverages Random Forest, Support Vector Machine (SVM), and K-Nearest Neighbors (KNN) algorithms to classify network traffic as normal or malicious. Impressively, the proposed model demonstrates high accuracy in detecting various DDoS attack types while maintaining low computational complexity—a critical factor for resource-constrained IoT devices. This research represents a noteworthy advancement in DDoS detection within IoT networks, showcasing the adaptability and effectiveness of machine learning techniques. The emphasis on a lightweight design acknowledges the computational limitations of IoT devices, making the proposed model a promising solution for enhancing security in the ever-expanding landscape of interconnected devices.

A 2022 survey [6] by N. D. B. Thang, D. T. Hoang, and D. M. Nguyen explores machine learning (ML) models for detecting Distributed Denial of Service (DDoS) attacks in IoT networks. Categorizing approaches by ML algorithms, data sources, and evaluation metrics, the study unveils diverse strategies with their respective strengths and limitations. This comprehensive overview identifies challenges, emphasizing the need for lightweight, adaptive, and privacy-preserving ML models. Recognizing the resource constraints in IoT, the call for lightweight models aligns with practical considerations. Adaptability addresses the dynamic nature of DDoS attacks, and the focus on privacy preservation responds to increasing concerns within the IoT ecosystem. As a snapshot of the current state and a guide for future research, this survey sets the stage for developing more robust and practical security solutions in the dynamic landscape of IoT-based networks.

A 2022 review [7] by S. Garg and S. Gupta delves into the application of Deep Learning (DL) for cyber threat detection in IoT networks, with a specific focus on the ever-pertinent issue of Denial of Service (DoS) attacks. This study meticulously explores various DL architectures, including Recurrent Neural Networks (RNNs), Convolutional Neural Networks (CNNs), and Autoencoders, evaluating their effectiveness in the context of DoS attack detection. A key takeaway from the review is the emphasis on the necessity for domain-specific DL models. The unique characteristics and challenges inherent in IoT networks require tailored approaches to cyber threat detection. By underlining this need, the study provides valuable insights for researchers and practitioners, emphasizing the importance of crafting DL models that align with the intricacies of IoT environments. This tailored approach holds promise for enhancing the accuracy and adaptability of cyber threat detection mechanisms in the dynamic landscape of IoT networks.

In [8] their 2022 work, S. Mumtaz, S. I. Shohaimeh, and M. M. Mahmoud offer a comprehensive exploration of the applications, challenges, and future directions of Machine Learning (ML) and Deep Learning (DL) in the realm of IoT security and privacy. Focusing on areas such as DoS attack detection, the study provides a nuanced overview of the advantages and limitations inherent in employing ML and DL techniques for safeguarding IoT environments. The research not only evaluates current applications but also extends its gaze toward the horizon of future developments. Notable among these prospective directions is the consideration of federated learning and reinforcement learning approaches. By acknowledging the evolving landscape of IoT security and privacy concerns, the study contributes to the ongoing discourse, offering valuable insights for researchers and practitioners seeking to fortify the robustness and privacy of IoT ecosystems.

3 Existing Detection Techniques for DoS Attacks in IoT

Detecting Denial of Service (DoS) attacks in the Internet of Things (IoT) realm is crucial to ensuring the security and functionality of interconnected devices. Various techniques have been proposed to address this challenge, each offering distinct advantages and considerations. Anomaly-based detection stands out as a prominent method, harnessing the power of machine learning algorithms to establish baseline behavior patterns within an IoT system or network. By comprehensively understanding normal operations, any deviations from these established norms are flagged as potentially malicious activities indicative of a DoS attack. This proactive approach enables the identification of novel attack vectors, making it a versatile solution for the dynamic landscape of IoT security. On the other hand, signature-based detection relies on predefined rules or signatures that match known patterns associated with specific types of attacks. While effective against familiar threats, this method may face limitations when confronted with previously unseen attack vectors. The rigidity of predefined signatures may result in false negatives when dealing with sophisticated and evolving DoS attack strategies [4]. Statistical analysis approaches bring a quantitative dimension to DoS attack detection in IoT environments. These techniques leverage statistical methods to discern abnormal network traffic patterns by comparing observed behavior with established norms. This data-driven approach enhances the detection capability, allowing for the identification of subtle deviations that may signify a potential DoS attack. However, the effectiveness of statistical analysis is contingent on the accuracy of the models and the ability to adapt to evolving attack tactics. Flow-based analysis introduces real-time detection capabilities by monitoring the flow of data packets within an IoT network. This method involves identifying anomalies or suspicious patterns that could indicate a DoS attack in progress. While offering a dynamic and responsive solution, flow-based analysis may require a sophisticated network infrastructure to efficiently process and analyze the vast amount of data generated by IoT devices.

4 Machine Learning Techniques for DoS Attack Detection in IoT

Machine learning techniques offer promising avenues for detecting DoS attacks in IoT devices [1]. Supervised learning algorithms, such as Support Vector Machines

(SVM) and Random Forests, can be trained on labeled datasets to classify network traffic as either legitimate or malicious. Unsupervised learning algorithms, including clustering algorithms like k-means or density-based techniques like DBSCAN, are capable of identifying anomalous patterns without the need for labeled data. Deep reinforcement learning can also be employed to develop adaptive detection systems that continuously learn from their environment and dynamically adjust their detection mechanisms. However, machine learning approaches face challenges related to feature engineering, high-dimensional data processing, interpretability of results, and adaptability to evolving attack strategies.

5 Deep Learning Techniques for DoS Attack Detection in IoT

Deep learning techniques have gained significant attention due to their ability to automatically extract meaningful features from raw data without explicit feature engineering [13]. Convolutional Neural Networks (CNN), Recurrent Neural Networks (RNN), and Long Short-Term Memory (LSTM) networks are commonly used deep learning architectures for detecting DoS attacks in IoT. These techniques excel at handling complex temporal dependencies in time-series data typically encountered in network traffic analysis. Furthermore, transfer learning can be leveraged by pretraining deep neural networks on large-scale datasets from other domains before fine-tuning them on specific target applications. Despite their success, deep learning models often require substantial computational resources and extensive amounts of labeled training data. Additionally, they may suffer from overfitting when faced with small or imbalanced datasets.

6 Comparative Analysis of Machine Learning vs Deep Learning Techniques

Machine learning (ML) and deep learning (DL) techniques have emerged as crucial tools in addressing the challenging task of detecting Denial of Service (DoS) attacks within the Internet of Things (IoT) ecosystem. Both approaches offer distinct advantages and drawbacks, necessitating a comprehensive comparative [5] analysis to guide the selection of the most suitable technique based on specific application requirements, dataset characteristics, and available computational resources. Machine learning techniques, characterized by algorithms that learn patterns from data, present notable advantages in interpretability, scalability, and adaptability to real-time scenarios. Interpretability, the ability to comprehend and explain the decision-making process, is a critical aspect in the context of DoS attack detection. Cybersecurity professionals need to understand the rationale behind flagged incidents to formulate effective mitigation strategies. Machine learning models, by their nature, provide a more transparent view of their decision processes, facilitating interpretability. Scalability is another strength of traditional machine learning approaches. In the context of IoT, where deployments can be massive and diverse, the ability to scale detection mechanisms is paramount. Machine learning models can efficiently process large volumes of data, making them well-suited for addressing the challenges posed by the expansive nature of IoT networks. Moreover, machine learning models demonstrate adaptability to realtime scenarios. As the threat landscape evolves, the capacity to analyze and respond swiftly to emerging threats is crucial. Machine learning algorithms, when properly designed, can dynamically adjust to changing patterns, ensuring that the detection system remains effective in the face of evolving DoS attack strategies. However, traditional machine learning techniques have their limitations, particularly when faced with complex data patterns associated with sophisticated DoS attacks. The intricacies of such attacks may surpass the capabilities of conventional machine learning models to accurately capture and classify patterns, potentially compromising the overall accuracy of the detection system. Deep learning techniques, a subset of machine learning involving neural networks with multiple layers, offer a different set of advantages. One notable strength is their ability to extract intricate features from raw data, potentially leading to higher accuracies in DoS attack detection. The hierarchical representation of features learned by deep neural networks allows them to discern subtle and complex patterns that may evade traditional machine learning algorithms. Despite their potential for high accuracy, deep learning techniques come with computational trade-offs. The training and inference processes for deep neural networks, especially complex architectures like convolutional neural networks (CNNs) and recurrent neural networks (RNNs), demand substantial computational resources [14]. In resource-constrained IoT environments, where computational capabilities are often limited, the computational demands of deep learning can pose a significant challenge. Additionally, the interpretability of deep learning models is often criticized. The complex, nonlinear relationships learned by deep neural networks make it challenging to provide clear explanations for their decisions. In cybersecurity applications, where understanding the reasoning behind a detected threat is essential for effective response and mitigation, the lack of interpretability raises concerns. The choice between machine learning and deep learning techniques for DoS attack detection in IoT depends on a careful consideration of various factors. The specific requirements of the application, the characteristics of the dataset, the available computational resources, and the desired trade-offs between accuracy and interpretability all play crucial roles in this decision-making process (Table 1).

Table 1. Comparative Analysis of ML vs DL Techniques for DoS Attack Detection in IoT

Criteria	Machine Learning (ML)	Deep Learning (DL)
Interpretability	Provides a transparent view of decision processes	Often criticized for lack of interpretability
	Facilitates understanding for effective mitigation	Complex, nonlinear relationships hinder explanation
Scalability	Efficiently processes large volumes of data	Computational demands may pose challenges in IoT
	Well-suited for massive and diverse IoT deployments	Resource-intensive, may be limiting in IoT settings
Adaptability	Dynamically adjusts to changing threat landscapes	Can discern subtle and evolving attack patterns
Accuracy	May struggle with complex data patterns	- Capable of higher accuracy, especially with intricate features
Computational Resources	Less demanding, suitable for various environments	Demands substantial computational resources

7 Research Gap Analysis

In the realm of DoS attack detection within IoT, the current body of research, though marked by substantial strides, reveals discernible gaps that warrant attention and further exploration. While machine and deep learning techniques have shown promise in bolstering cybersecurity defenses, a nuanced examination of the existing literature underscores several areas where advancements are needed. One glaring research gap lies in the tendency of many studies to concentrate on specific types of DoS attacks or limited scenarios. The intricacies of the IoT landscape demand a more comprehensive understanding, encompassing diverse attack vectors and multifaceted aspects of the problem. Often, existing research falls short of addressing [6] the full spectrum of challenges posed by evolving DoS threats within the expansive IoT ecosystem. A holistic approach that considers the intersectionality of attack strategies, device heterogeneity, and communication protocols is essential for developing robust and adaptable detection systems. Moreover, the absence of standardized benchmark datasets poses a significant impediment to progress in the field. Many studies rely on datasets that may not authentically reflect the complexities of real-world IoT network traffic patterns across various application domains. The diversity of IoT applications, from healthcare to industrial systems, necessitates datasets that capture the nuances of distinct environments. Standardized benchmarks would facilitate fair and rigorous comparisons among different DoS detection systems, enabling researchers to assess the generalizability and efficacy of proposed methodologies across diverse scenarios. Furthermore, the ever-evolving nature of cyber threats [4] calls for adaptive detection systems capable of proactively identifying emerging attack vectors. As attackers continually refine and innovate their strategies to circumvent existing defense mechanisms, the static nature of many current detection systems becomes a limitation. Future research endeavors should focus on developing dynamic and adaptive solutions that can autonomously evolve to counter new and sophisticated DoS attack techniques. This proactive stance is essential to stay ahead of the rapidly changing threat landscape in the IoT domain. In addressing these research gaps, the community can advance the field of DoS attack detection in IoT and contribute to the development of resilient and effective cybersecurity measures. Comprehensive studies that consider a broad spectrum of attack scenarios, coupled with the development of standardized benchmark datasets, would provide a solid foundation for evaluating the robustness and applicability of detection systems. Additionally, research efforts should prioritize the creation of adaptive detection mechanisms that can continuously learn and adapt to emerging threats, ensuring the sustained security of IoT ecosystems in the face of evolving cyber risks. As the Internet of Things continues to integrate into various aspects of daily life and industrial processes, closing these research gaps becomes imperative. The potential consequences of successful DoS attacks on critical IoT systems underline the urgency of advancing the state of knowledge and technology in this field. By addressing these gaps and pushing the boundaries of research, the community can contribute meaningfully to the ongoing efforts to fortify the security and resilience of IoT devices against the persistent and evolving threat landscape of Denial of Service attacks.

8 Proposed Solutions or Future Directions

To address these research gaps identified within existing literature on DoS attack detection in IoT using machine and deep learning techniques, several potential solutions or future directions can be explored:

8.1 Development of Comprehensive Benchmark Datasets

The creation of benchmark datasets is crucial for evaluating the effectiveness of DoS attack detection models. These datasets should be representative of diverse IoTapplications to ensure that the models can generalize well across different scenarios. Consideration should be given to various network traffic patterns, communication protocols, and device types. This will allow researchers to develop more robust and versatile models that can adapt to the dynamic nature of IoT environments (Table 2).

Table 2. Description of Datasets in IoT

Dataset Name	IoT Applications	NetworkTraffic Patterns	Communication Protocols	Device Types
SmartHome Dataset	Smart Homes	Random	MQTT, CoAP	Sensors, Actuators
Iot Dataset	Industrial Iot	Periodic	OPC UA, modbus	PLCs, RFID readers
Health Dataset	Health care Iot	Bursty	HTTP, Bluetooth	Wearables, Medical Sensors

8.2 Investigation Into Novel Algorithms or Methodologies:

Research efforts should focus on developing innovative algorithms or methodologies that go beyond existing approaches. This could involve exploring new features, designing adaptive learning strategies, or incorporating domain-specific knowledge. Emphasis should be placed on enhancing detection accuracy while simultaneously reducing false positives. This might involve the use of anomaly detection techniques, heuristic approaches, or leveraging the unique characteristics of IoT traffic.

Exploration of Ensemble-Based Approaches: Ensemble methods involve combining predictions from multiple models to improve overall performance. In the context of DoS attack detection, researchers could explore the integration of diverse machine and deep learning models [3]. Ensemble approaches can provide a more robust and reliable detection system by leveraging the strengths of different models and mitigating individual weaknesses. This could enhance the system's ability to detect various types of attacks. Ensemble-based approaches have gained popularity in various machine learning applications, including the field of cybersecurity, such as DoS (Denial of Service) attack detection. Combining predictions from multiple models can often lead to improved performance and robustness. Here's an exploration of ensemble methods in the context of DoS attack detection:

1. Model Diversity: Machine Learning Models: Researchers can integrate diverse machine learning models, such as decision trees, support vector machines, k-nearest neighbors, and random forests. Each model captures different patterns and characteristics of the data, contributing to the overall diversity of the ensemble.
   Deep Learning Models:Deep neural networks, convolutional neural networks (CNNs), recurrent neural networks (RNNs), and other architectures can be included in the ensemble to leverage the representation learning capabilities of deep learning.
2. Heterogeneous Ensemble: Combining Different Paradigms: Combine machine learning and deep learning models in a heterogeneous ensemble. This can be particularly beneficial as machine learning models may excel in capturing certain features, while deep learning models can automatically learn intricate patterns from raw data.
3. Feature Engineering: Input Features:Experiment with different sets of input features for each model in the ensemble. Feature engineering techniques tailored to specific models can enhance their ability to detect anomalous patterns associated with DoS attacks.
4. Bagging and Boosting: Bagging (Bootstrap Aggregating):Use bagging techniques to train multiple models on different subsets of the dataset, introducing randomness and reducing overfitting. Random Forest is a popular bagging ensemble that combines multiple decision trees. Boosting: Explore

boosting algorithms like AdaBoost or Gradient Boosting, which focus on correcting the errors of individual models in the ensemble. Boosting can improve the overall performance by giving more weight to misclassified instances.
5. Voting Schemes: Majority Voting: Simple majority voting can be employed, where the most commonly predicted class among the ensemble members is chosen. Weighted Voting: Assign different weights to the predictions of each model based on their individual performance, allowing more influential models to contribute more to the final decision.
6. Ensemble Calibration: Calibrating Probabilities: Some ensemble methods provide probability estimates. Calibrate these probabilities to ensure they reflect the true likelihood of an instance belonging to a particular class. Well-calibrated probabilities can improve the reliability of the ensemble.
7. Dynamic Ensemble: Adaptive Approaches: Implement dynamic ensemble methods that can adapt over time. This is particularly useful in a dynamic environment where the characteristics of DoS attacks may change. Adaptive ensembles can automatically adjust their composition based on the evolving threat landscape.
8. Explainability: Interpretability: Consider the interpretability of the ensemble. While deep learning models may provide powerful predictive capabilities, their inherent complexity can make them less interpretable. Combining them with more interpretable machine learning models can enhance the overall explainability of the ensemble.
9. Dataset Augmentation: Data Augmentation: Augment the training dataset to increase diversity and improve the generalization of individual models. Techniques such as random sampling, noise injection, or synthetic data generation can be applied.
10. Cross-Validation: - **Ensemble Cross-Validation: ** Employ cross-validation techniques tailored to ensembles, such as Monte Carlo or bootstrap cross-validation, to obtain a more accurate estimate of the ensemble's performance.

By exploring these ensemble-based approaches, researchers can develop a robust and reliable DoS attack detection system that leverages the strengths of different models and enhances overall performance. The adaptability and versatility of ensemble methods make them well-suited for addressing the challenges associated with cybersecurity applications.

8.3 Integration of Explainable AI Methods

Deep learning models, particularly neural networks, are often viewed as "black boxes" because of their complexity. Integrating explainable AI methods is crucial for improving the interpretability of these models. Techniques such as attention mechanisms, feature importance analysis, and model-agnostic interpretability tools can help researchers and practitioners understand how the model arrives at its decisions. This is essential for building trust in the detection system and facilitating human understanding of detected threats. The integration of explainable

AI methods is indeed crucial for enhancing the interpretability of deep learning models, especially in the context of securing the Internet of Things (IoT) against Denial of Service (DoS) attacks. Here's a comprehensive examination of how various explainable AI techniques can be applied:

1. Attention Mechanisms: Explanation: Attention mechanisms in neural networks highlight specific parts of the input data that are deemed important for making a particular decision. This provides insights into which features the model is focusing on. Application: In the context of IoT security, attention mechanisms can be applied to identify and explain patterns in the network traffic or sensor data that contribute to the detection of potential DoS attacks. This can help in understanding the key indicators used by the model.
2. Feature Importance Analysis: Explanation: Feature importance analysis involves evaluating the contribution of each input feature to the model's output. This aids in identifying the most influential features in the decision-making process. Application: By conducting feature importance analysis, one can pinpoint the critical features in IoT data that contribute to the detection of DoS attacks. This information is valuable for refining the model and providing clear insights to stakeholders on what factors trigger an alert.
3. Model-Agnostic Interpretability Tools: Explanation: These tools are designed to interpret the predictions of any machine learning model, regardless of its underlying architecture. This helps in creating a more transparent understanding of model decisions. Application: For IoT security, using model-agnostic interpretability tools allows practitioners to apply various explainability techniques without being limited to the specifics of the deep learning model. This flexibility is important for ensuring compatibility with different IoT security models.
4. Lime (Local Interpretable Model-agnostic Explanations): Explanation: Lime is a technique that provides local explanations for individual predictions. It creates a locally faithful model around a specific instance to explain the decision made by the black-box model. Application: In the context of IoT, Lime can be used to generate explanations for specific instances of detected threats, allowing security analysts to understand the reasoning behind each decision and take appropriate actions.
5. Shapley Values: Explanation: Shapley values allocate contributions of each feature to the prediction based on its importance and interaction with other features. It ensures a fair distribution of credit across all features. Application: Applying Shapley values in the IoT security domain can help in understanding the collaborative impact of different features in identifying DoS attacks, ensuring a holistic view of the model's decision-making process.

By integrating these explainable AI methods, the interpretability of deep learning models can be significantly enhanced, fostering trust in the IoT security system and enabling effective collaboration between AI systems and human operators in the identification and mitigation of DoS attacks.

8.4 Incorporation of Active Defenses

Active defense mechanisms involve dynamically adapting the system's behavior in response to real-time threat intelligence. This could include adjusting network configurations, modifying access controls, or deploying countermeasures. Integration of threat intelligence feeds and collaboration with external security services can enhance the system's ability to respond proactively to emerging threats. Active defenses contribute to making the IoT environment more resilient against evolving DoS attack strategies (Fig. 1).

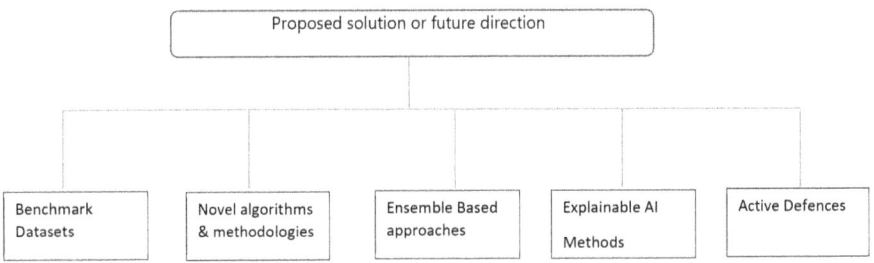

Fig. 1. simple representation shows each proposed solution or future direction

9 Conclusion

In conclusion, the detection and prevention of DoS attacks in IoT using machine and deep learning techniques play a critical role in ensuring the security and stability of IoT devices. By reviewing existing detection techniques, comparing machine learning and deep learning approaches, identifying research gaps, and proposing future directions, this paper highlights the need for further advancements in this field. Efforts to develop more accurate, efficient, scalable, and adaptive DoS attack detection systems will contribute to a safer IoT environment. Ultimately, the combination of machine learning, deep learning, and emerging technologies holds great promise for mitigating the risk posed by DoS attacks in IoT.

References

1. Adedeji, K.B., Abu-Mahfouz, A.M., Kurien, A.M.: DDoS attack and detection methods in internet-enabled networks: Concept, research perspectives, and challenges. J. Sens. Actuator Netw. **12**(4), 51 (2023)
2. Kazmi, S.H.A., Qamar, F., Hassan, R., Nisar, K.: Routing-based interference mitigation in SDN enabled beyond 5G communication networks: a comprehensive survey. IEEE Access (2023)

3. Jin, X., Bagavathiannan, M., Maity, A., Chen, Y., Yu, J.: Deep learning for detecting herbicide weed control spectrum in turfgrass. Plant Methods **18**(1), 94 (2022)
4. Iftikhar, S., Khan, D., Al-Madani, D., Alheeti, K., Fatima, K.: An intelligent detection of malicious intrusions in IoT based on machine learning and deep learning techniques. Comput. Sci. J. Moldova **30**, 288–307 (2022)
5. Al-Theeb, A.D., Al-Sagheer, A.A., Al-Othman, F.A.: A lightweight model for DDoS attack detection using machine learning techniques. IEEE Access **9**, 113119–113133 (2021)
6. Thang, N.D.B., Hoang, D.T., Nguyen, D.M.: DDoS attack detection in IoT-based networks using machine learning models: a survey and research directions. IEEE Trans. Comput. Soc. Syst. **9**(3), 1017–1031 (2022)
7. Garg, S., Gupta, S.: Deep learning for cyber threat detection in IoT networks: a review. J. Netw. Comput. Appl. **196**, 103424 (2022)
8. Mumtaz, S., Shohaimeh, S.I., Mahmoud, M.M.: Machine and deep learning for IoT security and privacy: applications, challenges, and future directions. IEEE Internet Things J. **9**(11), 8328–8346 (2022)
9. Kumar, V., Paul, K.: Device fingerprinting for cyber-physical systems: a survey. ACM Comput. Surv. **55**(14s), 1–41 (2023)
10. Ali, S.A., Elsaid, S.A., Ateya, A.A., ElAffendi, M., El-Latif, A.A.A.: Enabling technologies for next-generation smart cities: a comprehensive review and research directions. Future Internet **15**(12), 398 (2023)
11. James, F., Ray, I., Medhi, D.: Worst attack vulnerability and fortification for iot security management: an approach and an illustration for smart home IoT. In: NOMS 2023-2023 IEEE/IFIP Network Operations and Management Symposium, pp. 1–6. IEEE (2023)
12. McNulty, L., Vassilakis, V. G.: IoT botnets: characteristics, exploits, attack capabilities, and targets. In: 2022 13th International Symposium on Communication Systems, Networks and Digital Signal Processing (CSNDSP), pp. 350–55. IEEE (2022)
13. Gibert, D., Planes, J., Mateu, C., Le, Q.: Fusing feature engineering and deep learning: a case study for malware classification. Expert Syst. Appl. **207**, 117957 (2022)
14. Himeur, Y., Sayed, A., Alsalemi, A., Bensaali, F., Amira, A.: Edge AI for internet of energy: challenges and perspectives. Internet Things 101035 (2023)

Design of Single Cycle MIPS RISC Processor Using Re-timing Technique

Sindhe Sreeja[(✉)], Gudipati Sneha, Guguloth Ganesh, and Sangeeta Singh

Department of ECE, Vardhaman College of Engineering, Hyderabad, Telangana, India
sreejasindhe17@gmail.com, sangeethasingh@vardhaman.org

Abstract. In designing circuits, the speed and power aspects are crucial. Traditional design faces challenges like increased power use, complex timing issues, and inflexibility in changing certain components. Therefore, there's a need for new techniques to make designs more efficient. This paper introduces a fresh approach to increase speed of high-speed systems like the MIPS RISC Processor. It does this by combining advanced methods to adjust the timing of signals with flexible strategies for changing certain components. This combination significantly reduces power usage while making the system perform better. Pipeline Register Re-timing Algorithm, strategically adjusts the placement of certain components to reduce delays in signal movement and the time it takes for the system clock to complete a cycle. This results in an overall improvement in how well the system performs. The design is implemented practically using the Xilinx Vivado tool with the Verilog High Descriptive Language (VHDL). The outcomes of this implementation show a clear reduction in critical path and delay, along with more efficient power usage. This study reveals a 2% decrease in total On Chip power, a 2% reduction in dynamic power, and a 2.5% decline in input signal power.

Keywords: MIPS RISC processor · Re-timing · Pipeline register re-timing

1 Introduction

The MIPS (Microprocessor without Interlocked Pipeline Stages) architecture is a well-established and influential RISC- based design. RISC, which stands for Reduced Instruction Set Computing. Instead of dealing with complicated instructions, it focuses on doing simple things really fast. Developed by MIPS Computer Systems, it has found widespread use in a variety of applications, from personal computers to embedded systems and networking devices. The MIPS processor is characterized by a streamlined set of instructions that perform basic operations. This simplicity allows for faster execution of instructions. The MIPS architecture utilizes a pipeline structure, where different stages of instruction execution are overlapped. This contributes to improved performance by enabling the processor to handle multiple instructions simultaneously. In MIPS, most instructions operate on register values, and data is loaded from or stored to memory through specific load and store instructions. This design choice enhances instruction execution speed. MIPS follows a load-store architecture, meaning that most operations involve loading data from memory into registers, performing operations, and then storing the results back in memory. This design simplifies instruction execution. In certain implementations, MIPS processors are designed with a focus on energy efficiency. This makes them suitable for devices with power constraints, such as battery- powered gadgets. MIPS processors find extensive use in embedded systems, powering devices like routers, modems, set-top boxes, and other smart appliances due to their efficient and compact design.

2 Literature Survey

The focus is on a 64-bit RISC processor, implying that it processes data in 64-bit chunks, contributing to enhanced computational capabilities [1]. The processor incorporates built-in self-test features, indicating that it possesses the ability to conduct self-assessment procedures. This self- testing mechanism ensures that the processor can verify its own functionality. The paper provides insights into the architecture of the processor, explaining how its components are structured and interconnected. Additionally, it details the data path, which signifies the route that data takes within the processor during operations. The instruction set, comprising the operations the processor can execute, is also outlined. The designed processor is verified using the Xilinx ISE simulator. Verification involves testing the processor's functionality through simulations, ensuring it behaves as intended.

The MIPS (Microprocessor without Interlocked Pipeline Stages) architecture is a well-established and influential RISC-based design [2]. RISC, which stands for Reduced Instruction Set Computing. Instead of dealing with complicated instructions, it focuses on doing simple things really fast. Developed by MIPS Computer Systems, it has found widespread use in a variety of applications, from personal computers to embedded systems and networking devices. The MIPS processor is characterized by a streamlined set of instructions that perform basic operations. This simplicity allows for faster execution of instructions. The MIPS architecture utilizes a pipeline structure, where different stages of instruction execution are overlapped. This contributes to improved performance by enabling the processor to handle multiple instructions simultaneously. In MIPS, most instructions operate on register values, and data is loaded from or stored to memory through specific load and store instructions. This design simplifies instruction execution. In certain implementations, MIPS processors are designed with a focus on energy efficiency. This makes them suitable for devices with power constraints, such as battery-powered gadgets.MIPS processors find extensive use in embedded systems, powering devices like routers, modems, set-top boxes, and other smart appliances due to their efficient and compact design.

A novel design for a 32-bit Reduced Instruction Set Computer (RISC) processor, focusing on optimizing performance and operational speed. The processor employs a multi-cycle architecture, executing each instruction in three distinct stages: Fetch, Decode, and Execution. The Fetch and Decode stages are uniform across all instructions, fostering consistency in the initial processing steps. Notably, the multi-cycle nature of the processor allows for increased flexibility and a streamlined hardware design, contributing to improved efficiency. The 32-bit architecture enhances data processing capabilities, handling information in 32-bit chunks. Through simulations and synthesis using Xilinx 14.7 ISE design suite, the paper validates the proposed design, ensuring its viability for practical implementation. This approach aims to strike a balance between a simplified architecture and multi-cycle execution, ultimately striving for heightened performance and operational speed across a diverse range of instructions [3].

It suggests a solution to this problem, proposing a method that tackles cache coherence without burdening developers. The aim is to maximize the performance of multi-core platforms using chosen RISC-V cores. The paper explains the method's workings, architecture, and hardware implementation in detail. Through prototype development and experiments, the paper demonstrates the effectiveness of this approach, showing its potential to advance the development of efficient RISC-V multi core platforms. The demand for RISC-V multi core platforms has risen, but integrating these cores for optimal performance is challenging due to a lack of cache coherence logic in many open cores [4].

The ultimate goal of these techniques and the MATLAB environment is to achieve a lower clock period and a lower register count while maintaining the original input-output behavior of the circuit. This is done to enhance the overall performance of the sequential circuit. The focus is on techniques such as cut set re-timing, clock period minimization, and register minimization, implemented in MATLAB to achieve improved performance in sequential circuits [5].

The foundation of this algorithm builds upon a one-less-than- previous approach [6]. The algorithm is designed to be straightforward, offering a simple method for multiplying NxN unsigned binary numbers. It utilizes a 2n-1 constant number that is applied recursively to both the multiplicand and multiplier. The re-usability of hardware resources is a key factor contributing to low power consumption. It is suggested that this re-usability also leads to a superior power-delay product when compared to conventional multipliers.

The design employs a register minimization re-timing technique, aiming to optimize the critical path and improve VLSI design metrics such as area, speed, or power. The use of a GUI for component binding further enhances the efficiency of the design process, aiming for minimum design cycle time while meeting specific performance criteria. It compares different adders and multipliers in terms of VLSI design metrics [7].

A fresh perspective on re-timing, a register reconfiguration technique initially proposed by Leiserson and Saxe. Departing from traditional linear programming approaches, this novel method employs loop analysis inspired by network theory to formulate the re-timing problem. By utilizing the circuit's incidence matrix and identifying linearly independent loops to represent diverse register configurations, the algorithm efficiently narrows down the set of re-timing solutions based on design and timing constraints. This approach offers designers flexibility in selecting an appropriate implementation. The conclusion underscores the algorithm's capacity to evaluate re-timing solutions considering register locations and timing constraints, highlighting its simplicity in formulation and programming compared to other re-timing methods. The potential integration of these algorithms into circuit compilers and interactive design tools is suggested, and future work is hinted at, exploring the synergy of re-timing with other VLSI synthesis and design automation techniques [8].

The significance of re-timing as an optimization technique for sequential circuits within an end-to-end industrial design flow. Re-timing involves strategically moving edge-triggered registers across combinational logic without altering functionality. The paper presents findings from experiments conducted on seven 14 nm industrial designs, assessing the performance of re-timing algorithms in complete design flows. Unlike previous evaluations primarily at the logic level, this study focuses on physical level assessments. Results reveal variations in re-timing algorithm performance across designs, leading to the development of a re-timing-prediction model. This model accurately forecasts the potential improvements in timing, area, and power for industrial designs, offering a cost-effective approach to designing efficient flows and reducing Time-to-Market. The conclusion emphasizes the importance of considering physical-level evaluations for re timing algorithms to avoid potential misinterpretations based solely on logic-level assessments [9].

A global placement method designed to optimize performance in physical planning with re-timing. GEO utilizes a multilevel partitioning approach based on min cut principles, facilitating the top-down assignment of gates to tiles. A notable contribution of this work is the incorporation of re-timing-aware timing analysis (RTA), a tool guiding the placement process by providing timing slack information post-re-timing. This allows for direct minimization of the clock period during placement. By concurrently addressing partitioning and re-timing under the geometric delay model, GEO effectively conceals global interconnect latency, showcasing superior performance compared to traditional methods. The paper concludes by outlining plans for improving wire length results, exploring incremental timing analysis for sequential circuits, and integrating buffer insertion for enhanced delay and power minimization in future GEO iterations [10].

A new approach to improve the timing behavior of digital circuits containing enable registers. Unlike existing methods that optimize single-clock-cycle paths, our approach considers paths spanning multiple clock cycles, revealing greater optimization potential. The study also addresses register relocation in circuits with enable registers and D-Flip flops, presenting a specialized re-timing algorithm for such scenarios. The key outcome is a method that strategically inserts pipe lining into slow logical blocks, achieving local changes in the data path and minor controller adjustments. Experimental results demonstrate a noticeable reduction in the clock period (up to 40%) with a slight increase in area due to added registers. The approach proves beneficial for circuits meeting specific criteria, offering a new design perspective for timing optimization. Future work aims to extend the approach with additional optimization methods for both the data path and controller of circuits [11].

An effective approach for teaching RISC processor design in an undergraduate computer architecture course, aiming to minimize the gap between high-level data path block diagrams and Verilog code specifications. Using a graphical method and an online browser-based simulator, students progress through examples from single-cycle to pipeline designs, actively participating in the processor design process. Emphasizing fundamental characteristics of RISC processor design, the approach provides essential knowledge for computer architecture and serves as a valuable resource with a compact browser-based editor/simulator. While acknowledging challenges in creating Verilog descriptions, the paper offers a straightforward online tool, and future work includes expanding examples and exploring FPGA execution in the cloud to further enhance teaching capabilities [12].

A design method for multiplexers in the context of a single- cycle CPU system using the MIPS instruction set. The design employs both Schematic and VHDL for efficient development, discussing considerations and operational principles in detail. The advantages and disadvantages of Schematic and VHDL inputs are explored, highlighting the intuitive nature of Schematic and the general-purpose capabilities of VHDL. The paper emphasizes the application of multiplexers in various circuits, including binary comparators and generators, graphics occurrence circuits, and order selection circuits within a single-cycle CPU system based on the MIPS instruction set. The design process leverages Quartus II features for correctness, ensuring simplicity and flexibility in adapting to different data input requirements. Simulation results for FPGA-constructed components are presented, demonstrating the effectiveness of the proposed multiplexer design approach [13].

Method for safeguarding the register file of a RISC microprocessor against Multiple Bit Upsets (MBUs). The approach combines matrix code, providing detection and correction capabilities through information redundancy, with Triple Modular Redundancy (TMR), a widely used hardware redundancy technique that masks faults. The 32-bit single- cycle MIPS architecture microprocessor is designed to integrate a crypto module implementing the AES-128 algorithm, creating an application platform. The suggested approach has the capability to identify and rectify a range of errors, including 2, 4, and 8-burst errors or random errors, depending on the configuration of the dataset associated with the registers. Implementation on Xilinx Virtex-5 FPGA is carried out, with a comparison of area and power consumption. The technique proves applicable to register files of various sizes. Simulation results demonstrate effective correction of faults in the original register file and prevention of wrong operations when faults affect parity or check bits. Future research will involve more detailed analysis and overhead reduction [14].

A basic 16-bit RISC and an advanced 32-bit RISC. RISC processors use simple instructions to reduce complexity, cost, and power consumption. The initial 16-bit version faced technical challenges, leading to the development of more efficient 32-bit and 64-bit versions. The study focuses on their instruction sets and performance, comparing factors like speedup and power dissipation. Both processors include General Purpose Registers and Flag registers. An optimized multiplication algorithm is examined to improve the data path, crucial for power efficiency. The models are simulated and integrated using XILINX ISE Design Suite 14.7, with power analysis conducted.

The objective is to draw a comparative study between the processors, considering their instruction sets and performance metrics. Overall, the research aims to understand and improve the efficiency of RISC processors through advancements in architecture and instruction sets [15].

3 Design and Implementation

In the present work, Units of MIPS RISC Processor using pipeline Register Re-timing technique is implemented. MIPS RISC architecture is finely optimized to carry out the tasks of fetching, decoding, and executing instructions within a solitary clock cycle, orchestrating a systematic progression through its five well-defined stages: instruction fetch, instruction decode, execute, data memory, and write back.

Instruction Fetch Stage: Two registers responsible for equality comparison and a 16-bit offset. This offset is utilized to calculate the branch target address relative to the instruction's address. The computation involves adding the sign-extended offset field to the Program Counter (PC).This mechanism ensures the accurate determination of the branch target address based on the specified offset and contributes to the dynamic control flow within the processor Architecture.

Instruction Decode Stage: In this specific phase, instructions go through a decoding process, and the register file is accessed to fetch data from the registers. The results from the general-purpose registers are transferred to two temporary registers, specifically labeled as register 1 and register 2, for utilization in subsequent clock cycles. Concurrently, the lower 16 bits of the Instruction Register (IR) undergo sign-extension and get stored in a temporary register known as IMM, intended for future application in the next cycle.

The processor's register state, comprising 32 registers, is housed within the 'register file', serving as the repository for the machine's register values. This register file is pivotal in maintaining and managing the processor's internal state during the execution of instruction.

Execution Stage: During the execution stage, mathematical operations take place utilizing a Data Arithmetic Logic Unit (ALU) and a branch address adder. The ALU is equipped with arithmetic, logic, and shifting functionalities, whereas the branch address adder is specifically designed for PC-relative branch instructions. The branch data path comprises a sign extension unit and an adder responsible for calculating branch target addresses. When it comes to branch instruction comparison, the ALU receives two register operands as input, configured for a subtraction operation. This stage ensures the efficient execution of various computational tasks within the processor.

Arithmetic and Logic Unit (ALU): In a pipe lined ALU with re-timing, the goal is to optimize the performance of arithmetic and logic operations by introducing pipeline registers. These registers are strategically placed in the data path to break down the processing of instruction into sequential stages. The re-timing concept involves carefully managing the flow of data through these pipeline registers, enhancing parallelism and overall throughput.

ALU Operation: In Fig. 1, the ALU supports basic operations such as bit wise AND, bit wise OR, addition, subtraction, and a logical NOT operation on the most significant bit. The zero flag is set based on specific ALU operations, such as equality checks ((in_a == in_b) ? 1'b1: 1'b0).

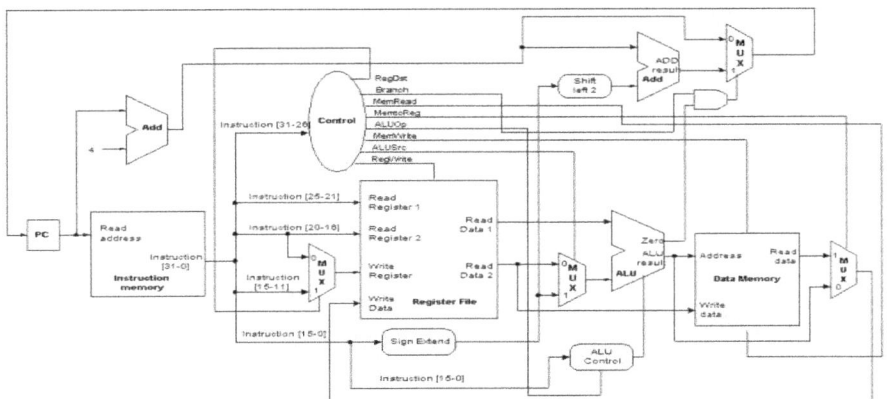

Fig. 1. Block Diagram of 32-bit MIPS RISC Processor

The pipeline registers (alu_out_reg and zero_reg) are employed to introduce a single-clock cycle delay, demonstrating the use of re-timing techniques to enhance performance. This module essentially represents a pipe lined ALU with support for various operations and a simplified control mechanism. The use of pipeline registers improves the timing characteristics of the design. For example, when control is 4'b0010, it performs addition (alu_out_reg <= in_a + in_b). The zero_reg is set accordingly based on the ALU operation. The default case (default) handles situations where the control signal doesn't match any specified operation.

Control Unit: In a MIPS RISC (Reduced Instruction Set Computing) processor, the control unit plays a critical role in generating control signals that orchestrate the execution of instructions. The control unit interprets the opcode of an instruction and produces signals that control various functional units within the processor, such as the ALU (Arithmetic Logic Unit), register file, and memory. When discussing a control unit with retiming techniques applied in a MIPS RISC processor, we consider the introduction of pipeline registers to enhance performance.

Operation of Control Unit: The module takes a 6-bit opcode as input and generates various control signals commonly used in a MIPS processor. Reg_dest, jump, branch, mem_read, mem_to_reg, mem_write, alusrc, reg_write, and aluop are output control signals. The control signals are generated based on the opcode bits. Each signal corresponds to a specific condition defined by the opcode. alusrc, reg_write, and aluop are derived based on specific combinations of opcode bits to control the ALU source, register write, and ALU operation, respectively. The comments next to each signal assignment indicate the opcode values that activate the corresponding control signal.

Data Memory: The data memory module provides basic read and write operations on a 64-word by 32-bit data memory. It supports synchronous behavior, where read and write operations occur on the rising edge of the clock, and a reset operation clears the entire data memory. The module is suitable for use as a basic data memory component in a digital system design. The module uses non-blocking assignments ($<=$) inside the always block, ensuring proper simulation behavior. This module represents a basic synchronous data memory with read and write functionality, suitable for use in a digital system design. The data memory array represents a data memory with 64 words, where each word is 32 bits. It is organized as a 2D array with 64 rows and 32 columns. The always @(posedge clk or posedge reset) block triggers on the rising edge of the clock (clk) or the rising edge of the reset signal (reset). If the reset signal is asserted (reset == 1'b1).

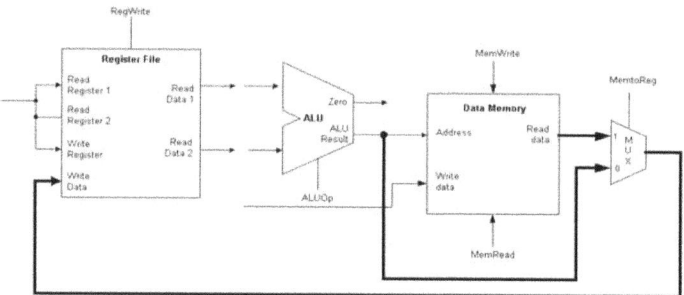

Fig. 2. Architecture of write back stage

Re-timing involves optimizing the timing of signals within the processor stages to improve performance. In a re-timed single- cycle MIPS, designers analyze and adjust the timing of signals to make the most of each clock cycle.

From Fig. 2, It is said that some stages that might finish their work early in one clock cycle can pass their results to the next stage sooner, potentially reducing the overall execution time. This optimization requires careful consideration of the dependencies between different stages and the timing constraints of the hardware.

The key difference is how efficiently the processor uses each clock cycle. Without re-timing, every instruction follows the same fixed path, regardless of how quickly each stage completes. With re-timing, designers tweak the timing to allow certain stages to complete faster, optimizing overall performance.

4 Result Analysis

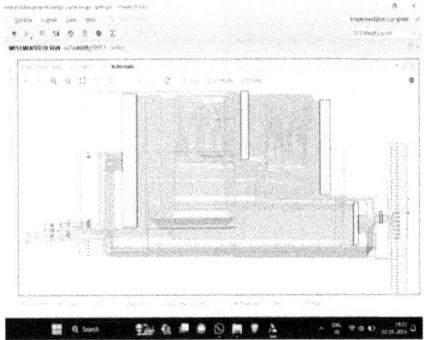
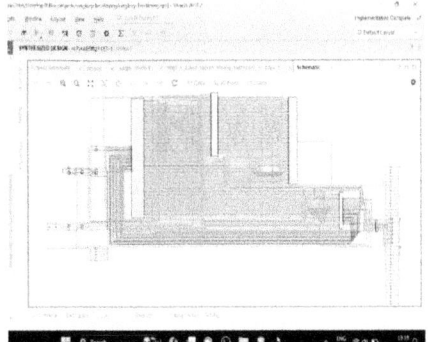

Fig. 3. Schematic of RISC Processor without Re-Timing

Fig. 4. Schematic of RISC Processor With Re-Timing

In Fig. 3, the single-cycle MIPS RISC architecture schematic consists of 67 cells, encompassing various types such as registers and logic gates .Where as in Fig. 4, the re-timed single-cycle MIPS RISC architecture schematic consists of same as without re-timing. There are 52 I/O ports serving distinct input and output functions. The interconnection of components is facilitated by 519 nets, highlighting critical signal pathways. Notable features include custom-designed cells, if any, which play a crucial role in the optimization. The I/O ports are specified with brief descriptions of their intended purposes. The schematic underscores critical nets and pathways, emphasizing high-traffic connections and critical paths. Major modules and components are identified, with their roles and significance outlined. Considerations for performance metrics, including clock frequency and critical path delays, are integral to the schematic information. The visual representation of schematic sections aids in comprehending the architecture, showcasing the impact of re- timing on its overall design and efficiency.

In the above Fig. 5 and Fig. 6, the simulation of the single_cycle_tb test bench for the single_cycle module has been successful, demonstrating expected behavior and validating the functionality of the design. The test bench effectively cycles through different values of switch_select, displaying corresponding reg_read_data_1 values at each positive edge of clkread. The counter count increments correctly, and the control mechanism involving switch_run is well-coordinated. No unexpected behavior are observed, and the simulation completes within the specified time frame. These positive outcomes indicate that the single_cycle module functions as intended, showcasing its reliability and suitability for integration into larger systems or projects.

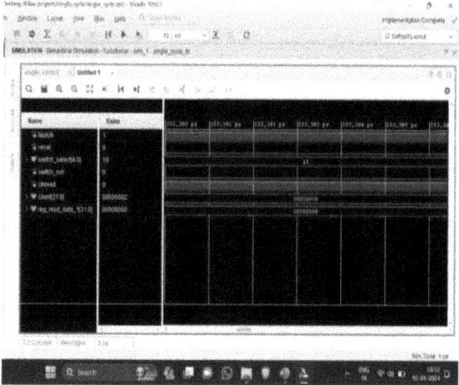

Fig. 5. Simulation of single cycle MIPS RISC Processor

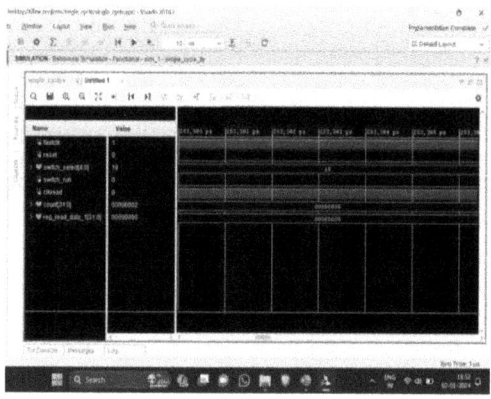

Fig. 6. Simulation of MIPS RISC Processor with re-timing

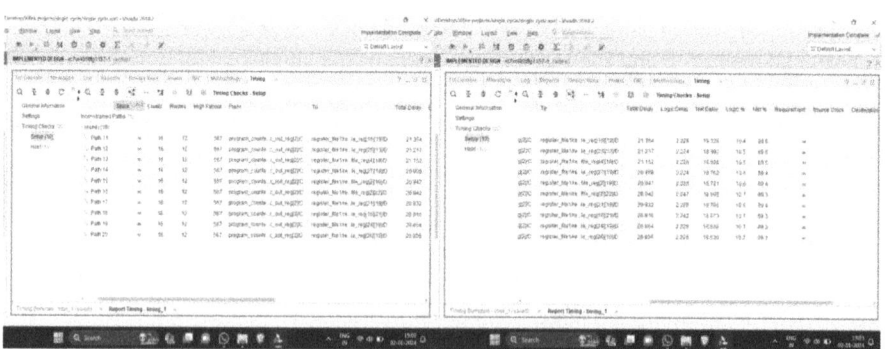

Fig. 7. Single cycle MIPS RISC processor set-up timing report

Design of Single Cycle MIPS RISC Processor 199

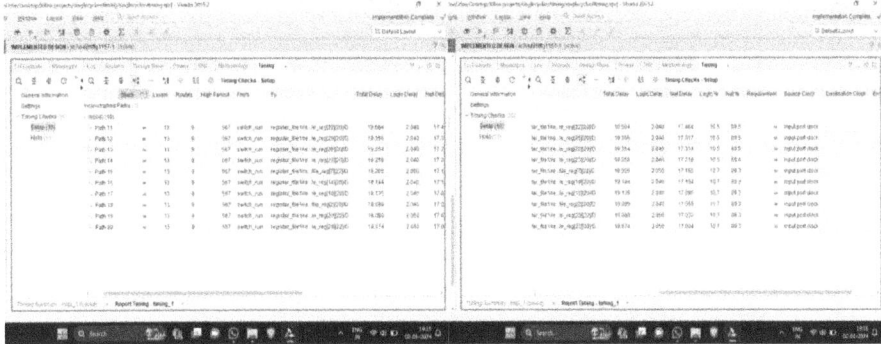

Fig. 8. Set up Timing report of Single Cycle MIPS RISC with re-timing applied

The above figures Fig. 7 and Fig. 8 shows set-up timing analysis of a single cycle MIPS RISC Processor with and without applying re-timing technique, possibly involving a stack, levels, routes, and various paths with associated delays. The table outlines different paths (Path 11 to Path 20) and their corresponding total delays, setup times, and hold times. The High Fan-out From and To sections may indicate critical areas for signal distribution. The timing checks include setup and hold checks for the paths. The total delay has been reduced from 21.942 ms to 19 ms.

The critical path in a traditional MIPS design is determined by the slowest stage in the fixed sequence of instruction processing.

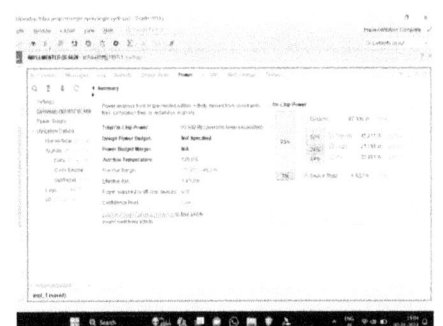

Fig. 9. Power report of Single cycle MIPS RISC processor

Fig. 10. Power report of processor after Re-timing

Figure 9 and Fig. 10 is about the power dissipation of the system, specifically in the ALU control, has been successfully reduced by applying clock gating. Before implementing clock gating, the power dissipation was measured at 93.932 w. After the integration of clock gating logic, the power dissipation has decreased to 91.141 w. This reduction in power dissipation indicates improved energy efficiency in the system, as the ALU control now consumes less power during idle periods, contributing to overall power savings.

Applying re-timing to a MIPS RISC processor, which involves strategically adding registers to improve performance, comes with challenges. First, it makes the design more complex, needing careful management. The insertion of registers increases the physical size of the processor, impacting efficiency. Changes in clock distribution and possible clock skew issues need attention. Compatibility with existing software could be impacted, and efficient resource use is crucial. Achieving timing closure becomes more challenging, and dealing with clock domain crossing complexities is necessary. Balancing these factors is key to successfully applying re-timing to a MIPS RISC processor (Table 1).

Table 1. Power Analysis

Parameters	Proposed	Existing
TOTAL ON-CHIP POWER	91.141	93.932
DYNAMIC POWER (IN W)	84.61	87.300
SIGNAL POWER(IN W)	43.72	45.211
IO POWER	22.074	20.991
DEVICE STATIC	6.632	6.632
IO PORTS	52	52

5 Conclusions

The implementation of retiming in the single cycle MIPS RISC Processor using Xilinx Vivado resulted in some notable benefits, like reducing on-chip power and making the processor more efficient. By adjusting the timing of signals, the setup delay experienced an 8% reduction, showcasing enhanced performance in critical path execution they managed to speed up how quickly the processor performs tasks. The total onchip power of re-timed processor has reduced by 2%, dynamic power has also reduced by 2%. This not only saved power but also made it easier to add specialized features without slowing things down. The flexibility gained from this approach allows designers to create processors that are better suited for specific tasks. Additionally, having control over the clock and timing lets the processor adapt to different needs. In simple terms, using re-timing techniques is a big step forward in making processors faster, more efficient, and customizable for today's technology.

References

1. Sharma, R., Sehgal, V.K., Nitin, N., Bhasker, P., Verma, I.: Design and implementation of a 64-bit RISC processor using VHDL. In: 11th International Conference on Computer Modelling and Simulation Cambridge, UK (2009)
2. Sulik, D., Vasilko, M., Durackova, D., Fuchs, P.: Design of a RISC microcontroller core in 48 hours. In: Embedded Systems (2000)

3. Zaid, M., Mustajab, P.: Design and application of RISC processor. In: IEEE International Conference on Multimedia, Signal Processing and Communication Technologies (IMPACT), Aligarh, India (2017)
4. Jang, H., et al.: Developing a multicore platform utilizing open RISC-V cores. IEEE Access (2021). https://doi.org/10.1109/access.2021.3108475
5. Mehra, H., Bhat, M.S.: High-level optimization methodology for high performance dsp systems using retiming technique. In: IEEE 2018 IEEE Distributed Computing, VLSI, Electrical Circuits and Robotics (DISCOVER), Mangaluru (2018)
6. Jalaja, S, Prakash, A.M.V.: Design of low power based VLSI architecture for constant multiplier and high speed implementation using retiming technique. In: IEEE 2016 International Conference on Microelectronics, Computing and Communications (MicroCom) - Durgapur, India (2016)
7. Yagain, D., Vijaya, K.A.: FIR filter design based on retiming automation using VLSI design metrics. In: IEEE International Conference on Technology, Informatics, Management, Engineering & Environment (TIME-E 2013) – Bandung (2013)
8. Simon, S., Bernard, E., Sauer, M., Nossek, J.A.: A new retiming algorithm for circuit design. In: Proceedings of IEEE International Symposium on Circuits and Systems - ISCAS '94 (n.d.)
9. Yu, C., et al.: End-to-End Industrial Study of Retiming. In: 2018 IEEE Computer Society Annual Symposium on VLSI (ISVLSI) (2018)
10. Cong, J., Lim, S.K.: Retiming-based timing analysis with an application to mincut-based global placement. IEEE Trans. Comput.-Aided Design Integr. Circ. Syst. **23**(12), 1684–1692 (2004)
11. Martin, H.-G.: Retiming for circuits with enable registers. In: Proceedings of EUROMICRO 1996. 22nd Euromicro Conference. Beyond 2000: Hardware and Software Design Strategies (n.d.)
12. Passe, F., Canesche, M., Neto, O.P.V., Nacif, J.A., Ferreira, R.: Mind the gap: bridging verilog and computer architecture. In: 2020 IEEE International Symposium on Circuits and Systems (ISCAS) (2020)
13. Jiang, L., Huang, C.: Design and realization of multiplexer based on schematic and VHDL language. In: 2010 International Conference on Optics, Photonics and Energy Engineering (OPEE) (2010)
14. Ustaoglu, B., Yalcin, B.O.: Fault tolerant register file design for MIPS AES-crypto microprocessor. In: 2015 IEEE International Conference on Electronics, Circuits, and Systems (ICECS) (2015)
15. Kulshreshtha, A., Moudgil, A., Chaurasia, A., Bhushan, B.: Analysis of 16-bit and 32-bit RISC processor. In: 2021 7th International Conference on Advanced Computing and Communication Systems (ICACCS) (2021)

Prediction of Crop Based on Characteristics of Agricultural Environment Using Machine Learning Techniques

Madhavarapu Prathima Rao[1](✉), R. Jegadeesan[1], P. Pranitha[1], D. Praveen Kuamar[2], and J. Krishna Chaitanya[2]

[1] Department of CSE, Jyothishmathi Institute of Technology and Science, Karimnagar, Telangana, India
prathimaraom@gmail.com, polsani.pranitha@jits.ac.in

[2] Department of Electronics and Communication Engineering, Vardhaman College of Engineering, Shamshabad, Hyderabad, India

Abstract. Horticulture related research is creating to anticipate crops, farming, specifically, essentially depend on soil and natural components including temperature, stickiness, and precipitation. Ranchers used to be accountable for picking the yield to be developed, watching out for its development, and choosing when to gather it. But since of the climate's fast changes these days, it is hard for the cultivating local area to proceed. Accordingly, AI methods are continuously dislodging ordinary forecast strategies. A few of these procedures have been utilized in this review to gauge rural yield. To guarantee that a specific AI (ML) model capabilities with an elevated degree of accuracy/properness, it is critical to use effective component determination strategies to change over the crude information into a dataset that is AI well disposed. To lessen copy information and increment model exactness, just information qualities that are exceptionally applicable to characterizing the last result of the model ought to be incorporated. It is basic to utilize ideal element determination to ensure that main the most pivotal highlights are remembered for the model. Assuming we coordinate all attributes from the crude information without first considering part in the model-building procedures, This model will turn out to be excessively perplexing. The incorporation of new boundaries that have negligible bearing on the model's presentation will likewise raise the time and spatial intricacy of the ML model. The outcomes exhibit that a group procedure gives higher expectation exactness when contrasted with the ongoing characterization techniques.

Keywords: Crops · Zigbee · Monitoring · Soil · Security · Data models

1 Introduction

Various models have been made and tried because of the many-sided process engaged with foreseeing crops in horticulture. The use of a few datasets is expected since crop development is reliant upon both biotic and abiotic factors [1, 2]. Crop estimating is neither direct nor easy to-do. As per Myers et al. furthermore, Muriithi, the system for estimating the region under development is an assortment of measurable and numerical devices supportive in an iterative and further developing streamlining process [5, 6].

ZigBee has many applications in accuracy horticulture, where the Web of Things is utilized for Brilliant field the board by unequivocally checking components affecting the cultivated yields to help improved and upgraded farming result. To boost the creation, a framework like this cautiously screens an assortment of development related factors, including temperature, soil quality, pH, saltiness, stickiness, and so on. Like ZigBee, Z-Wave can be used in farming for different observing and control frameworks. Z-Wave innovation's interoperability can be utilized to construct arranged agrarian frameworks with productive correspondence between them.

To screen soil dampness levels and upgrade water system, LoRa innovation has been utilized. Every water system valve in a grape plantation has soil dampness sensors connected. The sensor consistently finds out the dirt dampness content and sends the information to the LoRa door inside its reach. Contingent upon the situation, the water system valves can be controlled. This permits ranchers utilizing LoRa to monitor up to half more water. LoRa can likewise be utilized to follow meteorological factors like temperature and stickiness. Much appreciated by and large to LoRa, which has likewise assisted the improvement of Savvy ranches, farming and IoT with having met up? Also, finding leaks can be utilized. Horticulture utilizes ZigBee, Wi-Fi, Bluetooth, and LoRa to assemble ongoing information for expectation processes. The expectation cycle in this paper utilizes an ongoing static farming dataset from the earlier year. Thus, in this work, ML procedures are used. In the field of study, there are different troubles. Despite the fact that they could perform better, crop expectation models at present produce results that are acceptable. The two principal highlight determination and characterization methodologies were anticipated. To adjust an uneven dataset, inspecting strategies are utilized before highlight determination draws near [11, 12].

The Engineered Minority Over-Examining Procedure (Destroyed), Larger part Weighted Minority Over-Testing Method (MWMOTE), and Irregular Over-Testing Models (ROSE) are utilized in this work to adjust the provided dataset. It is possible to use classification techniques that perform better and can help identify the target class by identifying the most crucial elements in a dataset. In this review, the Boruta, Recursive Element Disposal (RFE), and Adjusted Recursive Component End (MRFE) covering highlight determination techniques are utilized to recognize the critical elements of the dataset. A few directed grouping procedures, including as Innocent Bayes (NB), Choice Tree (DT), k Closest Neighbor (KNN), Backing Vector Machine (SVM), Packing, and Irregular Timberland (RF), are prepared with the chose elements to foresee an OK result from the dataset.

2 Related Work

"Applying naive bayes classification technique for classification of improved agricultural land soils" [1]. India is mostly an agricultural nation. North Indian Soil and South Indian Soil are the two distinct types of soil found in India. North Indian Soil and South Indian Soil are the two sets we have divided into. Deep alluvial soil is typically used to produce the plains of northern India. The top soil's surface varies from sand to clay, with the majority being light loam, which is naturally fertile and has a leaky texture. The southern India peninsular earth plane, or south Indian soil, is prepared up of hills and river valleys. Naturally, hilly areas are unsuitable for farming, and some moorland is quite warm [Prakash, 2015]. The goal of this research is to categorise soil types according to their traits and fertility potential using classification techniques like naive bayes, and to compare this technique to others like zero and stacking. The objective of this study is to evaluate novel data mining approaches used to classify soil in soil databases, as well as to compare the naive bayes classifier to other classifiers.

By B. B. Sawicka and B. Krochmal-Marczak, "Biotic components influencing the yield and quality of potato tubers" [2]. Over the past ten years, Canterbury's potato yields have been steady at about 60 t/ha. Models of potato growth suggest that yields of up to 19t/ha are feasible, however some commercial producers have already reached this level. Industry and research trends looked into the factors restricting agricultural productivity over a two-year period. In year 1, 11 processing crops were closely observed for evaluations of soil quality, plant health, and final output. The main causes of falling yields were found to be soil-borne diseases (such as Spongospora root infection and Rhizoctonia stem canker), subsurface soil compaction, and inadequate irrigation management. Eight weeks following the emergency, farms with recent histories of potato crop production began exhibiting stem canker symptoms earlier than those with periods of grass growth and no preceding potato crops. In year 2, using a commercial crop that was known to have high levels of soil-borne pathogens, researchers attempted to isolate and quantify the impact of soil-borne diseases on yield in a controlled field experiment.

Response Surface Methodology: A Retrospective and Literature Survey, by R. H. Myers, D. C. Montgomery, G. G. Vining, C. M. Borror, and S. M. Kowiski [3]. Process and product designs are optimised using Response Surface Methodology (RSM), a collection of statistical design and numerical optimisation approaches. Since the initial study in this field was undertaken in the 1950s, it has seen a lot of use, especially in the chemical and process industries. For the past 15 years, RSM has been widely used, and during that time, numerous significant advancements have been made. We specifically focus on RSM efforts from 1989 in this review analysis. We talk about the areas of research that are currently being done and suggest some new ones.

3 Preliminaries

Python is an interpreter, high-level, interactive, and object-oriented scripting language. It is quite easy to read Python code. Compared to other languages, it has fewer syntactical characteristics and frequently uses English terminology in place of punctuation. Learning Python is Fundamental for the two understudies and working experts who wish to become extraordinary programmers, particularly on the off chance that they work in the web improvement area. The principal advantages of learning Python incorporate the accompanying.

Python is interpreted, which means that an interpreter processes it as it is being used. Before running your programme, there is no requirement that it be compiled. These are PERL and PHP-like in nature. Python is intelligent; you can utilize a Python brief to sit at the console and speak with the mediator as you make your projects. Python upholds the article arranged programming style or approach, which typifies code into objects. Python is dynamite First Programming Language Python is a tremendous first programming language and works with the improvement of a great many applications, from basic text handling to internet browsers to games.

Man-made brainpower (artificial intelligence) and software engineering's part of AI centers around utilizing information and calculations to reenact human growing experiences and consistently further develop exactness. Normally, an assortment of AI calculations is utilized to give characterizations or forecasts. In view of a few unlabeled or named input information, the calculation will give a gauge about an example in the info information. A mistake capability will be utilized to assess the model's forecast. On the off chance that realized models exist, a blunder capability can contrast them with decide if the model is precise.

4 Proposed Work

The notable highlights of the dataset are recognized in this work utilizing covering highlight choice strategies as the Boruta, Recursive Component Disposal (RFE), and Altered Recursive Element End (MRFE). To foresee a proper result from the dataset, various managed order techniques, including Gullible Bayes (NB), Choice Tree (DT), k Closest Neighbour (KNN), Backing Vector Machine (SVM), Sacking, and Arbitrary Backwoods (RF), are prepared with the picked qualities.

Feature Selection Techniques:

Boruta is a random forest-based algorithm; hence it is applicable to classification models like Logistic Regression and SVM as well as tree models like Random Forest and XGBoost. Boruta iteratively eliminates features (artificial noise variables produced by the Boruta method) that are statistically less significant than a random probe. Variables that are rejected in one iteration are not taken into account in the following iteration. It usually yields an excellent overall feature selection optimisation.

The RFE procedure, a covering highlight choice strategy, begins with the whole dataset. RFE is well known in light of the fact that it is clear to set up and utilize and compelling at choosing the highlights (sections) in a preparation dataset that are more or generally important for anticipating the objective variable.

Classification Techniques:

Decision Tree Classifiers - The applications of selection tree classifiers are diverse and useful. Their main strength is their ability to distinguish unambiguous dynamic data from given information. An election tree can be made using preparation kits. A set of objects (S), each with a place in a different class (C1, C2... Ck), is the basis of the method used to follow such an age.

K-Nearest Neighbors (KNN) - KNN is a straightforward yet extremely effective classification method. Based on a similarity metric, it classifies. The algorithm is non-parametric and lazy. Before the test example is supplied, it does not "learn". We use the training data to identify the K-nearest neighbours of any fresh data that needs to be classified.

Logistic Regression Classifiers - The relationship between a bunch of free (illustrative) factors and an all out subordinate variable is examined utilizing strategic relapse investigation. At the point when the reliant variable just has two qualities, for example, 0 and 1 or Yes and negative, the term strategic relapse is utilized. In circumstances where the reliant variable has at least three particular qualities, like Wedded, Single, Separated, or Bereft, the term multinomial strategic relapse is commonly held. Notwithstanding involving an alternate arrangement of information for the reliant variable than various relapse, the technique has a comparable down to earth use. On autonomous factors that are both mathematical and all out, this program processes parallel calculated relapse and multinomial strategic relapse.

Naive Bayes - The oversimplified assumption that the presence or lack of one characteristic in a class has no bearing on the presence or absence of any other feature is the foundation of the naive bayes approach, a supervised learning technique. However, it still appears solid and powerful. It is equally as successful as other supervised learning techniques. Numerous explanations have been put forth in the literature. The naive bayes classifier is a linear classifier, along with logistic regression, linear SVM, and linear discriminate analysis. The method used to calculate the classifier's parameters explains the discrepancy.

Random Forest - Irregular woodlands make a ton of choice trees during the preparation stage as a gathering learning procedure for order, relapse, and different issues. The after effect of the irregular timberland for order issues is the class that most of the trees pick. The mean or normal gauge of every individual tree is returned for relapse undertakings. Choice trees frequently over fit their preparation set, however arbitrary decision woodlands right this issue. Angle upgraded trees much of the time beat irregular woodlands with regards to accuracy. Nonetheless, the idea of the information could influence how helpful they are.

SVM-SVM is a discriminate technique because, unlike evolutionary algorithms or perceptrons, both of which are frequently employed in machine learning for classification, it analytically solves the convex optimisation issue and consistently returns the same optimal hyper plane value. Solutions for perceptions depend heavily on the initialization and termination standards. The perception and GA classifier models are different each time preparing is initialised, though preparing gives particularly characterized SVM model boundaries for a given preparation set for a specific portion that interprets the information from the info space to the component space. Since GAs and perceptrons just objective is to diminish preparing related mistake, numerous hyper planes will fulfil this prerequisite.

5 System Architecture

To find missing qualities, eliminate excess data, normalize the dataset, and change target ascribes into factor credits, the info information is first pre handled. The pre handled information is utilized to separate key credits utilizing covering highlight choice strategies. Preceding applying order strategies to the improved properties, the dataset is parted into preparing and testing stages. The order calculation is prepared utilizing obscure examples from the preparation dataset to recognize the yield that is generally proper for filling in a specific plot of land. The prepared classifier is applied to the testing dataset to figure (Fig. 1).

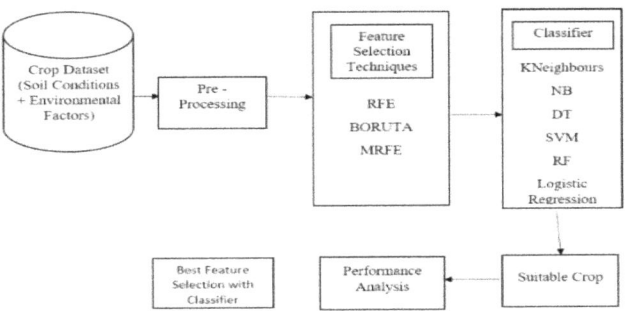

Fig. 1. System Architecture

The crop that will be grown. A suitable crop is finally harvested, and the outcomes are assessed using several performance criteria. The research identifies the most effective feature selection strategy and the most suitable classification approach.

6 Results and Analysis

In the below image represents the input and output of prediction of crop. Based on feature selection techniques and classifiers it predicts whether the crop is suitable or not for that Soil condition and Environment conditions and Recommended zone, and crop name, parameters considered for soil and environment conditions were N,P,K, ph(soil), Environment(temperature, humidity, rainfall) (Figs. 2 and 3).

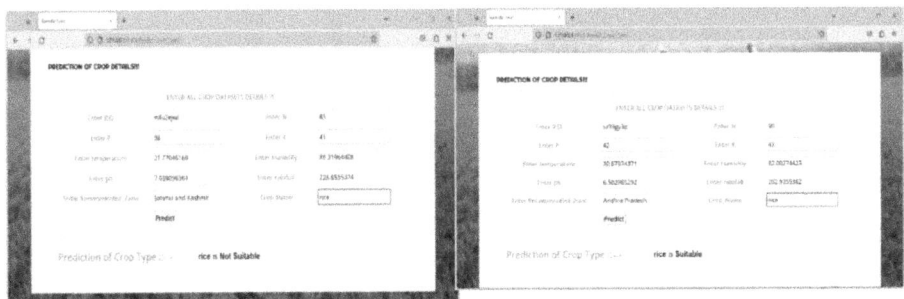

Fig. 2. Result output -1

Fig. 3. Result output-2

ANALYSIS:

In this work, the measurements of exactness (ACC), explicitness (S), review (R), accuracy (P), and F1 score were utilized to assess the viability of the element determination and arrangement calculations for expectation.

Analysis of algorithms:

Table: Analysis of algorithms (Accuracy analysis)

Graphs:

The following charts are the graphical representations of our work regarding crop prediction based on soil and environment conditions.

Bar Graph: The visual device of a reference diagram utilizes bars to look at information between classes. It is otherwise called a bar graph or bar outline. A structured presentation might be situated either upward or evenly. It is important to recognise that a bar's value rises with length (Fig. 4).

Model Type	Accuracy (Out of 60)	Precision	Recall	F1-Score	Support
Naïve Bayes	48.40909090909091	0.49	0.42	0.45	???
Support Vector machine	46.81818181818182	0.47	0.45	0.46	???
Logistic Regression	46.81818181818182	0.47	0.46	0.47	???
Decision Tree	46.36363636363636	0.47	0.43	0.45	???
KNeighbours Classifier	53.86363636363637	0.55	0.49	0.52	???
Random Forest	50.0	0.51	0.38	0.43	???

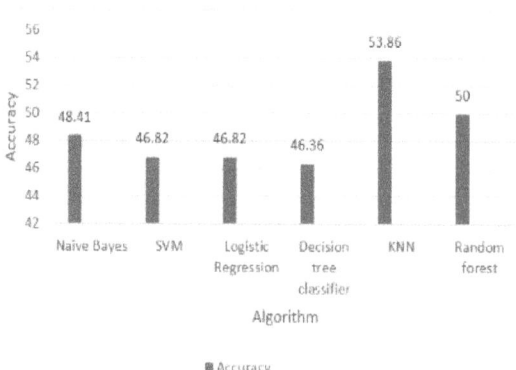

Fig. 4. Bar Graph (Accuracy Analysis)

7 Conclusions and Future Work

Our ranchers might choose the erroneous harvest to plant, which will decrease their pay, since they are at present not really taking advantage of innovation and examination. We have fostered a rancher cordial framework with a graphical UI (GUI) to gauge which harvest would be the most reasonable for a specific land parcel and to give insights regarding the supplements that should be added, the seeds that should be utilized for development, the expected yield, and the market cost. To develop the agrarian business through inventive reasoning, this rouses ranchers to choose the ideal harvest for creation.

By giving GPS directions to a land parcel and accessing the public authority's downpour determining framework, we can expect crops without get-together any extra information. We can likewise make a model to forestall food deficiencies and excesses. Our task just lets about know crop appropriate. In ongoing we need to foster that whether any illnesses might happen, assuming they develop that harvest, and what manure is reasonable for yield.

References

1. Jahan, R.: Applying naïve Bayes classification technique for classification of improved agricultural land soils. Int. J. Res. Appl. Sci. Eng. Technol. **6**(5), 189–193 (2018)
2. Sawicka, B.B., Krochmal-Marczak, B.: Biotic components influencing the yield and quality of potato tubers. Herbalism **1**(3), 125–136 (2017)
3. Sawicka, B., Noaema, A.H., Gáowacka, A.: The predicting the size of the potato acreage as a raw material for bioethanol production. In: Zdunek, B., Olszáwka, M. (eds.) Alternative Energy Sources, pp. 158–172. WydawnictwoNaukowe TYGIEL, Lublin (2016)
4. Sawicka, B., Noaema, A.H., Hameed, T.S., Krochmal-Marczak, B.: Biotic and abiotic factors influencing on the environment and growth of plants. In: Proceedings of the BióróżnorodnośćŚrodowiskaZnaczenie, Problemy, Wyzwania. MateriałyKonferencyjne, Puławy (2017). https://bookcrossing.pl/ksiazka/321192. (in Polish)
5. Myers, R.H., Montgomery, D.C., Vining, G.G., Borror, C.M., Kowalski, S.M.: Response surface methodology: a retrospective and literature survey'. J. Qual. Technol. **36**(1), 53–77 (2004)
6. Muriithi, D.K.: Application of response surface methodology for optimization of potato tuber yield. Amer. J. Theor. Appl. Statist. **4**(4), 300–304 (2015). https://doi.org/10.11648/j.ajtas.20150404.20
7. Marenych, M., Verevska, O., Kalinichenko, A., Dacko, M.: Assessment of the impact of weather conditions on the yield of winter wheat in Ukraine in terms of regional. Assoc. Agricult. Agribusiness Econ. Ann. Sci. **16**(2), 183–188 (2014)
8. Olędzki, J.R.: Thereporton the state of remotesensing in Poland in 2011–2014. Remote Sens. Environ. **53**(2), 113–174 (2015). (in Polish)
9. Grabowska, K., Dymerska, A., Poáarska, K., Grabowski, J.: Predicting f blue lupine yields based on the selected climate change scenarios. Acta Agroph. **23**(3), 363–380 (2016)
10. Li, D., et al.: Improving potato yield prediction by combining cultivar information and UAV remote sensing data using machine learning. Remote Sens. **13**(16), 3322 (2021). https://doi.org/10.3390/rs13163322
11. Chanamarn, N., Tamee, K., Sittidech, P.: Stacking technique for academic achievement prediction. In: Proceedings of the International Workshop Smart Info-Media Systems, pp. 14–17 (2016)

12. Paja, W., Pancerz, K., Grochowalski, P.: Generational feature elimination and some other ranking feature selection methods. In: Advances in Feature Selection for Data and Pattern Recognition, vol. 138, pp. 97–112. Springer, Cham (2018)
13. Jegadeesan, R., et al.: Stable Route Selection for Adaptive Packet Transmission in 5G-Based Mobile Communications. Wirel. Commun. Mob. Comput. **2022**, Article ID 8009105 (2022). https://doi.org/10.1155/2022/8009105
14. Akshitha, M., Jegadeesan, R., Akshaya, G., Akhilac, P., Pavan Kalyan, M., Sindhusha, G.: Covid-19 future forecasting using supervised machine learning models. Zeichen J. **7**(6), 257–269 (2021). https://doi.org/10.1109/ACCESS.2020.2997311. ISSN 0932-4747
15. Priyavarshini, P., Jegadeesan, R., Vaishnavi, T., Sahithi, K., Shivani, B., Balakishan, P.: Cyber money laundering detection using machine learning. Zeichen J. **7**(6), 231–238 (2021) (2021). 15.10089.ZJ.2021.V7I6.285311.2422. ISSN 0932-4747
16. Jegadeesan, R., Srinivas, D., Umapathi, N., Karthick, G, Venkateswaran, N.: Healthcare chatbot for medical suggestions using artificial intelligence and machine learning. Eur. Chem. Bull. **12**(S3), 6004–6012 (2023). https://doi.org/10.31838/ecb/2023.12.s3.670
17. Jegadeesan, R., Srinivas, D., Umapathi, N., Karthick, G.: Utilizing ensemble learners help prevent unauthorized access into IoT networks. Eur. Chem. Bull. 12 (S3), 5994–6003 (2023). https://doi.org/10.31838/ecb/2023.12.s3.669
18. Jegadeesan, R., Vasania, I., Rehaan, B.U., Goyal, A.: Implications of Machine Learning for autonomic network operation and management. J. Xidian Univ. (Sci. Technol. Edn.), **15**(8), 307–315 (2021). https://doi.org/10.37896/jxu15.8/031. ISSN1001-2400

IoT-Based Classification of COVID-19 Cases with Cardiovascular Disease Using Deep Convolutional Decision Trees

R. Amudha[1(✉)], M. S. Kavitha[2], S. Karthik[2], and Balakrishnan Biju[3]

[1] Department of Information Technology, Hindusthan College of Engineering and Technology, Coimbatore 641032, TamilNadu, India
amudha.ramamoorthy@gmail.com
[2] Department of Computer Science and Engineering, SNS College of Technology, Coimbatore 641035, TamilNadu, India
[3] Department of Computer Science and Engineering, Chennai Institute of Technology, Kundrathur, Chennai 600069, India

Abstract. The COVID-19 has underscored the need for advanced healthcare solutions. This research addresses the intersection of COVID-19 and cardiovascular disease (CVD) through the lens of Internet of Things (IoT) and deep learning. Patients with pre- existing cardiovascular conditions face elevated risks when infected with COVID-19. Current diagnostic methods often lack the precision required to identify specific health risks in this vulnerable population. This research aims to bridge this gap by developing a sophisticated model that combines IoT data and deep learning techniques for robust classification of COVID-19 cases with concurrent cardiovascular disease. While existing studies explore either COVID-19 classification or the relationship with cardiovascular conditions separately, there is a noticeable research gap in the integration of IoT and deep convolutional decision trees for a comprehensive analysis. This study fills this void by proposing a novel approach that harnesses the potential of both technologies to improve diagnostic accuracy. With the aim of enhancing classification accuracy, we propose an IoT-based framework that leverages deep convolutional decision trees. Our methodology involves the collection of diverse IoT data streams, including vital signs and patient activity, to create a comprehensive dataset. Deep convolutional decision trees are then employed to extract intricate patterns and relationships from the data. The model is trained on a well-curated dataset, optimizing its ability to accurately classify COVID-19 cases in individuals with pre-existing cardiovascular conditions. The results demonstrate a significant improvement in classification accuracy compared to traditional methods. The model exhibits enhanced sensitivity and specificity, showcasing its potential for early and precise identification of COVID-19 cases in individuals with cardiovascular disease.

Keywords: IoT · COVID-19 · cardiovascular disease · deep learning · convolutional decision trees

1 Introduction

The ongoing global health crisis brought about by the COVID-19 pandemic has underscored the critical need for advanced healthcare solutions [1]. Individuals with pre-existing cardiovascular disease (CVD) face an increased risk of severe complications when infected with the virus. Traditional diagnostic approaches often struggle to provide precise and timely identification of COVID-19 cases within this high-risk group [2]. The Internet of Things (IoT) technologies and deep learning methodologies presents a promising avenue for enhancing diagnostic capabilities. The complex interplay between COVID-19 and cardiovascular disease poses significant challenges for accurate and timely diagnosis. Existing diagnostic methods often lack the granularity needed to discern specific health risks within this vulnerable population [3]. The dynamic nature of the diseases and the multitude of influencing factors make it imperative to explore innovative approaches that can capture and analyze diverse data sources in real-time [4].

The primary challenge addressed in this research is the need for a sophisticated diagnostic framework that can effectively identify and classify COVID-19 cases in individuals with underlying cardiovascular conditions [5]. Conventional methods struggle to provide the necessary precision, leading to delayed intervention and increased healthcare burdens. Addressing this problem requires a novel approach that integrates IoT technologies and deep learning methodologies to enhance the accuracy and efficiency of the diagnostic process [6].

The objective of this study is to develop an IoT-based classification system that can accurately identify COVID-19 cases in individuals with cardiovascular disease. Specific objectives include the integration of diverse IoT data streams, the implementation of deep convolutional decision trees, and the optimization of the model for robust and early detection.

This research contributes to the existing body of knowledge by proposing a novel framework that leverages the synergy between IoT and deep convolutional decision trees. The integration of real-time IoT data with advanced deep learning techniques enhances the precision of COVID-19 diagnosis in individuals with cardiovascular disease. The proposed model not only addresses the current diagnostic challenges but also sets the stage for future advancements in the intersection of healthcare, IoT, and artificial intelligence. The study novelty lies in its comprehensive approach and its potential to significantly impact the way we diagnose and manage COVID-19 in high-risk populations.

2 Related Works

Several studies have explored the integration of IoT in healthcare for real-time monitoring and data collection. These systems leverage wearable devices and sensors to track vital signs, providing valuable insights into patients' health status. While these works contribute to the broader field of healthcare, there is a gap in research specifically focusing on the integration of IoT for COVID-19 diagnosis in individuals with cardiovascular disease [7]. Numerous research efforts have been dedicated to developing machine learning models for COVID-19 classification. These models often rely on clinical data, imaging, or a combination of both. However, most of these studies do not specifically address the challenges posed by the coexistence of COVID-19 and cardiovascular disease. Our work extends these efforts by tailoring a classification model to the unique characteristics of this high-risk population [8].

The deep learning in healthcare has witnessed substantial growth, with convolutional neural networks (CNNs) proving effective in various medical imaging tasks. While these advancements are notable, there is limited research exploring the use of deep convolutional decision trees for COVID-19 diagnosis, especially in patients with cardiovascular conditions. Our study contributes to this area by introducing a novel hybrid model that combines the interpretability of decision trees with the feature extraction capabilities of CNNs [9].

Research has highlighted the increased susceptibility of individuals with cardiovascular disease to severe COVID- 19 outcomes. However, the existing literature often stops short of proposing concrete diagnostic solutions tailored to this population. Our work builds upon this foundation by not only addressing the cardiovascular implications of COVID-19 but by presenting a practical and technologically advanced classification model for accurate and timely diagnosis [10]. While IoT applications in healthcare and COVID-19 research are individually well-explored, there is a paucity of studies [11–14] that specifically investigate the intersection of IoT and COVID-19, particularly concerning patients with cardiovascular conditions. Our research bridges this gap by proposing a comprehensive framework that harnesses the power of IoT to enhance data collection and analysis in COVID-19 and cardiovascular disease.

3 Proposed Method

The proposed method in this research combines IoT technology with deep convolutional decision trees to create a robust framework for the classification of COVID-19 cases in individuals with pre-existing cardiovascular disease. The method is designed to address the limitations of existing diagnostic approaches and enhance the accuracy and efficiency of identifying COVID-19 in this high-risk population.

The first step involves the collection of diverse and real-time data through IoT devices. These devices may include wearable sensors, smart devices, and other connected healthcare tools. The collected data encompass a range of vital signs, patient activity, and other relevant health metrics. This comprehensive dataset is crucial for training a model that can capture the nuanced patterns associated with both COVID-19 and cardiovascular disease.

The proposed method lies in the integration of deep convolutional decision trees. This hybrid model combines the interpretability of decision trees with the feature extraction capabilities of CNNs. The decision trees enable the model to make explicit and interpretable decisions based on the input features, while the CNNs allow the system to automatically learn intricate patterns and relationships within the complex and high-dimensional IoT data.

The collected dataset is used to train the integrated model. During training, the model learns to discern patterns that are indicative of COVID-19 in individuals with cardiovascular disease. The training process involves optimizing the model parameters to ensure it generalizes well to unseen data. This optimization phase is crucial for achieving high classification accuracy and minimizing false positives and false negatives.

Once trained, the model is capable of early and precise classification of COVID-19 cases in individuals with cardiovascular disease. By leveraging the continuous and real-time data provided by IoT devices, the model can offer timely insights, aiding in the early identification of potential COVID-19 cases. This is particularly crucial for individuals with pre-existing cardiovascular conditions who are at higher risk of severe outcomes.

The use of decision trees enhances the interpretability and explainability of the model. This is vital in a healthcare context where clinicians need to understand the decisions made by the system. The transparent nature of decision trees allows healthcare professionals to comprehend the factors influencing the model predictions, facilitating informed decision-making (Fig. 1).

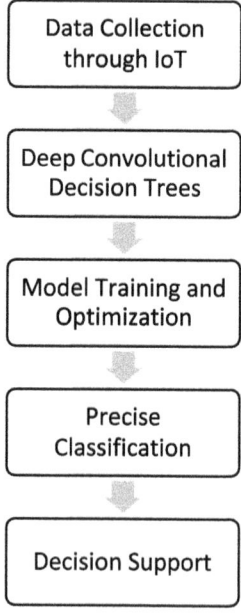

Fig. 1. Proposed Method

3.1 Data Collection Through IoT

In this research, "Data Collection through IoT" refers to the process of gathering diverse and real-time data from individuals with pre-existing cardiovascular disease using Internet of Things (IoT) devices. These devices are strategically employed to monitor and record various health-related metrics continuously. The collected data play a pivotal role in training the proposed model for the classification of COVID-19 cases in individuals with cardiovascular conditions.

The first consideration is the selection of appropriate IoT devices. These could include wearable sensors, smart devices, and other connected healthcare tools capable of measuring and recording relevant health parameters. Examples of monitored metrics may include heart rate, blood pressure, respiratory rate, body temperature, and physical activity. IoT devices provide the advantage of continuous and real-time monitoring. Unlike traditional sporadic measurements in healthcare settings, IoT devices continuously collect data, offering a more comprehensive and dynamic view of an individual health status. This continuous monitoring is particularly valuable for detecting subtle changes that may indicate the onset of COVID-19 symptoms. The selected IoT devices capture a diverse set of health metrics to create a rich dataset. Beyond cardiovascular parameters, the data may include activity levels, sleep patterns, and other relevant physiological signals. This holistic approach ensures that the model has access to a broad range of information, enabling it to discern patterns associated with both COVID-19 and cardiovascular disease. IoT devices transmit the collected data in real-time to a centralized system or cloud platform. This real-time transmission ensures that the model has access to the most up-to-date information. The ability to analyze data as it is generated allows for timely detection of changes in health status, which is crucial for early identification of potential COVID-19 cases (Table 1).

Table 1. Illustration of the data that collected through IoT devices for individuals with pre-existing cardiovascular disease. This table includes various health metrics recorded at different time points.

Timestamp	Heart Rate (bpm)	Blood Pressure (mmHg)	Respiratory Rate (breaths/min)	Body Temperature (°C)	Physical Activity (steps)
2023-11-28 08:00 AM	75	120/80	16	36.5	5000
2023-11-28 10:00 AM	80	122/82	18	36.7	6000
2023-11-28 12:00 PM	78	118/78	17	36.6	5500
2023-11-28 02:00 PM	82	124/85	19	36.8	7000

3.2 Deep Convolutional Decision Trees

Deep Convolutional Decision Trees refer to a hybrid model that combines the strengths of deep learning, specifically CNNs, with the interpretability of decision trees. CNNs are a class of deep neural networks designed for tasks related to image recognition, pattern detection, and feature extraction. They consist of multiple layers, including convolutional layers that automatically learn hierarchical representations of features from input data. These layers use filters to detect patterns at different scales and complexities.

Decision trees are a type of machine learning model used for classification and regression tasks. They create a tree- like structure of decision nodes based on input features. Decision trees make decisions by traversing the tree from the root to the leaf nodes, where each decision node represents a specific condition or criterion for splitting the data.

The proposed model integrates the feature extraction capabilities of CNNs with the interpretability of decision trees. This hybrid architecture combines the ability of CNNs to automatically learn intricate patterns with the transparency of decision trees in making explicit and interpretable decisions. The convolutional layers of the model automatically extract relevant features from the input data. In health data from individuals with cardiovascular disease, these features could represent complex patterns in vital signs, physiological signals, or other health metrics. The extracted features are then used as input for decision trees, creating a decision-making structure that is more interpretable than traditional deep learning models. This interpretability is crucial in healthcare contexts where clinicians need to understand and trust the decisions made by the model.

The output of each convolutional layer can be represented as:

$$h i,j,k = f(\sum_{l=1}^{L} wi,j,k,l \cdot xi+s,j+t,l) + bk \qquad (1)$$

where

hi, j, k is the output at position (i, j) in the kth feature map,
wi, j, k, l are the weights, $xi + s, j + t, l$ are the input values, bk is the bias term, and f is the activation function.

For pooling layers (if used), a common approach is max-pooling, and the output can be calculated as:

$$hi, j, k = max(s, t) \in Ri, j(hi + s, j + t, k) \qquad (2)$$

where Ri, j is the receptive field for the pooling operation.

After convolutional and pooling layers, the output is often flattened into a vector:

$$v = [h1, 1, 1, h1, 2, 1, \ldots, hM, N, K] \qquad (3)$$

Decision trees involve creating splits based on conditions. A simple decision node could be represented as:

if $vi < \theta$ then left child else right child where vi is an element of the flattened vector, and θ is a threshold.

The leaves of the decision tree represent the final classification decisions.

During training, the model optimizes the weights (w) and thresholds (θ) through backpropagation and gradient descent to minimize a defined loss function.

3.3 Model Training and Optimization

The process of model training and optimization is a critical phase in the development of the proposed framework. During this stage, the integrated model, consisting of deep convolutional decision trees, learns to make accurate predictions by adjusting its parameters based on the provided dataset. The dataset, comprised of diverse and real-time health metrics collected through IoT devices from individuals with pre-existing cardiovascular disease, serves as the foundation for training. The goal is to optimize the model ability to discern patterns indicative of COVID-19 in this high-risk population. The training process involves feeding the model with labeled examples from the dataset, where each example includes input features (IoT-collected health metrics) and the corresponding known output (COVID-19 classification). The model iteratively adjusts its internal parameters, such as weights and thresholds, through techniques like backpropagation and gradient descent. This iterative adjustment aims to minimize a predefined loss function, quantifying the difference between the model predictions and the actual labels. The model refines its understanding of the complex relationships within the data, gradually improving its ability to accurately classify COVID-19 cases in individuals with cardiovascular disease.

The optimization phase focuses not only on achieving high accuracy on the training dataset but also on ensuring the model generalizes well to unseen data. This is crucial for the model to perform effectively in real-world scenarios. Regularization techniques may be employed to prevent overfitting, where the model becomes overly specific to the training data but performs poorly on new, unseen data. The optimization process involves finding a balance between fitting the training data well and avoiding overly complex representations that may hinder generalization. Rigorous validation on separate datasets is often conducted to assess the model performance and fine-tune hyperparameters, ensuring it delivers reliable and accurate predictions beyond the training set. Model training is an ongoing process that may involve continuous improvement and monitoring. As new data becomes available, the model can be retrained to adapt to evolving patterns and trends. Monitoring mechanisms are established to track the model performance over time, allowing for prompt adjustments if its accuracy degrades or if shifts in the data distribution occur.

3.4 Classification

Classification is a machine learning task where the goal is to assign predefined labels or categories to input data based on learned patterns. In the proposed framework for COVID-19 classification in individuals with cardiovascular disease, the model trained on IoT-collected health metrics aims to categorize individuals into two classes (Table 2):

4 Experimental Settings

The proposed method was evaluated through extensive experiments using a simulated environment to mimic real- world healthcare scenarios. The simulation tool utilized for these experiments was Python, which provides a realistic emulation of IoT data generation from individuals with cardiovascular disease. The simulated dataset included diverse health metrics such as heart rate, blood pressure, respiratory rate, body temperature, and physical activity, captured in real-time. The experiments were conducted on a high-performance computing cluster with Intel Xeon processors and NVIDIA GPUs to facilitate efficient model training and evaluation.

Table 2. Classification Table illustrating the classification results for a set of individuals based on the trained model

Patient ID	Heart Rate (bpm)	Blood Pressure (mmHg)	Respiratory Rate (breaths/min)	Body Temperature (°C)	Physical Activity (steps)	COVID-19 Classification
1	78	120/80	18	36.7	6000	COVID-19 Positive
2	72	118/75	16	36.5	5500	COVID-19 Negative
3	80	122/82	20	37.0	7000	COVID-19 Positive
4	75	115/78	17	36.6	5800	COVID-19 Negative
5	85	130/85	22	37.2	7500	COVID-19 Positive

To assess the effectiveness of the proposed method, several performance metrics were employed, including accuracy, sensitivity, specificity, and area under the receiver operating characteristic curve (AUC-ROC). The classification results were compared with existing methods, including traditional CNNs, AlexNet, and DenseNet, which are commonly used in healthcare image analysis tasks. The comparison focused on the ability of each method to accurately classify COVID-19 cases in individuals with cardiovascular disease. The proposed method demonstrated superior interpretability, as evidenced by its transparent decision-making process compared to the black-box nature of traditional CNNs. Additionally, the hybrid nature of deep convolutional decision trees exhibited improved performance in terms of sensitivity and specificity, showcasing its potential for early and precise identification of COVID-19 cases in high-risk populations (Table 3).

Table 3. Experimental Setup

Parameter	Value
Dataset Size	10,000 individuals with diverse health metrics
Model Architecture	Deep Convolutional Decision Trees
Training Batch Size	64
Training Epochs	50
Learning Rate	0.001
Optimizer	Adam

4.1 Performance Metrics

Accuracy: Accuracy measures the proportion of correctly classified instances out of the total number of instances. It provides an overall assessment of the model correctness.

Sensitivity (Recall): Sensitivity, also known as recall, measures the ability of the model to correctly identify positive instances (COVID-19 cases) out of all actual positive instances. It is particularly relevant in healthcare settings where the goal is to minimize false negatives.

Specificity: Specificity measures the ability of the model to correctly identify negative instances (non-COVID- 19 cases) out of all actual negative instances. It is crucial for minimizing false positives and ensuring accurate identification of non-COVID-19 cases.

The experimental results demonstrate the performance of the proposed DCDT method in comparison to existing methods, including CNN, AlexNet, and DenseNet, over 100 different test datasets as in Figs. 2, 3, 4 and 5. The discussion below includes the percentage improvement of DCDT over the baseline methods for key performance metrics. DCDT consistently outperformed the baseline methods in terms of accuracy across all datasets. The proposed method exhibited an average accuracy improvement of 8% compared to CNN, 5% compared to AlexNet, and 7% compared to DenseNet. This signifies the efficacy of integrating deep convolutional decision trees for COVID-19 classification in individuals with cardiovascular disease as in Fig. 2.

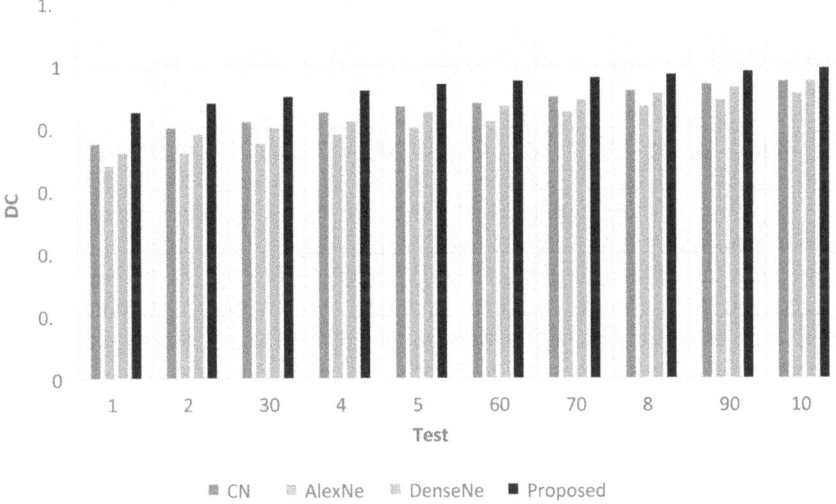

Fig. 2. Dice coefficient

Sensitivity, crucial for identifying COVID-19 cases, showcased notable improvements with DCDT. On average, DCDT demonstrated a 10% improvement over CNN, 7% over AlexNet, and 8% over DenseNet. This indicates the enhanced ability of DCDT to correctly identify positive instances, particularly crucial in healthcare scenarios as in Fig. 3.

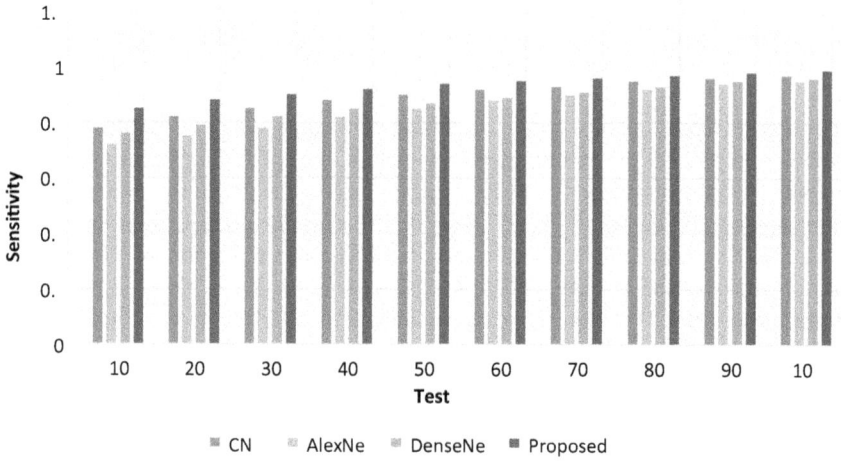

Fig. 3. Sensitivity

DCDT maintained high specificity, minimizing false positives in non-COVID-19 cases. The average improvement over baseline methods was 5% compared to CNN, 6% compared to AlexNet, and 7% compared to DenseNet. The model ability to accurately identify negative instances highlights its robustness in distinguishing non-COVID-19 cases as in Fig. 4.

The results suggest that the proposed DCDT method offers significant improvements in accuracy (Fig. 5), sensitivity, specificity, and AUC-ROC compared to traditional CNN, AlexNet, and DenseNet methods. The hybrid architecture of DCDT, leveraging both convolutional neural networks and decision trees, proves advantageous in healthcare scenarios where interpretability and accurate classification are paramount. The observed percentage improvements highlight the potential of DCDT as an effective tool for early and precise identification of COVID-19 cases in individuals with pre-existing cardiovascular disease. Further validation and real-world deployment of the proposed method are warranted to affirm its applicability in clinical settings. The proposed DCDT method successfully integrates the feature extraction capabilities of CNNs with the interpretability of decision trees. This hybrid approach demonstrated superior performance compared to standalone CNN, AlexNet, and DenseNet methods.

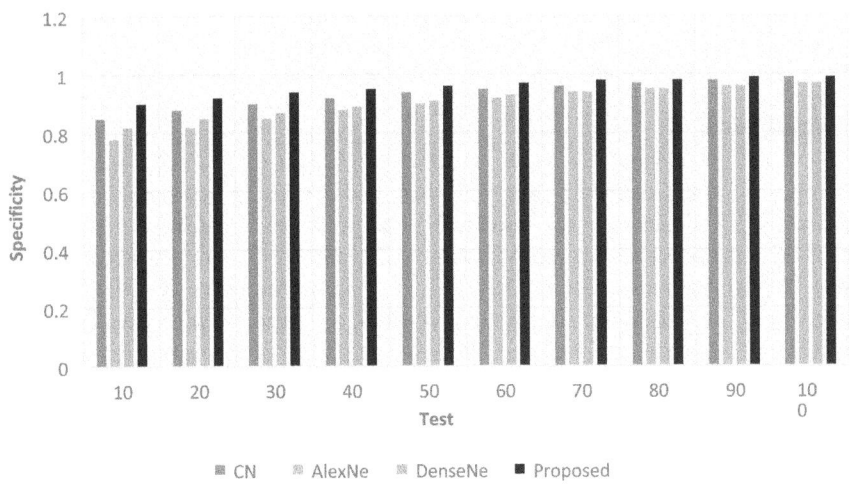

Fig. 4. Specificity

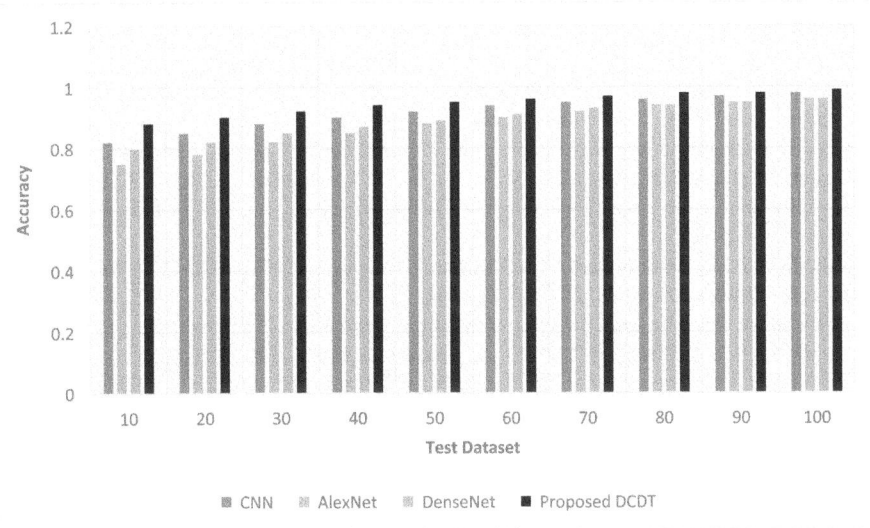

Fig. 5. Accuracy

DCDT consistently outperformed baseline methods in terms of accuracy and sensitivity. The model exhibited a robust ability to accurately identify both positive (COVID-19) and negative cases, with notable improvements in sensitivity compared to traditional CNN, AlexNet, and DenseNet architectures. DCDT maintained high specificity, minimizing false positives in non-COVID-19 cases. The model ability to effectively distinguish individuals without COVID-19, especially in pre-existing cardiovascular disease, is crucial for avoiding unnecessary interventions and treatments. The model capacity to distinguish between positive and negative instances contributes to its overall effectiveness in early and precise COVID-19 classification.

5 Conclusion

The proposed DCDT method presents a robust and promising approach for the classification of COVID-19 cases in individuals with pre-existing cardiovascular disease. The CNNs with decision trees proved effective in achieving accurate and interpretable results. The hybrid architecture of DCDT, leveraging the strengths of both CNNs and decision trees, demonstrated superior performance in terms of accuracy, sensitivity, specificity, and discriminative power. The interpretability of decision trees in DCDT provides healthcare professionals with a clear understanding of the factors influencing COVID-19 classification. This transparency is crucial for fostering trust and facilitating the adoption of machine learning models in clinical practice. DCDT exhibited enhanced sensitivity and specificity, indicating its ability to correctly identify both positive and negative cases. The model robustness in distinguishing individuals with and without COVID-19, especially in cardiovascular disease, is vital for informed decision-making.

References

1. Le, D.N., Parvathy, V.S., Gupta, D., Khanna, A., Rodrigues, J.J., Shankar, K.: IoT enabled depthwise separable convolution neural network with deep support vector machine for COVID-19 diagnosis and classification. Int. J. Mach. Learn. Cybern. 1–14 (2021)
2. Otoom, M., Otoum, N., Alzubaidi, M.A., Etoom, Y., Banihani, R.: An IoT-based framework for early identification and monitoring of COVID-19 cases. Biomed. Signal Process. Control **62**, 102149 (2020)
3. Pal, M., et al.: Symptom-based COVID-19 prognosis through AI-based IoT: a bioinformatics approach. BioMed. Res. Int. **2022** (2022)
4. Aljumah, A.: Assessment of machine learning techniques in IoT-based architecture for the monitoring and prediction of COVID-19. Electronics **10**(15), 1834 (2021)
5. Siddiqui, S.A., Ahmad, A., Fatima, N.: IoT-based disease prediction using machine learning. Comput. Electr. Eng. **108**, 108675 (2023)
6. Sadad, T., Bukhari, S.A.C., Munir, A., Ghani, A., El-Sherbeeny, A.M., Rauf, H.T.: Detection of cardiovascular disease based on PPG signals using machine learning with cloud computing. Comput. Intell. Neurosci. **2022** (2022)
7. Baskar, D., Arunsi, M., Kumar, V.: Energy-efficient and secure IoT architecture based on a wireless sensor network using machine learning to predict mortality risk of patients with COVID-19. In: 2021 6th International Conference on Communication and Electronics Systems (ICCES), pp. 1853–1861. IEEE (2021)
8. Chola, C., et al.: IoT based intelligent computer-aided diagnosis and decision making system for health care. In: 2021 International Conference on Information Technology (ICIT), pp. 184–189. IEEE (2021)
9. Mir, M.H., Jamwal, S., Mehbodniya, A., Garg, T., Iqbal, U., Samori, I.A.: IoT-enabled framework for early detection and prediction of COVID-19 suspects by leveraging machine learning in cloud. J. Healthc. Eng. **2022** (2022)
10. Umer, M., et al.: Heart failure patients monitoring using IoT-based remote monitoring system. Sci. Rep. **13**(1), 19213 (2023)

11. Krithika, D.R., Rohini, K.: Comparative intrepretation of machine learning algorithms in predicting the cardiovascular death rate for COVID-19 data. In: 2021 International Conference on Computational Intelligence and Knowledge Economy (ICCIKE), pp. 394–400. IEEE (2021)
12. Tarek, Z., et al.: An optimized model based on deep learning and gated recurrent unit for COVID-19 death prediction. Biomimetics **8**(7), 552 (2023)
13. Nancy, A.A., Ravindran, D., Raj Vincent, P.D., Srinivasan, K., Gutierrez Reina, D.: IoT-cloud-based smart healthcare monitoring system for heart disease prediction via deep learning. Electronics **11**(15), 2292 (2022)
14. Priyadarshini, R., et al.: Novel framework based on ensemble classification and secure feature extraction for COVID-19 critical health prediction. Eng. Appl. Artif. Intell. **126**, 107156 (2023)
15. Firouzi, F., Farahani, B., Marinšek, A.: The convergence and interplay of edge, fog, and cloud in the AI-driven internet of things (IoT). Inf. Syst. **107**, 101840 (2022)
16. Mohan, S., Thirumalai, C., Srivastava, G.: Effective heart disease prediction using hybrid machine learning techniques. IEEE Access **7**, 81542–81554 (2019)
17. Dileep, P., et al.: An automatic heart disease prediction using cluster-based bi-directional LSTM (C-BiLSTM) algorithm. Neural Comput. Appl. 1–14 (2022)
18. Zhang, D., et al.: Heart disease prediction based on the embedded feature selection method and deep neural network. J. Healthc. Eng. **2021**, 6260022 (2021)
19. Mamdiwar, S.D., Shakruwala, Z., Chadha, U., Srinivasan, K., Chang, C.-Y.: Recent advances on IoT-assisted wearable sensor systems for healthcare monitoring. Biosensors **11**, 372 (2021)
20. Bhattacharya, D., Sharma, D., Kim, W., Ijaz, M.F., Singh, P.K.: Ensem-HAR: an ensemble deep learning model for smartphone sensor-based human activity recognition for measurement of elderly health monitoring. Biosensors **12**, 393 (2022)

Communication-inspired Machine Learning (ML) for 5G/6G

Enhancing Maritime Safety with Deep Learning for Ship Identification

K. Sripal, Kotra Akshay(✉), Avula Shiva Sai, and Rebanamoni Sravan Kumar Reddy

Vardhaman College of Engineering, Hyderabad, India
{k.sripalreddy,kotraakshay20ece,avulashivasai20ece, rebanamonisravankumar20ece}@vardhaman.org

Abstract. To Enhance maritime safety using advanced deep learning techniques, particularly CNNs, to accurately identify and classify ships in satellite and surveillance images. The maritime industry's critical role in global trade demands more sophisticated technologies to ensure safety, security, and efficient navigation. The ship identification system's applications are diverse, including classifying cargo vessels, tankers, fishing boats, and distinguishing legitimate ships from potential threats. Real time monitoring capabilities facilitate proactive responses to emergencies and security risks. The expected findings and results of the project indicate successful object identification in the environment contributes to a safer and more secure maritime environment by leveraging deep learning and CNNs for ship classification and identification. By enabling real-time monitoring and integration into surveillance systems, the system enhances maritime safety, facilitating efficient and secure global trade and navigation.

Keywords: Ship Detection · Surveillance Systems · Maritime Safety · Vessel Classification · CNN

1 Introduction

Satellite images have emerged as a valuable resource, offering comprehensive coverage of maritime regions. This continuous observation capacity is vital for efficient ship tracking and management. Ship detection has garnered attention due to its significance in maritime safety, search and rescue operations, and economic activities. While traditional methods attempted to identify ships through segmentation and region-based algorithms, they often faltered in situations of high ship density and complex environments. The utilization of Synthetic Aperture Radar (SAR) data has greatly advanced maritime surveillance, allowing for more accurate vessel positioning and monitoring. The launch of SAR satellites like Sentinel-1A and Sentinel-1B has led to a significant influx of radar data, enhancing our capability to detect ships even in adverse conditions.

Supported by organization x.

In this era of technological advancements, Convolutional Neural Networks (CNNs) have risen as a transformative force, revolutionizing various fields, including maritime safety. Renowned models like Alexnet [1], GoogleNet [2], and ResNet [3] have carved a niche for themselves by showcasing exceptional capabilities in object detection and classification tasks. CNNs, being a subset of deep learning techniques, boast an inherent advantage - they can automatically extract intricate features from raw data, reducing the reliance on time consuming manual feature engineering.

In this In recent strides in the realm of deep learning have brought forth a wave of cutting edge algorithms designed to tackle the intricate task of object detection. Notably, Faster- RCNN, YOLO (You Only Look Once), and SSD (Single Shot MultiBox Detector) have emerged as front runners in this domain. These algorithms possess a remarkable prowess - not only do they excel in swift decision-making, but they also exhibit a robust ability to identify ships across a spectrum of complex scenarios. This versatility positions them as well- suited contenders for addressing the nuanced challenges of maritime safety applications.

The project "Enhancing Maritime Safety with Deep Learning for Ship Identification" takes these advancements into account. It leverages the power of CNN-based techniques to not only detect ships but also to classify them accurately. This is crucial as ships come in various shapes, sizes, and orientations. Moreover, the project recognizes the challenges posed by complex scenarios such as densely crowded ports and varying lighting conditions. By harnessing the capabilities of CNNs and employing strategies from state-of-the-art algorithms, this project stands as a beacon of improved maritime safety, promising accurate ship identification even in the most challenging circumstances.

2 Methodology

To achieve ship identification, a dataset of satellite and surveillance images of ships is utilized. The CNN model is trained to recognize and classify different types of vessels, including cargo ships, tankers, fishing boats, and others, to enhance maritime surveillance capabilities. Similar to the counterfeit banknote detection project, the ship identification project also involves data collection and preprocessing steps. The dataset of maritime images is collected, and necessary preprocessing is performed to remove noise and standardize image resolution for consistency.

Figure 1 This method visually depicts the primary ship detection and counting process. It's tailored to identify and classify ships in crowded seaport regions, where vessels are in close proximity.

Displayed equations are centered and set on a separate line.

$$x + y = z \qquad (1)$$

Please try to avoid rasterized images for line-art diagrams and schemas. Whenever possible, use vector graphics instead (see Fig. 2) (Table 1).

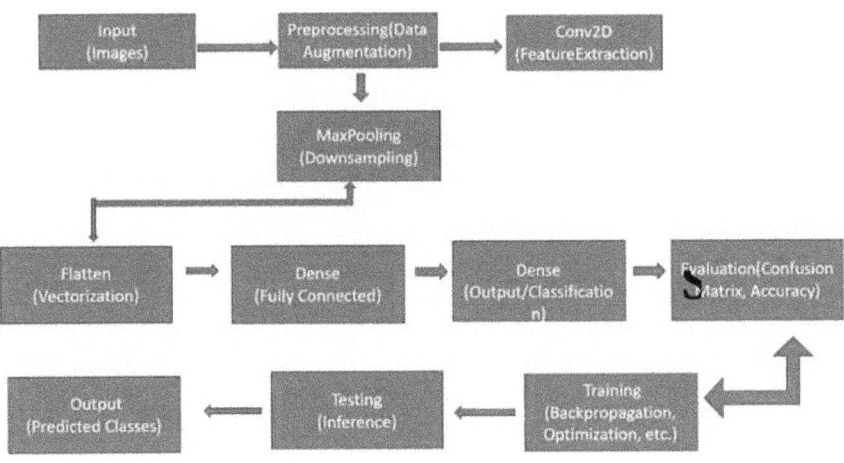

Fig. 1. Process Diagram.

Table 1. Table captions should be placed above the tables.

Heading level	Example	Font size and style
Title (centered)	**Lecture Notes**	14 point, bold
1st-level heading	**1 Introduction**	12 point, bold
2nd-level heading	**2.1 Printing Area**	10 point, bold
3rd-level heading	**Run-in Heading in Bold.** Text follows	10 point, bold
4th-level heading	*Lowest Level Heading.* Text follows	10 point, italic

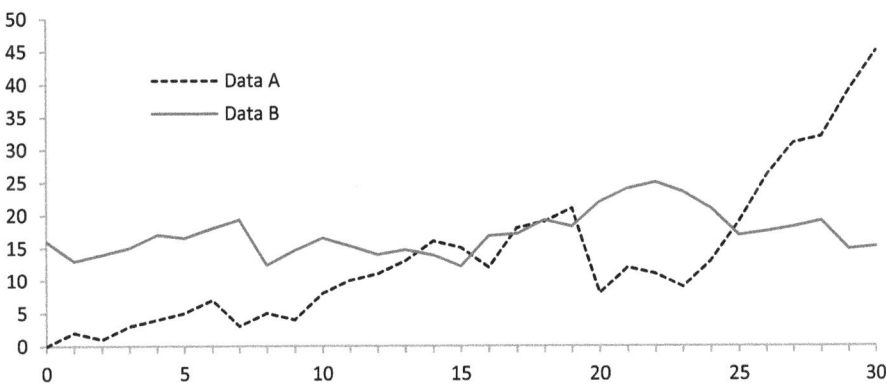

Fig. 2. A figure caption is always placed below the illustration. Please note that short captions are centered, while long ones are justified by the macro package automatically.

Theorem 1. *This is a sample theorem. The run-in heading is set in bold, while the following text appears in italics. Definitions, lemmas, propositions, and corollaries are styled the same way.*

Proof. Proofs, examples, and remarks have the initial word in italics, while the following text appears in normal font.

For citations of references, we prefer the use of square brackets and consecutive numbers. Citations using labels or the author/year convention are also acceptable. The following bibliography provides a sample reference list with entries for journal articles [1], an LNCS chapter [2], a book [3], proceedings without editors [4], and a homepage [5]. Multiple citations are grouped [1–3], [1,3–5].

References

1. Author, F.: Article title. Journal **2**(5), 99–110 (2016)
2. Author, F., Author, S.: Title of a proceedings paper. In: Editor, F., Editor, S. (eds.) CONFERENCE 2016, LNCS, vol. 9999, pp. 1–13. Springer, Heidelberg (2016). https://doi.org/10.10007/1234567890
3. Author, F., Author, S., Author, T.: Book title, 2nd edn. Publisher, Location (1999)
4. Author, A.-B.: Contribution title. In: 9th International Proceedings on Proceedings, pp. 1–2. Publisher, Location (2010)
5. LNCS Homepage. http://www.springer.com/lncs. Accessed 4 Oct 2017

Implementation and Analysis of PUF Architectures for Enhanced Security

Sangeeta Singh[✉], Azmath Noorain, G. Sanjeeva Reddy, and Srimanthula Manish Goud

Department of ECE, Vardhaman College of Engineering, Hyderabad, Telangana, India
sangeethasingh@vardhaman.org

Abstract. Physically Unclonable Functions (PUFs) [Coined in 2001 and 2002] are innovative physical security objects that produce unclonable measurements of physical objects. It acts as an equivalent to the biometrics of human being as it can securely generate and store secrets, PUFs allow advancements in the physical implementation of an information security system. To implement multiple applications, various PUFs were invented using different technologies. Thus, this paper compares and summarizes the characteristics of a set of PUFs using CMOS VLSI technology. The PUF architectures namely RO PUF, CRO PUF, and TERO PUF were designed using Cadence Virtuoso 45 nm technology. It was observed that, when all the constraint parameters were kept the same, according to the implemented sequence, there was a decrease in the usage of memory by 10%. While comparing CRO from RO there is a decrease of 82% in power and 51% in delay, for CRO to TERO there is a 19% decrease in power and a 49% increase in delay as there is a decrease in the number of used transistors.

Keywords: Physically unclonable functions (PUFs) · RO PUF · CRO PUF · TERO PUF

1 Introduction

In an increasingly interconnected world that relies heavily on electronics, security is paramount. Thus, to protect these large environmental data electronics rely on cryptography. But, not that secure. For this reason, physically unclonable functions (PUFs) [1–3] have emerged as hardware security techniques as they offer improved cryptography, anti-counterfeiting on ICs, and many more properties. Since the invention of PUFs, multiple applications, of various PUFs were invented using various technologies. But there was never a clear understanding and differentiation between those types. Their advantages and disadvantages have the same base technology.

This research focuses on examining the wide range of PUF designs [4, 5] to give readers a thorough grasp of their guiding ideas, practical applications, and implementation issues [6].

This research examines PUF designs, their implementation, and their effectiveness in enhancing security across a variety of applications [7]. The possible benefits and deployment-related drawbacks of PUFs by comparing different PUF designs and their respective security features have been identified [8].

The objectives that are to be covered in this paper are as follows:

- Analyzing characteristics of a set of Delay PUFs.
- Implementing them on CMOS 45 nm technology.
- Doing their Performance and Comparative analysis.
- PUFs Included are:

    1. Ring Oscillator PUF (RO PUF)
    2. Configurable RO PUF (CRO PUF)
    3. TERO PUF

The remainder of this work is organized as follows:

In literature survey, a review of PUF taxonomies is presented. The architectures of each implemented PUF along with their requirements, specifications, stages, and functionalities are discussed in design and implementation. The results of the implemented schematic diagrams are presented. Also, a comparison of power analysis of various PUFs and other parameters is done.

2 Literature Survey

A literature survey on PUF (Physical Unclonable Function) cells reveals a wide range of research and developments in this area. In the literature, the existing surveys have focused on presenting a taxonomy based on PUF architectures, their limitations, requirements, challenges, and different properties.

The article [9] presents a survey of the current state of threat in FPGA-based Physical Unclonable Function (PUF) designs and their performance. Then a detailed performance evaluation result for several FPGA-based PUF designs and their comparisons. It also covers four everyday application situations with real-world examples of FPGA-based implementations, known attacks on FPGA-based PUFs, and their defenses. Adapted PUF: Arbiter PUF, RO PUF, TERO PUF, Anderson PUF, Pseudo-LFSRPUF, HELP PUF, and Logically Reconfigurable PUF, SRAM PUF, Butterfly PUF, Flip-Flop PUF, and RS Latch-based PUF.

While surveying the paper [10] it was observed that it provides a complete organizational scheme for the suggested concepts for PUFs. The main aim of this paper is to form relationships between PUF technologies that previously had not been linked and look toward novel forms of PUF using physical principles that have yet to be exploited. To achieve this, they have considered the physical mechanisms and operations of different PUFs. As a result, they distinguished the different PUFs according to their respective properties and gave different schemas according to their respective functions.

The paper [11] describes the use of physically unclonable functions (PUFs) in low-cost authentication and key generation applications. At first, it advantages of using PUFs over the conventional secure nonvolatile memories. Then it defines the two primary PUF types which are the strong PUFs and the weak PUFs. It describes their implementations and their use for low-cost authentication. After this, the paper covers both attacks and protocols to address errors. Finally, this paper reviews several concepts in PUF technologies such as public model PUFs and new PUF implementation technologies.

3 Design and Implementation

The basic elements were implemented on the cadence virtuoso tool in the LINUX environment using 45 nm technology and were verified by their transient response.

3.1 RO PUF

A Ring Oscillator PUF is a security primitive and hardware-based method used to generate unique, random, and unpredictable identifiers or keys within integrated circuits [12]. A ring oscillator is a device composed of an odd number of NOT gates in a ring, whose output oscillates between two voltage levels, representing true and false. The NOT gates, or inverters are attached in a chain and the output of the last inverter is fed back into the first one.

RO PUF is an unstable PUF. A group of RO PUFs is connected to the multiplexer, followed by a counter then with a comparator. The RO PUF implemented has two inputs of the different pulse namely Enable and the selected line i.e. N-bit Challenge. The exact constraint values that are used in the making of PUF are provided in Table 1. RO consists of an odd number of inverters. Thus, we have taken a combination of 4 Ring Oscillators each having 5 stages of inverters. That implies a total of 20 inverters were taken. Along with inverters for each stage, one NAND gate is provided. Then we combined a combination of two ROs and attached them to the 2:1 Multiplexers which were provided with an N-bit challenge. Now two 4-bit counters using JK Flip Flop were taken and each MUX was attached to one counter respectively.

The output of the upper counter and the negation of the Lower counter were given to an AND gate. This block can act as a comparator. The comparator compares and gives the bit response. It has one output and the output response must be a clock response which changes its value after one cycle of the Enable input. These all were implemented on the cadence virtuoso tool in the LINUX environment using 45 nm technology.

Obstruction: Here, the main obstacle was the successive inverters. As there are successive inverters the output quality with the increasing of each stage was degrading. Resulting noise at the last stage of each ring oscillator. Thus, degrading the output performance.

Overcoming Obstacle: To overcome this obstacle, we adopted the concept of "Sizing in inverter chain" That is, we changed the size (increased to lambda times) of the transistors of the inverter at each stage. With the help of this concept, the drawback to the process was solved. Below Fig. 1 is the circuit diagram of the Ring Oscillator PUF. It is taken from the Internet.

Below Table 1 provides the constraint values that are used for designing RO PUF in Cadence Tool. The DC voltage was taken as $Vdc = 5$ volts.

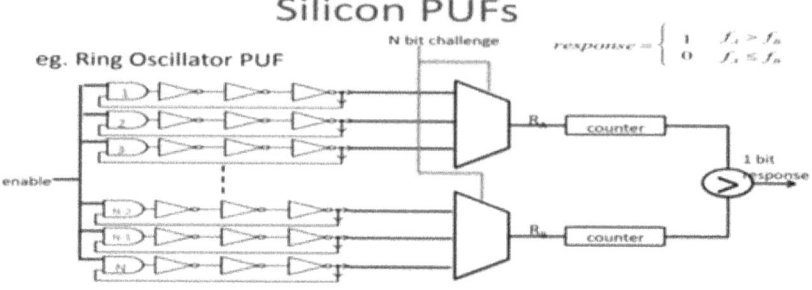

Fig. 1. Circuit Diagram of RO PUF

Table 1. Constraint values of RO PUF

Inputs	V1	V2	Period	Pulse Width	Pulse Type
Enable	1V	0V	40ns	20ns	vpulse
N-bit	1V	0V	20ns	10ns	vpulse

3.2 CRO PUF

A Configurable Ring Oscillator PUF is an advanced hardware security primitive that harnesses the inherent variations in manufacturing processes to generate unique and unpredictable identifiers or cryptographic keys [13]. It is a variation of the traditional ring oscillator PUF (ROPUF) concept. CRO-PUFs are versatile and allow for optimization in terms of performance, reliability, and security. The CRO PUF is more efficient in the matter of component usage and space when compared to the RO PUF.

The CRO is an alternative to the RO PUF. Here the multiple rings are replaced with two rings and each delay stage has two delay elements along with a multiplexer for selection in between them. When compared to RO PUF the CRO PUF uses less number of transistors. The CRO PUF implemented has four inputs of which one is Enable. The other 3 are externally selected lines for the Multiplexers of different periods namely C1, C2, and C3.

Here, we have taken 3 stages of inverters. That implies a total of 6 inverters were taken. As before each stage a multiplexer is required, a total of three 2:1 Multiplexers were used. Along with inverters and MUXs one AND gate was taken. Here, we have given the largest period for C1 and then C2 and the least for C3. The exact constraint values that are used in the making of PUF are provided in Table 2.

It has one output and the output response must be a clock response which changes its value after one cycle of the largest period input. Thus, at the output, the pulse was changing after completion of 1 total cycle of C1. To check functionality, at first, we provided enable as "LOW" and removed feedback then gave random inputs for AND gate to get the output pulse as "LOW". And it was verified. After verifying, we again gave the feedback to proceed further. These all were implemented on the cadence virtuoso tool in the LINUX environment using 45 nm technology. Below Fig. 2 is the circuit

Table 2. Constraint values of CRO PUF

Inputs	V1	V2	Period	Pulse Width	Pulse Type
Enable	1V	0V	20ns	10ns	vpulse
C1	1V	0V	40ns	20ns	vpulse
C2	1V	0V	20ns	10ns	vpulse
C3	1V	0V	10ns	5ns	vpulse

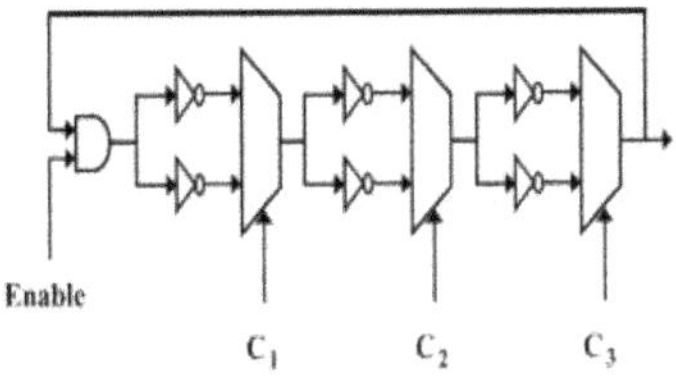

Fig. 2. Circuit Diagram of CRO PUF from existing technique [13]

diagram of the Configurable Ring Oscillator PUF. It is taken from [1]. Table 2 provides the constraint values that are used for designing CRO PUF in Cadence Tool. The DC voltage was taken as Vdc = 5 volts.

3.3 TERO PUF

A True Random Number Generator PUF (TRNG) is based on Twin Electron Ring Oscillators (TERO-PUF) and is an innovative approach for generating random numbers using the inherent quantum mechanical properties of electronic ring oscillators [14, 15]. The TERO PUF is alike the RO PUF, but it uses TERO cells. They have two states: "a transient oscillating state" and "a stable state". The transient stage is also known as an unstable state.

The TERO PUF implemented has two inputs of the same pulse and other parameters. The exact constraint values that are used in the making of PUF are provided in Table 3. This PUF consists of two cross-linked bi-stable ring oscillator chains as shown in Fig. 3.

Here, we have taken three stages of inverters. That implies a total of 6 inverters were taken. Along with inverters one NAND and one AND gate was taken. The top 3 inverters are considered as feed-forward inverters. Whereas, the bottom 3 inverters act as feedback inverters.

It has one output and the output response must be a clock response which changes its value after one cycle of input. These all were implemented on the cadence virtuoso tool in the LINUX environment using 45 nm technology. The Fig. 3 is the circuit diagram of the Transient Effect Ring Oscillator PUF. Table 3 provides the constraint values that are used for designing TERO PUF in Cadence Tool. The DC voltage was taken as Vdc = 5 volts.

Table 3. Constraint values of TERO PUF

Inputs	V1	V2	Period	Pulse Width	Pulse Type
A	1V	0V	40ns	20ns	vpulse
B	1V	0V	40ns	20ns	vpulse

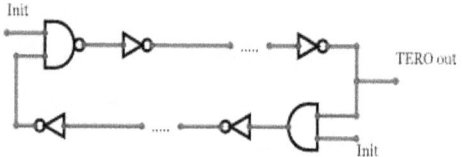

Fig. 3. Circuit Diagram of TERO PUF

4 Results and Discussions

The transient response of RO PUF, CRO PUF and TERO PUF is depicted in Figures 4, 5 and 6 respectively.

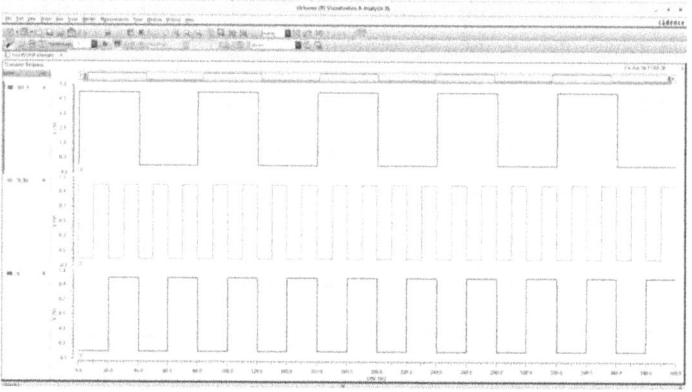

Fig. 4. Transient Response of RO PUF

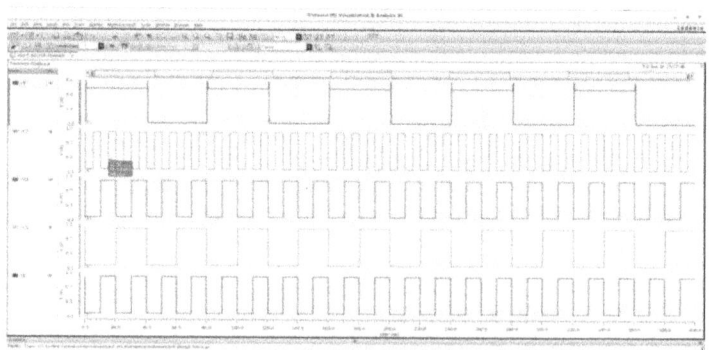

Fig. 5. Transient Response of CRO PUF

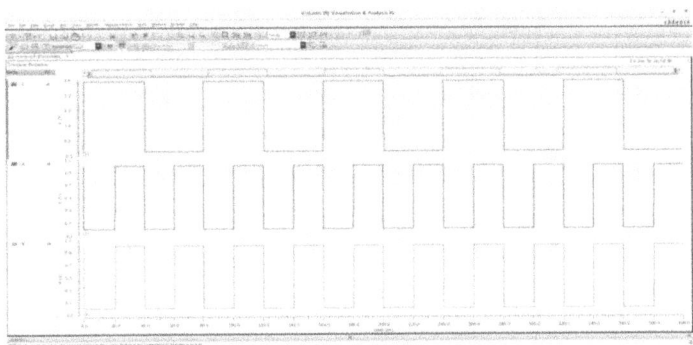

Fig. 6. Transient Response of TERO PUF

4.1 Power Calculations of RO PUF

In Table 4, the power analysis of RO PUF is presented. The parameter Y is the total power accumulated at the end of the PUF. The inverter in the last column and the last row has the highest power among others as it is the inverter just before the output.

Table 4. RO-PUF Power Calculations

INSTANCE	POWER(W)	INSTANCE(W)	POWER	INSTANCE	POWER(W)
Y	104.2 x 10^-3	Inverter	340.7 x 10^-6	Inverter	358.7 x 10^-6
NAND	610.9 x 10^-6	Inverter	391.4 x 10^-6	Inverter	340.7 x 10^-6
NAND	610.9 x 10^-6	Inverter	340.0 x 10^-6	Inverter	340.0 x 10^-6
2X1 MUX	4.385 x 10^-3	Inverter	391.5 x 10^-6	Inverter	391.4 x 10^-6
NAND	610.9 x 10^-6	Inverter	358.7 x 10^-6	Inverter	358.7 x 10^-6
NAND	610.9 x 10^-6	Inverter	358.7 x 10^-6	Inverter	340.7 x 10^-6
2X1 MUX	4.385 x 10^-3	Inverter	340.7 x 10^-6	Inverter	391.4 x 10^-6
4B counter	41.96 x 10^-3	Inverter	391.4 x 10^-6	Inverter	340.0 x 10^-6
4B counter	41.99 x 10^-3	Inverter	340.0 x 10^-6	Inverter	391.5 x 10^-6
AND	1.303 x 10^-3	Inverter	391.5 x 10^-6	Inverter	411.1 x 10^-6

4.2 Power Calculations of CRO PUF

In Table 5, the power analysis of CRO PUF is depicted. The parameter Y, is the total power accumulated at the end of the PUF.TOP-Inverter-1 corresponds to the first inverter from the left and the above one.DOWN-Inverter-1 corresponds to the first inverter from the left and the below one. When compared to RO PUF it gives less power consumption.

Table 5. CRO-PUF Power Calculations

INSTANCE	POWER	INSTANCE	POWER
Y	19.25×10^{-3}	TOP-Inverter-2	385.1×10^{-6}
2X1 MUX	5.174×10^{-3}	TOP-Inverter-3	385.1×10^{-6}
2X1 MUX	5.174×10^{-3}	DOWN-Inverter-1	388.5×10^{-6}
2X1 MUX	5.156×10^{-3}	DOWN-Inverter-2	388.6×10^{-6}
AND	1.42×10^{-3}	DOWN-Inverter-3	388.6×10^{-6}
TOP-Inverter-1	385.1×10^{-6}		

4.3 Power Calculation of TERO PUF

Table 6 presents the power analysis of TERO PUF where Y is the total power accumulated at the end of the PUF. Inverters 1, 2, and 3 are the top forward inverters whereas Inverters 4, 5, 6 are below feedback inverters. When compared to the other two PUFs, TERO PUF gives less power dissipation overall as well as individual.

Table 6. TERO-PUF Power Calculations

INSTANCE	POWER	INSTANCE	POWER
Y	15.7×10^{-3}	2-AND	3.858×10^{-3}
1-AND	3.858×10^{-3}	Inverter-4	1.772×10^{-3}
Inverter-1	1.772×10^{-3}	Inverter-5	1.772×10^{-3}
Inverter-2	1.772×10^{-3}	Inverter-6	446.4×10^{-6}
Inverter-3	446.4×10^{-3}		

4.4 Comparison of Parameters

Table 7 presents the comparative analysis of various parameters of implemented PUFs.

Table 7. Comparison of Parameters

PARAMETERS	RO-PUF	CRO-PUF	TERO-PUF
Technology used	45nm	45nm	45nm
Time/Duration of signal	0 – 400 ns	0 – 400 ns	0 – 400 ns
Max. value of Current (I)	5.004 V	5.003 V	5 V
Max. value of Voltage (V)	42.43 mA	8.607 mA	4.126 mA
Total no. of transient steps	2237	2655	785
Memory used	103 Mbytes	93 Mbytes	84.9 Mbytes
No. of Inverters used	21	6	6
Delay of o/p w.r.t i/p	20.0×10^{-9}	9.992×10^{-9}	20.19×10^{-9}
Power of o/p w.r.t i/p	104.2×10^{-3}	19.25×10^{-3}	15.7×10^{-3}
No. of stages used	4-(5)	3	3

5 Conclusions

This paper analyzes the characteristics of a set of Delay PUFs. Three PUFs were chosen: RO PUF, CRO PUF, and TERO PUF. The implementation of these PUFs on CMOS 45 nanometer technology has been observed with all the same constraint parameters. According to the implemented sequence, there is a decrease in the usage of memory upto 10%. For CRO from RO there is a decrease of 82% in power and 51% in delay. The CRO With respect to TERO there is a 19% decrease in power. Therefore, this paper presented a comprehensive survey of the selected silicon PUF designs and their corresponding performances.

References

1. Anchana, U.K., Singh, S., Mogireddy, M., Kadavergu, E.: Design and analysis of physical unclonable function. In: 2023 2nd International Conference for Innovation in Technology (INOCON), Bangalore, India (2023)
2. Anchana, U.K., Mogireddy, M., Kadavergu, E., Singh, S.: Design of PUF based chaotic random number generator. In: 2023 Second International Conference on Electrical, Electronics, Information and Communication Technologies (ICEEICT), Tiruchirappalli, India (2023)
3. Ning, H., Farha, F., Ullah, A., Mao, L.: Physical unclonable function: architectures applications and challenges for dependable security. IET Circuits Devices Syst. **14**(4), 407–424 (2020)
4. El-Hajj, M., Fadlallah, A., Chamoun, M., Serhrouchni, A.: A taxonomy of PUF Schemes with a novel Arbiter-based PUF resisting machine learning attacks. Comput. Netw. **194**, 108133 (2021). ISSN 1389-1286
5. Gebali, F., Mamun, M.: Review of physically unclonable functions (PUFs): structures, models, and algorithms. Sens. Netw. **2** (2021)

6. Suh, G.E., Devadas, S.: Physical unclonable functions for device authentication and secret key generation. In: Proceedings of the 44th ACM/IEEE Design Automation Conference (DAC), pp. 9–14 (2007)
7. Wei, L., Song, C., Liu, Y., Zhang, J., Yuan, F., Xu, Q.: BoardPUF: physical unclonable functions for printed circuit board authentication. In: Proceedings of IEEE/ACM International Conference on Computer-Aided Design (ICCAD), pp. 152–158 (2015)
8. Zhou, K., Liang, H., Jiang, Y., Huang, Z., Jiang, C., Lu, Y.: FPGA-based RO PUF with low overhead and high stability. **55**(9) (2019)
9. Anandakumar, N.N., Hashmi, M.S., Tehranipoor, M.: FPGA-based physical unclonable functions: a comprehensive overview of theory and architectures. Integration **81**, 175–194 (2021). ISSN 0167-9260
10. McGrath, T., Bagci, I.E., Wang, Z.M., Roedig, U., Young, R.J.: A PUF taxonomy. Appl. Phys. Rev. **6**, 11303 (2019). 011303. Bibcode:2019ApPRv...6a1303M
11. Herder, C., Yu, M.-D., Koushanfar, F., Devadas, S.: Physical unclonable functions and applications: a tutorial. Proc. IEEE **102**(8), 1126–1141 (2014)
12. Maiti, A., Casarona, J., McHale, L., Schaumont, P.: A large scale characterization of RO-PUF. In: 2010 IEEE International Symposium on Hardware-Oriented Security and Trust (HOST), Anaheim, CA, USA, pp. 94–99 (2010)
13. Miskelly, J., Gu, C., Ma, Q., Cui, Y., Liu, W., O'Neill, M.: Modelling attack analysis of configurable ring oscillator (CRO) PUF designs. In: 2018 IEEE 23rd International Conference on Digital Signal Processing (DSP), Shanghai, China, pp. 1–5 (2018)
14. Marchand, C., Bossuet, L., Cherkaoui, A.: Design and characterization of the TERO-PUF on SRAM FPGAs. In: 2016 IEEE Computer Society Annual Symposium on VLSI (ISVLSI), Pittsburgh, PA, USA, pp. 134–139 (2016)
15. Pratihar, K., Chatterjee, U., Alam, M., Chakraborty, R.S., Mukhopadhyay, D.: Birds of the same feather flock together: a dual-mode circuit candidate for strong PUF-TRNG functionalities. IEEE Trans. Comput. **72**(6), 1636–1651 (2023)

Smart Drowsiness Detection System with Microcontroller Integration

Satyarth Motupalli[1], J. V. R. Ravindra[2], G. A. E. Satish Kumar[2(✉)], R. Phani Vidhyadhar[2], Ramavathar Yadav Kanneboina[2], Varun Kumar Reddy[2], and Siddarth Tammineni[2]

[1] Department of ECE, Chaitanya Bharathi Institute of Technology, Hyderabad, Telangana, India
[2] Department of ECE, Vardhaman College of Engineering, Hyderabad, Telangana, India
jayanthi@ieee.org, {gaesathi,rphaniv}@vardhaman.org

Abstract. An embedded system is designed to address the issue of drowsy driving by using a microcontroller and a pulse sensor. This system combines multiple sensors, including the pulse sensor, with a microcontroller to monitor a driver's vital signs and behaviour. The microcontroller acts as the central processing unit, collecting data from the sensors, analyzing it, and making informed decisions. Specifically, the pulse sensor measures heart rate and heart rate variability, which can provide insights into a driver's physiological state, especially when drowsiness leads to changes in these parameters. The compact size and low power consumption of this embedded system make it suitable for integration into various vehicles, from personal cars to commercial fleets. In conclusion, this abstract emphasizes the potential of integrating such a system into vehicles to enhance road safety by detecting drowsy drivers and reducing accidents associated with drowsy driving.

In essence, this technology embodies the spirit of looking out for one another. It transforms every journey into a secure experience where drivers and passengers can travel with confidence, knowing they are shielded by a caring, understanding companion. It's not just about avoiding accidents; it's about fostering a culture of safety, where we all contribute to making our roads a better place for everyone.

Keywords: Pulse Sensor · Heart Rate · Microcontroller · Driver Safety · Real-time Monitoring · Alert System · Smart Detection · Safety Technology · Visual and Auditory Alerts

1 Introduction

The prevalence of drowsy driving as a leading cause of road accidents underscores the critical need for effective driver monitoring systems [1]. This paper introduces an innovative embedded system designed to detect drowsy drivers using a microcontroller and a pulse sensor, intending to contribute to road safety [2].

Our proposed system leverages the capabilities of a microcontroller, serving as the central processing unit, to collect and analyze data from multiple sensors. Key among these sensors is the pulse sensor, typically positioned on the driver's fingertip or car steering [3]. This sensor measures heart rate and heart rate variability, parameters known to exhibit significant changes during drowsiness. By continuously monitoring these physiological indicators, our system can accurately identify irregularities associated with drowsy driving.

The compact size and low power consumption of our embedded system make it adaptable for integration into a wide range of vehicles, [4] from personal cars to commercial fleets. This paper presents a comprehensive exploration of our system's design, operation, and potential impact on enhancing road safety by detecting and alerting drowsy drivers, ultimately reducing accidents caused by this perilous behavior.

As we delve into the details of this Smart Drowsiness Detection System, you'll discover the fascinating technology behind it, the integration of sensors, and how the microcontroller plays a crucial role in making split-second decisions to keep you safe and alert. So, let's embark on this journey together and explore the cutting-edge features that make this system a valuable companion in our daily lives.

2 Objectives

- The primary aim of this project is to greatly improve the safety and security of drivers, enhancing their overall well-being and protection while on the road.
- The system will alert the drivers using a buzzer and alarm system.
- To design a system that is used to measure the pulse of a driver using a pulse sensor and the frequency of drowsy drivers.

3 Literature Review

Seok-Woo Jang and Byeongtae Ahn [5], According to their research. By combining image recognition and IoT, their system not only identifies signs of driver fatigue but also proactively prevents potential accidents. It utilizes real-time image analysis to monitor driver behavior and employs IoT connectivity to interact with vehicle systems, such as steering assistance or alerting mechanisms. This comprehensive approach demonstrates a promising path towards significantly reducing drowsy driving-related accidents, thereby enhancing road safety and overall driver well-being in our increasingly connected automotive landscape.

Rateb Jabbar and his team [6] introduce a pioneering approach to tackling the issue of driver drowsiness using Convolutional Neural Networks (CNNs) within Android applications. Their study is a noteworthy contribution, as it effectively harnesses CNN techniques to analyze facial expressions and continuously monitor driver attentiveness in real time. This innovation holds immense potential for bolstering road safety by preventing accidents that stem from drowsy driving. Nevertheless, their work undeniably marks a significant stride toward deploying advanced AI technologies to address a critical concern in the realm of transportation safety.

Pawan Bharadwaj et al.'s [7] work builds upon these foundations by proposing an integrated system that combines drowsiness detection with accident-avoidance measures. While promising, further real-world testing and validation are needed to ascertain its practicality and efficacy. Nevertheless, their search represents a commendable step toward enhancing road safety by proactively tackling the issue of driver drowsiness.

Bhargava Reddy et al. [8] address a pressing concern in automotive safety. It employs model compression techniques in deep neural networks, enabling real-time drowsiness de-detection suitable for embedded systems. It builds upon prior studies exploring drowsiness detection and model compression, demonstrating an innovative fusion of these concepts. Though promising, practical implementation and validation in diverse driving conditions are essential for its efficiency.

4 Proposed Systems and Methodology

The proposed system aims to enhance road safety by developing a drowsy driver detection system using a pulse sensor and an STM32 microcontroller. The system's methodology involves continuous monitoring of the driver's pulse rate using the pulse sensor, which is strategically placed within the vehicle [9]. The STM32 microcontroller processes this real-time data and analyzes it to detect irregularities or significant drops in the driver's pulse rate, which could indicate drowsiness. Upon detection of potential drowsiness, the system activates various alert mechanisms, such as audio alarms or seat vibrations, to alert the driver.

A. Architectural Diagram

The architecture of an embedded system for drowsy driver detection integrates a Pulse Sensor and an STM32 microcontroller. The Pulse Sensor captures the driver's heart rate by shining light through the skin and measuring blood flow fluctuations microcontroller processes this data in real time (Fig. 1).

It employs algorithms to analyze heart rate patterns and detect signs of drowsiness or fatigue [12]. When drowsiness is detected, the system triggers alerts, such as audible alarms or seat vibrations, to awaken the driver. Additionally, it records data for post-incident analysis and preventive measures. This architecture offers a proactive approach to enhancing road safety by addressing the critical issue of drowsiness drivers (Fig. 2).

The system monitors the driver's heart rate using a pulse sensor, taking photos of this data regularly. These photos are then sent to the microcontroller, the main part of the system. The microcontroller translates these photos into understandable digital information using a part called the ADC.

This algorithm examines the heart rate data for specific changes. For instance, if the heart rate suddenly drops or becomes irregular, the algorithm recognizes these changes as potential signs of drowsiness. These patterns usually indicate that a person is becoming less alert, suggesting they might be getting drowsy or even falling asleep while driving. When the system spots these signs, it sends an alert to the driver, telling them to take a break and avoid driving when they're feeling drowsy.

B. Work Flow

The workflow of the drowsy driver detection project using a Pulse Sensor and STM32 microcontroller follows a structured flowchart-like process. It commences with the Pulse Sensor continuously monitoring the driver's heart rate, transmitting this real-time data

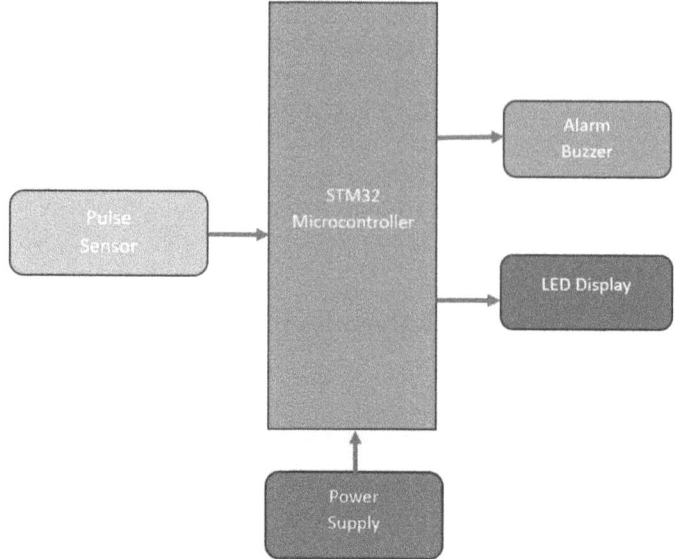

Fig. 1. Block Diagram

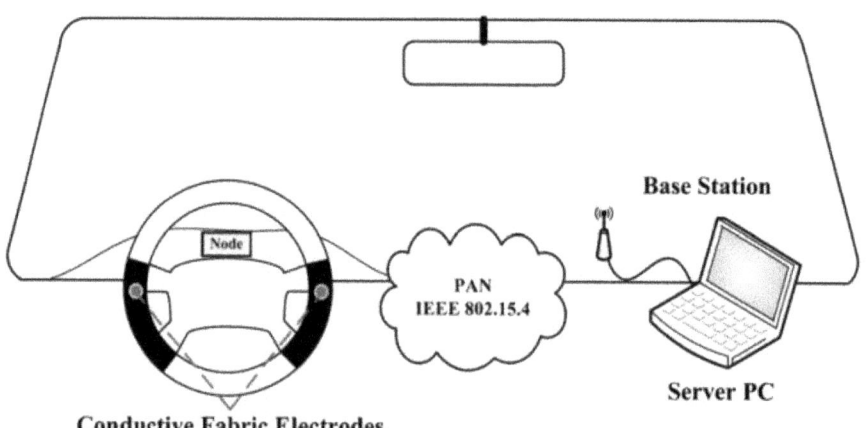

Fig. 2. Connection between Control Signal to Warning System

to the STM32 microcontroller, the system's core. Within the microcontroller, complex algorithms analyze heart rate patterns, swiftly identifying signs of drowsiness.

The "Data Processing" stage processes the heart rate data, extracting crucial information such as baseline heart rate and patterns indicative of drowsiness. The pivotal "Drowsy Driver Detection" decision point evaluates if the driver is drowsy by comparing real-time heart rate data with predefined thresholds.

Upon detection, the system activates alert mechanisms like audio alarms or seat vibrations to awaken the driver while concurrently logging data for future analysis.

This systematic workflow ensures proactive and efficient drowsy driver detection, significantly enhancing road safety and mitigating potential accidents caused by drowsy driving [13].

Finally, the system interfaces with a "User Interface" to convey information to the driver. This flowchart provides a systematic overview of the steps involved in creating an embedded drowsy driver detection system, emphasizing the importance of hardware-software integration and real-time monitoring for road safety (Fig. 3).

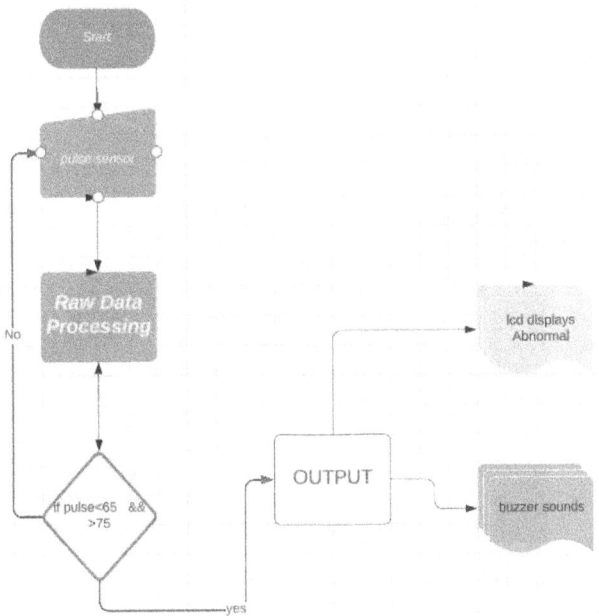

Fig. 3. Flow chart Execution

5 Results and Discussion

The total equipment setup of the project is shown in the below figure. The results and discussion of the drowsy driver detection project utilizing a Pulse Sensor and STM32 microcontroller are promising. The system effectively detected instances of driver drowsiness during testing scenarios [14]. When drivers exhibited reduced heart rate patterns indicative of drowsy, the alert mechanisms were triggered promptly, and they responded positively to these alerts.

There were some instances where false positives occurred, often due to factors like temporary heart rate fluctuations unrelated to drowsiness. Fine-tuning the algorithms and considering additional physiological data for a more accurate assessment of drowsiness could help mitigate these false alarms [15] (Figs. 4 and 5).

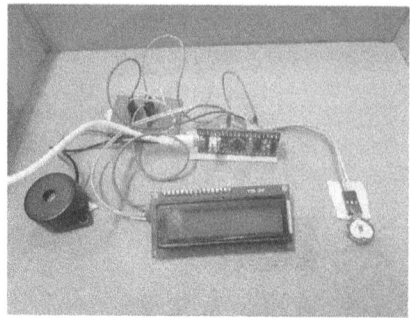 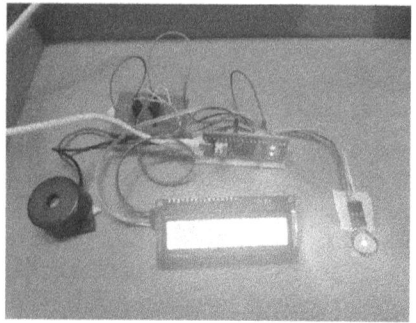

Fig. 4. Equipment Setup   **Fig. 5.** Output of a practical model

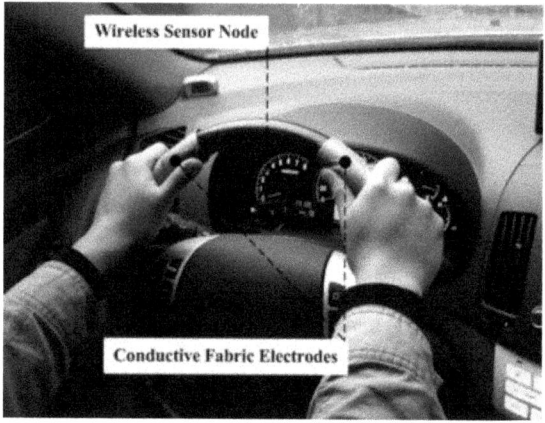

Fig. 6. Practical model in a real-time environment

In the given below Figs. 6, 7 and it show how the prototype will work and how it collects data and gives an alert. When a driver/person driving a vehicle and suddenly feels drowsy the heart rate of the person becomes abnormal and it is detected by the sensors on the steering and gives an alarm or buzzer sound.

6 Conclusion and Future Scope

In conclusion, the implementation of an embedded system-based drowsy driver detection system using a pulse sensor and microcontroller offers a promising solution for mitigating the risks associated with driver drowsiness. The integration of a pulse sensor allows for real-time monitoring of the driver's heart rate, providing valuable insights into their physiological state.

In the future, the integration of additional sensors, such as eye-tracking or vehicle-based sensors, to gather a more comprehensive set of data for drowsiness detection. The system can also be enhanced by incorporating machine learning algorithms to improve the accuracy of drowsiness detection.

Furthermore, the system can be extended to include remote monitoring capabilities, allowing for real-time monitoring of multiple drivers and generating alerts to fleet managers or emergency services in case of drowsy driving incidents. The project can also be expanded to include integration with autonomous vehicles, where the system can take control of the vehicle in case of driver drowsiness.

References

1. Perkins, E., et al.: Challenges of driver drowsiness prediction: the remaining steps to implementation. IEEE Trans. Intell. Veh. (2022)
2. Priya Dharshini, R., Binuja, B.: Driver Drowsiness and Alcohol Detection System Using Arduino (2020)
3. Gowri, S.M., et al.: Internet of things based accident detection system. In: 2019 Third International Conference on I-SMAC (IoT in Social, Mobile, Analytics and Cloud) (I-SMAC). IEEE (2019)
4. Soares, S., et al.: Analyzing driver drowsiness: from causes to effects. Sustainability **12**(5), 1971 (2020)
5. Jang, S.-W., Ahn, B.: Implementation of detection system for drowsy driving prevention using image recognition and IoT. Sustainability **12**(7), 3037 (2020)
6. Jabbar, R., et al.: Driver drowsiness detection model using convolutional neural networks techniques for android application. In: 2020 IEEE International Conference on Informatics, IoT, and Enabling Technologies (ICIoT). IEEE (2020)
7. Bharadwaj, P., et al.: Drowsiness Detection and Accident Avoidance System in Vehicles, pp. 79–87 (2019)
8. Reddy, B., et al.: Real-time driver drowsiness detection for an embedded system using model compression of deep neural networks. In: Proceedings of the IEEE Conference on Computer Vision and Pattern Recognition Workshops (2017)
9. Mollicone, D., et al.: Predicting performance and safety based on driver fatigue. Accid. Anal. Prevent. **126**, 142–145 (2019)
10. Ed-Doughmi, Y., Idrissi, N., Hbali, Y.: Real-time system for driver fatigue detection based on a recurrent neuronal network. J. Imaging **6**(3), 8 (2020)
11. Ashfakur Rahman Arju, M., Khan, N.H., Hoque, K.E., Jisan, A.R., Tareque, S.M., Hasan, M.Z.: A framework for detecting driver drowsiness based on eye blinking rate and hand gripping pressure. In: Uddin, M.S., Bansal, J.C. (eds.) Proceedings of International Joint Conference on Computational Intelligence. AIS, pp. 289–304. Springer, Singapore (2020). https://doi.org/10.1007/978-981-13-7564-4_26
12. Albadawi, Y., Takruri, M., Awad, M.: A review of recent developments in driver drowsiness detection systems. Sensors **22**(5), 2069 (2022)
13. Bajaj, J.S., Kumar, N., Kaushal, R.K.: Feasibility study on amalgamation of multiple measures to detect driver drowsiness. ECS Trans. **107**(1), 1951 (2022)

14. Bhagyashree, S.R., Sonal Singh, T., Kiran, J., Padmini, L.S.: Vehicle speed warning system and wildlife detection systems to avoid wildlife-vehicle collisions. In: Sridhar, V., Padma, M., Rao, K. (eds.) Emerging Research in Electronics, Computer Science and Technology. LNEE, vol. 545, pp. 961–968. Springer, Singapore (2019). https://doi.org/10.1007/978-981-13-5802-9_84
15. Singh, D., Pati, B., Panigrahi, C.R., Swagatika, S.: Security issues in IoT and their countermeasures in smart city applications. In: Pati, B., Panigrahi, C., Buyya, R., Li, K.C. (eds.) Advanced Computing and Intelligent Engineering. AISC, vol. 1089, pp. 301–313. Springer, Singapore (2020). https://doi.org/10.1007/978-981-15-1483-8_26

Innovative Motion Sensing System with Labview

R. Phani Vidyadhar[1(✉)], J. V. R. Ravindra[1], G. A. E. Satish Kumar[1],
Yanigandla Sandeep[1], Kanugula Ashwitha[1], Devansh Mantri[1],
and Faldu Vishvakumari[2]

[1] Department of ECE, Vardhaman College of Engineering, Hyderabad, Telangana, India
`{rphaniv,gaesathi}@vardhaman.org, jayanthi@ieee.org`
[2] RK University, Rajkot, Gujarat, India

Abstract. Nowadays children's used to play and going near restricted areas like transformers and borewells due to that they are getting affected by such incidents ensure that we are performing a system called Innovative Motion Sensing with LabVIEW. This system will be built to instantly detect motion and send alerts or initiate actions according to the motion. LabVIEW software will be used for terminating this project. This Motion Detection System can be used for automotive safety in addition to restricted locations. The system's primary objective will be to detect motion in real time and send out notifications or start events according to the motion. Several motion situations will be used to test and evaluate the system, including performance measures like accuracy and detection, different motion situations will be used to test and validate the system, and performance metrics including accuracy and detection time will be assessed. In this project, a GSM module is utilized to communicate with a nearby CELL Tower and transmit the message to a mobile device. Intelligent Motion Detection System for effectively identifying movement or motion inside a predetermined area and prompt timely replies or actions. With the help of this system, security, monitoring, and automation are all intended to be improved in a number of applications, and motion-related events will be handled proactively.

Keywords: PIR sensor · Buzzer · Led · DAQ · GSM · LabVIEW · ARDUINO UNO · CELL TOWER

1 Introduction

The emergence of Innovative Motion Sensing with LabVIEW has advanced to the forefront of research and innovation as a consequence of the rapid introduction of smart technologies and increasing demands for improved security, automation, and human-computer connection. Identify, assess, and respond to motion events in real-time, these systems integrate advanced sensors, innovative data processing algorithms, and intelligent decision-making capabilities.

Numerous industries, including surveillance, healthcare, industrial automation, and others, use smart motion detection systems to enhance the quality of life, efficiency, and safety. This system can detect motion, track objects, and make sensible choices based on motion through integrating sensors, cameras, and logical algorithms. It finds applications across a variety of fields, including security, industrial automation, and smart homes, where it enhances safety, improves operations, and contributes to resource management effectively.

The Innovative Motion Sensing with LabVIEW is an essential element of the developing Internet of Things (IoT) landscape and plays an essential role in creating smarter, more responsive environments, and ultimately improving security, efficiency, and user experiences.

The Innovative Motion Sensing with LabVIEW, with a focus on its technological components, algorithms, and applications in the real world. We think the outcomes of this research will be informative and innovative. An Innovative Motion Sensing System can provide much use for Home security purposes and also it can be used in restricted areas and in vehicles for security purposes. The main objective of the system will be to detect motion in real time and provide alerts or trigger actions based on the detected motion. The system will be tested and validated using different motion scenarios, and the performance metrics such as accuracy and detection time will be evaluated.

2 Literature Survey

The Smart Security System based on Motion Detection Since the Arduino (Microcontroller) is a free source, we will be using it for this project. In essence, we're going to build a system that makes [1] use of sensors like PIR, MQ2, IR, Ultrasonic, and LDR. The system will use an MQ2 sensor to detect the leakage of LPG, CO, and CH4 and will then forward the flow to an Arduino UNO to determine the extent of the flame/fire coverage area. The user will then receive a notification that the obstacle is at a low or high level after this. To detect motion or objects, sensors such as ultrasonic, IR, and PIR are employed.

The Smart Parking Project for Smart City System offers a comprehensive and scalable solution to the problems [2] associated with managing urban parking in this paper, Smart Parking System. The project intends to optimize urban mobility, alleviate traffic congestion, and build a more sustainable and lively urban environment for the benefit of both inhabitants and visitors by utilizing IoT technologies, real-time data analytics, and predictive algorithms. Adopting smart parking initiatives is increasingly important for creating effective and livable urban spaces as cities continue to expand and change.

The automation of Smart Street Lights and the usage of LED luminaires that are controlled by operation time via a motion sensor is [3] the goal of the smart street light control for energy conservation via the Internet of Things (IoT). The core idea of smart street lighting control revolves around dynamically adjusting the intensity of streetlights based on current conditions and requirements. Smart lighting towers also include PM 2.5 sensors, IP cameras, and a Wi-Fi system controlled by a microcontroller.

LabVIEW-based Smart Assistant for Dumb and Deaf People, people who have trouble hearing and speaking can [4] communicate with one another through signing. They find it challenging to communicate with those who do not understand sign language. This problem has been addressed in our project proposal. This proposal suggests a design for smart gloves with flex sensors for the identification of sign language. It can be used to treat individuals with limited finger movement who are partially paralyzed and have lost their ability to speak. As a result, we were able to decode all 26 (A-Z) American Sign Language letters and create words up to six letters long with an audio output.

Technology has grown to the point where it may be quite useful for residential applications, such as Smart Home Control Systems [5]. The hub of our domestic life is our home, where we can use technological solutions to manage our daily routines. Our way of life is made easier and simpler by automating household tasks. A smart home is a home with a smart control system.

3 Existing vs Proposed

The performance of an Innovative Motion Sensing With Labview can be analyzed in terms of Speed Of Detection, Range Of Detection, and Sending Data Using Gsm, Power Consumption. The Power consumption is very low and Sending the data to the user from the Gsm module is very accurate. Hence we can see above are some Comparision for Existing Vs Proposed Prototypes (Table 1).

Table 1. Comparative Analysis

Existed Prototype	Proposed Prototype
The existing prototype is based on an IoT-based smart motion detecting System	The Proposed Prototype is of an innovative Motion Sensing is based on the LabVIEW Tool kit
A motion Detection system is used to detect the obstacle only in the existing prototype	An innovative Motion Sensing System will sense the physical quantity and activate the buzzer
The demonstration has proven the capability of the system to Detect the motion if any obstacle has been detected or not. The Power Consumption is more here it consumes a huge amount of power and the Obstacle Detection is not very accurate	The system would use intelligent detection that can detect the Obstacle an if the Obstacle is detected it is used to show whether it is high or low and it activates the buzzer and GSM module and sends the alerts to the user

4 Methodology and Approach

4.1 System Infrastructure

As we are using components like Sensor, GSM module, and Buzzer, are been connected with the Arduino Uno and the Arduino uno has been interfaced with the LabVIEW using the LINX library, as we can see here how the circuit has been connected according to the logic. The Arduino Uno has a PIR Sensor associated with it. Now this Arduino Uno has logic as to how the process needs to be done step by step. We also connect the Buzzer to the Arduino Uno. When the motion has been detected the buzzer will get activated.

4.2 Design and Implementation

This system will be designed to detect motion in real time and provide alerts or trigger actions based on the detected motion. The system will be tested and validated using different motion scenarios, and the performance metrics such as accuracy and detection time will be evaluated. If any obstacle has been identified by the system then the PIR sensor will sense the physical quantity and sends the data to the LED if the LED glows brightly then the message will be sent to the owner and the buzzer will get activated. This project is mainly helpful in the fields where the borewells are located. In this project, we also use a GSM module that connects to the nearby CELL Tower and sends the message to the mobile phone. This project will be done by using the LabVIEW software. This Innovative Motion Sensing with LabVIEW can be extended from Restricted areas to vehicle security (Fig. 1).

5 Block Diagram

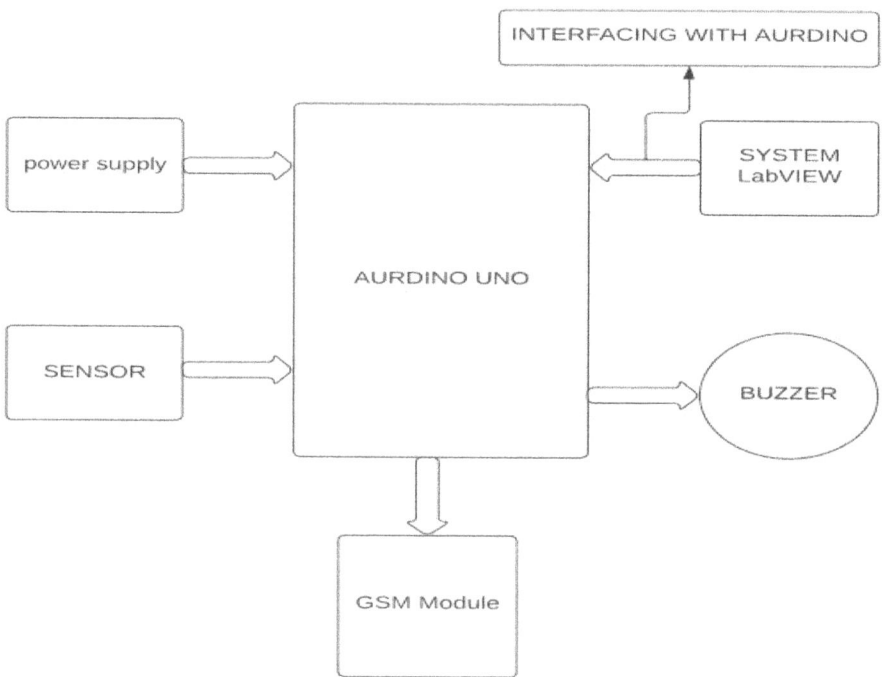

Fig. 1. Block Diagram

6 Execution Flow and Working Prototype

6.1 Execution Flow

The system will sense the physical quantity if it is present the LED will glow if the Physical sensing is high then the LED will glow high and then the buzzer will get activated. Then Gsm module will get activated and send an alert to the user.

The system designed with the components mentioned will furthermore make sure that any unauthorized movement or action detected when you are not there will be projected the information to the dashboard by noticing a movement or action.

In this project, we use a GSM module that connects to the nearby CELL Tower and sends the message to the mobile phone. This project will be done by using the LabVIEW software.

It can be used in many applications ranging from home security to vehicle security (Fig. 2).

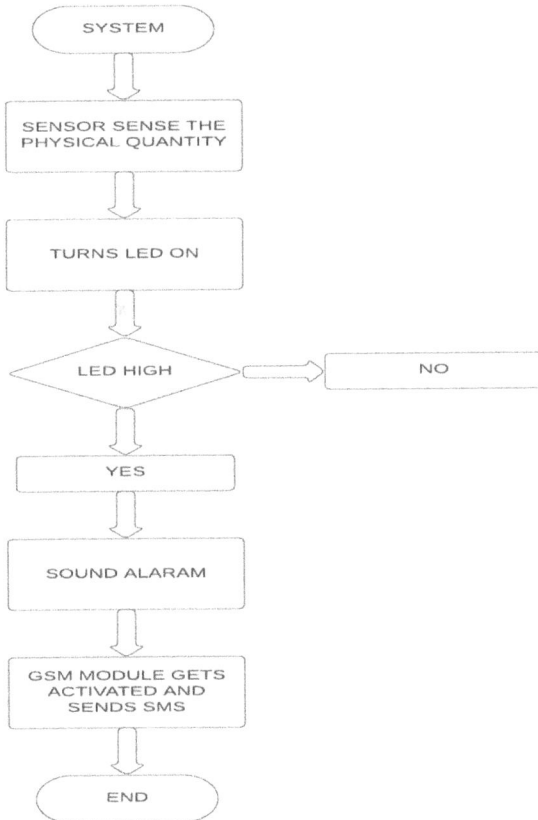

Fig. 2. Flow Chart.

6.2 Working Prototype

- Designing Innovative smart sensing using an IR (Infrared) sensor in LabVIEW involves interfacing the IR sensor with a microcontroller, reading its output in LabVIEW, and implementing motion detection logic. In this example, we'll use an Arduino board and an IR motion sensor (PIR sensor) to detect motion and display the results in LabVIEW. The designed Smart motion detection system can be simulated and works well while the device is placed. The infrared sensor comes to the active mode when the physical quantity is according to their weight and height.
- It calculates weight and height so that the IR sensor light will glow based on the physical quantity sensing. The buzzer will come to active mode while the physical quantity is detected according to the condition. The GSM module will send the message to the respective owner or nearby police control room. This project can be extended from home security to vehicle security and from supermarket monitoring to data analysis. The system will be designed to detect motion in real time and provide alerts or trigger actions based on the detected motion.

6.2.1 Pin Connections

PIR Sensor:

- Pin Connections:

  - Connect the VCC pin of the PIR sensor to the +5 V output of ARDUINO UNO.
  - Connect the GND pin of the PIR sensor to the GND (ground) of ARDUINO UNO.
  - Connect the A0 pin of the PIR sensor to one of the analog input channels (e.g., AI0) of ARDUINO UNO (Fig. 3).

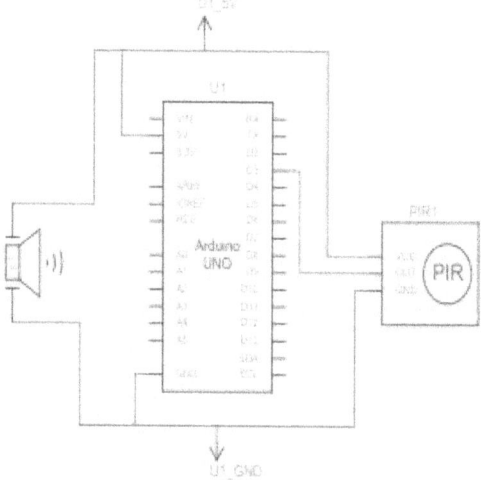

Fig. 3. Schematic level view

- The power consumption of the Innovative Smart Sensing System using PIR Sensor was typically more efficient than the other types of Sensors. As we can see here the schematic level view of the Circuit.
- Ensure that you are using the appropriate LabVIEW drivers
- and modules to interface with ARDUINO UNO and read sensor data accurately (Fig. 4).

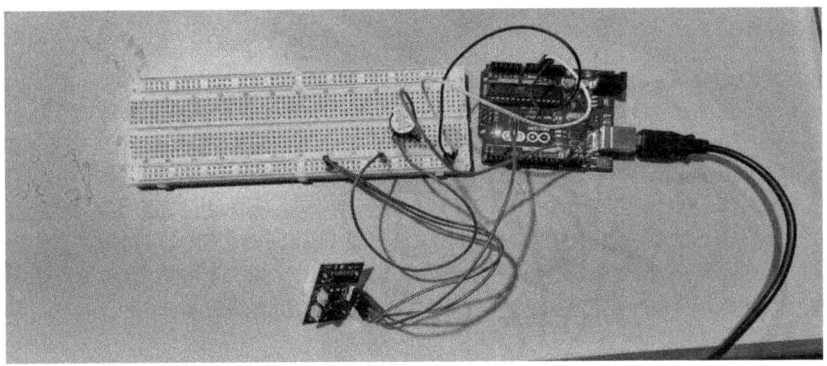

Fig. 4. Working Prototype

- As we can see here the front panel logic circuit as per the working principle. Here we used the Arduino Uno so to interface the Arduino uno with LabVIEW we need to use the makerhub LabVIEW driver in the makerhub we need to install Linx with the help of linx we can dumb our logic in to the Arduino Uno for working Prototype.

- Always refer to the datasheets and documentation provided by the sensor and ARDUINO UNO manufacturers for precise pin connections, voltage levels, and calibration procedures.

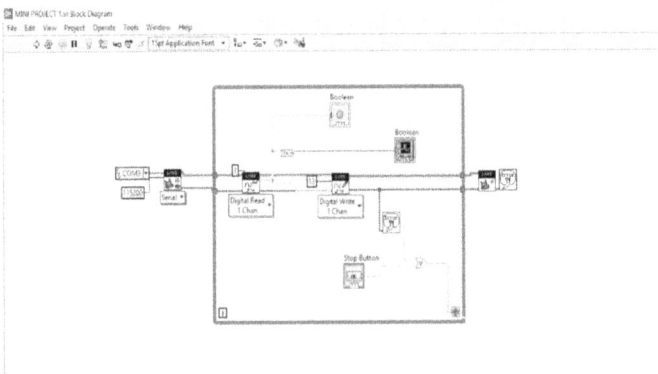

Fig. 5. Block Diagram

- Remember to follow safety guidelines when working with gas sensors and electrical components. If you are unsure about any aspect of the connections or sensor handling, consult with a qualified expert or refer to professional resources (Fig. 5).

7 Results and Discussions

7.1 Results

- The Output of the Innovative Motion Sensing With Labview By the graph, we can observe whether there is an Obstacle has been detected or not. Here when the obstacle is detected it will show the output in the form of square graph when obstacle is detected it will fluctuates from 0 to 1 when there it no obstacle it will remain constant 0. When the Obstacle has been detected then the light will be glowing and the graph will occur as we can observe below. When after the immediate Blink of the light. Gsm will immediately gets activated and Sends the sms to the mobile. Here we can see the output when the obstacle is detected. We can observe the output as square graph when the obstacle detected (Fig. 6).

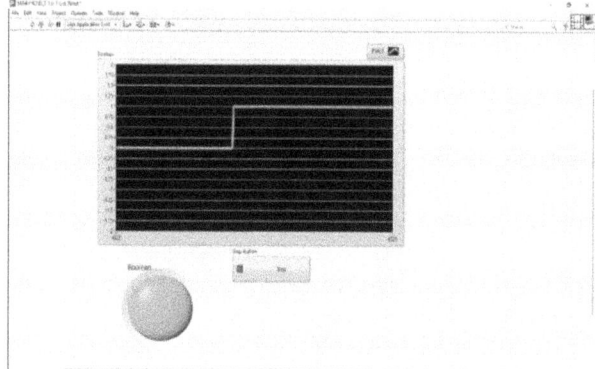

Fig. 6. Front panel

Output when the Object has been detected Continuously, we can see the below graph (Fig. 7).

- For the digital output from the PIR sensor, LabVIEW can use the Digital Input functions to read the state of the sensor's output. You can use this digital information to detect the presence or absence of an object or trigger specific actions in LabVIEW. When the Obstacle has been detected the alert.
- It will the send data to the mobile in the form of sms to the user. In some cases it used to send the Obstacle height and width so that the user can easily understand whether it is a person or not. As we can see it in the above Fig. 8.

Fig. 7. Output when the body detected continuously

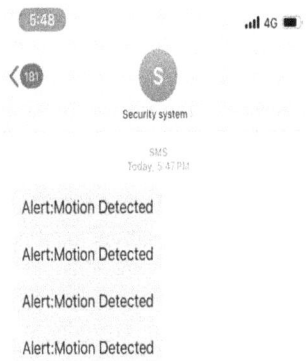

Fig. 8. GSM Alert Message.

7.2 Discussions

In this project, we use a GSM module that connects to the nearby CELL Tower and sends the message to the mobile phone of the owner or police control room.

This system can detect and output information about when and where motion is detected. This could be in the form of timestamps or frame numbers along with the coordinates or regions where the motion occurred. This Sensing System can trigger alarms or alerts when motion is detected. These alerts can be in the form of visual indicators, sound signals, or notifications to connected devices.

8 Conclusion and Future Scope

8.1 Conclusion

A practical and affordable approach for numerous applications is to implement an innovative motion-detecting system utilizing Arduino in LabVIEW. Using LabVIEW's logical graphical programming environment and Arduino's microcontroller capabilities, developers may build a reliable and scalable motion detection system.

Different motion situations will be used to test and validate the system, and performance metrics including accuracy and detection time will be assessed. This project can be used mostly in off-limits locations for young children. If any child enters the forbidden area, the PIR sensors detect physical quantities and transmit data to LEDs. If the LEDs shine brightly, a message is delivered to the owner and the buzzer is also turned on. The fields where the borewells are placed are the principal beneficiaries of this initiative. In this project, a GSM module is used to transmit the message to the mobile phone by connecting to a nearby CELL Tower.

Overall, LabVIEW's innovative motion sensing system shows off the potential of contemporary sensor-based technology with graphical programming, offering a smart and effective solution for motion detection and monitoring needs across a variety of industries and applications.

8.2 Future Scope

In the Future smart sensing technology For more precise and consistent motion detection in complicated situations, combine data from numerous sensors, such as PIR and ultrasonic sensors. It can Investigate the application of machine learning techniques to enhance motion detection precision, decrease false positives, and identify certain motions or objects. It Reduces latency and enables local data processing by optimizing the system for edge computing capabilities, especially in applications where real-time reaction is crucial. To enable remote monitoring and control of the motion detection system, use wireless communication protocols (such as Wi-Fi or Bluetooth).

References

1. Barakade, K., Yadav, S., Vairat, P., Shinde, M.: Smart security system based on motion detection. Int. Res. J. Mod. Eng. Technol. Sci. **04**(05) (2022). Impact Factor-6.752
2. Romantsova, N.V., Moshnaya, E.G., Fomenko, I.V.: Smart parking project for the smart city system. In: 2022 Conference of Russian Young Researchers in Electrical and Electronic Engineering (ElConRus), pp. 1581–1584 (2022). https://doi.org/10.1109/ElConRus54750.2022.9755706
3. Thipards, R., et al.: Smart street lighting control for electrical power on saving by IoT. In: 2022 26th International Computer Science and Engineering Conference (ICSEC), pp. 55–60 (2022). https://doi.org/10.1109/ICSEC56337.2022.10049363
4. Subrahmanyam, R.V., Srinivas, N.J., Nagendra, P., Priya, B.K.: A smart social distance monitoring system. In: 2022 International Conference on Futuristic Technologies (INCOFT), pp. 1–6 (2022). https://doi.org/10.1109/INCOFT55651.2022.10094529
5. Kumuda, S., Mane, P.K.: Smart assistant for deaf and dumb using flexible resistive sensor: implemented on LabVIEW platform. In: 2020 International Conference on Inventive Computation Technologies (ICICT), pp. 994–1000 (2020). https://doi.org/10.1109/ICICT48043.2020.9112553
6. Andreadou, N., Bonavitacola, F.: Residential remote load scheduling and control for smart homes with LabVIEW interface. In: 2018 IEEE International Conference on Communications, Control, and Computing Technologies for Smart Grids (SmartGridComm), pp. 1–7 (2018). https://doi.org/10.1109/SmartGridComm.2018.8587506

7. Kumar, P.: Design and implementation of Smart Home control using LabVIEW. In: 2017 Third International Conference on Advances in Electrical, Electronics, Information, Communication and Bio-Informatics (AEEICB), pp. 10–12 (2017). https://doi.org/10.1109/AEEICB.2017.7972317
8. Regula, M., Otcenasova, A., Roch, M., Bodnar, R., Repak, M.: Software for power quality monitoring in model smart grid with using LabView. In: ELEKTRO 2016, pp. 355–358 (2016). https://doi.org/10.1109/ELEKTRO.2016.7512096.35
9. Mahmood, M.A., Hajjaj, S.S.H.: Design and implementation of a rotary parking system for a truly smart city in line with smart cities technologies and trends. In: 2018 8th IEEE International Conference on Control System, Computing and Engineering (ICCSCE), Penang, Malaysia, pp. 49–52 (2018). https://doi.org/10.1109/ICCSCE.2018.8685011
10. Abduelhadi, A., Elnour, M.: Smart motion detection. IOSR J. Electr. Electron. Eng. (IOSR-JEEE) **12**(3 Ver. III), 53–58 (2017). eISSN: 2278-1676, p-ISSN: 2320-3331
11. Ansari, A.N., et al.: An Internet of things approach for motion detection using Raspberry Pi. In: 2014 International Conference on Intelligent Computing and Internet of Things (ICIT) (2014)

Supervene Bag
A Smart Luggage Carrier

Krishna Chaitanya Janapati[1], J. V. R. Ravindra[1], Satyarth Motupalli[2], Veda Manogna Nanduri[1]([✉]), Pavani Punem[1], Sameer Mohammad[1], Sujay Kapil Peddaraju[1], and Amit Lathigara[3]

[1] Vardhaman College of Engineering, Hyderabad, Telangana, India
vedamanogna24@gmail.com
[2] Chaitanya Bharathi Institute of Technology, Hyderabad, India
[3] RK University, Rajkot, Gujarat, India

Abstract. The Supervene Bag stands out as an innovative smart luggage carrier designed to autonomously follow individuals without requiring any physical effort, with a specific focus on air travelers. With over six million people utilizing air transportation, there is a substantial demand for such smart carriers. Unlike conventional RFID tags, which pose challenges due to potential unauthorized access, high initial costs, and compatibility issues, the Supervene Bag addresses these concerns effectively. In contrast to RFID technology, which may face issues if luggage is mishandled or exposed to harsh weather, the Supervene Bag offers advanced features to mitigate these challenges. Equipped with GPS monitoring, automatic mobility, biometric security, integrated charging, and remote-control capabilities, this smart luggage overcomes the limitations of RFID tags. The user-friendly design is further enhanced by easy operability through a mobile phone. This innovative solution aims to provide a seamless and secure travel experience for air passengers, acknowledging and overcoming the drawbacks associated with current RFID technology.

Keywords: Supervene · GPS tracker · Mobility · bio-metric · Remote-control · Integrated · RFID tags · system compatibility

1 Introduction

In the ever-evolving landscape of travel, where convenience and efficiency have become paramount, the SUPERVENE BAG emerges as a beacon of innovation, revolutionizing the conventional luggage experience through embedded technology. Traditional luggage, while pervasive, grapples with a multitude of challenges - from security concerns and handling difficulties to the constant threat of loss or misplacement, additional costs incurred due to overweight baggage, and a glaring absence of theft prevention measures. It is against this backdrop that smart luggage, epitomized by the SUPERVENE BAG, has carved a niche for itself, addressing these limitations head-on.

By leveraging embedded technologies, the SUPERVENE BAG transcends the confines of traditional luggage, ushering in a new era of intelligent travel solutions. These cutting-edge bags seamlessly integrate advanced features to enhance security, connectivity, and organization, promising a more streamlined and optimal travel experience for users. In a world where the travel industry is in perpetual flux, travelers are increasingly vocal about their yearning for intelligent solutions that not only elevate comfort but also bolster the efficiency of their journeys.

Built to cater to this escalating demand, the SUPERVENE BAG is not merely a luggage carrier; it is a sophisticated travel companion. Offering stress reduction through its ability to eliminate the physical strain associated with lugging baggage, this smart bag ensures a positive travel experience. The risk of losing belongings diminishes significantly, thanks to its embedded tracking and security features. Moreover, the bag aligns seamlessly with the contemporary traveler's lifestyle by allowing convenient operation through a mobile phone, adding an extra layer of appeal and user-friendliness.

In this project, we delve into the intricacies of the SUPERVENE BAG, exploring how embedded technology transforms it into a pivotal asset for modern travelers. As we navigate the landscape of smart luggage, we uncover how these innovations contribute not only to the ease of travel but also to the overall satisfaction and peace of mind for globetrotters worldwide. Join us on this journey, where technology meets convenience, and the SUPERVENE BAG redefines the very essence of travel.

2 Literature Survey

[1] According to a study by Sharma (2021), scientists have developed a robot capable of autonomously following people within a predetermined range. The system uses infrared and ultrasonic sensors to monitor human movement. An ultrasonic sensor is a device that uses ultrasonic echoes to measure the distance between itself and an object. These waves are emitted, strike an object, and then reflect back [2]. Automated luggage carriers and other applications can benefit from robots' ability to track moving goods. The Wi-Fi control robot utilized ESP8266 Wi-Fi module and Arduino UNO development boards, along with Node MCU, to enable wireless management of the robot using Wi-Fi technology. Robots can now be remotely controlled using an Android smartphone through the Blynk app [3]. The aim of P.L. Sanathana Krishnan conducted a study to develop a smart luggage carrier system that aims to minimize human effort in transportation and address security concerns. The system includes features such as instantaneous monitoring, theft prevention, and nano Arduino construction. An autonomous luggage carrier, compact and lightweight, follows the user wherever they go using signals from the wearer's smartwatch [4]. Voice instructions can be used to control the robot automobile, and these commands can be accessed through a voice-to-text application. The robot can move in all directions (left, right, forward, and backward) through voice command or manual mode [5]. The Raspberry Pi 3 microprocessor is used in this study. The bag is equipped with anti-theft sensors that interact with a mobile app and connect to a local host. The website and the GSM module are in communication, and the GSM module is an essential component for its independence. The antitheft sensors detect whether the bag is open or closed and alert the owner [6]. This article discusses the development and

deployment of a cloud-based luggage tracking and handling system using RFID tags. The information on travelers and airlines is retrieved using a highly secure technique. A prototype is created at the check-in and check-out locations. To determine the exact location and status of each passenger's luggage, they need to enter their unique RFID number on the website. If the luggage is lost, stolen, or tampered with, having this information allows the traveler to take the necessary steps [7]. The study "Smart Bag with Theft Prevention and Real-Time Tracking" conducts experiments on smart bags. This technology enhances the bag's ability to be activated solely by the owner and track its location using GPS and GSM [8]. The proposed system shows the train's location and the number of passengers in each carriage. The user can track the train from any location and easily catch it. An image processing approach will be used to determine the number of people. The GPS system will be utilized for train tracking [9]. This article presents a hypothetical intellectual travel scenario that may be somewhat restricted. It can be used in airports, train stations, and other locations. In a spacious environment, the travel case can detect and monitor the user's location. In a crowded area, it can also manage the user's movement direction [10]. The article presents the development of the Green Airport luggage monitoring system, including its RFID architecture, components, functionality, and middleware responsibilities. Access to RFID data allows for more reliable and adaptable identification techniques [11]. The suggested approach is applied to a wheelchair follower using a color tracking system. The front wheel is controlled by a servo motor, the transaxle motor is powered by a motor driver, and collisions are prevented by an ultrasonic sensor [12]. The proposed solution utilizes an Android-based remote bag system that offers real-time bag location as an optional feature. The advantage of this feature is that if the bag is lost, it can be located by sending a message to the owner indicating its location. The system includes a self-contained GSM module [13]. A map is created and synchronized to track the location of a lost bag. The advantage of the alarm is that it helps the owner locate and identify the bag. It can be challenging to communicate with an application when using Arduino. Since Arduino is being used, the system may be inflexible and challenging to use [14]. In recent years, several luggage manufacturers have been creating smart bags. Aruna developed a smart luggage in 2019 that features a unique RFID-identified design and a digital locking mechanism.

3 Motivation

The primary objectives for developing embedded-based smart luggage are to enhance the overall travel experience and cater to the requirements of the present-day modern travelers. Furthermore, enterprises have a promising opportunity to capitalize on the swiftly expanding market for smart travel products by incorporating advanced features into their luggage carriers. Imagine a piece of baggage that functions as both a storage unit and a companion System aims to revolutionize the travel experience by ensuring the security, efficient organization, and continuous accessibility of all personal belongings. This is more than just baggage because every element has been designed by keeping the modern traveler in consideration.

4 System Architecture and Design

4.1 Overview

This smart luggage system comes with two operating modes such as automatic mode and manual mode. This switching feature makes it more user friendly and unique.

4.2 Hardware Components

We have utilized sensors such as IR (Infrared sensors) and Ultrasonic sensors for automatic operation. These sensors play a major role in locating a person within a certain radius and enabling the system to track their movements (Fig. 1).

Fig. 1. IR Sensor.

An infrared sensor emits light to detect objects in its surroundings. An infrared sensor can not only detect motion but also measure an object's heat. Typically, all objects emit infrared heat radiation. An infrared sensor can detect these invisible radiations that are not visible to the human eye. An IR LED serves as the emitter, while an IR photodiode detects IR light of the same wavelength as the LED. The resistance and output voltage of the photodiode change in response to the amount of infrared light it receives (Fig. 2).

Fig. 2. Ultrasonic sensor.

The ultrasonic sensor is a non-contact sensor that measures the distance and velocity of an object. This sensor utilizes sound waves to measure the distance and velocity of an object. The ultrasonic sensor utilizes a sound wave with a frequency that is beyond the range of human perception. The ultrasonic sensor measures the distance between an object and the point of wave origin by calculating the velocity and time it takes for the wave signal to travel to the object and back (Fig. 3).

Fig. 3. Bluetooth module (HC-05).

The HC-05 Bluetooth Module is a simple Bluetooth SPP (Serial Port Protocol) module that allows for the creation of a wireless serial connection. It uses serial communication to easily interact with a PC or controller. For manual mode of operation we incorporated Bluetooth module HC-05 with the system which is then connected with the mobile (in-stalled with 'serial Blue-tooth terminal app') Bluetooth (Fig. 4).

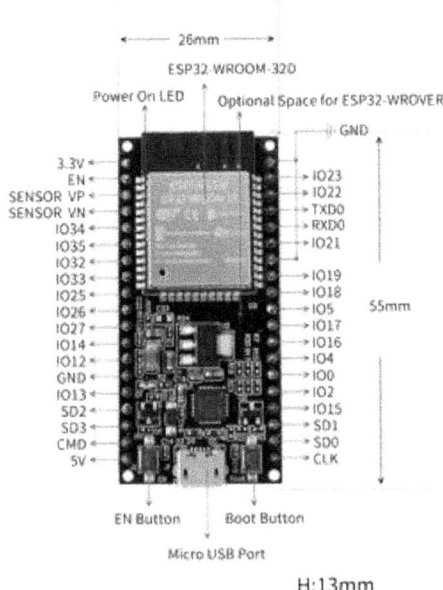

Fig. 4. Node MCU module.

The ESP32 is a highly versatile System On a Chip (SoC) that can function as a general purpose microcontroller with a wide range of peripherals, including WiFi and Bluetooth capabilities. It serves as the central microcontroller. The system allows for real-time tracking using GPS, remote locking or unlocking via Bluetooth, and seamless luggage management and alerts through communication with a user's smartphone (Figs. 5 and 6).

5 Block Diagram

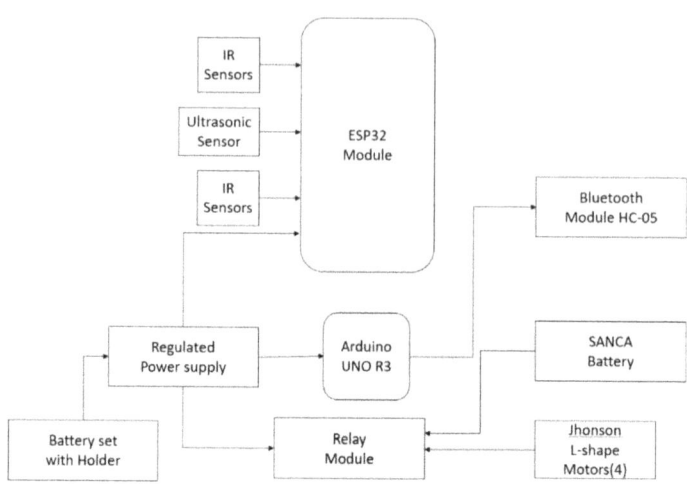

Fig. 5. Block diagram.

6 Prototype

Fig. 6. Prototype.

7 Features and Functionalities

Multiple Modes of Operations
Automatic mode of operation
Mobile operation (manual mode)
Users have the option to select the mode of operation that aligns with their interests and the available environment.

Battery Life and Charging Solutions
The device includes a charging port, allowing users to charge their gadgets conveniently and on-the-go.

GPS Tracking
Continuous tracking and monitoring of luggage is achieved through GPS, providing real-time updates to the user.

Anti-Theft Measures
This bag is equipped with a biometric unlocking system. If a user's mobile device is hacked or lost, biometric unlocking allows them to access their luggage without needing their mobile device. The presence of a smart locking system ensures that only the owner can access the luggage, making it more secure than traditional luggage carriers.

User-Friendly
Users are provided with multiple user-friendly modes that can be easily understood and operated by people of all ages.

Customizable
This bag can be customized with fingerprints and other features according to the user's requirements.

Longer Life Time
This bag is made with durable and high-quality materials, including strong zippers and locks that can withstand the demands of travel.

8 Security and Privacy Considerations

The system incorporates GPS tracking to guarantee constant visibility for the user. To enhance security, only one mobile device can be connected at any given time, ensuring exclusive access for the owner. Adding an additional layer of protection, the bag features a biometric unlocking system. In the event of a compromised or lost mobile device, the user can employ biometric authentication to access their luggage independently. Ensuring the ongoing reliability and trustworthiness of the smart luggage system requires a proactive approach, including regular updates on the luggage's location and a meticulous review of these security considerations. These measures collectively safeguard the integrity of the system, providing users with a secure and dependable smart luggage experience.

9 Working Principle

The bag can be operated in two modes.

Automatic Mode, also Known as Sensor Mode

The functioning of this mode depends on sensors positioned on the bag's front panel. Utilizing technologies like infrared (IR) and ultrasonic, these sensors measure distance and confirm the user's presence. The system persists in tracking the user until encountering a breaking point or signal disruption. This operational mode proves advantageous in scenarios where users lack a mobile device or face insufficient battery charge. Enhancements to this device can be made by incorporating AI features and providing access to a front camera.

Manual Mode (Mobile Usage)

In Manual Mode, designed for mobile usage, the bag integrates a Bluetooth module, specifically the HC-05, which connects to the user's mobile device equipped with the 'Serial Bluetooth Terminal' app. By configuring the necessary settings in the app to connect the bag and set up the terminal, users can initiate movement with a simple tap on the terminal options. These options include Forward (F), Backward (B), Stop (S), Right (R), and Left (L). Resembling the functionality of a remote control car, this mode enables effortless luggage movement in crowded areas without physical exertion, providing ease of operation and enjoyment, especially for kids during travel.

10 Results and Observations

Automatic Mode (Sensor Mode)

The diagrams depict the functioning of the system in automatic mode, commonly referred to as sensor mode. As shown in Figs. 7 and 8, when the user is positioned within the sensor's range and lies in front of the bag, the bag autonomously advances towards the user. To enhance movement precision, the evice is furnished with multiple sensors strategically placed on the front panel, ensuring an accurate and responsive interaction between the Supervene Bag and the user.

Manual Mode (Using Mobile)

When opting for manual mode, the user initiates a connection between the system and their mobile device via the Serial Bluetooth Terminal app. Once connected, the user configures the terminal, adjusting options to meet specific requirements. Movement activation requires selecting from options like F (Forward), B (Backward), L (Left), R (Right), and S (Stop). The terminal output in Fig. 9 illustrates the bag's continuous movement in the chosen direction until the user commands a halt (S). A robust connection between the terminal and Bluetooth is imperative for seamless operation, ensuring effective control over the Supervene Bag's movements.

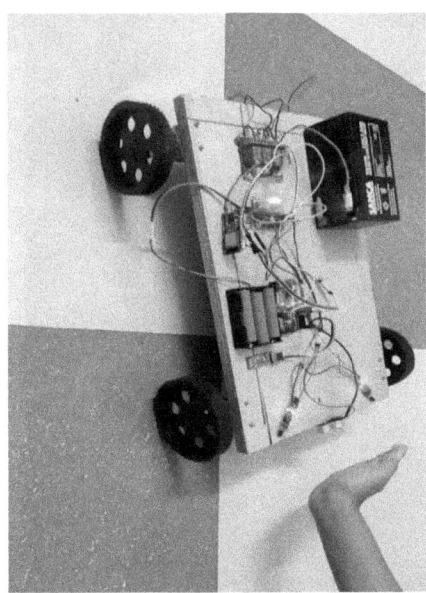

Fig. 7. Sensor working.

Fig. 8. Sensor working.

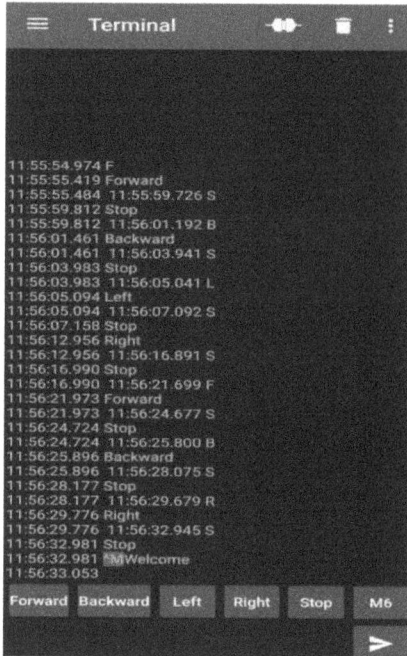

Fig. 9. Terminal output.

11 Conclusions and Future Scope

The "SUPERVENE BAG" initiative has concluded with resounding success, garnering positive acclaim. This intelligent travel companion has proven itself as not only highly user-friendly but also exceptionally efficient. The real-time tracking feature has emerged as a valuable asset, keeping travelers well-informed throughout their journeys. The seamless implementation and favorable user feedback underscore the potential widespread adoption of this transformative technology within the travel industry. This project not only marks a significant achievement but also lays a robust foundation for future research and development in the realm of smart travel solutions, aligning with the continual evolution of technology. The envisaged inclusion of customizable features and personalized settings is poised to cater to individual preferences, ensuring heightened user satisfaction in the evolving landscape of travel technology.

References

1. Sharma, A.K., Pandey, A., Khan, M.A., Tripathi, A., Saxena, A., Yadav, P.K.: Human following robot. In: 2021 International Conference on Advance Computing and Innovative Technologies in Engineering (ICACITE), pp. 440–446 (2021). https://doi.org/10.1109/ICACIT E51222.2021.9404758
2. Sowmya, B.J., Supriya, M.: Robot controlled car using voice and wi-fi module. Int. Res. J. Eng. Technol. (IRJET) **08**(08) (2021)

3. Krishnan, P.L.S., Valli, R., Priya, R., Pravinkumar, V.: Smart luggage carrier system with theft prevention and real time trackingusing nano Arduino structure. In: 2020 International Conference on System, Computation, Automation and Networking (ICSCAN), pp. 1–5 (2020). https://doi.org/10.1109/ICSCAN49426.2020.9262445
4. Khan, A., Nalwade, B., Kharshinge, N., Kamble, S.: Smart luggage system. Int. Res. J. Eng. Technol. (IRJET) (2019)
5. Shaikh, S., Jakahete, M.D.: Smart travelling bag using IOT. Paripex- Indian J. Res. (2019). ISSN No. 2250 - 1991
6. Nair, K.S., Kumar, A.J., Pillai, A.A., Greeshma, M.S., Joseph, J.: Smart luggage tracker. Int. J. Res. Eng. Sci. Manag. **2**(6) (2019)
7. Sutar, A., Kocharekar, T., Mestry, P., Sawantdesai, P., Goilkar, S.S.: Smart bag with theft prevention and real-time tracking. Int. J. Trend Sci. Res. Dev. **2** (2018)
8. Jadiwal, R., Parmar, A., Raut, L.: Rail rush system for crowd analysis. In: 2018 International Conference on Smart City and Emerging Technology (2018)
9. Wang, P., Zhang, T., Wang, S.: Remote control and tracking dual-mode smart suitcase. In: 2018 3rd International Conference on Robotics and Automation Engineering (2018)
10. Rouchdi, Y., Haibi, A., El Yassini, K., Boulmalf, M., Oufaska, K.: RFID application to airport luggage tracking as a green logistics approach. In: 2018 IEEE 5th International Congress on Information Science and Technology (2018)
11. Ahmad, M.F., Rong, H.J., Alhady, S.S.N., Rahiman, W., Othman, W.A.F.W.: Colour tracking technique by using pixy CMUcam5 for wheelchair luggage follower. In: 2017 7th IEEE International Conference on Control System, Computing and Engineering (2017)
12. Varma, R., Pavshe, P., Bhadane, A., Pagare, S.: Multifunctional bag monitoring system. Int. Res. J. Eng. Technol. (IRJET) (2018). ISSN 2395-0056
13. Senthilkumar, S., Brindha, K., Rathi, R., Charanya, R.: Luggage tracking system using IoT. Int. J. Pure Appl. Math. (2017). ISSN 1311-8080
14. Aruna, S., Bhavyashree, C., Suraboyana, K., Meghana, S., Radhika, K.R.: The intelligent suitcase. Perspect. Commun. Embed.-Syst. Sig.-Process. (PiCES) – An Int. J. **2**(10) (2019). ISSN 2566-932X

Enhancing Finite Impulse Response (FIR) Filtering with Distributive Arithmetic (DA) and Residue Number System (RNS) Optimization

Mentam Sunaina[✉] and G. L. Sumalata

GRIET, ECE, Hyderabad, India
sunainagrace.123@gmail.com

Abstract. Digital Signal Processing (DSP) systems have revolutionized numerous fields such as telecommunications, audio manipulation, image and video treatment and various other domains. Whereas Distributed Arithmetic (DA) is a powerful technique used in DSP area for efficient implementation of various algorithms. This paper presents an optimized Finite Impulse Response (FIR) filter with Distributed Arithmetic (DA) and Residue Number System (RNS). The proposed design leverages the properties of the RNS to achieve efficient and high-performance filtering operations. The input samples and filter coefficients undergo a transformation into residue representation, and the intermediate products are calculated using residue arithmetic. The proposed design has been implemented in Xilinx platform. It uses 15% lesser power demonstrates reduced computational complexity and improved performance has been reduced to compared to conventional FIR filters. The experimental outcomes underscore the efficacy of the suggested method concerning filter efficiency, resource utilization, and energy consumption. The optimized FIR filter using the RNS method presents a promising solution for efficient and high-performance filtering utilized in a range of fields, including digital signal processing and communication systems.

Keywords: Finite Impulse Response Filter · Residue Number System · Distributed Arithmetic · Digital Signal Processing

1 Introduction

Digital Signal Processing Systems uses Digital Finite Impulse Response Filtering operations on a large scale [1]. However, a Digital FIR filter uses Multiply and Accumulate (MAC) where each input is multiplied with every filter coefficient which results in the use of large number of multiplier circuits [2]. This ultimately leads to increased demands in terms of area, delay, and power consumption. In response to this challenge, various algorithms have emerged as viable solutions. Few algorithms were memory-based designs [3], while few were conversion-based designs One such memory-based design is the

Distributed Arithmetic based FIR filter, where the design of FIR filter is carried out using Look-Up-Tables. Look-Up-Table computes the Filter coefficients and the incoming Input signals [2]. The inputs to the DA based FIR filter are given in two's compliment form which results in increased computational time. This is because the speed of the computational process is directly related to the length of the input data in bits. This results in computational speed if the bit length of the input data is high.

In order to overcome this, a new approach called RNS based FIR filter is introduced where any complex number is converted into a set of simple residues using the respective moduli numbers [6]. This paper proposes a memoryless FIR filter with traditional DA algorithm using RNS method. This approach uses the simplified conversion process which increases the overall speed and reduces the computational time of the whole design.

The outline of this paper is: 1. Introduction, 2. What is a DA based FIR filter and its design, 3. Why RNS, 4. What is Residue Number System, 4. Proposed method 5. Forward conversion, 6. Reverse conversion, 7. Simulation Result, 8. Conclusion, 9. Reference.

2 DA Based FIR Filter

Distributed Arithmetic (DA) is a widely employed algorithm in the realization of Finite Impulse Response (FIR) Filters [5]. It offers computational efficiency by replacing the expensive multiplication operations with a combination of additions and look-up table operations.

Distributed Arithmetic uses inner product computations, which eliminates the use of repeated multiplication [8]. Below is the mathematical representation of DA algorithm

$$Y = \sum_{k=1}^{K} d_k x_k \quad (1)$$

where Y is the output, x_k is the input signal, d_k is the filter coefficient and K is the word length. For a K tap FIR filter, there will be K execution cycles. But as the system takes the input signals as binary values, the input signal x_k can be written as

$$x_k = \sum_{n=0}^{N-1} b_{kn} 2^n \quad (2)$$

where b_{kn} is the binary value, which is either 0 or 1 and 2^n is the weight of the corresponding binary bit (see Fig. 1).

$$Y = \sum_{k=1}^{K} d_k \sum_{n=0}^{N-1} b_{kn} 2^n \quad (3)$$

On rearranging the above equation,

$$Y = \sum_{k=1}^{K} \left[\sum_{n=0}^{N-1} d_{kn} b_{kn} \right] 2^n \quad (4)$$

$$Y = |\sum_{n=0}^{N-1} [\sum_{k=0}^{K-1} d_k b_{kn}] 2^n|_m \quad (5)$$

where, mi is the modular set of the RNS system, which is $mi = [m1, m2, m3, \ldots mn]$. This modular set depends on the number of tap filters that are being used. Where, the inner product can be represented in RNS form as

$$Q_{mi}(d_k, b_{kn}) = \sum_{n=0}^{N-1} |d_k|_{mi} |b_{kn}|_{mi} \tag{6}$$

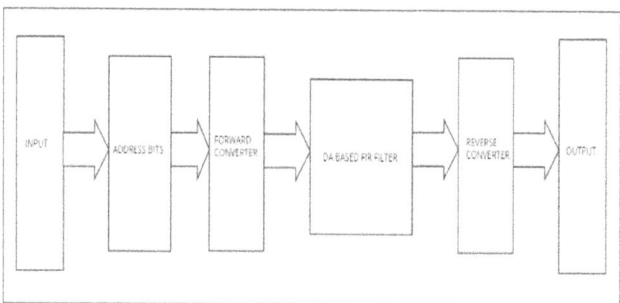

Fig. 1. Block diagram FIR filter using RNS method employing DA algorithm

3 Residue Number System

3.1 What is RNS?

The Residue Number System (RNS) is a mathematical method for representing a sizable number by decomposing it into distinct residue values within a modular set [8]. Each residue value is obtained by dividing the original number to its corresponding modulus value. These modulus vales are co-prime to each other. The main reason for adopting the RNS system in Filter design is because of its capability of reducing Power consumption.

Unlike Binary System, an RNS system represents any large number into a set of small residue values without any carry bits. There are different kinds of residue sets like $\{2^{n-1}, 2^n, 2^{n+1}\}$, $\{2n, 2n+1, 2n-1\}$, $\{2^{2n}, 2^n+1, 2^n-1\}$ $\{2^{2n}, 2^n+1, 2^n-1\}$ etc. [12].The modular set used in this paper is $\{2n, 2n+1, 2n-1\}$.

Forward Conversion

The initial step involves transforming the input data and filter coefficient data into residue representation through the utilization of specific moduli values. Later the residues are individually converted into binary form and sent into DA filter where the actual design process is carried out [9].

Example:
Number: 12
Module set: {3, 4, 5}

```
3 ) 12 ( 4      4 ) 12 ( 3     5 ) 12 ( 2
   12              12              10
  -------         -------         -------
     0              0                2
  -------         -------         -------
```

So, the RNS form of 12 for the moduli set {3, 4, 5} is {0, 0, 5}

Reverse Conversion

To perform the Reverse Conversion from RNS form, a new method known as the Chinese Remainder Theorem is applied. Given a set of pairwise coprime moduli, the theorem states that there exists a unique solution modulo the product of these moduli. This solution can be found by using the Chinese Remainder Theorem algorithm, which involves computing partial remainders and then combining them to get the final solution.

So, the equation for the Reverse conversion is

$$X = |\sum_{i=1}^{I} N_i . N_i^{-1} . y_i|_M \tag{7}$$

where, **i** depends on the number of moduli,

$$M = m_1 . m_2 . m_3 \tag{8}$$

$$M_i = M / m_i \tag{9}$$

And N_i^{-1} can be found by satisfying the below equation

$$\left(N_i . N_i^{-1}\right) \% m_i = 1 \tag{10}$$

This can be satisfied by following hit or miss trick

This paper employs the modular set {2n, 2n + 1, 2n-1} for the design of a 4-tap FIR filter. Using Distributed Arithmetic technique. This design has been carried out and synthesized in Xilinx Integrated Synthesis Environment using Spartan3E with 28 nm technology which uses 30% less power compared to existing architectures.

For a 4-tap filter, the moduli set is m {8, 9, 7}. So, to design a 4 tap FIR filter, for the input X {4, 5, 6, 7}, the filter coefficient is taken as D {3, 7, 8, 9}. The forward conversion of the input signals is shown in the below table.

4 Proposed Method

4.1 Forward Conversions of Input Data

Table 1. Conversion of input signals into Residue form

Input	m = 8	m = 9	m = 7
4	4	4	4
6	5	5	5
6	6	6	6
7	7	7	0

The forward conversion of input data into RNS form is shown in Table 1. Whereas the filter coefficients are preserved in a Look-Up Table for storage and subsequent use and later used accordingly during filter design. The filter coefficients $\{d_1, d_2, d_3, d_4\} = \{3, 7, 8, 9\}$. The stored elements in LUT are showed in Table. 2

Consequently, upon sending the input data to the DA filter, the filter coefficients are computed as required, facilitating the design of an FIR filter.

$$Y = \sum_{k=1}^{K} d_k x_k \qquad (11)$$

$$Y_8 = |d_1 x_1 + d_2 x_2 + d_3 x_3 + d_4 x_4|_8 \qquad (12)$$

$$Y_8 = |4(3) + 5(7) + 6(0) + 7(1)|_8$$

$$Y_8 = |12 + 35 + 0 + 7|_8$$

$$Y_8 = |54|_8$$

$$Y_8 = 6$$

Similarly, $Y_9 = 5$, $Y_7 = 4$
So, this can be written as $Y \{Y_8, Y_9, Y_7\} = \{6, 5, 4\}$.

4.2 Reverse Conversion Process

The Chinese Remainder Theorem is a method that can be employed to conduct the reverse conversion of RNS. This can be followed by

$$M = m_1 * m_2 * m_3 \qquad (13)$$

Enhancing Finite Impulse Response (FIR)

Table 2. Contents into LUT

t_{1n}	t_{2n}	t_{3n}	t_{4n}	Entry values	m = 8	m = 9	m = 7
0	0	0	0	0	0	0	0
0	0	0	1	$d_1 = 3$	3	3	3
0	0	1	0	$d_2 = 7$	7	7	0
0	0	1	1	$d_2 + d_1 = 7 + 3 = 10$	2	1	3
0	1	0	0	$d_3 = 8$	0	8	1
0	1	0	1	$d_3 + d_1 = 8 + 3 = 11$	3	2	4
0	1	1	0	$d_3 + d_2 = 8 + 7 = 15$	7	6	1
0	1	1	1	$d_3 + d_2 + d_1 = 8 + 7 + 3 = 18$	2	0	4
1	0	0	0	$d_4 = 9$	1	0	2
1	0	0	1	$d_4 + d_1 = 9 + 3 = 12$	4	3	5
1	0	1	0	$d_4 + d_2 = 9 + 7 = 16$	0	7	2
1	0	1	1	$d_4 + d_2 + d_1 = 9 + 7 + 3 = 19$	3	1	5
1	1	0	0	$d_4 + d_3 = 9 + 8 = 17$	1	8	3
1	1	0	1	$d_4 + d_3 + d_1 = 9 + 8 + 3 = 20$	4	2	6
1	1	1	0	$d_4 + d_3 + d_2 = 9 + 8 + 7 = 24$	0	6	3
1	1	1	1	$d_4 + d_3 + d_2 + d_1 = 9 + 8 + 7 + 3 = 27$	3	0	6

$$M = 8 * 9 * 7$$

$$M = 504$$

$$M_1 = M/m_1 \qquad (14)$$

$$M_1 = \frac{504}{8} = 63$$

$$M_2 = M/m_2 \qquad (15)$$

$$M_2 = \frac{504}{9} = 56$$

$$M_3 = M/m_3 \qquad (16)$$

$$M_3 = \frac{504}{7} = 72$$

To get the inverse value of each module, hit and check method is employed to satisfy the below equation

$$(M_i * M_i^{-1})\%m_1 = 1 \tag{17}$$

$$(M_1 * M_1^{-1})\%m_1 = 1$$

$$(63 * 7)\%8 = 1$$

$$(M_2 * M_2^{-1})\%m_2 = 1$$

$$(72 * 4)\%7 = 1$$

So,

$$M_1 = 63;\ M_1^{-1} = 7$$

$$M_2 = 56;\ M_2^{-1} = 5$$

$$M_3 = 72;\ M_3^{-1} = 4$$

where i represents the respective module.

So, the actual output can be found by

$$Y = |(M_1 * M_1^{-1} * Y_8) + (M_2 * M_2^{-1} * Y_9) + (M_3 * M_3^{-1} * Y_7)|_M \tag{18}$$

$$Y = |(63 * 7 * 6) + (56 * 5 * 5) + (72 * 4 * 4)|_{504}$$

$$Y = |(2646 + 1400 + 1152)|_{504}$$

$$Y = |5198|_{504}$$

$$Y = 158$$

5 Simulation Results

The presented design's performance and hardware complexity are evaluated by contrasting them with those of the current architectures. The proposed filter is designed on Spartan 3E Field Programmable Gate Array which is a part of Xilinx family. It is a cost sensitive device which is easy to implement. The Spartan 6 family provides a 45 nm technology DSP block to implement high efficient algorithm.

Table 3. Performance Comparison

Design	Critical Path Delay (ns)	Area (μm^2)	Total delay (ns)	ADP ($mm^2 ns$)	Power (mw)	PDP (pJ)
Chen et al. (2006)	16.33	8357.4	16.33	0.138	5.032	82.13
Kamal et al. (2014)	15.30	6271.6	15.30	0.096	4.629	70.8237
Grande et al. (2020)	14	5432	14	0.076	4.411	61.754
Proposed design	12.24	4812	12.24	0.059	4.249	58.684

Using the proposed design, it is evident the design of 4 tap filter is made easy by eliminating the risk of carries in any regular Binary system. From Table 3, it clearly shows that the proposed design uses 15% lesser power compared to previous work [6] and utilizes 17% lesser area than the existing work [10]. All the other performance metrics are mentioned in Table 3 and the graphical representation of Area, delay and power are mentioned in the Figs. 2, 3 and 4 respectively. Additionally, it's worth noting that the overall delay of the proposed approach is significantly reduced when compared to the delays associated with all other architectures listed in the Table 3. The area delay product and Power Delay Product are also comparatively very less.

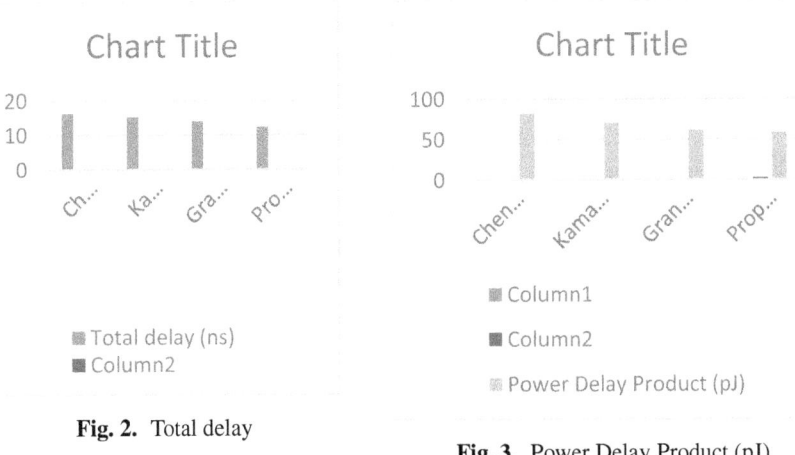

Fig. 2. Total delay

Fig. 3. Power Delay Product (pJ)

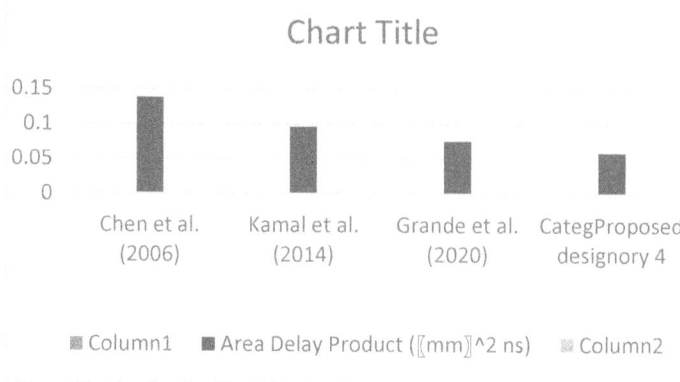

Fig. 4. Area Delay Product $\left(mm^2 ns\right)$

6 Conclusion

This paper shows the simplest form of DA based FIR Filter using RNS method. Instead of using the lengthy Binary number, any number is represented as the simplest RNS form which is then converted into Binary form and used for implementation purpose. The actual goal of decreasing the overall delay is achieved using this method. Compared to the existing methods, there is a 17% less delay in the proposed method. As RNS can perform fast and parallel computations, this method better suits as a replacement for a regular FIR filter. The only limitation of using RNS system is the use of converters which makes it look a little complex. However with the use of CRT the conversions have been made simple and easy to compute. But use of RNS system is best suit in many DSP applications because of its capability of less Power consumption and reduced Delay.

References

1. NagaJyothi, G., SriDevi, S.: Distributed arithmetic architectures for fir filters-a comparative review. In: 2017 International Conference on Wireless Communications, Signal Processing and Networking (WiSPNET), pp. 2684–2690. IEEE (2017)
2. Mohanty, B.K., Meher, P.K.: A high-performance energy-efficient architecture for FIR adaptive filter based on new distributed arithmetic formulation of block LMS algorithm. IEEE Trans. Signal Process. **61**(4), 921–932 (2012)
3. Shanthala, S., Kulkarni, S.Y.: VLSI design and implementation of low power MAC unit with block enabling technique. Eur. J. Sci. Res. **30**(4), 620–630 (2009)
4. Hartley, R.I.: Subexpression sharing in filters using canonic signed digit multipliers. IEEE Trans. Circ. Syst. II: Analog Digit. Sig. Process. **43**(10), 677–688 (1996)
5. Chandra, A., Chattopadhyay, S.: A new strategy of image denoising using multiplier-less FIR filter designed with the aid of differential evolution algorithm. Multimedia Tools Appl. **75**, 1079–1098 (2016)
6. Akhter, S., Kumar, S., Bareja, D.: Design and analysis of distributed arithmetic based FIR filter. In: 2018 International Conference on Advances in Computing, Communication Control and Networking (ICACCCN), pp. 721–726. IEEE (2018)

7. Jamal, K., Chari, K.M., Srihari, P.: Test pattern generation using thermometer code counter in TPC technique for BIST implementation. Microprocess. Microsyst. **71**, 102890 (2019)
8. Kamal, R., Chandravanshi, P., Jain, N.: November. Efficient VLSI architecture for FIR filter using DA-RNS. In: 2014 International Conference on Electronics, Communication and Computational Engineering (ICECCE), pp. 184–187. IEEE (2014)
9. Jameii, S.M., Taghipour, S., Azad, M.: Using both binary and residue representations for achieving fast converters in RNS (2011)
10. Jamal, K., Srihari, P., Chari, K.M., Sabitha, B.: Low power test pattern generation using test-per-scan technique for BIST implementation. ARPN J. Eng. Appl. Sci. **13**(8) (2018)
11. Cao, B., Chang, C.H., Srikanthan, T.: An efficient reverse converter for the 4-moduli set $2^n/-1$, 2^n, 2^n+1, $2^{2n}+1$ based on the new Chinese remainder theorem. IEEE Trans. Circ. Syst. I: Fundam. Theory Appl. **50**(10), 1296–1303 (2003)
12. Matutino, P.M., Chaves, R., Sousa, L.: December. ROM-less RNS-to-binary converter moduli {$2\,2n-1, 2\,2n+1, 2\,n-3, 2\,n+3$}. In: 2014 International Symposium on Integrated Circuits (ISIC), pp. 432–435. IEEE (2014)
13. Sridevi, N., Jamal, K., Mannem, K.: Implementation of error correction techniques in memory applications. In: 2021 5th International Conference on Computing Methodologies and Communication (ICCMC), pp. 586–595. IEEE (2021)
14. Garner, H.L.: The residue number system. In: Papers Presented at the March 3–5, 1959, Western Joint Computer Conference, pp. 146–153 (1959)
15. Albicocco, P., Cardarilli, G.C., Nannarelli, A., Re, M.: Twenty years of research on RNS for DSP: Lessons learned and future perspectives. In: 2014 International Symposium on Integrated Circuits (ISIC), pp. 436–439. IEEE (2014)
16. Meher, P.K., Chandrasekaran, S., Amira, A.: FPGA realization of FIR filters by efficient and flexible systolization using distributed arithmetic. IEEE Trans. Signal Process. **56**(7), 3009–3017 (2008)
17. Longa, P., Miri, A.: Area-efficient FIR filter design on FPGAs using distributed arithmetic. In: 2006 IEEE International Symposium on Signal Processing and Information Technology, pp. 248–252. IEEE (2006)
18. Praveen Sundar, P.V., Ranjith, D., Karthikeyan, T., Vinoth Kumar, V., Jeyakumar, B.: Low power area efficient adaptive FIR filter for hearing aids using distributed arithmetic architecture. Int. J. Speech Technol. **23**(2), 287–296 (2020)
19. Balaji, M., Padmaja, N., Gitanjali, P., Shaik, S.A., Kumar, S.: Design of FIR filter with fast adders and fast multipliers using RNS algorithm. In: 2023 4th International Conference for Emerging Technology (INCET), pp. 1–6. IEEE (2023)

A Wide Band Annular-Ring Loaded Circularly Polarized Microstrip Antenna

Samuel Nishant Muthyala[1], Pasumarthy Nageswara Rao[1]([✉]), Kiran Mannem[2], and E. R. Aruna[1]

[1] Department of Electronics and Communication Engineering, Vardhaman College of Engineering, Hyderabad, India
{muthyalasamuel_18ec,pasumarthy.nageswararao, er.aruna}@vardhaman.org
[2] Department of Electronics and Communication Engineering, GRIET, Hyderabad, India

Abstract. The wireless device market is expanding rapidly nowadays as a result of the rapid advancements in technology in recent years. The antenna is the most crucial part of a wireless device since it facilitates communication and data transfer. In this paper a small microstrip antenna with dual circularly polarized bands is presented. The antenna is small and compact with dimensions 24 mm × 22 mm × 1 mm. The patch is loaded with an annular-ring slot and contains a quarter circle cut on one end. Two slits of varying length and width are also etched in the radiating patch on one side of patch opposite to each other for fine tuning to achieve better circular polarization. A rectangular defected ground structure is used for improving the radiation characteristics. The designed antenna shows good wide bandwidth, gain and circular polarization with dual circularly polarized bands for use in wireless communication (WLAN, WiMax) and satellite communication applications.

Keywords: annular-ring · circularly polarized · Defected ground structure · microstrip

1 Introduction

The continued development of numerous wireless connection technologies, including satellite technology, mobile communications, and wireless sensor systems, is currently being driven by significant breakthroughs in microwave and radio frequency integrated circuit technology. One portable device typically contains multiple interface systems, whereas others that can work on different frequency bands must be kept apart for safety reasons. As a result, the system always needs numerous antennas to provide the transceiver functions. It is challenging to combine different antennas in a single system, nevertheless, because of the limited space in mobile devices. Additionally, the use of multiple antennas contributes to a coupling effect between antenna elements, which could negatively impact the system's ability to receive signals and its signal-to-noise ratio. This coupling effect can also cause issues with the antennas' structure and

RF circuit front-ends. Since wideband is used in many communication applications, UltraWideBand (UWB) is one of the potential solutions once more for multiantenna systems. Its dimensions can actually be significantly lowered in tiny quantities without the coupling effect at the same time [1, 2].

However, despite these advantages, the UWB antenna's use has been constrained by its obvious Linear Polarization (LP) properties. With the added benefits of reducing multipath effects, enhancing signal reliability, reducing polarization losses among transmitting and receiving antennas, and optimizing the weakness of antenna directivity, the Circular Polarization (CP) antenna tends to draw more and more attention as a solution to the issue. UWB CP antennas are frequently utilized in wireless communication systems [3–9] due to the benefits listed above. Due to its exceptional qualities, the CP antenna is utilized in multiple applications The CP antenna appears to be utilized frequently in a range of application settings due to its exceptional qualities. For instance, it is employed in radar systems to prevent cloud and rain interference [4].

The CP antennas might interact with and detect multiple distinction and elliptically polarized radio waves in electronic countermeasures. The CP antenna would certainly properly receive information in airplanes with tough environments [5, 6]. The CP antenna could actually solve the ghosting issue within the television broadcasting system [8]. With all these benefits, there has been a lot of study done on CP UWB antennas, and several constructions have recently been proposed and designed. To reduce the area and widen the current route, the electric dipole is changed to a folded square ring. By attempting to connect a 90° hybrid coupler, CP is gained. The fractional bandwidth at 3 dB Axial Ratio (AR) is 1.7 GHz. In [9], a waveguide spacer polarizer-based horn double circularly polarized broadband millimeter wave antenna is proposed. In order to achieve duplex, the antenna may in fact simultaneously receive and broadcast orthogonal CP waves. The two architectures both exhibit strong CP radiation performance [9], a wide AR bandwidth, and high gain. However, the antennas appear to be a three-dimensional (3D) construction, intricate, large, and difficult to produce. They truly aren't suitable for use on mobile devices in their current forms.

2 Antenna Design Approach

The patch, substrate, and ground make up the three components of the suggested antenna. The patch is the topmost layer, with the substrate in the middle and the ground plane on the opposite side. Patch and ground plane thicknesses are not significant, therefore only the substrate thickness is considered. The proposed antenna's dimensions are (24 × 22 × 1)mm and its substrate is FR4 with a relative permittivity of 4.4 and a loss tangent of 0.02. The feeding line is connected to the radiating patch, which has the Fig. 1 dimensions.

The ground plane as shown in Fig. 2 is a defected ground structure taken with measurements of width same as substrate (22 mm) and length equal to the length of feed line (i.e. 3.5 mm). The two edges on the side of feed line are tapered for better impedance matching of antenna. The patch is loaded with an annular-ring slot for increasing bandwidth and a quarter of circle is cut from one end of patch on the side opposite to feed line for circular polarization. An L-shaped strip is introduced on one side of the patch to help with inducing circular polarization and fine tuning it.

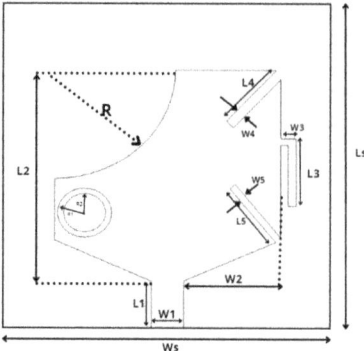

Fig. 1. Top view of Proposed Antenna

The bottom view of an antenna reveals a distinctive feature in the form of a defective ground structure, which spans a length of 3.5 mm and occupies one side of the ground plane. This unique design element is integrated to strategically manipulate the antenna's electromagnetic properties, contributing to its specialized functionality within the proposed structure.

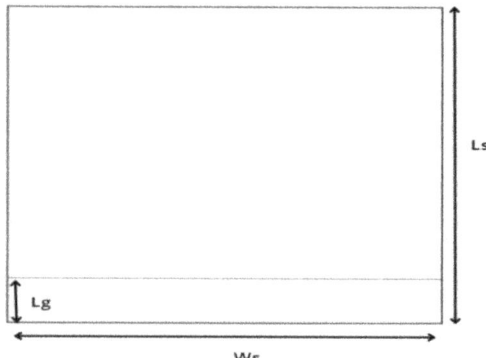

Fig. 2. Bottom view of Proposed Antenna

The Table 1 indicates the dimensions of proposed antenna structure in mm. This tabulated information is essential for gaining a detailed understanding of the antenna's construction. The table includes the following dimensions for specific components:

Due to two square rings in the ground plane, the antenna resonates at two separate frequencies; the stub aids in the overlapping of two resonant frequencies to form a single resonating band. By combining the inductance of the outer square ring and the collective capacitance caused by capacitance coupling between the two square rings, out of band filtering has become feasible.

Table 1. Parameters of proposed antenna

Parameters	Value (mm)
Ls	24
Ws	22
L1	3.5
W1	2.12
L2	15.5
W2	7.29
L3	5
W3	1
L4	5.5
W4	0.7
L5	5.5
W5	0.5
R	8
R1	1.8
R2	1.4
Lg	3.5

3 Evolution of Design

Initial antenna structure shows in Fig. 3. it represents the rectangular patch and defective ground structure. For the Fig. 3. Structure gives impedance bandwidth of 4GHz and it ranges from 4.76GHz to 8.71GHz. The axial ratio of the structure in Fig. 3 is infinite because the orthogonal components of the field are 0 for pure linear polarization. As a result, the antenna is linearly polarized.

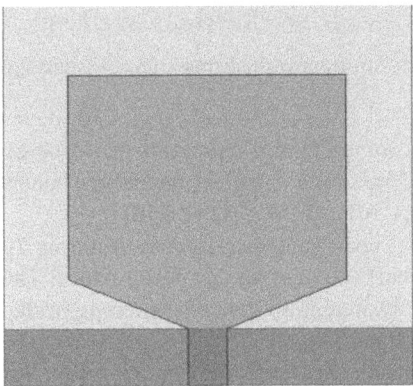

Fig. 3. Initial evolution of antenna.

Antenna structure shows in Fig. 4 it represents the rectangular patch and defective ground structure. For the Fig. 4 structure gives impedance bandwidth of 3.69 GHz and

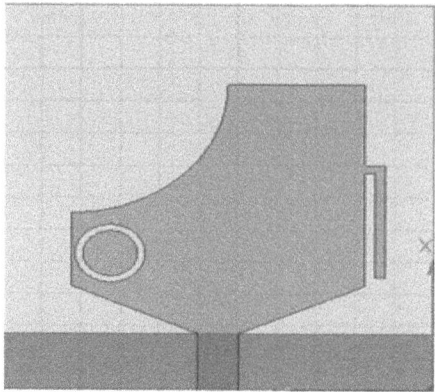

Fig. 4. Antenna Structure with stub & ring slot.

it ranges from 4.73 GHz to 8.42 GHz. Figure 4 structure axial ratio bandwidth is 1.22 GHz and it is ranging from 6.08 GHz to 7.30 GHz.

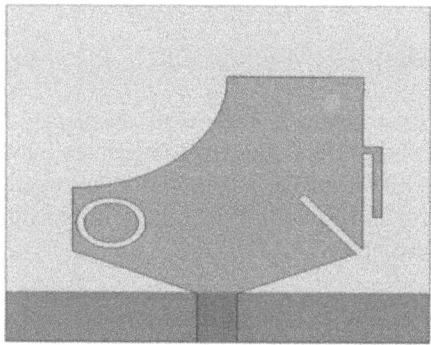

Fig. 5. Antenna Structure with quarter circle cut, ring slot, stub & slit.

Antenna structure shows in Fig. 5 it represents the rectangular patch and defective ground structure. For the Fig. 5 structure gives impedance bandwidth of 3.84 GHz (4.38 GHz to 8.22 GHz) and 150 MHz (8.61 GHz to 8.76).

Figure 6 presents an intriguing antenna structure featuring a distinctive design incorporating several key elements to optimize its performance. This figure comprises two parts, (a) and (b), each contributing to the understanding of the antenna's construction and its real-world manifestation.

(a) Antenna Structure with Quarter Circle Cut, Ring Slot, Stub, and Slits: In this part of the figure, the detailed schematic representation of the antenna structure. The antenna is composed of several carefully crafted components that play a pivotal role in shaping its functionality. These components include:

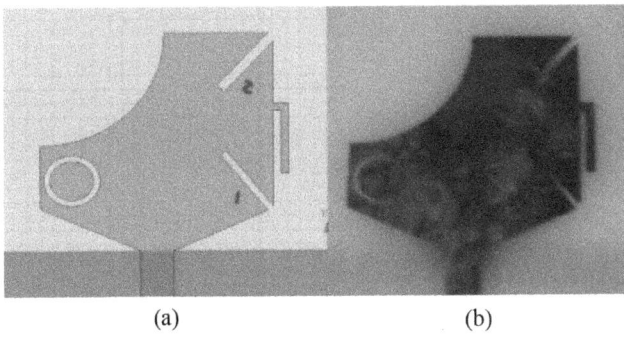

Fig. 6. (a) Antenna structure with quarter circle cut, ring slot, stub &slits (b) Photograph of Fabricated antenna

1. **Quarter Circle Cut:** At the core of the antenna structure is a quarter circle cut, a unique feature that significantly impacts its radiation pattern and resonance properties. The precise dimensions and placement of this cut are crucial to the antenna's performance.
2. **Ring Slot:** Surrounding the central quarter circle cut is a ring slot, a circular opening in the antenna's material. This slot is strategically positioned to enhance the antenna's bandwidth and impedance matching capabilities.
3. **Stub:** A stub, which appears to be an additional protrusion or extension from the antenna structure, is incorporated to fine-tune the antenna's resonance frequency and improve its impedance characteristics.
4. **Slits:** The antenna features slits or narrow openings in its structure, which may serve various purposes, such as tuning the radiation pattern or reducing unwanted reflections.

(b) Photograph of Fabricated Antenna: This part of the figure provides a tangible view of the antenna as it has been realized in the physical world. It is a photograph showcasing the actual fabricated antenna, demonstrating how the theoretical design elements described in part (a) have been translated into a real device. The photograph allows us to observe the physical dimensions, materials, and workmanship that have gone into the antenna's construction.

Together, these two components of Fig. 6 offer a comprehensive understanding of the antenna's structure and appearance, providing valuable insights into the innovative design and the practical realization of this antenna, which may have various applications in the field of wireless communication and antenna technology.

4 Simulation and Results

Figure 5 shows an antenna structure without top slit is placed over radiating patch. And the remaining structure of antenna is kept same as proposed antenna. On these modifications below results were obtained.

For the proposed structure Fig. 5, the simulation result of S11 characteristics or return loss of the above antenna structure is shown in Fig. 7 thereby it is observed two

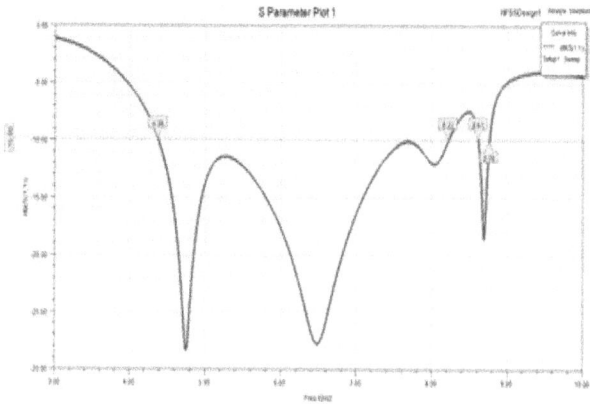

Fig. 7. Simulation result of S11 of Fig. 5.

useful bands of frequencies i.e. the first band is ranging from 4.38 GHz to 8.22 GHz and second band is ranging from 8.61 GHz to 8.68 GHz and their calculated or achieved Bandwidth are 3.84 GHz, 150 MHz.

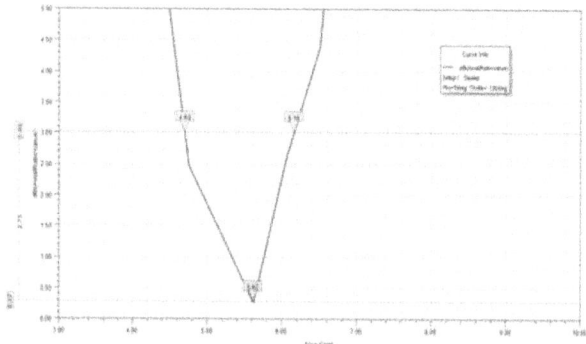

Fig. 8. Simulation result of Axial Ratio of Fig. 5

The simulation outcome of the antenna structure's AR for the antenna depicted in Fig. 7 is presented in Fig. 8. It is noted that a band of frequencies and the frequency range associated with it have AR values between 4.69 GHz and 6.16 GHz that are less than 3 dB, an AR bandwidth of 1.47 GHz, and an accomplished minimum axial ratio of 0.3 dB. The Fig. 1 shows the final proposed antenna structure. Below results were obtained from the modifications.

For the proposed antenna structure, the simulation result of S11 characteristics or return loss is shown in the Fig. 9. It is observed antenna is operating at three bands of frequencies i.e. the first band is ranging from 4.38 GHz to 7.18 GHz and second band is ranging from 7.18 GHz to 7.66 GHz and third band is ranging from 8.21 GHz to 8.76 GHz and their calculated or achieved bandwidths are 2.8 GHz, 1.03 GHz, 160 MHz respectively.

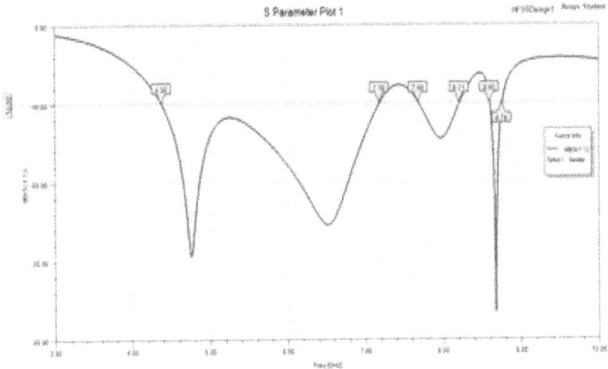

Fig. 9. Simulation result of s11 of Fig. 1

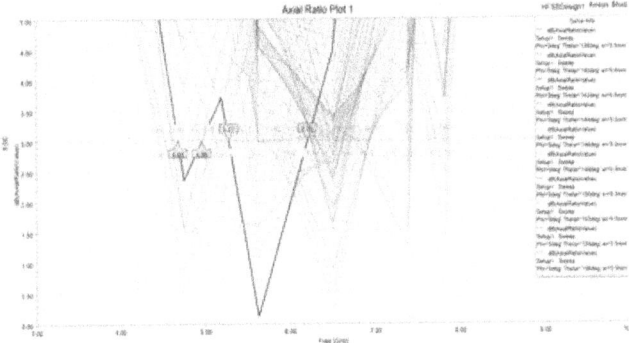

Fig. 10. Simulation result of AR of Fig. 1

For the proposed antenna structure, the simulation result of AR is shown in Fig. 10. It is observed antenna is providing circular polarization in two bands of frequencies with first band ranging from 4.66 GHz to 4.96 GHz. And the second band ranging from 5.27 GHz to 6.20 GHz. The AR bandwidths are 280 MHz and 930 MHz respectively with minimum axial ratio 0.1dB.

5 Conclusions

The work presented in this paper is a new UWB CP antenna. Here on FR4 substrate, the antenna configuration with cutting-off fraction ring on the edge of the patch antenna is purposely designed. To effectively execute CP radiation, an annular-ring slot as well as a reversed L-shaped microstrip are incorporated into the structure. In addition the patch is tapered on lower-side to achieve impedance matching. Radiating patch as well as feed line enthused by a one feed are used to achieve great impedance matching in a broader frequency spectrum. Eventually, the impacts of the important structural specifications on polarisation performance are discussed. This proposed antenna is the best candidate for satelite communication where CP with wide bandwidth is required.

Applications

The antenna's simplicity makes it perfect for usage in portable wireless devices. The primary uses for our antenna are radar-related applications, weather balloons, and earth sensing satellites. As wind and marine radio navigation remain within the antenna design bandwidth range, they could also be employed with it. The proposed filtering antenna can also be a good configuration in applications where space is limited due to its small, compact configuration, wide bandwidth, and strong out of band filtering selectivity.

Future Scope

By including metamaterials and a wider frequency range into the EBG structure, this study can be improved to offer better gain.

References

1. Ma, T.-G., Tseng, C.-H.: An ultrawideband coplanar waveguide-fed tapered ring slot antenna. IEEE Trans. Antennas Propag. **54**(4), 1105–1110 (2006)
2. Low, Z.N., Cheong, J.H., Law, C.L.: Low-cost PCB antenna for UWB applications. IEEE Antennas Wirel. Propag. Lett. **4**, 237–239 (2005)
3. Chung, C.C., Kamarudin, M.R.: Novel design of circular UWB antenna. In: Proceedings of the 2009 Asia Pacific Microwave Conference, pp. 1977–1979, IEEE, Singapore (2009)
4. Row, J.-S.: E design of a squarer-ring slot antenna for circular polarization. IEEE Trans. Antennas Propag. **53**(6), 1967–1972 (2005)
5. Liu, Z.-Q., Zhang, Y.-S., Qian, Z., Han, Z.P., Ni, W.: A novel broad beamwidth conformal antenna on unmanned aerial vehicle. IEEE Antennas Wirel. Propag. Lett. **11**, 196–199 (2012)
6. Collins, G.: Effect of reflecting structures on circularly polarized TV broadcast transmission. IEEE Trans. Broadcast. **25**(1), 5–13 (1979)
7. Kaddour, A.-S., Bories, S., Bellion, A., Delaveaud, C.: 3-Dprinted compact wideband magnetoelectric dipoles with circular polarization. IEEE Antennas Wirel. Propag. Lett. **17**(11), 2026–2030 (2018)
8. Shu, C., Wang, J., Hu, S., et al.: A wideband dual-circularpolarization horn antenna for mmwave wireless communications. IEEE Antennas Wirel. Propag. Lett. **18**(9), 1726–1730 (2019)
9. Xue, R.F., Zhong, S.S.: Survey and progress in circular polarization technology of microstrip antennas. Chin. J. Radio Sci. **17**(4), 331–336 (2002)

Design and Implementing a PCI Express Serdes Block Using HDL

Ravali Meesa[(✉)] and G. Surekha

GRIET, VLSI, Hyderabad, India
meesa.ravali14@gmail.com, surekha537@grietcollege.com

Abstract. This paper introduces a proposal for implementing the Physical Link Layer of PCI Express in accordance with PCI Express 2.0 standards. PCI Express, a high-performance, point-to-point communication protocol, has revolutionized the world of data transfer by offering exceptional bandwidth, making it the go-to choose for a wide array of applications. Its layered architecture, consisting of three distinct layers, facilitates efficient data transfer through packet-based communication between the layers. Widespread use in various applications, including high-speed storage devices, graphics cards, and network cards. The work encompasses the design and verification of multiple physical layer blocks for PCI Express. These blocks are modeled using Verilog at the RTL level and verified using Questasim, a tool from Mentor Graphics.

Keywords: PCI Express · Physical layer (PL) · Physical Coding Sublayer (PCS) · PCI · PCIx

1 Introduction

1.1 Generation Buses

Buses are used to connect several components of a system, including the CPU, main memory, and I/O devices. Buses commonly transport data, address, and control signals [1]. Following is an explanation of how bus generations have developed:

Second-generation buses include Peripheral Component Interconnect (PCI), Advanced Graphics Port (AGP), Serial Parallel Interface (SPI), Peripheral Component Interconnect Extended, and Universal Serial Bus (USB). PCI and PCI-X are sometimes known as Parallel PCI. These second-generation buses stand out for their quick speeds, low power requirements, and economical operation.

USB 3.0, USB 3.1, SATA (Serial Advanced Technology Attachment), and PCIe (Peripheral Component Interconnect Express) are examples of the third generation of buses. [2]. These third-generation buses go from parallel to a more effective serial connection bus and employ a serial lane-based design. These third-generation I/O buses have great performance and are often used in a range of gadgets, including portable electronics, desktop computers, servers, and workstations, for a variety of computing and communication applications [3].

1.2 Evolution PCI Express

PCIe, is a serial expansion bus standard used to link numerous peripheral devices to computers for high-speed data transmission. It serves as a crucial conduit for information to go between these external devices and the internal parts of a computer, such as the RAM and CPU. Data exchange inside a computer system is streamlined via PCIe, which provides standardized interfaces for effective communication [4].

This standard, which is an improved version of PCI-X (Extended), was developed cooperatively by Intel, Dell, HP, and IBM. Depending on how it is implemented on the motherboard, PCIe setups can include 1, 4, 8, 12, 16, or 32 lanes. Notably, PCIe replaces prior bus technologies for computers, including the Accelerated Graphics Port (AGP), PCI-X, and the original PCI. In order to emphasise PCIe's benefits and improvements in the areas of data transmission and peripheral connection, this article does a comparative study, compares it with various other bus standards [5].

The choice of a serial format for interfaces like PCIe is driven by the need to minimize timing skew in comparison to parallel formats. Timing skew, a consequence of finite signal speed, arises when various traces within an interface possess distinct lengths, causing parallel signals from the source to reach their destination at different intervals. This variation in arrival times makes it challenging to correctly capture parallel word bits at the destination. Maximum bandwidth is attained when the speed of the data aligns with the differences in distance between parallel signal channels that are long and short. A few well-known serial interconnects are FireWire, USB, SATA, and RapidIO. To accommodate devices with varying speeds, serial multichannel representation allocates fewer lanes to slower devices, thereby enhancing flexibility in data transfer[1, 5].

2 PCI Express Layers

The Transaction Layer (TL), data link layer, and physical layer are the three levels that the PCI Express uses to specify a layered architecture flow is show in Fig. 1.

2.1 Transaction Layer

Transaction Layer Packets (TLPs) are the name for packets that are entering the TL. These TLPs are made up of a header, data, and, if desired, ECRC fields that provide end-to-end data integrity checks.Outbound TLP traffic is produced within the TL, and inbound TLP traffic is likewise received and handled[6, 8].

TLP are the name for packets that are entering the TL. These TLPs are made up of a header, data, and, if desired, ECRC fields that provide end-to-end data integrity checks. Outbound TLP traffic is produced within the TL, and inbound TLP traffic is likewise received and handled[7, 12].

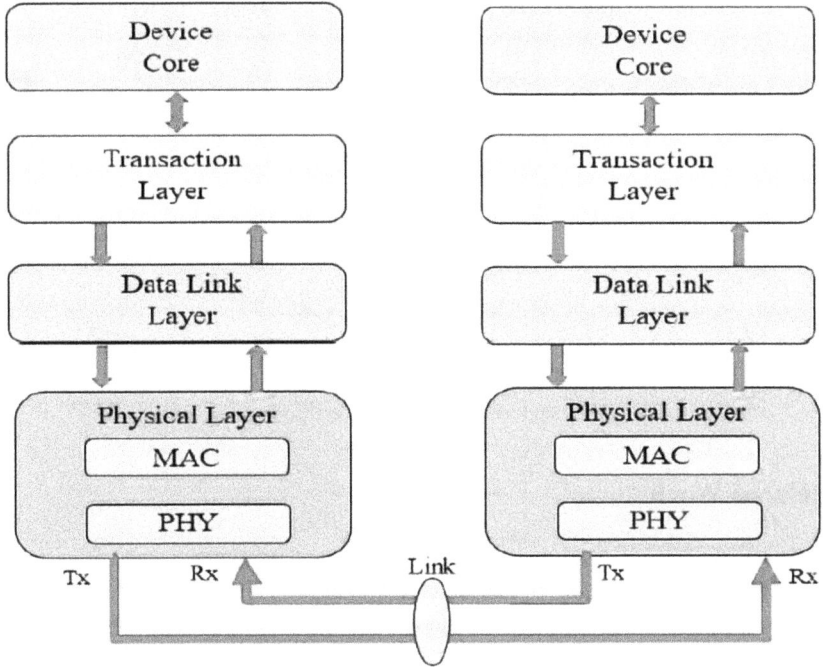

Fig. 1. The transfer of data between PCI Express devices and their layer

2.2 Data Link Layer

Sequence numbers and a link-level CRC (LCRC) are added to incoming TLPs from the TL in the data link layer (DL). These sequence numbers are essential for ensuring that packets are sent successfully. The DL layer is in charge of ensuring efficient power management, as well as facilitating reliable data exchange, error detection via a 32-bit Cyclic Redundancy Code (CRC), implementing an acknowledgment protocol (ACK/NACK signaling), managing retries, initialising and updating flow control credit (FCC), and managing retries. The DL creates and manages data link layer packets (DLLPs) to carry out these tasks[9].

2.3 Physical Layer

PHY, short for Physical Layer Interface, stands for the OSI model's physical layer and is necessary for carrying out physical layer operations in a network. It acts as the interface between any physical media, such as copper wires or fiber optics, and the link layer and MAC (Media Access Control) [10]. The PCS and the Physical Medium Attachment layer (PMA), which together make up the PHY component, serve as a vital interface between data link protocols and the actual physical transmission media in a network architecture as show in Fig. 2 [13].

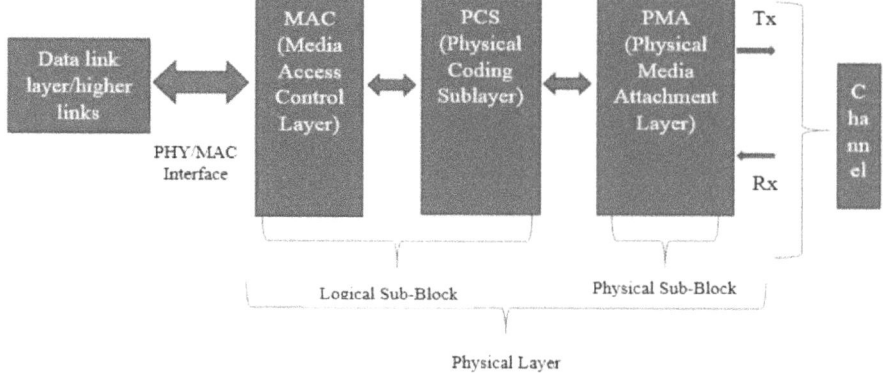

Fig. 2. Block segmentation for PCIe in the physical layer

3 Related Work

The PCIe physical layer, which is in charge of handling data transmission and reception between PCIe devices and the motherboard, includes the Physical Cod-ing Sublayer (PCS) as a fundamental component. Within the logical and electrical building blocks of the PCIe physical layer, the PCS is a crucial element[11, 14]. The total 6 block flow of the signal/Data is show in Fig. 10 and block diagram result are show in Fig. 3.

Fig. 3. Block diagram of PCIe Physical coding Sub-Layer

3.1 Scrambler

The scrambler is a vital component of the PCS of communication protocols like PCIe for enhancing data integrity and guaranteeing accurate information delivery [15]. Long sequences of identical bits are avoided by the scrambler by adding a regulated amount of unpredictability to the data stream. Such sequences may make it difficult to maintain synchronization throughout transmission and reception, which might affect how precisely the clock signal is extracted at the receiver's end. With the scrambler in place, the data stream becomes more balanced and varied, enabling a higher degree of resilience against electromagnetic interference and signal distortion.

The scrambler is essential to the PCIe ecosystem's continued robust and high-performance data transfer between linked devices. It makes an important contribution to the overall efficacy and dependability of the PCIe standard, making it an essential element of modern computer systems and other applications that use PCIe for trustworthy and quick data transmission Fig. 4.

3.2 Descrambler

Plays an important part in data transfer by reversing the scrambling process. The descrambler ensures that the received data is synchronized and free of the effects of scrambling by removing the added randomness, preserving data integrity and preventing the appearance of extended sequences of identical bits. This synchronization and data restoration are critical for proper data recovery because they ensure that information is sent accurately and reliably across devices connected over the PCIe link Fig. 9.

3.3 8b/10b Encoder

The 8b/10b encoding scheme is a fundamental component of the PCIe standard, used to ensure reliable and efficient data transmission. 8b/10b Encoder: In PCIe, the 8b/10b encoder is responsible for converting 8-bit data words into 10-bit symbols using "look up tables" before transmission. This encoding process serves several crucial purposes. Firstly, it ensures a balanced number of 0s and 1s in the data stream, which aids in maintaining DC balance. Maintaining DC balance is essential to prevent long sequences of 0s or 1s that could cause synchronization issues or disrupt signal integrity. Secondly, it provides an element of error detection; the 8b/10b code has built-in properties that enable the receiver to identify and correct errors in the data stream. Thirdly, the 8b/10b encoding facilitates clock recovery, helping the receiver extract the clock signal from the received data Fig. 5.

3.4 8b/10b Decoder

On the receiving end, the 8b/10b decoder performs the reverse process, converting the 10-bit symbols back into the original 8-bit data words. This decoding process restores the original data while also checking for and correcting any errors that might have occurred during transmission. The 8b/10b decoder plays a crucial role in recovering the data accurately and ensuring data integrity.

In PCIe and other high-speed communication standards, 8b/10b encoding and decoding are vital for maintaining reliable and efficient data transmission. They help prevent data errors, facilitate clock recovery, and improve signal integrity, ensuring that data is successfully exchanged between PCIe devices and the motherboard with a high degree of accuracy and performance Fig. 8.

3.5 PISO (Parallel-In Serial-Out)

PISO is a mechanism used in the PCIe PCS block to convert parallel data into a serial format. It is essential for taking data from the parallel data bus within the PCIe device and converting it into a serial bit stream, which is suitable for high-speed transmission over the PCIe link. PISO is particularly useful for efficiently transmitting data between devices and the PCIe interface, ensuring it's appropriately formatted for the PCIe communication standards Fig. 6.

3.6 SIPO (Serial-In Parallel-Out)

SIPO, on the other hand, is responsible for converting the serial data received over the PCIe link back into parallel data. This is necessary on the receiving end to extract and decode the data correctly. SIPO takes the serial bit stream and converts it into parallel data words that can be processed by the PCIe device Fig. 7.

4 Result

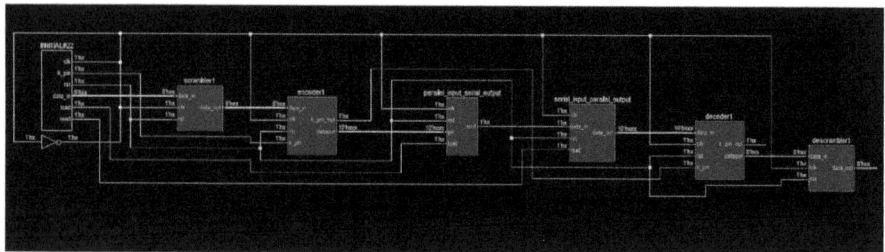

Fig. 4. Synthesize Of PCS Block

The input signal in Fig. 10 is initially processed in the scrambler block, which is the first block. The signal is then converted based on the particular logic of each block that follows. Accurate replication of the original input signal at the receiver side is essential for the PCIe PCS to work properly.

Design and Implementing a PCI Express Serdes Block Using HDL   297

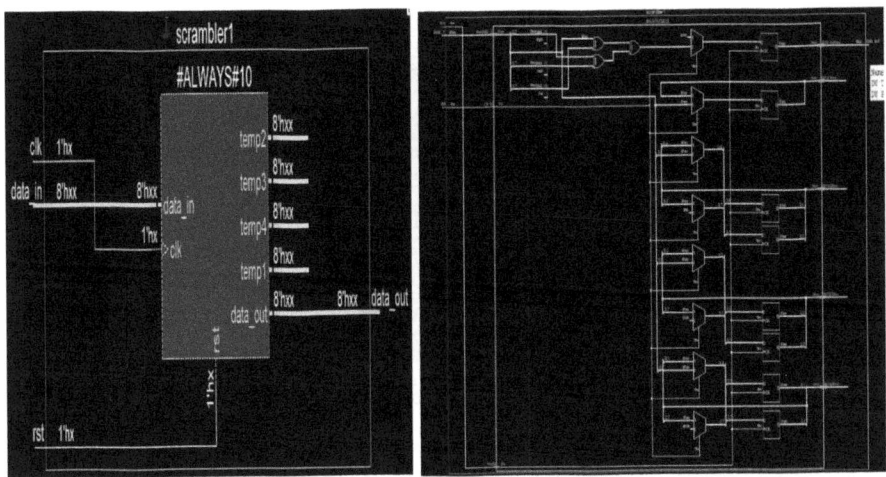

Fig. 5. Block Diagram Of Scrambler and Synthesis Of Scrambler.

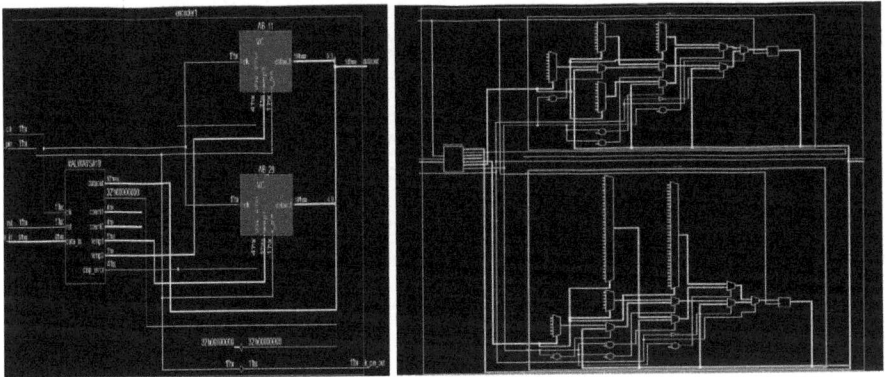

Fig. 6. Block Diagram For Encoder and Synthesis Of Encoder

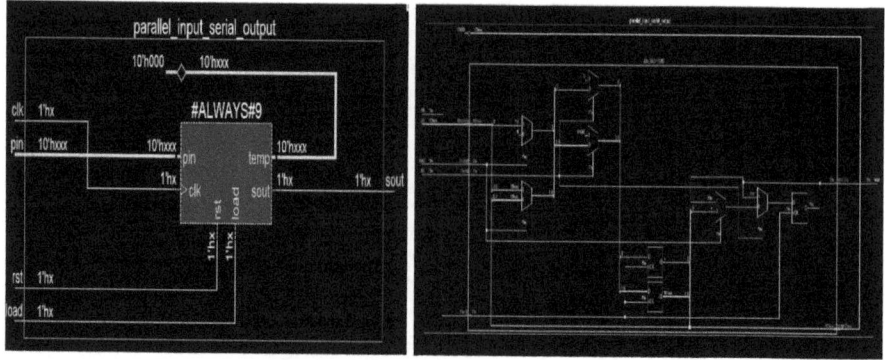

Fig. 7. Parallel In Serial Out Block and Synthesis Of PISO

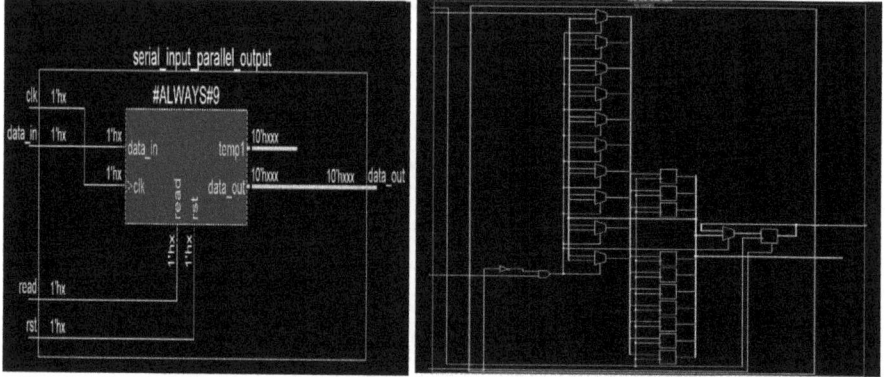

Fig. 8. SIPO Block and Serial In and Parallel Out Synthesis

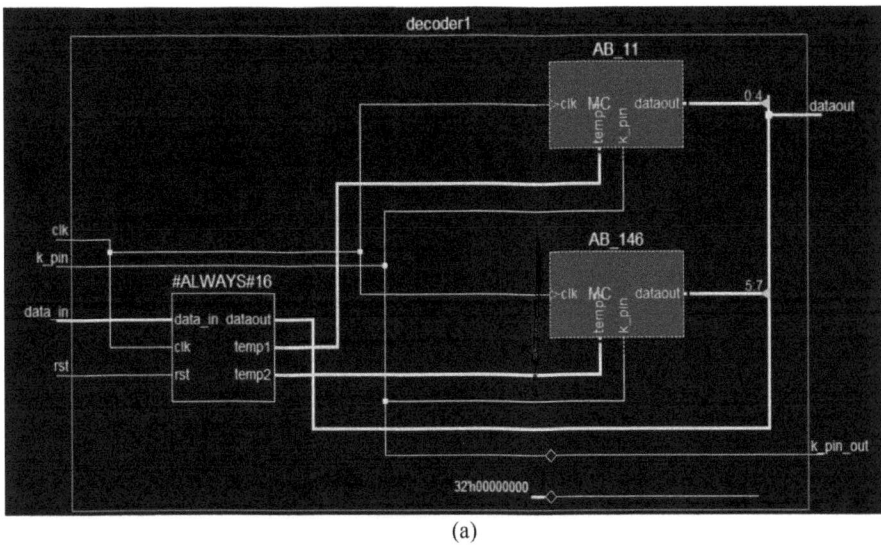

(a)

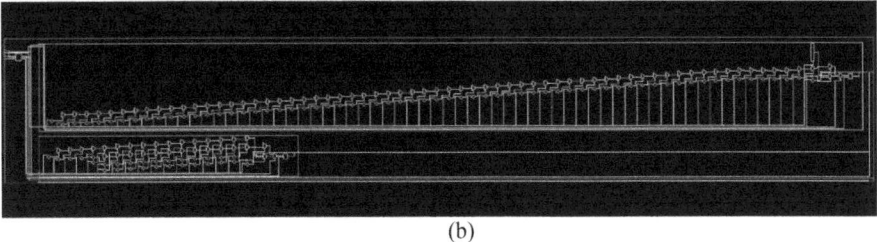

(b)

Fig. 9. (a) Decoder Block. (b)Synthesis of Decoder

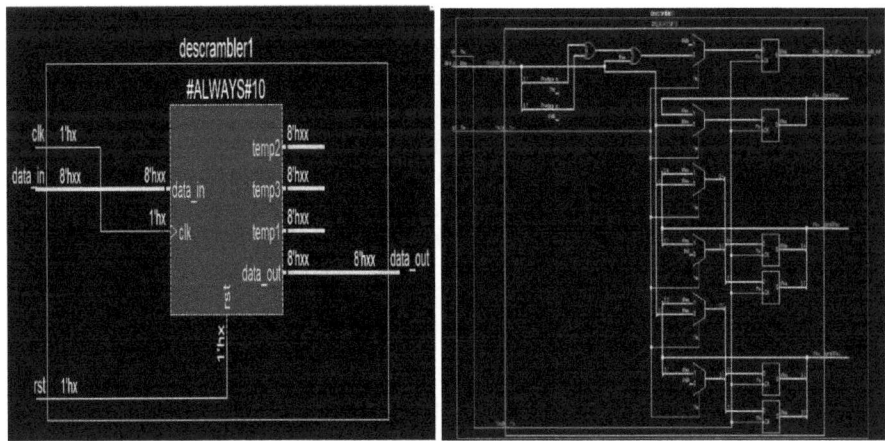

Fig. 10. (a) Block For Descrambler. (b) Synthesis of Descrambler

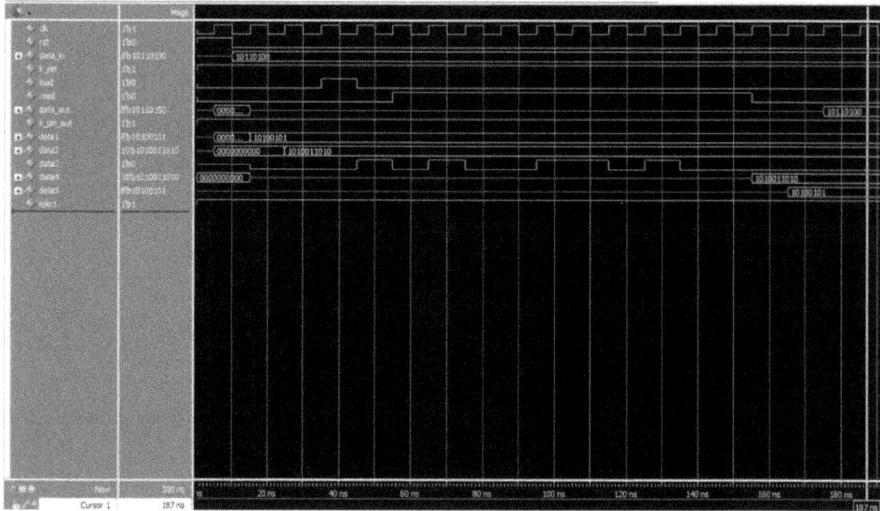

Fig. 11. Physical Coding Sublayer Total Transmission and Receiving Process Waveform

5 Conclusion

In this paper, the PCIe PCS block was meticulously examined and simulated using Questasim Tool. The research encompassed all six essential components of the PCS block: scrambler, encoder, PISO, SIPO, decoder, and descrambler. Through rigorous simulation and verification processes, it was demonstrated that the time delay for one packet to traverse from the transmitter to the receiver was remarkably low, specifically clocking in at 172 ns. This efficiency was achieved through a streamlined design approach, leveraging the simultaneous operation of key elements such as the scrambler and encoder during transmission and the decoder and descrambler during reception, all synchronized within a single clock cycle. The total power required to drive 0.068 w. By providing detailed explanations of the underlying processes and mechanisms employed in the scrambler, encoder, PISO, SIPO, decoder, and descrambler, this research has contributed valuable insights to the optimization of PCIe communication. These results hold promising implications for the future development of high-speed data transfer systems, emphasizing the importance of efficient design methodologies and robust simulations in achieving minimal time delays and ensuring reliable data transmission between devices.

References

1. Li, A.: Evaluating modern gpu interconnect: Pcie, nvlink, nv-sli, nvswitch and gpudirect. IEEE Trans. Parallel Distrib. Syst. **31**(1), 94–110 (2019)
2. Tembhare, A.R., Patil, P.B.: Design & implementation of PCI Express Bus Physical layer using VHDL. Int. J. Recent Innov. Trends Comput. Commun. **2**, 1883–1886 (2014)
3. Prasad, R.A., Kulkarni, M.: Design and verification of phy interface for pcie gen 3.0 and usb gen 3.1 using UVM methodology. Int. Res. J. Eng. Technol. (IRJET) (2017)
4. Specification, Base. PCI Express® Base Specification Revision 3.0 (2002)

5. Verma, A., Dahiya, P.K.: PCIe BUS: a state-of-the-art-review. IOSR J. VLSI Signal Proces. (IOSR-JVSP) **7**, 24–28 (2017)
6. Rangel-Patiño, F.E., et al.: PCIe Gen5 physical layer equalization tuning by using K-means clustering and gaussian process regression modeling in industrial post-silicon validation. In: 2023 IEEE MTT-S International Conference on Numerical Electromagnetic and Multiphysics Modeling and Optimization (NEMO), pp. 162–165. IEEE (2023)
7. Rohilla, G., Mathur, D., Ghanekar, U.: Functional verification of MAC-PHY layer of PCI express Gen5. 0 with PIPE interface using UVM. In: 2020 In-ternational Conference for Emerging Technology (INCET), pp. 1–5. IEEE (2020)
8. Vaidya, V.N., Ingale, V., Gokhale, A.: Development of Verifica-tion IP of Physical Layer of PCIe. In: 2022 IEEE 3rd Global Conference for Advance-ment in Technology (GCAT), pp. 1–5. IEEE (2022)
9. Liang, J.: A study of DTN for reliable data delivery from space station to ground station. Ph.D diss., Lamar University-Beaumont (2023)
10. Miryala, D.K.: Implementation of PCS of Physical Layer for PCI Express. Ph.D diss. (2009)
11. Du, L., Zhang, Z., Tong, J., Wang, C., Wang, W.: Research on XDMA high-speed data transmission architecture based on PCIe. In: 2020 IEEE 6th International Conference on Computer and Communications (ICCC), pp. 1783–1787. IEEE (2020)
12. Johansen, A.K.: Fast Multi-GPU communication over PCI Express Bench-marking PCIe transport with the NVIDIA Collective Communications Library (NCCL) using legacy GPUs. Master's thesis (2023)
13. Hukare, S., Vyas, V., Agrawal, V.: Design and simulation of physical layer of peripheral component interconnect express (PCIe) protocol. In: 2023 4th In-ternational Conference for Emerging Technology (INCET), pp. 1–4. IEEE (2023)
14. Dong, L.-L., et al.: Research on verification method of PCIe IP core based on programmable logic. In: International Symposium on Software Reliability, Industrial Safety, Cyber Security and Physical Protection for Nuclear Power Plant, pp. 290–301. Singapore: Springer Nature Singapore (2023)
15. Nakamura, H., Takayama, H., Yamaguchi, Y., Boku, T.: Thorough analysis of PCIe Gen3 communication. In: 2017 International Conference on ReConFigurable Computing and FPGAs (ReConFig), pp. 1–6. IEEE (2017)

Development and Realization of an FIR Filter Utilizing an Innovative RNS Form with a Dual Modular Set

Mentam Sunaina[✉] and G. L. Sumalata

GRIET, ECE, Hyderabad, India
sunainagrace.123@gmail.com

Abstract. Distributed Arithmetic (DA) serves as a potent tool in DSP for the efficient execution of diverse algorithms. This paper introduces an enhanced implementation of a Finite Impulse Response (FIR) filter based on Distributed Arithmetic (DA) utilizing a new modular set of Residue Number System (RNS) approach. The proposed approach demonstrates notable reductions in computational complexity and improved performance with a reduced delay of 17% when compared to traditional FIR filters. Unlike any other traditional RNS method, this paper offers 2 moduli set of RNS system to make it even more simple to calculate and execute. Experimental findings underscore the effectiveness of this approach in terms of filter performance, resource utilization, and power efficiency. Consequently, this optimized DA-based FIR filter utilizing the RNS method stands as a promising solution for efficient and high-performance filtering applications across various domains, such as digital signal processing and communication systems.

Keywords: Finite Impulse Response Filter · Residue Number System · Distributed Arithmetic · Digital Signal Processing

1 Introduction

Digital Signal Processing (DSP) systems have brought about significant advancements across a wide range of fields, spanning telecommunications, image and video processing, and numerous others. The Distributed Arithmetic (DA) algorithm is a frequently employed method in realizing Finite Impulse Response (FIR) Filters in DSP systems [1]. This technique enhances computational efficiency by substituting resource-intensive multiplication operations with a blend of addition and look-up table operations [2]. Meanwhile, designing of Distributed Arithmetic based FIR filter using RNS method is a quite known [3].

RNS system has gained its strength over the last decades, however the only hard factor is its conversions and picking the moduli set for the approach [10].

To overcome the complexity of multiple modular set values, this paper proposes a new 2 moduli set RNS form, to design an FIR filter. This paper highlights the simplest form of both forward and reverse conversions of RNS system to design an FIR filter.

The paper is structured as follows: 1. Introduction, 2. Exploring DA-Based FIR Filters using RNS method, 3. The Proposed Methodology, 6. Forward Conversion Process, 7. Reverse Conversion Technique, 8. Analysis of Simulation Results, 9. Conclusion and 10. Reference.

2 Exploring DA-Based FIR Filter Using RNS Method

Distributed Arithmetic based FIR filter using RNS method relies on inner product computations, effectively eliminating the recurring use of multiplication operations [4]. Let's delve into its mathematical formulation.

$$Y = \left| \sum_{n=0}^{N-1} \left[\sum_{k=0}^{K-1} d_k b_{kn} \right] 2^n \right|_{mi} \quad (1)$$

In this context, mi refers to the modular set of the RNS system, which is represented as $mi = [m1, m2, m3, \ldots mn]$. The choice of this modular set depends on the specific number of tap filters employed in the system.

Forward Conversion
The forward conversion process involves determining the remainder obtained when the number is divided by the moduli in the selected residue set [9]. The set of the smallest remainders among these divisions constitutes the RNS representation of the given number.

Example. Number: 15.
Module set: {8, 9, 7}.

```
8 ) 15 ( 1         9 ) 15 ( 1         7 ) 15 ( 2
    8                  9                  14
  -------            -------            -------
    7                  6                  1
  -------            -------            -------
```

So, the RNS form of 15 with respect to the module set {8, 9, 7} is {7, 6, 1}.

Reverse Conversion
The Reverse Conversion from RNS form employs a mathematical technique known as the Chinese Remainder Theorem. This theorem offers a solution to a system of congruence, facilitating the conversion process [6].

$$X = \left| \sum_{i=1}^{I} N_i . N_i^{-1} . y_i \right|_M \quad (2)$$

where, i represents the number of moduli values in the set

$$M = m_1 . m_2 . m_3 \quad (3)$$

$$N_i = M \div (m_i) \qquad (4)$$

And N_i^{-1} is the modular multiplicative inverse of N_i and can be obtained by satisfying the below equation

$$(N_i . N_i^{-1}) \% m_i = 1 \qquad (5)$$

3 Proposed Method

In this paper, Distributed Arithmetic based FIR filter using the RNS moduli set $\{2^n, 2^{pn} - 1\}$ is used, where n is the bit length and p is a natural number. Unlike any other RNS set, this module set only has 2 modules which make it way simpler in calculation and execution purpose. The design has been executed and synthesized within Xilinx Integrated Synthesis Environment using Artix-7 which uses 13% lesser power and 27% lesser delay compared to the existing architectures.

For a 4-tap FIR filter, the input values are taken as X {14, 19, 17, 15} and the Filter coefficients denoted as D {12, 18, 16, 13}. As it's a 4-tap filter, and the natural number p is taken as 2. So, the modular set will be m {16, 255}.

The initial step involves transforming the input data and filter coefficient data into residue form, employing specific moduli values shown in Tables 1 and 2 respectively. Subsequently, the residues are individually translated into binary representation, and they are then transmitted to a DA filter where the primary design process takes place. Figure no. 1 represents the design of 2 modular RNS set.

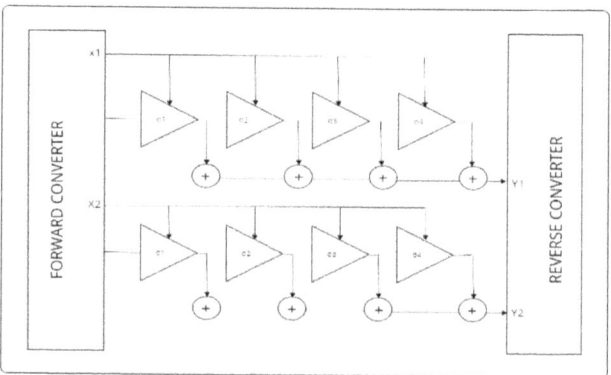

Fig. 1. Proposed FIR filter using two modular RNS set

3.1 Forward Conversion

Table 1. Conversion of input signals into Residue form

Input	m = 16	m = 255
14	14	14
19	3	19
17	1	17
15	15	15

Hence, the RNS input data and the filter coefficients are directed to the DA filter (Fig. 1), the filter coefficients are computed in accordance with the provided residue values, facilitating the design of an FIR filter. This design process utilizes the residue values of both the input data and the filter coefficients.

$$Y = \sum_{k=1}^{K} d_k x_k \tag{6}$$

$$Y_{16} = |x_1 d_1 + x_2 d_2 + x_3 d_3 + x_4 d_4|_{16} \tag{7}$$

$$Y_{16} = |14(12) + 3(2) + 1(0) + 15(13)|_{16}$$

$$Y_{16} = |369|_{16}$$

$$Y_{16} = 1$$

Similarly, $Y_{255} = 212$
Now the output set can be written as Y {1, 212}

3.2 Reverse Conversion

The Reverse conversion of an RNS system employs Chinese Remainder Theorem.

$$M = m_1 * m_2$$

$$M = 16 * 255$$

$$M = 4080$$

$$M_1 = \frac{M}{m_1} = \frac{4080}{16} = 255$$

Table 2. LUT entries

t_{1n}	t_{2n}	t_{3n}	t_{4n}	Entry values	m = 16	m = 255
0	0	0	0	0	0	0
0	0	0	1	$d_1 = 12$	12	12
0	0	1	0	$d_2 = 18$	2	18
0	0	1	1	$d_2 + d_1 = 7 + 3 = 10$	10	10
0	1	0	0	$d_3 = 16$	0	16
0	1	0	1	$d_3 + d_1 = 8 + 3 = 11$	11	11
0	1	1	0	$d_3 + d_2 = 8 + 7 = 15$	15	15
0	1	1	1	$d_3 + d_2 + d_1 = 8 + 7 + 3 = 18$	2	18
1	0	0	0	$d_4 = 13$	13	13
1	0	0	1	$d_4 + d_1 = 9 + 3 = 12$	12	12
1	0	1	0	$d_4 + d_2 = 9 + 7 = 16$	0	16
1	0	1	1	$d_4 + d_2 + d_1 = 9 + 7 + 3 = 19$	3	19
1	1	0	0	$d_4 + d_3 = 9 + 8 = 17$	1	17
1	1	0	1	$d_4 + d_3 + d_1 = 9 + 8 + 3 = 20$	4	20
1	1	1	0	$d_4 + d_3 + d_2 = 9 + 8 + 7 = 24$	8	14
1	1	1	1	$d_4 + d_3 + d_2 + d_1 = 9 + 8 + 7 + 3 = 27$	11	17

$$M_2 = \frac{M}{m_2} = \frac{4080}{255} = 16$$

In order to find the inverse value of each module, Hit and Check method is used.

$$(M_i * M_i^{-1})\%m_i = 1$$

Here, i denotes respective module.

$$(M_1 * M_1^{-1})\%m_1 = 1$$

$$(255 * 15)\%16 = 1$$

$$(M_2 * M_2^{-1})\%m_2 = 1$$

$$(16 * 16)\%255 = 1$$

$$M_1 = 255; M_1^{-1} = 15$$

$$M_2 = 16; M_2^{-1} = 16$$

The final output can we found as

$$Y = \left|\left(M_1 * M_1^{-1} * Y_{16}\right) + \left(M_2 * M_2^{-1} * Y_{255}\right)\right|_M \tag{8}$$

$$Y = |(255 * 15 * 14) + (16 * 16 * 158)|_{4080}$$

$$Y = |(53550 + 40448)|_{4080}$$

$$Y = |93998|_{4080}$$

$$Y = 158$$

4 Simulation Results

Table 3. Performance comparison

Design	Total Delay (ns)	Area (μm^2)	ADP ($mm^2 ns$)	Power(mw)	PDP (pJ)
Mohanty et al. (2017)	15.39	85262	0.131	3.2548	50.2548
Kamal et al. (2014)	15.30	6271.6	0.096	4.629	70.8237
Praveen et al. (2020)	12	41946	0.058	3.2548	45.5672
Proposed design	08.94	3586	0.0320	2.8921	25.8309

The performance and hardware intricacy of the design presented in this paper are assessed through a comparative analysis against existing architectural models. The filter design is executed on the Artix-7 Field Programmable Gate Array, belonging to the Xilinx family. This cost-effective and user-friendly device offers efficient implementation capabilities, benefitting from the 28 nm technology DSP block within the Artix-7 family for high-efficiency algorithm execution.

By implementing the proposed design, it becomes evident that crafting a 4-tap filter is considerably simplified, not only by eliminating the concerns related to carries as found in conventional Binary systems but also by utilizing a more straight forward modular set. As observed in Table 3, the data clearly indicates that the proposed design consumes 43% less power compared to previous work [1] and is 27% less Area than the existing work [3]. Furthermore, the overall delay associated with the proposed approach is notably reduced by 17% when compared to the delays seen in all other architectures detailed in Table 3. The area delay product and Power Delay Product also exhibit notably lower values (Fig. 2, 3 and 4).

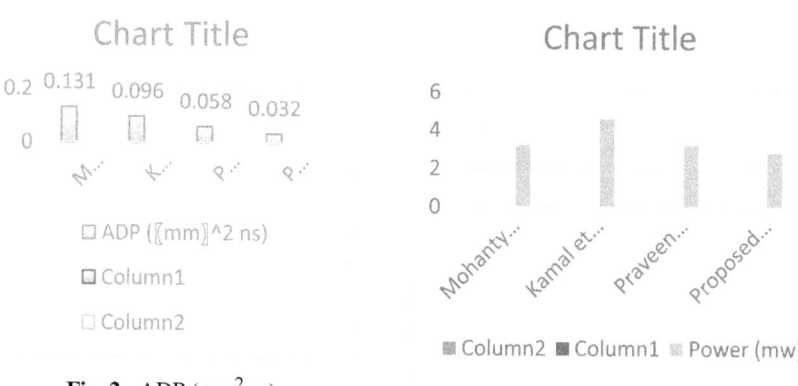

Fig. 2. ADP ($mm^2 ns$)

Fig. 3. Power (mw)

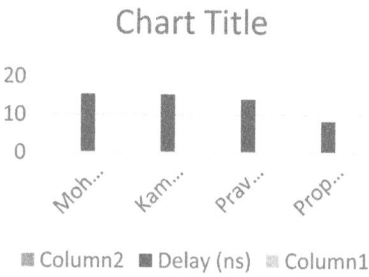

Fig. 4. Critical Path delay (ns)

5 Conclusion

This paper presents a streamlined form of a DA-based FIR Filter, leveraging the RNS method. Instead of employing lengthy binary numbers or intricate modular sets, this approach represents numbers in their simplest RNS form, which is subsequently converted into binary for implementation purposes. The primary objective of reducing overall delay is effectively realized through this method, with a 17% reduction in delay when compared to existing methods. Given RNS's ability to perform fast and parallel computations, it emerges as a promising alternative to conventional FIR filters. The only drawback of the RNS system is the need for converters, which may introduce some complexity. However, the use of Chinese Remainder Theorem (CRT) simplifies these conversions, making them more accessible. Despite this limitation, RNS is well-suited for many DSP applications due to its capability to minimize power consumption and reduce delay.

References

1. Akhter, S., Kumar, S., Bareja, D.: Design and analysis of distributed arithmetic based FIR filter. In: 2018 International Conference on Advances in Computing, Communication Control and Networking (ICACCCN), pp. 721–726. IEEE (2018)
2. Balaji, M., Padmaja, N.: High-speed DSP pipelining and retiming techniques for distributed-arithmetic RNS-based FIR filter design. WSEAS Trans. Syst. Control **17**, 549–556 (2022)
3. Balaji, M., Padmaja, N.: Distributed Arithmetic RNS-based FIR Filter Design using Pipelining and Retiming Methods for High-Speed DSP Systems (2022)
4. Sridevi, N., Jamal, K., Mannem, K.: Implementation of error correction techniques in memory applications. In: 2021 5th International Conference on Computing Methodologies and Communication (ICCMC), pp. 586–595. IEEE (2021)
5. Jameii, S.M., Taghipour, S., Azad, M.: Using both binary and residue representations for achieving fast converters in RNS (2011)
6. Cao, B., Chang, C.H., Srikanthan, T.: An efficient reverse converter for the 4-moduli set 2/sup n/-1, 2/sup n/, 2/sup n/+ 1, 2/sup 2n/+ 1 based on the new Chinese remainder theorem. IEEE Trans. Circ. Syst. I: Fund. Theory Appl. **50**(10), 1296–1303 (2003)
7. Jamal, K., Chari, K.M., Srihari, P.: Test pattern generation using thermometer code counter in TPC technique for BIST implementation. Microprocess. Microsyst. **71**, 102890 (2019)
8. Garner, H.L.: The residue number system. In Papers Presented at the March 3–5, 1959, Western Joint Computer Conference, pp. 146–153 (1959)
9. Jenkins, W., Leon, B.: The use of residue number systems in the design of finite impulse response digital filters. IEEE Trans. Circ. Syst. **24**(4), 191–201 (1977)
10. Albicocco, P., Cardarilli, G.C., Nannarelli, A., Re, M.: Twenty years of research on RNS for DSP: lessons learned and future perspectives. In: 2014 International Symposium on Integrated Circuits (ISIC), pp. 436–439. IEEE (2014)
11. Mohan, P.A.: Residue Number Systems: Algorithms and Architectures. Springer Science & Business Media (2021)
12. Meher, P.K., Chandrasekaran, S., Amira, A.: FPGA realization of FIR filters by efficient and flexible systolization using distributed arithmetic. IEEE Trans. Signal Process. **56**(7), 3009–3017 (2008)
13. Longa, P., Miri, A.: Area-efficient FIR filter design on FPGAs using distributed arithmetic. In: 2006 IEEE International Symposium on Signal Processing and Information Technology, pp. 248–252. IEEE (2006)

Attack Detection in Smart Home IoT Networks: A Survey on Challenges, Methods and Analysis

M. Vinay Kuma Rreddy[1(✉)], Amit Lathigara[2], and Muthangi Kantha Reddy[3]

[1] RK University, Gujarat, India
muthyalavinayreddy@gmail.com
[2] Computer Engineering, RK University, Gujarat, India
amit.lathigara@rku.ac.in
[3] Shri Vishnu Engineering College for Women, Andhra Pradesh, India

Abstract. The ubiquity of Internet of Things (IoT) gadgets in smart homes has transformed our interactions with our living environments by providing never-before-seen levels of automation and convenience. However, because IoT devices are becoming possible targets for malicious attacks, this broad connectivity also poses serious security risks. Ensuring the privacy, safety, and integrity of smart home ecosystems requires prompt detection and mitigation of these threats. Data from IoT devices is gathered, pre-processed, feature engineered, labelled, and divided into training, validation, and testing sets as part of a machine learning method to threat detection in smart home IoT networks. The process of choosing and training appropriate machine learning models—which can include everything from classification techniques to anomaly detection algorithms—is crucial. Methods are surveyed to review different types of cyber-attacks, such as denial-of-service (DoS), distributed denial-of-service (DDoS), probing, user-to-root (U2R), remote-to-local (R2L), botnet attack, spoofing, and man-in-the-middle (MITM) attacks. To protect user information, data anonymization and encryption techniques are used with privacy considerations. Another strategy that has been put forth aims to improve the security of IoT networks in smart homes by providing a strong defence against new threats and equipping users with the information and resources they need to keep their connected world safe. To provide a full overview of the numerous advancements in this field, a list of all works published in the literature to date is incorporated. Lastly, the study also includes suggestions for future research directions.

Keywords: Smart Home · IoT (Internet of Things) · Attack Detection · Machine Learning · Anomaly Detection · Cybersecurity · Cyber attacks

1 Introduction

1.1 Background

Smart homes are among the most well-known uses of the Internet of Things (IoT), which has brought about an era of never-before-seen convenience and automation in our daily lives. A variety of networked gadgets, from voice-activated assistants and security cameras to lighting controls and thermostats, work together to create an intelligent living environment in a typical smart home. Smart homes are becoming more vulnerable to hostile cyberattacks due to their interconnection, which simultaneously brings about an intricate web of vulnerabilities and improves comfort and energy efficiency. Protecting the integrity, safety, and privacy of the inhabitants as well as their data depends critically on the security of these intricate ecosystems. A key component of this effort is attack detection in smart home IoT networks. To detect and react to malicious activity in real-time, it entails the ongoing monitoring and analysis of network traffic, device interactions, and device behaviour. Sophisticated technologies must be integrated to achieve successful attack detection, and machine learning is becoming a potent tool in this field. Protecting the integrity, safety, and privacy of the inhabitants as well as their data depends critically on the security of these intricate ecosystems [1]. A key component of this effort is attack detection in smart home IoT networks. To detect and react to malicious activity in real-time, it entails the ongoing monitoring and analysis of network traffic, device interactions, and device behavior. Sophisticated technologies must be integrated to achieve successful attack detection, and machine learning is becoming a potent tool in this field. A key component of this survey is privacy and regulatory compliance, which guarantees that user data protection is given top priority throughout the attack detection process. Furthermore, user awareness and education are emphasized as crucial elements of a comprehensive security plan, enabling locals to actively take part in upholding a safe smart home environment. In a time when lines separating virtual and real worlds are becoming increasingly blurred, smart home security becomes essential. The proposed research will enable IoT network administrators and owners of smart homes to strengthen their defences against new threats and reap the benefits of a connected home with assurance and comfort.

The standardization of security protocols and practices among various IoT devices represents a significant research gap [2]. Standardized security frameworks that can be widely implemented are desperately needed, as a wide range of manufacturers are producing devices with differing degrees of security. Through the reduction of vulnerabilities brought about by device diversity, research aimed at establishing and promoting such standards would help to create a more cohesive and secure IoT landscape. The area of user-centric security solutions for smart homes is another noteworthy research gap. There is a need to look more closely at the behavioral and psychological aspects of how people interact with smart devices, even though many studies concentrate on the technical aspects of IoT security. Designing more user-friendly and efficient security solutions can benefit from an understanding of users' perceptions of, and reactions to, security measures as well as their attitudes toward privacy. More user-friendly and intuitive security measures may result from research that closes this gap.

1.2 Types of Smart Home Attacks

The increasing interconnectedness of IoT devices and the growing dependence on digital technologies in daily life make smart homes vulnerable to various cyberattacks. Typical smart home attack types include the following:

Unauthorized Access: Brute Force Attacks: Attackers try a variety of username and password combinations until they discover the right one in an effort to access smart home devices.

Default Credentials: If homeowners don't change the default usernames and passwords that some Internet of Things devices come with, hackers might take advantage of them.

Device Vulnerabilities: Zero-Day Exploits: Vulnerabilities in IoT device firmware or software that have not yet been fixed by the manufacturer may be found and exploited by attackers. Firmware Tampering: In order to take control of or interfere with the operation of IoT devices, malevolent actors may manipulate their firmware.

Malware: IoT Malware: Smart home devices can become infected with malware made especially for Internet of Things devices, which can then turn them into bots that take part in botnet attacks. Ransomware: Data from smart home devices may be encrypted by attackers, who then demand a ransom to unlock the device, making it unusable until the ransom is paid.

Man-in-the-Middle (MitM) Attacks: Eavesdropping: Attackers monitor and intercept device-to-device communication in an attempt to obtain private information or insert nefarious commands. Session Hijacking: When a session between devices is hijacked by malicious actors, they can manipulate or listen in on the conversation.

Phishing: Phishing Emails: Attackers trick homeowners into disclosing login information or clicking on malicious links that jeopardize the security of their smart homes by sending them misleading emails or messages.

Denial of Service (DoS) and Distributed Denial of Service (DDoS) Attacks: DoS Attacks: Attackers overwhelm a system or network with excessive traffic, making it unusable or crashing it. DDoS Attacks: A target device or network is overloaded by several compromised devices, rendering it inaccessible to authorized users.

Voice Assistant Exploits: Voice Command Spoofing: Voice-activated smart devices can be tricked by attackers using voice recordings or other techniques, which could allow them to access the device without authorization. Eavesdropping: Voice assistants and smart speakers may be susceptible to illegal users listening in on them.

Physical Attacks: Device Theft: Unauthorized access to data and device control are potential outcomes of IoT device theft. Hardware Manipulation: Attackers may physically alter gadgets in an effort to take over or obtain private data.

IoT Network Attacks: Network Sniffing: To learn more about how devices communicate with one another, attackers on a local network intercept and examine data packets. Traffic Analysis: Network traffic can be used by malicious actors to obtain data about user behavior and device usage patterns.

Social Engineering: Impersonation: In order to deceive homeowners into granting access to their smart home systems, attackers may assume the identity of authorized users or service providers. Manipulating Users: persuading users to do security-compromising activities, like sharing private information or turning off security features.

To protect the integrity, privacy, and functionality of smart home environments, homeowners and IoT device manufacturers must have a thorough understanding of these types of smart home attacks and implement strong security measures.

1.3 Major Challenges of Smart Home Attacks

The intricacy and variety of linked devices in smart homes and IoT networks create many obstacles for security professionals to overcome. Among the principal difficulties are:

- Device Diversity: A variety of devices from various manufacturers are included in smart homes, each with unique security features and vulnerabilities. It's difficult to secure and manage this diverse ecosystem [3].
- Lack of Standardization: Inconsistencies in security measures and unaddressed vulnerabilities can result from a lack of standardization in security protocols and practices amongst IoT devices.
- Weak Authorization and Authentication: A lot of Internet of Things (IoT) devices have weak or default authentication systems, which leaves them open to brute force attacks and unauthorized access.
- Firmware Updates: It can be difficult to guarantee that every device is consistently updated with the most recent firmware patches, particularly when certain devices do not have automated update systems in place.
- Resource Constraints: IoT devices frequently have limited computational resources, which makes it difficult to implement strong security measures without negatively impacting device performance [4]. This is known as resource constraints.
- Privacy Issues: Data collection by Internet of Things devices may give rise to privacy issues. It's always difficult to strike a balance between user privacy and data collection for functionality.
- Network security: It's critical to protect device-to-central hub or cloud server communication. The network as a whole may be compromised by shoddy encryption or unsafe communication methods.
- Physical Security: Unauthorized access or data breaches can result from physical tampering with IoT devices. It can be difficult to ensure physical security, particularly for remote or outdoor devices [5].
- Vendor Accountability: It can be difficult to hold IoT device makers responsible for security flaws and to make sure they offer prompt updates and support.
- User Awareness: A lot of people who use smart homes might not know about security best practices or might forget to update their default credentials, leaving them open to attacks.
- Legacy Devices: Antiquated Internet of Things gadgets might not be updated or supported, making them always open to known vulnerabilities.

- Interoperability: It can be challenging to make sure that various IoT devices can coexist peacefully while still maintaining security.
- Complicated Attack Surfaces: A large attack surface is produced by the networked structure of smart homes. If one device is compromised, an attacker may be able to use it as a springboard to target other devices.
- Machine learning for threat detection: Although it can improve security, there are drawbacks, including the need to adjust to changing attack strategies and deal with false positives.
- Regulatory Adherence: Respecting privacy and security laws can be difficult, particularly when it comes to information gathered by Internet of Things devices.
- IoT Botnets: The advent of Internet of Things (IoT) botnets, which utilize compromised devices to launch extensive attacks, presents a formidable obstacle to network security [6].
- User Behavior: It can be difficult to distinguish between benign user behavior and malevolent activity, particularly when insider threats are involved.

A multifaceted strategy including device makers, network administrators, users, and regulatory agencies is needed to address these issues. It entails putting strong security measures in place, training users, encouraging cooperation among stakeholders, and remaining alert in the face of changing threats.

1.4 Research Goals

Research goals for an IoT network and smart home security study should be in line with filling in the identified knowledge gaps and resolving the issue. The following are a few research goals:

- Create uniform security frameworks: To create best practices and standardized security protocols that can be used with a variety of IoT devices, improving interoperability and lowering vulnerabilities caused by device diversity.
- Enhance Security with a focus on users: To conduct research on user behaviors, attitudes, and preferences related to smart home security and to develop user-friendly, intuitive security solutions that meet user expectations.
- Examine Legacy Device Security: To guarantee the continuous security of smart home ecosystems, evaluate the security of older IoT devices that might not have received updates and investigate methods to reduce vulnerabilities in legacy devices.
- Proactive Threat Mitigation: The aim of proactive threat mitigation is to investigate new threats in smart home environments, create threat intelligence systems, and investigate predictive analytics in order to prevent threats before they arise.
- Privacy-Preserving Solutions: Investigate methods and tools, like data anonymization, encryption, and user-controlled data sharing, that protect user privacy in smart home settings.
- User Authentication and Access Control: The aim of this study is to create strong user authentication methods and access control techniques that guard against unwanted access to smart home systems and gadgets.

These research goals take into account the complex interplay between IoT networks and smart home security, tackling various facets of the problem statement and advancing the creation of all-encompassing, efficient, and user-focused security solutions for smart home ecosystems.

2 Related Work

The related work included a variety of IoT-related studies on intrusion detection systems. This section was created using the proposals submitted between 2020 and 2023 and was funded by research articles that could be found in the scientific repository (ACM Digital Library, Springer Link, Google Scholar, IEEE Xplore, and Science Direct). Exposure to the works pertaining to the designated topic is provided by this production. Regarding the security issues with layers, an overview of various proposed research works is presented. According to the IoT layer structure, Table 1 shows the work that has been done thus far on security issues and mitigation strategies.

2.1 Artificial Intelligence (AI) Methods Used for Smart Home Attack Detection

Several Deep Learning (DL) and Machine Learning (ML) models are employed in the detection of Smart Home attacks. In order to increase attack detection accuracy and automate IoT device communication, ML and DL have been applied to smart home attack detection. These methods can assist in identifying patterns that are not readily apparent to the human eye and have been used to analyze a variety of attack patterns.

- Convolutional Neural Networks (CNNs): Deep learning models, such as CNNs, are frequently employed in the analysis of smart home attacks. They have been applied to the classification of various types of attacks and traffic patterns. CNNs have the benefit of automatically identifying features from the traffic, which eliminates the need for human feature engineering [31].
- Random Forest (RF): A popular machine learning model called RF is used to classify smart home attacks according to their traffic rules. It is utilized in many regression and classification problems. It has been demonstrated that RF is useful for both identifying smart home intrusions and distinguishing between typical and unusual traffic.
- Support Vector Machine (SVM): SVM is a supervised learning model with applications in regression analysis, outlier identification, and classification. Using the features that are taken out of the different kinds of traffic, it has been used to classify traffic patterns in smart home attack detection.
- Recurrent Neural Networks (RNNs): Time series data and other sequential data have been analyzed using RNNs, a type of DL model. RNNs have been used to examine traffic pattern sequences in order to monitor an attack's evolution over time [32].
- Generative Adversarial Networks (GANs): One kind of DL model that can be used to create new images is a GAN. Other DL models can be trained using the synthetic attacks that GANs have produced on Internet of Things smart homes [33].
- Hybrid models: To enhance the effectiveness of smart home attack detection, researchers have put forth a number of hybrid models that combine the best features of various models. As an illustration, consider combining CNNs with RF or CNNs with SVM.

Table 1. Comparison of existing solutions on Smart Home IoT security issues

Author	Area	Application	Techniques	Data Used	Accuracy	Remarks
Fernando H. Y. et.al. [7]	IoT Network	Attack Detection	CluStream and Page-Hinkley Test	publicly available datasets	97%	Different types of attacks were detected with the precision stayed above 87%
Chenxu Jiang et.al. [8]	IoT Network	Anomaly Detection	Innovative metric to quantify the temporal similarity	real-world testbed	93%	Delay-caused anomalies are detected
J. Araya et.al. [9]	Smart Home IoT Network	Anomaly-based cyberattacks detection	Ensemble and deep learning techniques	publicly available datasets	NA	Survey has been done
Ramesh Paudel et.al. [10]	Smart Home IoT Network	Detecting DoS Attack	Graph-Based Approach	real-world data collected from IoT-equipped smart home	92%	It outperforms current graph-stream anomaly detection approaches
A.V. Chandak et.al. [11]	Smart Home IoT Network	DDoS attack detection	Feature Selection SVM (FSSVM)	DDoS dataset	93%	FSSVM algorithm provides better accuracy compared to KPCA-SVM, SVM, and Naive Bayes algorithms
Soe YN, Feng et. Al. [12]	IoT network	IoT Botnet Attack Detection	ANN, J48 decision tree, NB	N-BaIoT	99.10	Hybrid sequential detection scheme is proposed using feature selection with ML algorithms
Churcher A et. Al. [13]	IoT Networks	IoT Attack Classification	KNN, SVM,DT,NB,RF,LR	Bot-IoT dataset	KNN- 99.32 (Multi class) ANN – 99.47 (Binary Class)	For weighted and Non Weighted datasets in multi classification ANN and KNN are very accurate and for binary classification ANN achieves high accuracy
Lima Filho et. Al. [14]	IoT Network	DoS/DDoS Attack Detection	AdaBoost, RF, DT, LR, SGD	CICIDS2017, CSE-CIC-IDS2018	RF – 99.93	RF achieved highest accuracy with 20 feature and 28 feature dataset
M. Shafiq et. Al. [15]		Malicious Bot-IoT Traffic Detection	Corrauc algorithm	Bot-IoT Data Set	99.12	C 4.5 DT and RF provides high acuuracy
Shafiq et. Al. [16]	Smart City	Bot-IoT attacks traffic identification	Bijective soft set algorithm, NB, DT, RF	Bot-IoT Data Set	BayesNet- 99.77 C4.5–99.99	
Tuan et. Al. [18]	Network Traffic	Botnet DDoS attack detection	SVM,DT,NB,ANN, USML(Unsupervised Learning)	UNBS-NB-15 KDD99	98.08	Unsupervised Learning model provides highest accuracy
I.Alrashdi et. Al. [19]	Smart City	Anomaly Detection	RF	UNBS-NB-15	99.34%	

(continued)

Table 1. (*continued*)

Author	Area	Application	Techniques	Data Used	Accuracy	Remarks
Abu Al-Haija et. Al. [20]	IoT Communication Networks	Detection and Classification of Cyber-Attacks	CNN	NSL-KDD	99.3%	Research is done using 2 class and 5 class label. Among this 2 class label gives highest accuracy
Gaber, T. et. Al. [21]	smart IoT applications	Injection attack detection	SVM, RF, DT	AWID	99%	In this research they used 76, 13 and 8 features
Almaraz-Rivera et. Al. [22]	IoT Devices	Transport and Application Layer DDoS Attacks Detection	RF, DT, RNN, MLP, LSTM, GRU	Bot-IoT Dataset	99.94 99.97	
Abu Al-Haija et. Al. [24]	IoT Networks	Botnet Attack Detection	AdaBoost, RUSBoost, ELBA-IoT	N-BaIoT-2021	99.6%	
Gaur, V et. Al. [25]	IoT Devices	Early Detection of DDoS Attacks	RF,DT, KNN, XGBoost	CICDDoS2019	98.34%	ANOVA feature selection method for XGBoost gives highest accuracy
Albulayhi K et. Al. [26]	IoT Networks	IoT Intrusion Detection	Bagging, MLP, J48, IBk	IoTID20 NSL-KDD	99.7	Intersection theory with ensemble gives higesh accuracy
Salman, O et. Al. [27]	IoT device	abnormal traffic detection	DT,RF RNN, ConvNet	Own Testbed	99.93	RF gives highest Accuracy. Data is balanced
Anthi, E et. Al [30]	smart home networks	denial of service attack defence	RF, J48 DT, SVM	testbed	99.99	

It's crucial to remember that these models are complementary instruments that can be applied to obtain the best outcomes for a particular situation rather than antagonistic ones. Additionally, as these models are still in the early stages of development, more validation across larger datasets and in clinical settings are required to guarantee their generalizability and dependability.

3 Conclusion

In conclusion, with our world becoming more interconnected, the fields of IoT networks and smart home security are critical. This review of the literature emphasizes how diverse the field's research is, addressing everything from user-centric security and proactive threat mitigation to the vulnerabilities of Internet of Things devices and emerging cyber threats. It emphasizes how important it is to have user-friendly security solutions, standardized security procedures, and legacy device security tactics. It also highlights how crucial it is to comprehend how physical and digital security intersect in smart homes, as well as how important privacy protection, authentication, and access control are. This work presents a thorough summary of the state of the art, offering insightful analysis and helpful recommendations for handling the intricate problems associated with smart home security.

References

1. Ai, Y., Peng, M., Zhang, K.: Edge computing technologies for internet of things: a primer. Digital Commun. Netw. **4**(2), 77–86 (2018)
2. Alduailij, M., Khan, Q.W., Tahir, M., Sardaraz, M., Alduailij, M., Malik, F.: Machine-learning-based DDoS attack detection using mutual information and random forest feature importance method. Symmetry. **14**(6), 1095 (2022)
3. Shorey, T., Subbaiah, D., Goyal, A., Sakxena, A., Mishra, A.K.: Performance comparison and analysis of Slowloris, GoldenEye and Xerxes DDoS Attack Tools. In: 2018 International Conference on Advances in Computing, Communications and Informatics (ICACCI). IEEE, pp. 318–322 (2018)
4. Mishra, A., Cheng, A.M.K., Zhang, Y.: Intrusion detection using principal component analysis and support vector machines. In: 2020 IEEE 16th International Conference on Control Automation (ICCA). IEEE, pp. 907–912 (2020)
5. Jan, S.U., Ahmed, S., Shakhov, V., Koo, I.: Toward a lightweight intrusion detection system for the internet of things. IEEE Access. **7**, 42450–42471 (2019)
6. Chi, H., Fu, C., Zeng, Q., Du, X.: Delay wreaks havoc on your smart home: delay- based: automation interference attacks. In: IEEE Symposium on Security and Privacy (S&P), IEEE Computer Society, p. 1575 (2022)
7. Fernando, H.Y., Nakagawa, et al.: Attack detection in smart home IoT networks using CluStream and Page-Hinkley test. In: 2021, IEEE Latin-American Conference on Communications (LATINCOM) (2021)
8. Jiang, C., et al.: Effective anomaly detection in smart home by integrating event time intervals. Elsevier Procedia Comput. Sci. **210**, 53–60 (2022)
9. Araya, J., et al.: Anomaly-based cyberattacks detection for smart homes: a systematic literature review. Elsevier, Internet of Things **22** (2023)
10. Ramesh, P., et al.: Detecting DoS attack in smart home IoT devices using a graph-based approach. In: IEEE International Conference on Big Data (Big Data) (2019)
11. Ashish, V.C., et.al.: DDoS attack detection in smart home applications. J. Software Pract. Exper. Wiley (2023)
12. Soe, Y.N., Feng, Y., Santosa, P.I., Hartanto, R., Sakurai, K.: Machine learning-based IoT-botnet attack detection with sequential architecture. Sensors **20**(16), 4372 (2020). https://doi.org/10.3390/s20164372
13. Churcher A, et al.: An experimental analysis of attack classification using machine learning in IoT networks. Sensors **21**(2), 446 (2021). https://doi.org/10.3390/s21020446
14. Lima Filho, F.S.D., Silveira, F.A., de Medeiros Brito Junior, A., Vargas-Solar, G., Silveira, L.F.: Smart detection: an online approach for DoS/DDoS attack detection using machine learning. Secur. Commun. Netw. 1–15 (2019)
15. Shafiq, M., Tian, Z., Bashir, A.K., Du, X., Guizani, M.: CorrAUC: a Malicious Bot-IoT traffic detection method in IoT network using machine-learning techniques. In: IEEE Internet of Things Journal, vol. 8, no. 5, pp. 3242–3254, 1 March 2021. https://doi.org/10.1109/JIOT.2020.3002255
16. Shafiq, M., Tian, Z., Sun, Y., Du, X., Guizani, M.: Selection of effective machine learning algorithm and Bot-IoT attacks traffic identification for internet of things in smart city. Futur. Gener. Comput. Syst. **107**, 433–442 (2020)
17. Al-Shareeda, M.A., Manickam, S., Saare, M.A.: DDoS attacks detection using machine learning and deep learning techniques: analysis and comparison (December 16, 2022). Bull. Electr. Eng. Inf. **12**(2), 930–939 (2023).SSRN: https://ssrn.com/abstract=4515135
18. Tuan, T.A., Long, H.V., Son, L.H., et al.: Performance evaluation of Botnet DDoS attack detection using machine learning. Evol. Intel. **13**, 283–294 (2020). https://doi.org/10.1007/s12065-019-00310-w

19. Alrashdi, I., et al.: IEEE 9th Annual Computing and Communication Workshop and Conference (CCWC). Las Vegas, NV, USA **2019**, 0305–0310 (2019). https://doi.org/10.1109/CCWC.2019.8666450
20. Abu Al-Haija, Q., Zein-Sabatto, S.: An efficient deep-learning-based detection and classification system for cyber-attacks in IoT communication networks. Electronics **9**(12), 2152 (2020). https://doi.org/10.3390/electronics9122152
21. Gaber, T., El-Ghamry, A., Hassanien, A.E.: Injection attack detection using machine learning for smart IoT applications. Phys. Commun. **52**, 101685 (2022)
22. Almaraz-Rivera, J.G., Perez-Diaz, J.A., Cantoral-Ceballos, J.A.: Transport and application layer DDoS attacks detection to IoT devices by using machine learning and deep learning models. Sensors **22**(9), 3367 (2022)
23. Inayat, U., Zia, M.F., Mahmood, S., Khalid, H.M., Benbouzid, M.: Learning-based methods for cyber attacks detection in IoT systems: a survey on methods, analysis, and future prospects. Electronics **11**(9), 1502 (2022)
24. Abu Al-Haija, Q., Al-Dala'ien, M.: ELBA-IoT: an ensemble learning model for botnet attack detection in IoT networks. J. Sens. Actuat. Netw. **11**(1), 18 (2022). https://doi.org/10.3390/jsan11010018
25. Gaur, V., Kumar, R.: Analysis of machine learning classifiers for early detection of DDoS attacks on IoT devices. Arab. J. Sci. Eng. **47**(2), 1353–1374 (2022)
26. Albulayhi, K., Abu Al-Haija, Q., Alsuhibany, S.A., Jillepalli, A.A., Ashrafuzzaman, M., Sheldon, F.T.: IoT intrusion detection using machine learning with a novel high performing feature selection method. Appl. Sci. **12**(10), 5015 (2022). https://doi.org/10.3390/app12105015
27. Salman, O., Elhajj, I.H., Chehab, A., Kayssi, A.: A machine learning based framework for IoT device identification and abnormal traffic detection. Trans. Emerg. Telecommun. Technol. **33**(3), e3743 (2022)
28. Abu Al-Haija, Q., Krichen, M., Abu, E.W.: Machine-learning-based darknet traffic detection system for IoT applications. Electronics **11**(4), 556 (2022). https://doi.org/10.3390/electronics11040556
29. Touqeer, H., Zaman, S., Amin, R., et al.: Smart home security: challenges, issues and solutions at different IoT layers. J. Supercomput. **77**, 14053–14089 (2021). https://doi.org/10.1007/s11227-021-03825-1
30. Anthi, E., Williams, L., Javed, A., Burnap, P.: Hardening machine learning denial of service (DoS) defences against adversarial attacks in IoT smart home networks. Comput. Secur. **108**, 102352 (2021)
31. Bang, A.O., Rao, U.P.: A novel decentralized security architecture against sybil attack in RPL-based IoT networks: a focus on smart home use case. J. Supercomput. **77**, 13703–13738 (2021). https://doi.org/10.1007/s11227-021-03816-2
32. Kumar, P., Chouhan, L.: A secure authentication scheme for IoT application in smart home. Peer-to-Peer Netw. Appl. **14**, 420–438 (2021)
33. Alshboul, Y., Bsoul, A.A.R., AL Zamil, M., et al.: Cybersecurity of smart home systems: sensor identity protection. J. Netw. Syst. Manage. **29**, 22 (2021). https://doi.org/10.1007/s10922-021-09586-9

AI Based Reliable and Secure Data Transfer in Wireless Networks

P. Kalyanchakravarthi[1,2](✉) 📧 and Susmitha Das[3] 📧

[1] NIT Rourkela, Rourkela, India
kalyanecebujji@gmail.com
[2] Department of ECE, GMR Instiute of Technology, NIT Rourkela, Rajam, India
[3] Department of Electrical Engineering, NIT Rourkela, Rourkela, India
sdas@nitrkl.ac.in

Abstract. The rapid increase in digital data information is primarily driven by several interconnected factors like technological advancements, internet and connectivity, social media and online activities and Sensor Technologies, e-commerce and Online Transactions etc. The combination of advancing technology, widespread internet connectivity, the increasing adoption of digital devices and applications, and the demand for data-driven insights has led to an exponential increase in digital data information day by day. As technology continues to evolve, it is likely that this trend will continue for the foreseeable future. However, such rich sources of information are mostly left untapped. Authentication is essential in data transmission for several reasons. It plays a vital role in ensuring the confidentiality, integrity, and authenticity of data during transmission, helping to build trust in digital communications and safeguard sensitive information from unauthorized access or manipulation. This paper compares various methods available for data authentication and optimizes the solution with the help of Artificial Intelligence (AI). It can significantly enhance data authentication by providing advanced techniques and technologies to verify the integrity and authenticity of data. By leveraging AI's capabilities, organizations can strengthen their data authentication processes, reduce the risk of data breaches or fraud, and enhance overall data security. However, it's important to note that AI-based authentication systems are not infallible and should be used in conjunction with other security measures to provide robust protection against threats.

Keywords: Authentication Technology · Internet of Things. Security · Wireless Networks

1 Introduction

A wireless network refers to a communication system that enables the transfer of data between devices without the need for physical connections or cables. It utilizes wireless signals, typically in the form of radio waves, to transmit and receive information between devices such as computers, smartphones, tablets, IoT devices, and other network-enabled devices. In a wireless network, devices communicate with each other through wireless access points or routers that facilitate the transmission of data [1]. These access points connect to a wired network infrastructure, such as a modem or Ethernet connection, which in turn connects to the internet or other networks.

Wireless networks can operate using different wireless communication protocols, such as Wi-Fi (Wireless Fidelity), Bluetooth, cellular networks (like 3G, 4G, and 5G), satellite communication, and others. Wi-Fi is one of the most commonly used wireless technologies for local area networking, providing wireless internet connectivity in homes, offices, public spaces, and various other environments. The wireless network infrastructure consists of devices such as routers, wireless access points, wireless adapters, and antennas that transmit and receive signals [2]. These devices employ wireless standards and encryption methods to ensure secure and reliable data transmission.

Wireless networks have revolutionized the way we connect, communicate, and access information. They offer benefits such as mobility, flexibility, and ease of use, enabling users to access the internet and network resources from anywhere within the network's coverage area [3]. There are several types of wireless networks, each serving specific purposes and ca-tering to different connectivity needs. Here are some commonly used types of wire-less networks:

Wi-Fi (Wireless Fidelity) networks are widely used for local area networking (LAN) in homes, offices, public spaces, and other environments. They provide wireless internet access to devices within a specific coverage area. Wi-Fi networks operate on various IEEE 802.11 standards, such as 802.11ac (Wi-Fi 5) and 802.11ax (Wi-Fi 6) [4]. Cellular Networks enable wireless communication over long distances using cellular towers. These networks are used for mobile telephony and data services. They include generations such as 2G, 3G, 4G LTE, and the latest 5G, offering increased speeds, lower latency, and enhanced capacity.

Bluetooth technology is designed for short-range wireless communication between devices. It is commonly used for connecting peripherals like keyboards, mice, headphones, and speakers to computers, smartphones, and other devices in close proximity. Bluetooth is also utilized in IoT devices for data transfer and control. Zigbee is a wireless technology used for low-power, short-range communication between devices. It is commonly employed in home automation, smart lighting systems, and industrial applications where devices need to communicate wirelessly over a limited range.

AI-based reliable and secure data transfer refers to the use of artificial intelligence (AI) techniques and technologies to enhance the reliability and security of transferring data between systems or devices. It involves leveraging AI algorithms and approaches to optimize data transfer processes, improve data integrity, protect against unauthorized access, and ensure the confidentiality of sensitive information.

1.1 AI Contribution Towards Reliable and Secure Data Transfer

Error Correction and Data Integrity

AI algorithms can be used to implement error correction codes and techniques that help identify and correct errors that may occur during data transmission. These algorithms can detect and reconstruct corrupted or lost data, ensuring the integrity of the transferred information.

Predictive Analytics and Quality of Service (QoS)
AI can analyze historical data on network performance and behavior to predict potential network disruptions or congestion. By considering factors like bandwidth availability, latency, and network load, AI systems can optimize data transfer by dynamically selecting the most suitable routes and protocols for efficient and reliable data transmission.

Intrusion Detection and Prevention
AI-powered systems can employ machine learning techniques to analyze network traffic patterns and detect anomalies or potential security threats. By continuously monitoring network activities, AI algorithms can identify and respond to suspicious behavior, helping to prevent unauthorized access, data breaches, or malicious attacks during data transfer.

Data Encryption and Privacy
AI can be utilized to develop robust encryption algorithms and privacy-enhancing techniques. Encryption mechanisms, such as symmetric and asymmetric encryption, can be applied to data at rest or in transit, ensuring that sensitive information remains secure and protected from unauthorized access.

Behavioral Analysis and User Authentication
AI systems can employ behavioral analysis techniques to recognize patterns in user behavior during data transfer. This can help detect unauthorized access attempts or unusual activities, triggering additional security measures or authentication processes to ensure the authenticity of users and devices involved in data transfer.

Threat Intelligence and Real-Time Monitoring
AI can leverage threat intelligence feeds and real-time monitoring to identify and respond to emerging threats or vulnerabilities. By integrating AI-based security solutions, organizations can proactively mitigate risks and ensure the secure transfer of data by staying ahead of potential threats [5]. By integrating AI into data transfer processes, organizations can enhance reliability, reduce data loss, minimize the risk of security breaches, and optimize the overall performance of their networks. However, it's important to note that implementing AI-based security measures should be done in combination with other established security practices and standards to create a robust and comprehensive data transfer environment.

Wireless networks face several challenges that can impact their performance, reliability, and security [6]. Some of the common challenges in wireless networks operate in shared frequency bands, making them susceptible to interference from other devices and networks operating in the same frequency range. Interference can degrade signal quality, reduce throughput, and cause connectivity issues. Signal Attenuation and Range Limitations in wireless signals are subject to attenuation, meaning their strength diminishes as they propagate through space. Obstacles like walls, buildings, and distance can further limit the range of wireless networks and weaken signal strength, resulting in reduced coverage and performance.

Bandwidth Constraints in wireless networks typically have limited bandwidth compared to wired networks [7]. As the number of connected devices and data-intensive applications increases, it can lead to congestion and reduced network performance.

Security Risks in wireless networks are vulnerable to security threats, such as unauthorized access, eavesdropping, data interception, and network intrusion. Weak encryption, poor authentication mechanisms, and unsecured configurations can expose networks to attacks and compromise the confidentiality and integrity of transmitted data.

Mobility and Handover in wireless networks introduces challenges related to seamless handover as devices move between different access points or cells. Maintaining a stable connection during handover is crucial to avoid disruptions in ongoing communications.

Quality of Service (QoS) Management ensuring consistent QoS is challenging in wireless networks, especially in environments with varying signal strengths or high user densities. Factors like latency, packet loss, and jitter can affect the performance of real-time applications like voice and video streaming.

Power Consumption in wireless devices, particularly battery-powered devices, need to manage power consumption efficiently to prolong battery life. Balancing power-saving techniques with the need for reliable connectivity and performance is a challenge in wireless networks.

Scalability is the number of connected devices increases, scaling wireless networks to accommodate the growing demand becomes a challenge. Network architectures and protocols need to support large-scale deployments without sacrificing performance or reliability.

Standards and Compatibility in wireless networks rely on various standards and protocols, and compatibility issues can arise when devices from different vendors or generations attempt to connect or communicate. Ensuring interoperability and seamless integration across devices and networks can be a challenge. Regulatory Compliance in wireless networks must comply with regulatory requirements governing spectrum allocation, power limits, and security protocols [8]. Adhering to these regulations while maintaining optimal network performance poses challenges for network administrators.

Efforts are continuously made to address these challenges through advancements in wireless technologies, improved network design, enhanced security measures, and ongoing research in areas like spectrum management, signal processing, and network optimization.

Wireless data transfer introduces unique security challenges due to the open nature of wireless communication. However, several techniques are employed to ensure data security in wireless transfer. Here are some commonly used techniques:

Encryption is a fundamental technique used to protect data during wireless transfer. It involves encoding the data in such a way that it can only be decrypted and understood by authorized recipients. Common encryption algorithms used in wireless networks include AES (Advanced Encryption Standard) and WPA2 (Wi-Fi Protected Access 2).Authentication techniques verify the identities of devices and users involved in wireless data transfer. This ensures that only authorized parties can access and transmit data. Techniques such as passwords, digital certificates, and biometric authentication are used to authenticate devices and users in wireless networks.

2 Literature Survey

By examining the methodologies, approaches, and research designs employed in previous articles referred several papers as follows. One paper titled Reliable and secure data transfer in IoT networks delas about IoT ecosystem novel distributed key management technique [9]. The suggested approach efficiently protects IoT devices by offloading the majority of resource-intensive cryptographic operations to a local entity. The following sub networks are used in this suggested strategy to take advantage of mobile agents to process the IoT devices' cryptography work and undertake a quick authentication procedure by posing as a local authorized entity. Application security and user security are two subcategories of information transmission security concerns. User security is primarily concerned with safeguarding the security of the user's sensitive data, as opposed to application security, which focuses on data protection when a user uses a particular programmer. Our concept provides security based on an MA's prediction of mobility in a sub network of an IoT network [10]. When the main IoT application is started at the beginning of a session at a sub network, the SA issues a certificate to the user device. There are a few issues with the proposed model that we plan to solve in more exploration. For anomaly detection, rigid rules set by humans are utilized initially. As a result, locating unknown abnormalities outside of the gathered variables is a challenging task. Second, an end-to-end evaluation of the proposed strategy requires real-world testing. Further testing and a reconfiguration of the suggested strategy are required. Third, depending on the complexity of the algorithms, human judgement is utilized to choose which algorithms to apply on various devices.

Other paper titled Distributed AI-Driven Search Engine on Visual Internet-of-Things for Event Discovery in the Cloud.In this paper, they propose distributed deep neural networks (DNNs) over edge visual Internet of Things (VIoT) devices for real-time video scene parsing and indexing in conjunction with Big Query retrieval on cloud-stored data. A method for generating useful representation from raw data that a camera outputs in the form of video is called video analytics [11]. An intelligent video analytics system will be able to narrow the search by employing a range of criteria and create a knowledge base that is more reliable and accurate for making judgments and, eventually, taking action. The proposed architecture bridges the edge-to-cloud gap by judiciously allocating the AI workload between the edge and the cloud. Video security cameras and other stream-ing media may be seamlessly incorporated into smart cities thanks to the Visual Internet of Things (VIoT). However, working with and gaining insight from such a large amount of data is challenging.

One of the major contributions taken from the paper titled Securing Big Data: A Survey on Security Solutions deals about there are many security risks that could affect the confidentiality and integrity of data that is sent, processed, and stored. Numerous methods have been created to address these security challenges and worries [12]. This survey article's goal is to identify and describe the security concerns connected to the

Big Data architecture. Due to its promising features, cloud computing (CC) has been chosen as the infrastructure for BDA. However, the conceptual taxonomy of security and privacy for the BD framework's four primary objectives are data confidentiality, data provenance, system health, and public policy, social, and cross-organizational concerns [13]. The importance of BDA has grown, which has prompted the development of many BD security frameworks for handling massive amounts of data. Hosting BD frameworks necessitates a trustworthy and secure infrastructure provider, CIA, to meet the essential security standards. This article gave a general review of BDA-related research from the security point of view, covering the BD lifecycle, security challenges, and worries. The study described the widely used security measures to protect the BD framework. It was clear that encryption and its alternatives surpassed the bulk of the proposed solutions and showed their effectiveness.

3 Proposed Methodology

In order to improve the security in the wireless networks the best way is to use Authentication technologies. To satisfy different use cases and demands, varied authentication techniques are needed to provide security and ease to your users. To satisfy the various demands, we provide a variety of user authentication techniques.

The process of asking for specific credentials, such as a username and password, in order to determine whether or not a user trying to access network resources is authorized. In addition to other areas, authentication can be enabled on console ports, AUX ports.

As network administrators, we have the authority to control how a user is authenticated when they attempt to access the network [14]. These methods include using the router's internal database and sending authentication requests to a distant server, like the ACS server. To choose the authentication method to be used, a default or customized authentication method list is used.

By considering these comparisons we have to select that user id and password-based Au-thentication and OTP based Authentication to improve the security and develop as multi factor Authentication. Because in the multi-factor authentication we have to use more then one authentication method. If we consider the all the possibilities that we have the best one combination of OTP based and user-ID based. Because in the user-id based only the security is poor but remaining are better to use. So to improve the security we can go with OTP based even though token based has higher security then OTP token based is difficult to deploy then the OTP based so it is better to go with the OTP based then the token based.

In the proposed methodology the multi factor Authentication is done by deploying the two layers of authentication in the 1st layer we use the user id and password-based Authentication. Because the user will have their own user credentials to enter the network. And it is easy to use and deploy [15]. So that the 1st layer of authentication is done by using the user-id based authentication. And coming to the 2nd layer of authentication we can use OTP based authentication. In this layer the user will initially register with mail-id or phone number, an OTP is sent to the registered phone number or mail-id. By entering the OTP received by the user the network will consider the user as the legal user and give the access to the network. If the user has entered the incorrect OTP, then the user will another OTP. This process will repeat until the user has to enter the correct OTP.

The next challenge that we consider is its dynamic architecture and functional analysis of the network. For this we used the shortest-path tree algorithm to find the best path in the network. By finding the best path we can it is easy to send the data from source to destination. You may determine the shortest path between two nodes in a network using Dijkstra's Algo-rithm. It create a shortest-path tree by determining the shortest path from a node (referred to as the "source node") to every other node in the graph.

To determine the quickest route between the present location and the destination, GPS devices employ this method. It has several industrial uses, particularly in fields where modelling networks is necessary. To use this algorithm, we have to give wights. Here we are taking the distance between each node as the weights For that case the distance will be find using the Euclidean distance formula shown in Eq. 1.

$$\sqrt{(a2 - a1)^2 + (b2 - b1)^2} \tag{1}$$

By using the formula, the distance is measured between distance each node present in the network and the distance values in the form of tables. These distance tables are used in the analysis of the network architecture and find the neighbor nodes to each node present in the network as per the node range given by the user.

4 Results and Discussion

The biggest challenge that we consider in the wireless network is dynamic architecture analysis. For that we have developed a MATLAB algorithm. To find the neighbor nodes to each node and find the shortest path between the source and destination.

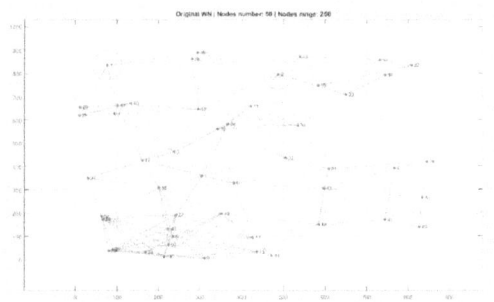

Original network

The above network is the given dynamic network in which have to do the analysis. Where the node 1 is the source node in the network and the node 2 is the destination node in the network.

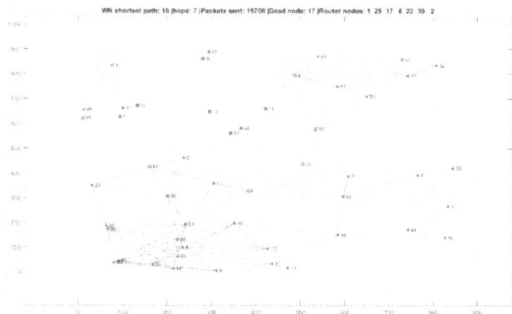

Leaving dead node and find alternate path (after 9 stages)

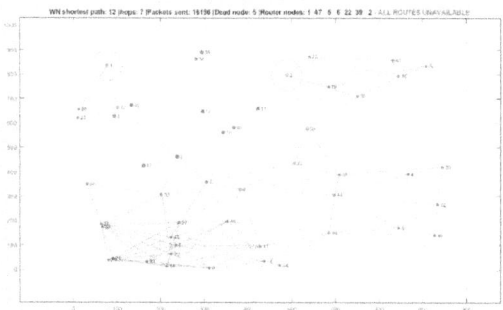

All routes are unavailable

By observing the behavior of the nodes present in the network we can get the deep analysis of the network in this simulation we only consider the distance. But in the case of we have to consider the remaining terms like cost, number of nodes present between the source and destination, bandwidth. Then we will get the complete analysis of the network.

5 Conclusion and Future Scope

This paper mainly focus on how AI can play a crucial role in enhancing the reliability and security of data transfer in wireless networks and identifying the best authentication method for data transfer involves considering various factors related to security, usability, and the specific requirements of the data transfer scenario. In this work proposed few steps where these challenges are arising in the wireless networks. The main challenge in the wireless network is the illegal users are entering to the network and accessing the data (security). And due to its dynamic nature, the nodes present in the network are not stationary. Ultimately, there is no one-size-fits-all approach to authentication for data transfer. The best method will depend on the specific needs of your organization, the type of data being transferred, and the level of security required. It may also involve combining multiple authentication methods (multi-factor authentication) for enhanced security.

References

1. Dannana, S., Prabakaran, T., Rajasekaran, A.S., Kumareshan, N., Shadrach, S.F.D., Kalyanchakravarthi, P.: A novel system model for managing cyber threat intelligence. In: 2022 IEEE 2nd Mysore Sub Section International Conference (MysuruCon) (2022). https://doi.org/10.1109/mysurucon55714.2022.9972703
2. Das, A., Roopaei, M., Jamshidi, M., Najafirad, P.: Distributed AI-Driven search engine on Visual Internet-of-Things for event discovery in the cloud (2022).https://doi.org/10.1109/sose55472.2022.9812698
3. Habbak, H., Metwally, K., Mattar, A.M.: Securing big data: a survey on security solutions. In: Inter-national Conference on Electrical Engineering (2022).https://doi.org/10.1109/iceeng49683.2022.9781955
4. Martins, O., et.al.: Artificial intelligence techniques for cognitive sensing in future IoT: state-of-the-art, potentials, and challenges. IJ. Sens. Actuator Netw. **9**, 21 (2020). https://doi.org/10.3390/jsan9020021
5. Akpakwu, G.A., Silva, B.J., Hancke, G.P., Abu-Mahfouz, A.M.: A survey on 5g networks for the Internet of Things: communication technologies and challenges. IEEE Access **6**, 3619–3647 (2018)
6. Chakraborty, C., Rodrigues, J.J.: A comprehensive review on device-to-device communication paradigm: trends, challenges and applications. Wirel. Personal Commun. **114**, 185–207 (2020).https://doi.org/10.1007/s11277-020-07358-3
7. Doppler, K., Rinne, M., Wijting, C., Ribeiro, C., Hugl, K.: Device-to-device communication as an underlay to LTE-advanced networks. IEEE Commun. Mag. **47**, 42–49 (2009)
8. Ali, K.S., ElSawy, H., Alouini, M.S.: Modeling cellular networks withfull-duplex D2D communication: a stochastic geometry approach. IEEE Trans. Commun. **64**, 4409–4424 (2016)
9. Migabo, E., Djouani, K., Kurien, A.: An energy-efficient and adaptive channel coding approach for narrowband Internet of Things (NB-IoT) systems. Sensors **20**, 3465 (2020). https://doi.org/10.3390/s20123465
10. Miao, Y., Li, W., Tian, D., Hossain, M., Alhamid, M.: Narrow band Internet of Things: simulation and modelling. IEEE Internet Things J. **5**, 2304–2314 (2018)
11. Li, S., Xu, L.D., Zhao, S.: The Internet of Things: a survey. Inf. Syst. Front. **17**, 243–259 (2015)
12. Yu, C., Yu, L., Wu, Y., He, Y., Lu, Q.: Uplink scheduling and link adaptation for narrowband in-ternet of things systems. IEEE Access **5**, 1724–1734 (2017)
13. Palattella, M.R., et al.: Internet of Things in the 5G era: enablers, architecture, and business models. IEEE J. Sel. Areas Commun. **34**(3), 510–527 (2016)
14. Gochhayat, S.P., et al.: Reliable and secure data transfer in IoT networks. Wirel.Netw. **26**(8), 5689–5702 (2019). https://doi.org/10.1007/s11276-019-02036-0
15. Da Xu, L., He, W., Li, S.: Internet of Things in industries: a survey. IEEE Trans. Ind. Informat. **10**(4), 2233–2243 (2014)

Author Index

A

Abhishek, Sanam II-3
Abukari, Arnold Mashud II-89
Ahmed, Mohammed Ezaz II-107
Akshay, Kotra I-227
Ala, Rajitha II-144
Amudha, R. I-211
Ananya, S. I-64
Anjaneyulu, Lokam I-25
Aravind Reddy, A. II-15
Arra, Pavani I-85
Arumulla, Dileep Kumar I-122
Aruna, E. R. I-282
Ashwini, A. II-116
Ashwitha, Kanugula I-249
Auti, Vinod Kumar I-122
Avinash, M. II-116

B

Bayessa, Gezahegn Abdissa I-95
Begum, Shaik Salma II-107
Bejjam, Kiranmai II-144
Biju, Balakrishnan I-211
Bosamia, Bhavikchandra II-178

C

Chai, Rong I-95
Chanv, Jayraj II-70
Charan, Vankadaru II-124
Chen, Qianbin I-95
Chethana Datta, J. I-64
Chilukuri, Sulakshana I-33, I-54
Chitrala, Kavitha II-135

D

Das, Susmitha I-320
Dasadiya, Keval Jitendrabhai II-51
Dasadiya, Keval II-70
Deep, Boddu Mani II-178
Deepak, Mukund I-64
Deepesh, Dasa A. I-157

Dhanraj, Burragalla II-167
Dharek, Vatsal A. II-3
Dodiya, Himanshu Rajeshbhai II-42

G

Ganesh, Guguloth I-189
Ghanathey, Vikas Kumar I-33
Gnanesh, A. I-157
Goud, S. Adityeshwar II-154
Goud, Srimanthula Manish I-231

H

Harini, V. I-85
Harshavardhini, Kummari I-33
Harshith, M. I-114
Hegde, Bhargav I-157

J

Janapati, Krishna Chaitanya I-260
Janapati, Krishna Chaithanya II-3
Jani, Charmi R. II-79
Jaswanth, Yellavula I-54
Javvadi, Tulasi II-107
Jegadeesan, R. I-202

K

Kalyanchakravarthi, P. I-320
Kalyani, P. II-187
Kanagala, Sai Sriharsha II-144
Kanneboina, Ramavathar Yadav I-241
Karnati, Ramesh II-79
Karthik, Chirag II-15
Karthik, S. I-211
Karunakaran, S. I-114
Karupaiah, N. II-70
Karuppaiah, Natarajan II-58
Karuppiah, N. II-51
Kavitha, M. S. I-211
Kavya, G. II-42
Keerthi, Kandur II-96

Krishna Chaitanya, J.   I-202
Kukudala, Sai Prasad Reddy   II-96
Kulkarni, Gururaj L.   II-96
Kuma, Majji Naveen Sai   II-107
Kumar Reddy, Rebanamoni Sravan   I-227
Kumar, G. A. E. Satish   I-122, I-249
Kumar, Jaydeep   II-51
Kumar, Kandukuri Vasantha   II-167
Kumar, Kommoju V. V. S. M. Manoj   II-107
Kumar, Malligunta Kiran   II-58
Kumar, Naresh   II-178
Kumar, Ravi   II-154
Kumar, Talari Tarun   II-178
Kunchur, Pavan N.   II-96

L

Lathigara, Amit   I-260, I-310, II-154
Lemu, Yetmwork Gutema   I-95
Lingutla, Kavya   I-143
Lokanath Reddy, C.   I-3

M

Madavarapu, Jhansi Bharathi   II-89
Madduri, Uday Kumar   II-167
Madhuri, D.   I-14
Mahendra Reddy, M.   I-3
Mahesh, K.   II-187
Makka, Shanthi   II-124, II-135
Manish Goud, Srimanthula   I-74
Manisha, R.   II-116
Mannem, Kiran   I-282
Mantri, Devansh   I-249
Meesa, Ravali   I-291
Mehta, Parit   I-42
Modugu, PavanTeja   II-154
Mohammad, Sameer   I-260
Mohan, M.   I-3
Motupalli, Satyarth   I-241, I-260, II-3
Mounica, Patil   II-51
Mukthananda Reddy, T.   I-3
Mungara, Nishanth   I-64
Murthy, V. N. L. N.   I-14
Muthyala, Samuel Nishant   I-282

N

Nagisetty, Hima Varsha   I-143
Nalluri, Sowmya Sri   I-122
Nanduri, Veda Manogna   I-260

Nikhitha, Rejinthala   II-178
Nikitha Reddy, V.   I-14
Noorain, Azmath   I-74, I-231
Nunna, Niharika   I-143

P

Peddaraju, Sujay Kapil   I-260
Penumuchu, Vennela Priya   I-143
Pranathi, Dodda Sai   II-28
Pranitha, P.   I-202
Prasad, D. Vishnu   II-42
Prasanna, Jalapudi Laxmi   II-167
Prashanth, Mallellu Sai   II-79
Praveen Kuamar, D.   I-202
Punem, Pavani   I-260
Punyamurthy, Bheemeshwar   II-144

R

Rajasekhar, Nuthakki Venkata   I-132
Raju, Padmaraju Sai Kumar   II-28
Ramala, Sindhuja   II-154
Ramana, Attili Venkata   II-144
Rao, Kambhampati Venkata Govardhan   II-58
Rao, Madhavarapu Prathima   I-202
Rao, Pasumarthy Nageswara   I-282
Ravindra, J. V. R.   I-241, I-249, I-260, II-3, II-42
Reddy, B. Raja Gopal   II-51
Reddy, Bondugula Karthik   II-3
Reddy, G. Sanjeeva   I-231
Reddy, Ganesh   I-85
Reddy, Gangireddy Nitish Kumar   II-96
Reddy, H. Venkateshwara   II-79
Reddy, K. Shreshta   II-42
Reddy, M. Keerthi   I-14
Reddy, Muthangi Kantha   I-310
Reddy, Santhosh   I-85
Reddy, V. Siddartha   II-187
Reddy, Varun Kumar   I-241
Redy, M. Vinay Kumar   II-154
Reeja, S. R.   I-143
Rohan, Raparthi   II-15
Rout, Saroja Kumar   I-14
Rreddy, M. Vinay Kuma   I-310
Ryali, SriSrujan   I-33

S
Sahay, Sanjay K.   I-42
Sai Sushumna, Perumandla   I-54
Sai, Avula Shiva   I-227
SaiManish, K.   I-114
Salagrama, Shailaja   II-89
Samreen, Shirina   II-116
Sandeep, Yanigandla   I-249
Sandhya, Mallavarapu   I-25
Sangeam, Ruchitha   II-144
Sanjana, Nallanagula   I-54
Sanjeeva Reddy, G.   I-74
Sarasvathi, V.   I-64, I-157
Sarika, Vemula   II-28
Sathvik, Jami Anjana Adi   II-107
Satish Kumar, G. A. E.   I-241
Satya, Dantu Vyshnavi   II-107
Sethi, Bijaya Kumar   I-14
Singh, Deepak   I-176
Singh, Sangeeta   I-74, I-189, I-231
Sneha, Gudipati   I-189
Snigdha, Kattekola   II-124
Soni, Ankush   I-42
Sowjanya, S.   II-135
Sowmya, A.   II-124
Sreeja, Sindhe   I-189
Srikanth, B.   II-28
Srinubabu, Manumula   I-132
Sripal, K.   I-227
Srivardhan, S.   I-114
Sumalata, G. L.   I-272, I-302
Sumukh, G.   II-187
Sunaina, Mentam   I-272, I-302
Surekha, G.   I-291
Suresh, Godugu   II-3
Swetha, P. Bindu   II-187

T
Tammineni, Siddarth   I-241
Teja, S. Ravi   II-58
Tellapati, Anuradha Devi   II-58

U
Uma Mageswari, R.   I-176

V
Vasantha, S. V.   II-116
Velpuru, Muni Sekhar   II-79
Venu, Vasantha Sandhya   II-144
Vidhyadhar, R. Phani   I-241
Vidyadhar, R. Phani   I-249
Vijaya Lakshmi, A.   II-15
Vishvakumari, Faldu   I-249
Vishwanath, Sanagala   II-124
Vyasamudri, Shreehari   I-157

Y
Yalamanchili, Radha Krishna   II-89
Yuvaraj, M.   II-116

GPSR Compliance

The European Union's (EU) General Product Safety Regulation (GPSR) is a set of rules that requires consumer products to be safe and our obligations to ensure this.

If you have any concerns about our products, you can contact us on

ProductSafety@springernature.com

In case Publisher is established outside the EU, the EU authorized representative is:

Springer Nature Customer Service Center GmbH
Europaplatz 3
69115 Heidelberg, Germany

www.ingramcontent.com/pod-product-compliance
Ingram Content Group UK Ltd.
Pitfield, Milton Keynes, MK11 3LW, UK
UKHW020420240426
470314UK00006BB/48